DATA COMMUNICATIONS
A COMPREHENSIVE APPROACH

Data Communications Book Series

Computer Message Systems. By Jacques Vallee. 1984, 163 pp., clothbound.

Data Communications Procurement Manual. By Gilbert Held. 1979, 150 pp., clothbound.

Data Network Design Strategies. Edited by Ray Sarch. 1983, 270 pp., softcover.

Interface Proceedings. Edited by Data Communications magazine. Annual Editions, softcover.

The Local Network Handbook. Edited by George R. Davis, 1982, 256 pp., softcover.

McGraw Hill's Compilation of Data Communications Standards (Edition II). Edited by Harold C. Folts, 1982, 1,923 pp., clothbound.

Practical Applications of Data Communications. Edited by Harry R. Karp. 1980, 424 pp., softcover.

Teleconferencing and Beyond: Communications in the Office of the Future. By Robert Johansen, with others contributing. 1984, 185 pp., clothbound.

Teletext and Videotex in the United States: Market Potential, Technology, and Public Policy Issues. By J. Tydeman, H. Lipinski, R. Adler, M. Nyhan, and L. Swimpter, 1982, 312 pp., clothbound.

Basic Guide to Data Communications. Edited by Ray Sarch, 1984, 360 pp., softcover.

DATA COMMUNICATIONS

A COMPREHENSIVE APPROACH

Gilbert Held
4-Degree Consulting
Macon, Georgia

Ray Sarch
Executive Technical Editor
Data Communications
New York, New York

 **Data Communications**
McGraw-Hill Publications Company

1221 Avenue of the Americas
New York, New York 10020

Project supervison was done by The Total Book.
The typesetter was Comgraph Inc.
The cover was designed by Cathy Canzani, Design Works.
Kingsport Press, Inc. was printer and binder.

First Printing, October 1983
Second Printing, August 1984

DATA COMMUNICATIONS:

A Comprehensive Approach

1 2 3 4 5 6 7 8 9 0 KGP 0 9 8 7 6 5 4 3 2 1

ISBN 0-07-600003-6

Library of Congress Cataloging in Publication Data

Held, Gilbert, 1943–
    Data communications.

    Bibliography: p.
    Includes index.
    1. Data transmission systems. I. Sarch, Ray,
II. Title.
TK5105.H425 1983   384   83-10054
ISBN 0-07-600003-6

5012286

The authors are indebted to Harry R. Karp, founding editor of *Data Communications,* for his guiding force in establishing the Data Communications Institute, for which this book was originally developed.

CONTENTS

FOREWORD

This book has been specially created to guide readers who are coming out of a data processing or computer environment but are new to the field of data communications. Materials are presented to provide readers with an in-depth understanding of the underlying principles of this rapidly expanding discipline.

The authors present the materials using a step-by-step approach to clearly define the conceptual foundation of the field. They cover most major topics in data communications: components, network design and configurations, transmission media, protocols, topologies, architectures, cost structures, and future technologies. Technical, regulatory, and historical aspects of data communications are detailed, along with both public and private network strategies.

To help the general reader, numerous technical illustrations are provided. Review questions are included where appropriate. These questions can also facilitate the use of the book as a textbook in courses or seminars dedicated to data communications.

Over five hundred attendees of the Data Communications Institute's Basic Data Communications Seminar have used earlier versions of this book. Their overwhelming positive response to its quality suggests that new readers will find the book to be of value also.

OVERVIEW

The following overview defines data communications, its functions, and its scope. Its purpose is to provide an understanding of the significance of data communications technology in today's business-communications environment. It is adapted from an article written by Raymond Sarch, executive technical editor of DATA COMMUNICATIONS magazine, that appears in the 1982 edition of *The Encyclopedia of Management,* edited by Carl Heyel.*

Data Communications is, as the name indicates, the means of communicating data—as opposed to communicating analog (telephone) voice. It comprises communications between digital computers, between terminals and these computers, and between terminals themselves. Thus, it is the means of tying together coherently all local and far-flung computerized devices.

Strictly speaking, data communications has existed as long as data processing, but its growth was severely restrained by the tariff restrictions imposed on and by the telephone industry. Telephone networks were the major means of connecting a remotely located terminal user to a centrally located mainframe computer. However, on June 26, 1968, the ground rules were drastically changed, and a "new" industry was spawned. On that date, the Federal Communications Commission rendered its landmark Carterfone Decision permitting direct interconnection to the telephone network of non-telephone company devices. Although the telephone companies remained free to maintain standards for the protection of their networks, this proved no deterrent to the growth of the newly liberated data communications applications. This growth is a major reason for the increasing computer orientation of our society.

Besides the telephone companies—especially AT&T—the other major influence affecting this growth has been and is IBM. This company is primarily known for its computers, typewriters, and other business machines, but its impact on data communications is twofold: in the interconnection of its own products, and in the connection of other manufacturers' "plug-compatible" products to IBM computers and other devices. The company's extremely strong position in the large-computer industry, and its strong position in other business-equipment areas, has enabled it to establish de facto standards for both the EDP and data communications fields.

Networks. The user realizes the full potential of data communications in the application of networks. The most elementary connection method of a remote terminal to a computer is via a leased line, point-to-point. When there are several terminals at a remote location requiring connection to the computer, instead of leasing an individual line for each terminal, it is possible and less costly to use only the one line in combination with a "multiplexing" (line-sharing) device. The multiplexer, representing an elementary form of networking, is commonly available today in several forms and variations of "intelligence."

As terminals from different remote sites require access to the centrally located computer, the network grows in complexity. Waystations, called nodal processors or nodes, become necessary within the network to interact with the terminals and the computer, storing, forwarding, and controlling the network's data flow. As more computers and terminals are added, the network design becomes ever more complex to provide the capability for any terminal to reach any computer or any other terminal.

The user firm is faced with a major design and implementation effort to provide a private network—which yields many control and security benefits—or it can avail itself of a public network to move its data. Among the different types of network designs are circuit-switching, which involves a straightforward transfer of data from one path onto another. Message-switching, on the other hand, adds a store-and-forward function: the message is stored at a network node, possibly checked for errors, then transferred onto another circuit (path). Depending on the distances involved and the network complexity, these nodal "stops" may occur from one to several times.

A variation of the message-switched network, growing in popularity, is the packet-switched network. Here, as the message enters the network, it is divided into discrete segments, called packets. Each packet travels the network independent of the others, with suitable identification. A packet is routed over the "freeest" path, node by node, until it reaches its exit node. There, all the packets are reassembled in their proper order, and presented to the destination device as the entered message.

An increasingly important element of the data communications network is the satellite—particularly, the geostationary satellite. Its orbit matches the earth's angular rotation, and it is positioned over the equator. To an observer on the earth, it appears stationary in space. In this position, it acts as a relay and disseminating station for all forms of electrical signals. When a firm's network requires satellite use, "dish" antennas may be positioned on building roofs, to minimize land-line use. The increasing use of digital data—as typified by Satellite Business Systems' services—makes the satellite of growing importance in data communications. SBS is a consortium of IBM Corp., Comsat General Corp., and Aetna Life and Casualty Co.

One drawback in the application of satellites to data transmission is the inherent propagation delay of this technique. There are several schemes to negate the delay's effect—especially noticeable in interactive (inquiry-response) applications—but the user must balance their cost against that of transmission via cable and normal microwave links. For non-interactive transmission, such as batch data, video, and facsimile, the delay is more readily absorbed.

Among the established public packet-switched networks in the United States are those of GTE-Telenet and Tymnet. Each interconnects internationally to Canada's Datapac, and via international record carriers to Europe and Japan. A private network that meets the interface requirements of one of the public ones could establish an economical combination of the two network types. International and overseas access is also available to the private network, with the proper interface.

The Terminal. The most ubiquitous data communications device is the operator's terminal. Commonly, it has a typewriter-like keyboard, and either a cathode-ray-tube (CRT) screen or a hard-copy capability (the two are not mutually exclusive). It permits the user to gain access to a wide range of databases (information sources), including business, training, entertainment, and interactive applications. These services are usually available on a timeshared basis—meaning accessible to many users "simultaneously" (i.e., it appears so to the user).

The business office is where the terminal and all its attendant peripherals find their potential increasingly realized. Office automation—sometimes referred to as the "office of the future"—is driven by the need for higher office productivity. Until recently, this drive has been fueled by the replacement of discrete office equipment with electronic counterparts. But significantly higher productivity is gained by the application of data communications concepts.

One of these concepts is the local network. In its most common form, it consists of a loop of coaxial cable interconnecting offices in adjacent buildings, operating at megabit/second data rates. This is about two orders of magnitude greater than what is available over common leased lines. Ideally, the local network enables the user to attach any communicating office device to the loop, automatically gaining access to all the other devices so connected. This idea is exemplified by Xerox's Ethernet offering. The user thus gains one of the most significant elements toward productivity improvement: resource sharing. Each office terminal device may readily access common databases, rather than having to maintain its own. Also, with the advent of digitized voice transmission, the office network becomes the common shared medium for all office transmissions, thus avoiding the need for separate, costlier facilities.

Standards for local networks are being established by such groups as the Institute of Electrical and Electronics Engineers (IEEE) and the International Federation of Information Processing Societies (IFIPS). To enable resource sharing on a global scale, by allowing local networks to connect to each other, standards bodies are specifying the functions of the internetwork interface, called a gateway. These functions include responsibility for end-to-end accountability, data routing, and traffic flow control. With gateway availability, local networks will interconnect and will also gain access to existing long-haul networks.

The business-office terminal is evolving into a multifunctional device. Depending on the amount of intelligence its owner is willing to purchase, it can not only handle interoffice message communications—such as "electronic mail"—but also do a considerable amount of data processing. With today's integrated-circuit chip technology, the terminal will include microprocessors—each with its own designated function. The information processing power is limited only by the imagination and ability of its designers and programmers.

Facsimile terminals are also evolving. New digital techniques enable scanning in seconds the material to be transmitted. Among these techniques is the terminal scanner's ability to skip over or "compress" redundant characters, including "white space." Of course, the receiving machine interprets the received compression codes and restores the original material in its entirety.

The Network Minicomputer. One "older" device still much in evidence in network applications is the minicomputer. As a communications processor, it "front-ends" a mainframe computer to handle the network traffic, thus freeing its host for the "number-crunching" tasks it handles more efficiently. The communications processor also functions as a switch, connecting terminals to each other as required. When a user desires access to the host's database, the front end opens a path to the mainframe.

Other network functions of the minicomputer are as a stand-alone message switch, as a cluster controller (directly controlling a group of terminals), as a gateway processor, and as a distributed processor. In the latter role, the mini may operate totally independent of a host computer, in conjunction with other minis. The resultant distributed data processing (DDP) network thus has no one element—such as a mainframe—that can make the network fail. Instead, if any of the DDP units becomes inoperative, only those functions it controls become unavailable. Of course, the coordination and programming tasks required by a DDP network are considerable, and the distributed database techniques are still evolving.

Network Control. A network does not run itself. For greatest efficiency, a control function is part of the basic network design. And the primary purpose of network control is to minimize—or better, avoid—downtime. The method used requires some specialized equipment, proven cost-effective, to acquire and interpret operational statistics. In this way, as a variable such as response time approaches its tolerance limit, the preprogrammed control mechanism apprises the network supervisor terminal of the condition. Depending on the control's complexity, corrective action may be automatic as the tolerance limit is reached, or the supervisor may key in suitable instructions to alleviate the condition.

When a network component experiences an outage, before the condition can be corrected, it must first be located and diagnosed. A properly designed network, with sufficient detection devices and diagnostic routines, and with built-in redundancy of critical components, will have minimum downtime. The problem will be located quickly, its extent readily evaluated, and the proper corrective measures promptly taken. The lesson to be learned is not to wait for trouble to decide how to handle it, but to anticipate and design for it at a very early stage of the overall project.

Protocols. The rules under which data communications devices communicate with each other are called protocols. They range from the simple, one-way-only simplex transmission to the packet-network high-level data link control (HDLC). They include transmission modes such as half duplex (one direction at a time), full duplex (both directions simultaneously), and multilayered interfaces. The more complex the protocol, the more intelligence required of the terminal/computer device and of the network. To the operator, protocols are "transparent," i.e., not visible, requiring minimal or no user reaction. As these protocols become standardized, the programming efforts needed to formulate them become susceptible to production methods such as solid-state chip technology, which makes the protocol a less-expensive hardware function.

An example of this protcol standardization sequence is the access to packet-switched networks. After much negotiation, the International Consultative Committee for Telegraphy and Telephony (CCITT) formulated its Recommendation X.25. Chips are available that implement packet-network access. As the standard is further refined, access implementation will require even less software as the functions are increasingly handled by hardware.

Software. Some firms specialize in software packages to optimize network design. The number of network alternatives is growing so fast that the demand for optimization—both in private-network design and in the interface to, and use of, public-network facilities—can be satisfied only through computer aids. These aids range from simple memory devices that compile and store network statistics to complex data traffic simulators, network design configurators, and software for data-distribution modeling. Much time and effort can be spared by computer modeling of a proposed network prior to implementation. The effects of traffic variables and equipment changes may be examined in the model, leading to network design optimization.

Other data communications software is concerned with accessing of mainframe computers by remotely located terminals. For example, among the software packages implementing this function are IBM's Virtual Telecommunications Access Method (VTAM) and Telecommuncations Access Method (TCAM), two of the more common ones. A software product that is designed to manage access methods and protocols is the teleprocessing (or telecommunications) monitor. The TP monitor optimizes a computer's processing time by off-loading the data communications software functions from the mainframe's operating system. The monitors are available from many software firms, as well as from computer vendors.

A software-related function of increasing importance to the network planner and user is database management, especially in DDP networks. A database management system (DBMS) provides users with a method of readily accessing data no matter where the data resides in a network. The aim of DBMS designers is to approach the ideal concept of totally distributed network processing. In this DDP environment, the user accesses a database by subject, and the network connects the user terminal to the proper computer. The user is completely unaware of this network operation. Common communications-related DBMS problems are contention, deadlock (simultaneous access), and recovery in a distributed environment.

To facilitate DBMS development, computers are needed that are capable of storing and retrieving information in an efficient manner. Ideally, they would handle these functions by information content, rather than by the customary techniques of physical addressing. To achieve the greater efficiencies of a computer architecture dedicated to information storage and retrieval, a database computer is needed. In its most efficient application, the database computer acts as a network node, totally decoupled from the data processing functions of the other network computers. The ideal database machine is still to be a reality, but when its role is more fully understood, it will be a significant part of DBMS and networking.

Current Trends. Spurred on by technological advancements, and enjoying an increasingly competitive climate, the data communications industry's influence on business will be considerable. With the recent FCC ruling, AT&T is free to enter the computer field. And with that other industry giant, IBM, well into the data communications field, the considerable research and development capabilities of the two companies are expected to respond to the competitive pressures of each other and of the growing number of "outsiders" with more and more technical breakthroughs.

Another giant business, the United States Postal Service, intends to pursue its electronic computer-originated mail (ECOM) plans. Fallout from this and the enhanced services expected from Satellite Business Systems will be far ranging. Access to SBS's satellite network is available to both large and small companies. Such access provides computer-to-computer links, high-speed document communications, video teleconferencing, and telephone communications. SBS offers two forms of service: one dedicated to a sole user, the other to be shared among smaller user firms.

The pace of local-network growth is accelerating. One developed by Ungermann-Bass Inc. of Santa Clara, California, is believed to be the first over which traditionally incompatible computer equipment can communicate. As expected, the key to this network—as to so many recent computer-related developments—is the microprocessor. In the Ungermann-Bass local network, the network interface unit is microprocessor-equipped to manage data-packet processing, circuit connection, and error detection.

Another notable business-office development is the digital private branch exchange. As an office's communications interface to the outside world, the PBX is undergoing considerable transformation. Besides handling both data and voice, more recent versions of the device integrate the two by digitizing the voice signals. Digitized information from word processors, "intelligent" typewriter terminals, facsimile equipment, and other devices are all funneled through the digital PBX.

Its own memory and switching functions, and interfaces to analog and digital networks (including packet-switched types), are all made possible by the application of microprocessor and chip technology.

The Future. One data communications technology showing extremely encouraging results in ongoing field tests and initial implementations is lightwave transmission. The medium in greatest use is glass, in the form of optical fibers. Using a light-emitting diode (LED) or a laser beam as the light source, data rates in the multimegabit-per-second range have been achieved. Other advantages are the material's ready availability, light weight (lighter than copper), and narrow gauge (less than coaxial cable)—all made available in a sufficiently strong packaged product.

Speech recognition and voice response technology are being applied to data communications devices in several areas. One is voice mail, where a computer synthesizes messages for the user who dials up his "mailbox." Another is the voice-activated typewriter terminal (both with and without a data communications interface), which at this writing is expected by 1990. In its ultimate form, the operator will speak to it, and the machine will print the words as spoken and correctly spelled, and the text will appear as typical typed material. Companies expected to lead with this development are IBM, Xerox, and Matsushita. The first commercial versions are expected to recognize correctly about 95% of "typical" business English as spoken by the "average" executive.

A growing phenomenon outside the United States, but starting to appear here in several versions, is interactive home TV, called videotex. Services expected are electronic mail, timeshared computing, remote shopping and banking, and travel and event reservations, besides the already vast array of home entertainment modes.

Of less visibility outside the data communications industry, but of tremendous importance, are the efforts of standards bodies to formulate specifications permitting interconnection of devices no matter which company is the manufacturer. Called Open Systems Interconnection (OSI), considerable progress is reported, but much work remains.

The increasingly competitive climate that evokes more and more advanced versions of data communications devices is starting to meet the productivity needs of inflation-plagued corporations. Just as standalone computers were seen as an aid in earlier troubled times, distributed data processing and allied data communications techniques are seen as the vehicles to help overcome the problems of more recent and near-future financially anxious eras.

Information References

Associations:
American Federation of Information Processing Socities.
American National Standards Institute.
Electronic Industries Association.
Institute of Electrical and Electronic Engineers.

International Consultative Committee for Telegraphy and Telephony.
International Federation of Information Processing Societies.
International Organization for Standardization
International Telecommunications Union.

Periodicals:
Data Communications
(See also periodicals listed under ELECTRONIC DATA PROCESSING.)

Texts:
"Data Communications Buyers' Guide," New York, McGraw-Hill, issued annually.
"Datacomm for the Businessman," Cherry Hill, N.J., Management Information Corp., 1981
Doll, Dixon R., "Data Communications Facilities, Networks, and Systems Designs," New York, Wiley, 1978.
Folts, Harold C., ed., "Data Communications Standards," New York, McGraw-Hill, 1982.
Karp, Harry R., ed., "Basics of Data Communications," New York, McGraw-Hill, 1976.
Karp, Harry R., ed., "Practical Applications of Data Communications," New York, McGraw-Hill, 1980.
Liebowitz, Burt H. and Carson, John H., "Distributed Processing," Silver Spring, Md., IEEE Computer Society Press, 1978.
McQuillan, John M. and Cerf, Vinton G., "A Practical View of Computer Communications Protocols," Silver Spring, Md., IEEE Computer Society Press, 1978.

CHAPTER 1

HISTORICAL DEVELOPMENT OF COMMUNICATIONS

1.1 INTRODUCTION

Man's inability to make his voice heard beyond a very limited distance was perhaps the governing factor in the early development of communications techniques. In the 11th century B.C., Homer, describing the fall of Troy, wrote about a chain of fires which were used to transmit news of the capitulation of that city. In the 18th century, as the pioneers moved westward across the Missouri, two shots from the scout's revolver were used as the all clear signal to the wagon train several miles to the rear.

As man's level of technological development progressed, there was a corresponding advancement in the level of communications techniques employed. In the 18th and 19th centuries, complex messages of war and peace, trade and art, science and history were transmitted in written form over distances of hundreds or thousands of miles, with the Pony Express linking the North American continent from shore to shore in a matter of days.

Wanting to communicate between greater distances on a faster scale, man experimented to develop more rapid and reliable communications systems. The development of these systems was based upon the utilization of a variety of machines that transmit information electronically to other machines located in another room or in a remote part of the world.

No matter what technology is employed or the type of communications used, three common items are required in order to communicate. First, a source or transmitter must exist. The transmitter can range from the tom-tom, to the more modern telegraph key, to a present-day communications terminal. Second, for the transmission to reach its destination, it must travel over an appropriate medium. This medium can be the atmosphere for the signal of the tom-tom, a wire for the transmission of telegraph signals, or a combination of media. An example of the latter could be outer space and wires within a building to connect an antenna receiving telemetry information to a computer. Third, a sink or receiver must be present to capture the signals that are transmitted.

1.2 TELEGRAPH SYSTEMS

The era of electronic communications began on May 24, 1844, when Samuel Morse transmitted the well-known "What hath God wrought?" from the United States Capitol in Washington to his partner, Alfred Vale, in Baltimore. Shortly thereafter the telegraph line was extended to New York City and additional lines were rapidly installed throughout the United States. The explosive growth of the telegraph system can be attributed to the simplicity of the code Morse developed as well as to the expansion of the railroad system across the North American continent. A major portion of telegraph message volume consisted of information concerning train dispatching. That telegraph lines could share a right of way with railroad lines resulted in the growth of each system complementing the other.

Due to the lack of a satisfactory system for sending and receiving information automatically, the use of telegraphy for many years was limited to the hand keying of the Morse code. The transmitter in the Morse telegraph system was a telegraph key, which is simply a switch with a handle so that it can be operated by trained personnel. This switch was used to open or close an electrical circuit whose power was provided by a battery or another source of direct current. The receiver consisted of an electromagnet with a moving armature.

When the transmitting operator depressed the telegraph key, he would close the circuit, which in turn would cause current to flow, making the movable armature click at the receiving end as it was pulled by the electromagnet to its stop position. These clicks of the armature could be "read" by a trained ear, and the sequence of clicks—a series of short and long contact closures—was used to represent different characters in Morse code.

A simple one-way telegraph circuit is illustrated in Figure 1.2.1.

This type of circuit is also referred to as a simplex circuit since information flows in one direction. When information can travel in either direction, but not at the same time, the circuit is known as half-duplex; and in either direction simultaneously, full duplex. (See Sec. 4.3.)

Although the Morse code was extensively utilized on telegraph systems, two factors hampered the development of automatic transmission with the use of that code. First, the structure of Morse code was not suitable for reception of transmitted information since different characters have a different number of elements consisting of a series of short (dot) and long (dash) contact closures to identify the character. Secondly, since there were no prescribed time intervals between characters, a method to synchronize the transmitting and receiving units was lacking.

These problems persisted until 1874 when a Frenchman, Emil Baudot, devised a constant-length code, which was an important step toward the development of automatic transmission systems. In the constant-length code, the number of

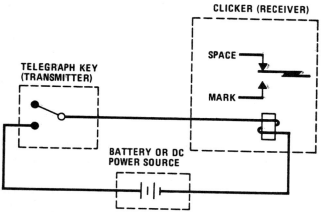

FIGURE 1.2.1   Simplex Telegraph Circuit

elements or signals used to represent a character is the same (constant) for every character, and the duration of each element is also a constant.

The Baudot code is commonly referred to as a five-level code since five elements or signals are used to represent a character. It is interesting to note that the Baudot code is considered by many to be the forerunner of most data processing codes in use today.

In 1910, an American, Howard Krum, devised a technique for synchronizing the transmission and reception of each character by appending a standard element to be used as an identifier to denote the beginning and end of each character. Krum's technique, known as start/stop synchronism, combined with the constant-length Baudot code, resulted in the development and widespread utilization of automatic telegraph equipment.

Commercial operation of automatic telegraph equipment, normally referred to as teleprinter service, began in 1910 with the Postal Telegraph System and later with the Western Union System. From a handful of teleprinters in 1910, rapid expansion resulted in tens of thousands of teleprinters in use today, serving private, commercial, and governmental users. Two of the largest and best known teleprinter networks are TWX and Telex.

Both TWX and Telex permit subscribers to transmit messages through the network to other subscribers. These message-switching systems are operated by Western Union. (TWX was developed by AT&T and sold to Western Union in 1971.) In 1956, Western Union introduced Telex service in the United States. This service originated in Germany in 1934 and was expanded into an international communications service. Currently, Telex susbcribers must employ teleprinters capable of using the 5-level Baudot code, whereas TWX users can connect to that service with terminals that use the Baudot code as well as terminals that use the more recently developed 8-level American Standard Code for Information Interchange (ASCII code).

Within the Department of Defense, the Army, Navy, and Air Force operate very large worldwide teleprinter networks. Many commercial organizations have developed corporatewide teleprinter networks for message switching by integrating teleprinters, lines, and computers to form specialized data communications networks.

1.3 TELEPHONE SYSTEMS

In 1874, thirty years after the first telegraph transmission, Alexander Graham Bell built a device that permitted an electrical current to vary in intensity within the device as the density of the surrounding air varied in passing through the device. Using a rudimentary diaphragm, Bell was able to pick up the sound waves generated by the twang of a clock spring, convert the waves into an electric current, and then reconvert that current back into sound at the distant end of the electrical circuit.

Bell continued experimenting with his device, which was known as a harmonic telegraph, until, on March 10, 1876, he transmitted the now famous sentence over a wire from his laboratory in Boston to his associate in the adjoining room: "Mr. Watson, come here, I want you!"

A simplified one-way telephone circuit is illustrated in Figure 1.3.1.

Here, the sound waves from the speaker cause the diaphragm to vibrate, thus causing the carbon grains behind it to be compressed or released according to the speaker's inflection. The change in the carbon grains causes varying resistance in the circuit, which in turn causes the current flow to vary. The resultant alternating current is similar in wave shape to that of the sound waves producing it. The alternating current, in turn, is passed into the primary winding to induce current into the secondary winding, from which the current is passed onto the telephone line.

FIGURE 1.3.1 Elementary Telephone Circuit

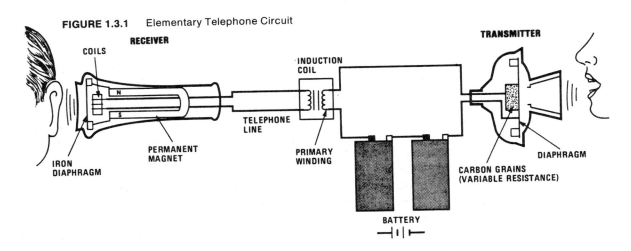

At the receiver, the coils in the electromagnet are connected across the pair of wires that forms the telephone line, and alternately attract or repel the iron diaphragm. The diaphragm in turn acts on the air next to it, to create sound waves similar in form to those that the speaker originated. Electrical power for the circuit is supplied by a battery or other direct current source. The permanent magnet in the receiver holds the diaphram in a central or neutral position when no alternating current is flowing, permitting the diaphragm to move either backward or forward.

In 1877, a telephone line was constructed between Boston and Somerville, Mass. Over the next three years additional lines and more than 50,000 telephones were installed in the United States. Approximately 100 years after the invention of the telephone, the United States was covered by a network of about one-half billion miles of telephone circuits, with 100 million telephones in use. Also in 1877, the first manual telephone switchboard was introduced; in 1882 the first dial-system switchboard (no manual intervention) was placed into operation. Today, almost 100 percent of the telephones in the United States have direct distance dialing (DDD) capability.

1.4 NEW TECHNOLOGICAL DEVELOPMENTS

Two recent technological developments have resulted in significant advances in the state of communications: satellites and lasers.

A communications satellite is basically a microwave radio relay station normally suspended (geostationary) at a point above the earth. First used by the military in the 1960s, the reliability and flexibility offered by satellites when compared to conventional methods of communications resulted in a number of commercial satellite offerings. By 1980, over one-hundred companies had earth stations installed on their premises to enable them to communicate directly via satellite to other company locations. There, connections were provided by other ground stations or by a telephone line connecting a satellite communications carrier's ground station to the customer's premises.

New developments in satellite technology permit thousands of simultaneous connections from different locations to be retransmitted via the satellite to ground stations distributed over a wide geographical area. The communications satellites' key limitation is that they are required to be in a line-of-sight position to both receive transmitted data and retransmit that data to the receiving ground station. One typical customer's satellite network is illustrated in Figure 1.4.1.

The second technological development that holds promise for significant advances in communications is the application of lasers. It has been demonstrated that the coherent light of the laser can transmit tremendous quantities of data when compared to conventional communications systems. Fiber optics, which is a grouping of glass fibers bundled together, permits light to be transmitted in other than a straight path. When combined with lasers, it holds an exciting potential for advances in the state of communications.

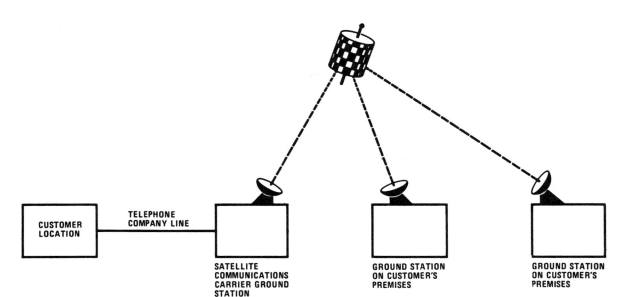

FIGURE 1.4.1   Satellite Network

1.5 SUMMARY

As man developed, he sought to transfer information between persons and locations by meaningful sounds and symbols. When the requirement arose to communicate at a more rapid rate between locations separated by great distances, new communications systems were developed, resulting in a series of progressively more sophisticated electronic communications systems. Man is both a communications system as well as the manipulator of machines that transfer information by wire, radio, and optical signals.

QUESTIONS

1.1 What three items are required for all communications? Discuss two different types of communications systems and how the three items required for communications relate to one another.

1.2 Why was the Morse code not suitable for utilization by an automatic transmission system?

1.3 What two developments resulted in the development and widespread utilization of automatic telegraph equipment?

CHAPTER 2

DEVELOPMENT OF COMPUTATIONAL MACHINERY

2.1 INTRODUCTION

During the last three decades we have witnessed two of the most incredible technological revolutions in the history of the world. The first (described in Chapter 1) is the advent of a truly global communications system, linking remote locations via satellites. The second revolution was the advent and evolution of the digital computer. In a short period of time computer technology has become so profound that the term "generation" has been applied to the sequences of machines that have been developed.

The first device used to help man perform calculations was the abacus, which was developed in China around 450 B.C., and is still used today in many areas of the world. The next significant development occurred more than 2,000 years later when man started to design and build mechanical calculators. In 1812, a British mathematician, Charles Babbage, designed a machine to aid in the computation of mathematical tables. This machine, which he called a "difference engine," was completed in 1822. Other mathematicians of that period also attempted to build calculating machines; however, a calculator is not a computer. In 1833, Babbage designed an "analytical engine," which was to be completely automatic. This heralded the dawn of the computer era. Although the machine was not constructed because the parts it required could not be built with sufficient precision in those days, the device had all the elements of a modern digital computer. It had a storage area for holding information (memory), components to perform calculations (arithmetic unit), and a means of controlling the operation (control unit).

The modern history of digital computation began in 1939 with Howard Aiken and his associates at Harvard University. Their work on an automatic-sequence-controlled electromechanical calculator called the Mark I was completed in 1944.

This machine was primarily designed to solve differential equations, and followed a sequence of programmed instructions stored on punched paper tape.

Like Babbage's analytical engine, the Mark I used binary arithmetic and had the same three basic elements of memory, arithmetic, and control units. An input/output unit however was added to the Mark I to enter data and return answers, providing a firm foundation for further computer development. The Mark I could perform any specified sequence consisting of the four basic arithmetic operations (addition, subtraction, multiplication, division) and references to tables of previously computed results. Information was supplied on punched cards and by the setting of switches on the machine, while answers were punched on cards or printed by a typewriter. The Mark I was in use for over 15 years, and a typical multiplication on that machine required about 3 seconds.

In 1946 the second key development of modern computer technology occurred. J.P. Eckert and J.W. Mauchley at the University of Pennsylvania designed the Eniac (electronic numerical integrator and computer). This machine was the forerunner of the first generation of electronic digital computers and contained 18,000 vacuum tubes. Since the device had no moving parts, its development represented a significant advance in computer technology. Addition required 0.2 milliseconds and multiplication took 2.8 milliseconds. The Eniac was programmed by the wiring of circuit boards on the machine, which was a slow process that limited its versatility.

In 1946 Dr. John von Neumann at the Institute of Advanced Study in Princeton introduced the concept of the stored program, which is used in all modern computers. In a stored program, a sequence of instructions maintained in memory are examined by the device to determine what sequence of computations is to be followed. The computer proposed by von Neumann was completed in 1950. Called an Edvac (electronic discrete variable automatic computer), it had twelve different instructions and performed additions in 0.9 milliseconds and multiplications in about 2.9 milliseconds.

The first commercially produced electronic digital computer was the Univac I. This computer was used by the United States government to perform all the calculations of the 1950 national census and was sold to commercial organizations in 1951. The Univac I and most of the following computers developed during the 1950s used vacuum tubes.

Vacuum tube technology, while permitting computation to occur at a rate thousands of times that expected from Babbage's analytical engine, had a number of drawbacks. First, tubes were bulky devices that consumed large amounts of power and correspondingly produced a large amount of heat that had to be removed from the environment. Second, the vacuum tubes were short-life devices, and at any given time the probability was quite high that at least one tube had failed in the computer.

These early machines were predominantly used for scientific work and there was very little desire to add to the hazards of computing by transmitting information to remote locations via telephone or telegraph lines. As the volume of information from computing grew, and as decisions became more time critical, new developmental efforts turned toward the existing telegraph lines and the Telex message-switching network, fostering the beginning of data communications technology as we know it today.

By 1960 the semiconductor industry had been formed, and during the early 60s a second generation of computers was developed that used discrete solid state electronic components in place of vacuum tubes. These computers performed operations hundreds of times faster, with instructions executed in microseconds, and were less expensive than the machines they replaced.

By the mid-1960s advances in technology resulted in the replacement of discrete electronic components (transistors) by integrated components that combined hundreds of functional units on one chip. A dramatic price/performance breakthrough in computational capability occurred, fostering the third generation of computers, with computer instructions now executed in nanoseconds (billionths of a second).

Advances in semiconductor technology have led to chips replacing tens of thousands of discrete units, resulting in computer developments that some consider to be the fourth generation of computer technology. These chips are called LSI (large-scale integrated) and VLSI (very-large-scale integrated) types.

2.2 COMPUTATIONAL NUMBERING CONCEPTS

The basic building block mathematics of a digital computer is Boolean algebra. Named after the English mathematician, George Boole, who pioneered in the field of symbolic logic, it is an important tool in the design and analysis of computers.

The simple circuit illustrated in Figure 2.2.1 shows why mathematical logic is important in the design of digital computers. Let us assign the value of 0 to the switch when it is open and the value of 1 when it is closed. These two switch states then correspond to the value of false (0) and true (1) of the symbolic logic of Boolean algebra.

For the simple series circuit illustrated in Figure 2.2.1 there will be continuity to the output point C only when both switch A and switch B are closed. This situation can be described by the Boolean statement A AND B, which is written symbolically as A·B.

In the lower portion of Figure 2.2.1, a parallel circuit is represented. This is a circuit where there will be continuity to point C if either A or B is closed and is described by the Boolean statement A OR B, which is written symbolically as A + B.

Although George Boole's book, "An Investigation of the Laws of Thought," concerning mathematical logic, was published in 1854, it was not until the 1930s that bistable electronic components were available from which computers could be constructed. A bistable electronic component is so named because it exists in one of two states. Consider the action of a bistable electronic component illustrated in Figure 2.2.2. This component could be a vacuum tube as found in a first generation computer, a semiconductor such as a diode common in a second generation computer, or one functional unit on a chip found in a third generation computer.

As illustrated in Figure 2.2.2, the bistable component is initially at state A; then

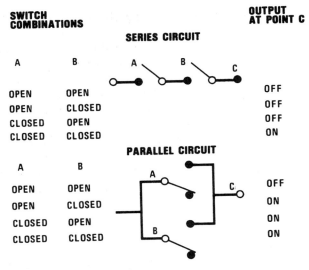

FIGURE 2.2.1   Switching circuit analysis

an energy pulse drives it to a new state B. If the component is in state B, then the removal of the energy pulse will return it to state A. This can be thought of as being similar to turning on and off a transistor. If we define state A to represent the number 0 and state B to represent the number 1, we can—through the binary numbering system—use bistable components to represent any number.

Prior to examining the binary numbering system let us review a commonly used but infrequently dissected numbering system—the decimal system.

The Decimal System

The decimal system is also known as the base-10 number system. It has 10 different symbols that make up all its numbers—0 through 9. Consider the number 575. This

FIGURE 2.2.2   Action of bistable electronic component

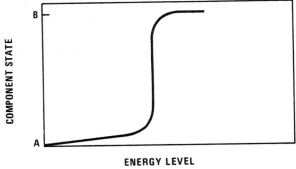

TABLE 2.2.1   DECIMAL SYSTEM POWERS OF THE BASE

1 =							$= 10^0$
10 =	10						$= 10^1$
100 =	10	×	10				$= 10^2$
1,000 =	10	×	10	× 10			$= 10^3$
10,000 =	10	×	10	× 10	× 10		$= 10^4$
100,000 =	10	×	10	× 10	× 10	× 10	$= 10^5$

number really means 5 hundreds plus 7 tens plus 5 ones. Each digit corresponds to a place value that is obtained by multiplying 10 by itself over and over, resulting in the 10s place, the 100s places, and so on. The place values can thus be represented as powers of the base, meaning the number of times the base is multiplied by itself, as shown in Table 2.2.1. From Table 2.2.1 note that 10 to the zero power (10^0) is 1. In fact, any number to the zero power is 1. Note also that 10 to the first power (10^1) is 10. Returning to our decimal number 575, it may also be read as follows:

$$575 = 5 \times 10^2 + 7 \times 10^1 + 5 \times 10^0$$
$$= 5 \text{ hundreds} + 7 \text{ tens} + 5 \text{ ones}$$

The Binary System

In the binary or base-2 system, only the digits 0 and 1 are used. When using binary numbers, the place values are found by multiplying 2 by itself over and over to obtain the 2s place, the 4s place, the 8s place and so on. The place values can be represented as powers of the base as shown in Table 2.2.2. Using the information in Table 2.2.2, the binary number 11010 can be expressed as its decimal equivalent:

$$11010 = 1 \times 2^4 + 1 \times 2^3 + 0 \times 2^2 + 1 \times 2^1 + 0 \times 2^0$$
$$= 16 + 8 + 0 + 2 + 0$$
$$= 26$$

To alleviate the confusion that can occur when working with different number systems, we can employ the use of a subscript to indicate the numbers base. Thus, $11010_2 = 26_{10}$, which is read as "11010" in base 2 is equal to "26" in base 10.

TABLE 2.2.2   BINARY SYSTEM POWERS OF THE BASE

1 =										$= 2^0$
2 =	2									$= 2^1$
4 =	2	×	2							$= 2^2$
8 =	2	×	2	×	2					$= 2^3$
16 =	2	×	2	×	2	×	2			$= 2^4$
32 =	2	×	2	×	2	×	2	×	2	$= 2^5$
64 =	2	×	2	×	2	×	2	×	2	× 2	$= 2^6$

To go in the opposite direction and convert a decimal number to binary, two methods can be employed. The easier but more laborious method is to write out all the binary place values up to the highest one you will require for the decimal number. Thus, for converting the number 26_{10}, we would write:

$$16\ 8\ 4\ 2\ 1$$

We do not require the next higher place number, which would be 32, because the decimal number to be converted (26_{10}) is smaller than that one.

Now all that remains is for us to put a 1 under each of the terms via trial and error until they add up to 26. After some fast addition, our result would be as follows:

$$16\ 8\ 4\ 2\ 1$$
$$1\ 1\ 0\ 1\ 0$$

A second method to convert decimal numbers to binary is by continuous division by 2, where the remainder is used to indicate the binary place value while the quotient is divided again and again by 2 until it becomes zero, as illustrated in Table 2.2.3.

Although binary numbers are the basis of computer technology, they are difficult for people to use, especially when such numbers are long. This makes the

TABLE 2.2.3   DECIMAL TO BINARY CONVERSION BY REPEATED DIVISION

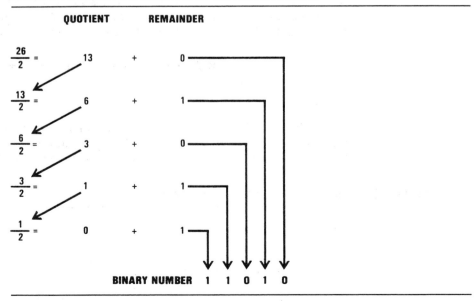

TABLE 2.2.4   OCTAL SYSTEM POWERS OF THE BASE

1 =					= 8^0
8 =	8				= 8^1
64 =	8	×	8		= 8^2
512 =	8	×	8	×	8	= 8^3

probability of an error occurring relatively high when they are written or read. Since binary numbers tend to be long, it is often convenient to group the binary digits in sets of digits. These sets of digits now produce different bases with different numbering systems and provide man with a shorthand method of binary representation.

Most digital computers are designed for one or another of these shorthand systems. As an example, a computer may be designed so that humans can easily use the octal number (base-8) system with it, as is the Honeywell Series 700. The IBM System/360 and 370 computers have been designed so that the hexadecimal (base-16) system can be easily used with it. In any case, the computer itself always uses the binary system for internal data manipulation, and the shorthand systems based upon the octal and hexadecimal number systems are only for human convenience.

Octal and Hexadecimal Number Systems

By grouping the binary digits into sets of 3, the numbers are converted into octal format. The octal number system is based on 8 and has eight different symbols, 0 through 7, whose place values are powers of 8, as illustrated in Table 2.2.4.

To convert an octal number to decimal is just like converting a binary number to decimal, with the exception that one uses powers of 8 rather than powers of 2. Thus, the octal number 512 can be represented as:

$$5 \times 8^2 + 1 \times 8^1 + 2 \times 8^0 = 330_{10}$$

To convert a decimal number to an octal number, one may use either of the two methods for converting a decimal number to a binary number which were previously explained. As an example, consider the decimal number 330. To convert to octal, we divide the decimal number by 8 and save the remainder, continuing the process by dividing the quotient by 8 until no further division is possible, with the remainders forming the octal number as illustrated in Table 2.2.5.

Now that we have examined octal as a number system let us explore how it can be used as a shorthand for the binary number system. The first eight octal numbers and their binary equivalents are illustrated in Table 2.2.6.

From Table 2.2.6 we can see that the highest number that can be written with a single digit in octal is 7, and its binary equivalent requires three binary digits. By

TABLE 2.2.5 DECIMAL TO OCTAL CONVERSION BY REPEATED DIVISION

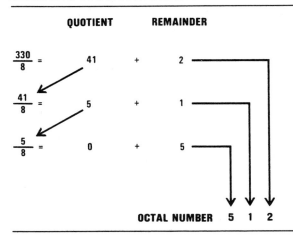

grouping binary digits into sets of 3 we can therefore convert the number into octal format. Thus, the binary number

$$1 1 1 0 1 1 0 1 0 1_2$$

can be grouped into 3 sets of 3 digits and a most significant digit.

$$1 \quad 110 \quad 110 \quad 101$$

Converting to octal, the binary number becomes 1665_8.

The hexadecimal number system, whose base is 16, uses the symbols 0 through 9 for the first ten digits and the letters A through F to stand for 10, 11, 12, 13, 14, and 15. By grouping the binary digits into sets of 4, the number is converted to hexadecimal format. Thus, the binary number 1 1 1 0 1 1 0 1 0 1 can be grouped into 2 sets of 4 digits and 1 set of 2 digits to produce:

TABLE 2.2.6 OCTAL AND BINARY EQUIVALENTS

Octal	Binary
0	0
1	1
2	10
3	11
4	100
5	101
6	110
7	111

TABLE 2.2.7   NUMBERING SYSTEM RELATIONSHIPS

Hexadecimal	Decimal	Octal	Binary
0	0	0	00000
1	1	1	00001
2	2	2	00010
3	3	3	00011
4	4	4	00100
5	5	5	00101
6	6	6	00110
7	7	7	00111
8	8	10	01000
9	9	11	01001
A	10	12	01010
B	11	13	01011
C	12	14	01100
D	13	15	01101
E	14	16	01110
F	15	17	01111
10	16	20	10000

$$1\ 1 \quad 1\ 0\ 1\ 1 \quad 0\ 1\ 0\ 1$$
$$3 \qquad B \qquad 5$$

the hexadecimal number $3B5_{16}$. In Table 2.2.7, the relationships between the first 17 numbers of the hexadecimal, decimal, octal, and binary number systems are listed.

2.3 BINARY ARITHMETIC

Now that we have examined several numbering systems, let us investigate how we can use one such system. Binary numbers can be operated on in the same manner as decimal numbers, with a carry occurring when 1 is added to 1, which is similar to the carry when 1 is added to 9 in the decimal system. The four possible combinations in binary addition are:

AUGEND	+	ADDEND	=	RESULT	+	CARRY
0	+	0	=	0	+	0
0	+	1	=	1	+	0
1	+	0	=	1	+	0
1	+	1	=	1	+	1

Like decimal arithmetic, the carry is added to the next higher position. As an example, consider the following:

```
   1          carries        1
   6                         0110
 + 5     in decimal becomes  0101    in binary.
  11                         1011
```

Binary subtraction can be performed by following decimal system rules where we borrow from the next position of the minuend when the present value of the subtrahend is greater than the present value of the minuend. Since many computers perform subtraction by doing a special type of addition operation to minimize circuitry, let us examine how this process can occur.

Subtraction can be performed by the implementation of complement binary arithmetic. The ones complement of a binary number is formed by changing every one to zero and every zero in the number to one. For example, the ones complement of 0110 is 1001. The twos complement of a binary number is obtained by adding 1 to the ones complement of that number, as shown below:

```
binary number        0110
Ones complement      1001
Twos complement      + 1
                     1010
```

In the binary number system, subtraction can be performed by adding the twos complement of the subtrahend to the minuend and discarding the final carry. For example, to perform the binary subtraction

```
Minuend        0110
Subtrahend     0101
```

we form the twos complement of the subtrahend, which is obtained by adding 1 to the ones complement (1010 + 1 = 1011). Next, the twos complement of the subtrahend is added to the minuend and the final carry is discarded as shown below:

```
                   Minuend              0110
Twos complement of subtrahend         + 1011
                                   1) 0001        Difference
                                         ↙
          discard final carry
```

The discarded final carry provides the sign of the answer. If the final carry is 1, then the answer is positive. Conversely if the final carry is 0, then the answer is negative.

In many computers, binary multiplication is performed by repeated additions, since each partial is either zero or exactly the multiplicand. For example:

$$
\begin{array}{r}
6 \\
\times 5 \\
\hline
30_{10}
\end{array}
\quad \text{in decimal becomes} \quad
\begin{array}{r}
110 \\
\times\ 101 \\
\hline
110 \\
000 \\
110 \\
\hline
11110_2
\end{array}
\quad \text{in binary}
$$

The last operation to be considered in this section, binary division, is performed in most computers by a series of repeated subtractions. For example:

$$
\begin{array}{r}
110 \quad \text{Quotient} \\
101\,\overline{)\,11110} \quad \text{Dividend} \\
\underline{101} \\
101 \\
\underline{101} \\
0000 \\
\underline{0000} \\
0
\end{array}
$$

(Divisor)

2.4 COMPUTER HARDWARE ORGANIZATION

Architecturally, computers generally resemble one another to a very high degree. In Figure 2.4.1 a simplified block diagram is used to show the hardware organization of a typical digital computer.

Today most computer memories are implemented using high-speed semiconductors or magnetic core elements. They are random-access devices where data can be written to or read from any addressed section of memory.

As the name implies, the arithmetic and logic unit performs arithmetic operations on data transferred within the computer, the memory, and from and to input and output devices.

Referred to as the computer's "brain" because it coordinates all the computer units in timed logical sequence, the control unit receives sequences of instructions from memory. These sequences, called programs, reside in memory and are best known as "software."

In order to communicate with a wide variety of devices, data transfers occur via the input or output sections of a computer. In most cases the input/output unit of a computer is bidirectional and referred to as the I/O unit. Devices connected to a computer's I/O unit are known as computer peripherals and include line printers, cathode ray tube displays, card readers and punches, magnetic storage disks and drums, paper or magnetic tape units, and assorted communications devices and lines.

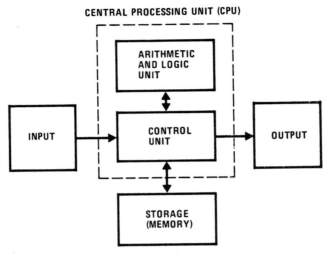

FIGURE 2.4.1   Hardware organization of a digital computer

In addition to the five functional units illustrated in Figure 2.4.1, every computer contains a set of registers, and circuits linking the five functional units to the registers. A register can be thought of as a box that provides intermediate storage of data and instructions. As an example, when two numbers are to be added, they might first be loaded into two registers. Then the circuitry to add the contents of the two registers would be activated to store the result in a third register.

Memory Organization

At any instant during the execution of a program, the memory is equivalent to a grid of binary digits (bits) consisting of a pattern of ones and zeros as illustrated in Figure 2.4.2. Since a single bit can only represent two states, 0 or 1, we must code larger numbers by grouping bits into "words" to convey greater amounts of information.

Common computer word sizes include 8, 12, 16, 18, 24, 32, and 64 bits. A computer that groups bits into 16-bit words, for example, is referred to as a 16-bit

FIGURE 2.4.2   Computer memory during program execution

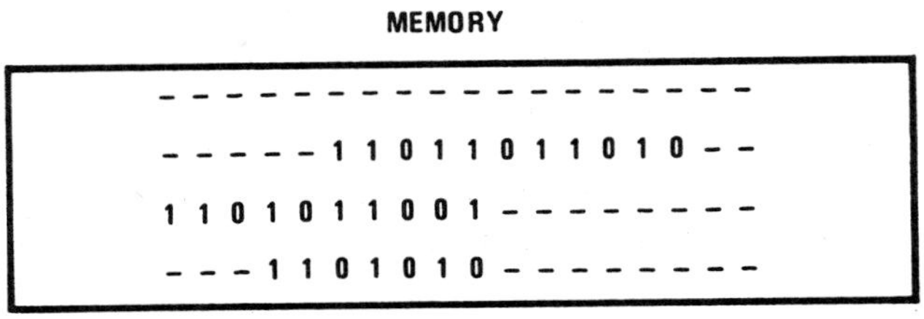

MEMORY

```
- - - - - - - - - - - - - - - - -
- - - - - 1 1 0 1 1 0 1 1 0 1 0 - -
1 1 0 1 0 1 1 0 0 1 - - - - - - - -
- - - 1 1 0 1 0 1 0 - - - - - - - -
```

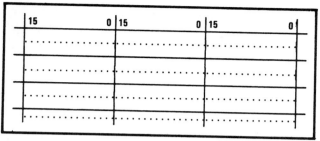

FIGURE 2.4.3   Organization of 16-bit-word computer memory

machine, while a computer whose logic is based on 32-bit words is referred to as a 32-bit machine. Memory in a 16-bit computer can be visualized as illustrated in Figure 2.4.3. By convention, the bits of a computer word are numbered from right to left. In Figure 2.4.3 the low order or least significant bit is 0 and the most significant or high order bit is 15.

Within the computer's memory, every word has a unique address. Thus, in addition to consisting of a grouping of bits, a computer word is also a group of bits that represents the largest addressable unit of information in memory.

Numeric Representations

Depending upon the architecture of the machine, numeric data can be represented in one of several ways. In a 16-bit computer, each word might be subdivided as shown in the top portion of Figure 2.4.4. Here, the 16-bit word is subdivided to contain 5 octal digits, while the 15th bit represents the sign of the data. Thus, numeric data would fall within the range:

$$1\,7\,7\,7\,7\,7_8 = -3\,2\,7\,6\,7_{10}$$

to

$$0\,7\,7\,7\,7\,7_8 = +3\,2\,7\,6\,7_{10}$$

FIGURE 2.4.4   Numeric representation based on word structure

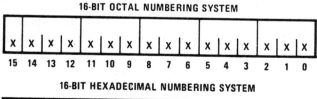

16-BIT OCTAL NUMBERING SYSTEM

X	X	X	X	X	X	X	X	X	X	X	X	X	X	X	X
15	14	13	12	11	10	9	8	7	6	5	4	3	2	1	0

16-BIT HEXADECIMAL NUMBERING SYSTEM

X	X	X	X	X	X	X	X	X	X	X	X	X	X	X	X
15	14	13	12	11	10	9	8	7	6	5	4	3	2	1	0

In the bottom portion of Figure 2.4.4, the 16-bit word is subdivided into 4 hexadecimal digits. If the high order bit is used to represent the sign (one convention), then the numeric data would fall within the range:

$$F F F F_{16} = -3 2 7 6 7_{10}$$

to

$$7 F F F_{16} = +3 2 7 6 7_{10}$$

Character Representation

In addition to entering, processing, and outputting numeric data, the computer must interpret letters of the alphabet and special characters such as $, +, -$. Then, by having appropriate software and peripheral devices, a payroll program (for example) could be executed and employee checks with names, addresses, and remuneration could be printed. To represent characters, a set of bits are grouped together to form what is referred to as a byte.

Two of the most common codes used to represent data with bytes are the American standard code for information interchange (ASCII) and the extended binary coded decimal interchange code (EBCDIC). If a character is represented by an 8-bit byte, then a computer will relate its word to character bytes as illustrated in Figure 2.4.5.

If the computer's word size is 6 bits, the two high-order bits from the 8-bit byte are eliminated, which reduces the number of different characters that can be represented on such a machine. In the middle portion of Figure 2.4.5, an 8-bit-word computer directly represents one byte with one 8-bit word. When the computer's word size is 16 bits or greater, more than one byte may be packed into the computer word. This is illustrated in the bottom portion of Figure 2.4.5 where two 8-bit bytes have been packed into one 16-bit computer word. Although we have seen that at its lowest level a computer's memory consists of a sequence of binary digits, we can now recognize that both numbers and characters can be read, manipulated, and transmitted to peripheral devices by the computer.

2.5 COMPUTER SOFTWARE CONCEPTS

A digital computer is constructed to perform calculations by executing a sequence of operations called instructions. The sequence of instructions is called a program.

In early digital computer applications, programming was accomplished by logically and electrically inserting binary digits into the computer's memory. Here, a particular string of bits, say 8 or 16, constitutes a language instruction, such as "store the results." The computer hardware then interprets each coded instruction for program execution. Such numeric coding, called machine language programming, makes excellent use of computer resources. But the effort is so tedious and time consuming that few computers are now programmed this way.

6-BIT COMPUTER WORD CONTAINS A PORTION OF A BYTE

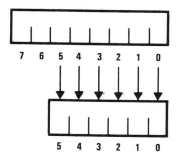

8-BIT COMPUTER WORD CONTAINS 1 FULL BYTE

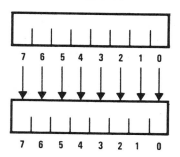

16-BIT COMPUTER WORD CONTAINS 2 FULL BYTES

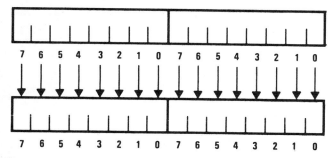

FIGURE 2.4.5   Relationships between 8-bit byte and computer words

Assembly-language programming uses easy-to-remember symbolic notations, or mnemonics, instead of strings of 1s and 0s, to define an operation or instruction. The mnemonic ADD (for addition), for example, when inserted by the programmer, is interpreted by the computer to generate the corresponding machine-language instructions. That is, there is a one-to-one correspondence in that each assembly-language mnemonic symbol produces an equivalent machine-language instruction. The result of the assembly translation is called an object program. The object program is then executed by the computer as illustrated in the top portion of Figure 2.5.1.

The chief advantage of the assembly language is that the programmer only needs to remember and use simple symbols instead of a long string of 1s and 0s. The net result is that assembly-language programming is easier, faster, and more accurate than machine-language programming.

Applications programmed in assembly language appropriate to a particular computer are, however, usually valid only for that computer or generic family of computers. So, if circumstances warrant a changeover to another vendor's computer, the application must be reprogrammed for the new computer. In other words, machine-language and assembly-language programs are both "machine-dependent."

With a procedure- or higher-level-oriented language, the programming of a particular application becomes independent of the computer—provided that the computer vendor can supply a compiler, translator, or interpreter that converts the procedure-oriented language program into a machine-language object program suited to his computer. This is illustrated in the bottom portion of Figure 2.5.1.

With a procedure-oriented language, programmers can produce with one statement a segment of a program that in assembly language would require many more individual statements. In Figure 2.5.2, the relationship between machine-language, assembly-language and procedure-oriented-language programming for a simple application involving the summing of two numbers is illustrated.

What the programmer has to code for each of these methods is enclosed in boxes. Note that in both the machine-language and assembly-language methods, the programmer writes five "lines" of instructions and two lines of data. The procedure-oriented language requires the same two lines of data but just one statement, which the computer's translator automatically converts to the equivalent machine-language instructions.

In more complex programs, five procedure-oriented language statements might perform the equivalent of 50 or more assembly-language instructions. Thus, speed

FIGURE 2.5.1 Program processors

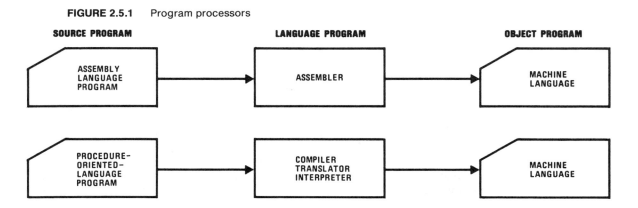

LANGUAGE COMPARISON	MACHINE LANGUAGE	MACHINE LANGUAGE EQUIVALENT (BINARY)	ASSEMBLY LANGUAGE			PROCEDURE - ORIENTED LANGUAGE
MEMORY LOCATION	FUNCTIONAL DESCRIPTION OF INSTRUCTION		SYMBOLIC LOCATION	MNEMONIC OPERATION	OPERAND	
770	PICK UP DATA IN LOC 774	0 0 0 0 1 0 0 1 1 1 1 1 1 1 1 0		LDA	DATA1	
771	ADD DATA IN LOC 775	0 0 0 1 1 0 0 1 1 1 1 1 1 1 0 1		ADD	DATA2	
772	STORE RESULT	0 0 0 1 0 0 0 1 1 1 1 1 1 1 1 0		STA	RESULT	
773	STOP EXECUTION	0 0 0 0 0 0 0 0 0 0 0 0 0 0 0 0		STOP		
774	DATA (DECIMAL 1)	0 0 0 0 0 0 0 0 0 0 0 0 0 0 0 1	DATA1 (=1)	DEC	1	DATA (=1)
775	DATA (DECIMAL 100)	0 0 0 0 0 0 0 0 0 1 1 0 0 1 0 0	DATA2 (=100)	DEC	100	DATA (=100)
776	RESULTS GO HERE	0 0 0 0 0 0 0 0 1 1 0 0 1 0 1	RESULT	BSS	101	RESULT = DATA1 + DATA2 101

FIGURE 2.5.2   Language relationships

of programming in a procedure-oriented language is one of the key advantages over programming in assembly language.

Early procedure-oriented languages were certainly less efficient and slower in program execution than equivalent assembly-language programs since the procedure-oriented language invokes a greater number of machine instructions than would be required by the equivalent assembly-language program. This is mainly due to the fact that the required compiler, translator, or interpreter is designed to perform generalized translations while the assembly language program can be code optimized, reducing the size of the object program and thus permitting the assembly-language program to execute in less time.

In general, procedure-oriented languages are easy to learn and use, hence they reduce training and program writing time. They also simplify program checkout, maintenance, and documentation, and speed program conversion from one computer to another. Overall, procedure-oriented languages save expensive programming manpower, the cost of which keeps going up.

However, procedure-oriented languages are inefficient on object (machine-language) code. They also require more memory for program execution and extend program run time. In addition, sometimes they cannot express all the operations required in specialized applications, such as bit and byte manipulation extensively used in data communications programming.

Since the introduction of procedure-oriented languages, substantial improvements have occurred in their efficiency, speed, and scope. Such popular procedure-oriented languages as Cobol (common business-oriented language), Fortran (formula translation), Basic (beginners all symbolic instruction code), RPG (report program generator), and others have been developed to meet specific business and scientific requirements. However, none is specifically designed for programming data communications applications.

Currently, computer programming for data communications must rely on an assembly language or an extended version of a language specifically tailored for other applications. Due to this fact, a substantial portion of the effort expended in programming a data communications application on one computer may be lost if for some reason a new computer is acquired. Many persons in the industry view communications programming as a frontier for further progress since even today it is comparatively primitive and expensive, a situation that belies the sophisticated design and advanced technology of modern communications networks.

Part of the problem may be that the growth of data communications followed the introduction and initial expansion of scientific and business data processing. Thus, while specialized procedure-oriented languages were being developed for scientific and business use, communications programmers were just starting to use assembly language, which permits a large degree of bit and byte manipulation that is well suited to such programming.

2.6 DATA PROCESSING DEVELOPMENTS

Until the early 1960s most computers were used only by persons at the computer's location. Programmers would have their programs keypunched and the resulting cards were sent to the computer center, where they were batched together with other programs and executed one at a time. This process is known as batch data processing.

The development of magnetic disks permitted millions of additional bits of storage to be rapidly loaded into and transmitted from the computer's memory. Coupled with the development of multiprogramming, which allowed a computer to process a number of programs simultaneously by interleaving their execution, more efficient utilization of computer resources was possible. One job could now be executing while a second job was perhaps having its output listed on a peripheral device.

This resulted in the development of remote-access data processing systems. Here, data is transmitted from many locations via communications links to and from a computer performing the required data processing functions. This permitted many users to simultaneously access the computer. Since the computer's processing speed was many millions of operations per second, to each user it appeared that he was the only one using the computer's facilities.

The number and variety of remote-access data processing systems are already large and rapidly growing in both number and scope of operation. Through the mixture of computers and communications, many users can now obtain the immediate use of computational power regardless of location, while preserving on one site the expertise required to operate the system. A few of the more commonly used remote-access data processing systems include:

- Conversational timesharing systems—These systems permit the simultaneous sharing of a central computer among a group of users located at remote terminals and connected to the computer via a variety of communications lines. These systems permit a user to "interact" with a computer. The user develops, debugs, and executes programs "on-line," and receives the program results at his terminal.

- Remote batch processing systems—These systems permit the computer processing of tasks transmitted from distant locations. In contrast to conversational systems where the quantities of data input or output are limited, remote batch processing provides a mechanism for transmitting large quantities of data to and from the central computer. Due to the large amount of data that is transmitted in comparison to conversational systems, remote batch terminals usually operate at higher data rates than timesharing terminals.

- Inquiry systems—These systems are usually limited in scope since they are designed to provide information on a particular subject. One widely used inquiry system is a stock quotation service where many terminals are connected to a computer via communications lines. This system permits remote users to enter a stock symbol and obtain such data as the stock's current price, its latest earnings per share, and other financial data.

- Data collection systems—These systems involve the transmission of information—gathered at many remote points—to a central computer for processing and storage. One common data collection system is a series of badge readers located at many entry points in a building. As workers enter the building after normal working hours, the coding on the badge is read by the reader and transmitted to the computer.

The computer may then compare the badge number against a list of authorized badge numbers, and, if a match occurs, transmit a signal to unlock the door. If required, the computer may also be programmed to prepare a report of all after-hour entries and other information required by management.

In order to connect the computer to communications lines, it is necessary to add clocking and buffering circuitry that makes the computer compatible with the particular speed and code of the terminal connected at the remote end of the line. In addition, it is necessary to indicate to the computer that a complete unit of information has been received or is ready to be transferred to the terminal. Such a unit of information could be a bit. However, in most cases it is a byte, which is a grouping of bits that represent a character. By acting upon bytes of information instead of bits, the computer can spend more time processing information than keeping track of communications.

Early computers usually interfaced one, or at most a few, terminals by the use of single-line controllers. In addition to providing the clocking and circuitry necessary to interface the communications line, these controllers buffered incoming bits into bytes of information that were then passed to the computer. This is illustrated in Figure 2.6.1.

As remote-access networks evolved, more and more terminals were linked to the computer. To minimize the effect of interfacing a large number of communications lines, multiline controllers were designed. They provided the buffering capability and clocking circuitry to interface a large number of communications lines to the computer, as illustrated in Figure 2.6.2.

These controllers relieved some of the computer's communications processing functions. At the same time, they not only required the execution of computer instructions for their operation but also placed a large memory buffering allocation

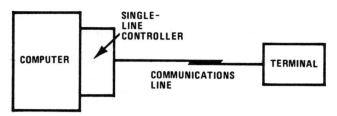

FIGURE 2.6.1 Single-line controller

burden on the computer. This was because incoming and outgoing information had to be buffered to compensate for the difference between the computer's internal operating speed and the slower data rate permissible over the communications line.

With remote access systems growing in size, number of terminals, and complexity, it became obvious that a computer with one or more multiline controllers would be able to handle only a limited number of lines and still maintain efficient processing of data. Beyond that point, the overhead in processing instructions for data transmission would tend to decrease significantly the computer's capability and throughput that remained for processing data. In recognition of these facts, computer manufacturers realized that if the communications function was to be performed efficiently and the overhead on the computer was to be minimized, it would have to be removed from the computer and performed elsewhere. This resulted in the development of data communications processors—small-scale computers with a mixture of single and multiline controllers and the necessary hardware to interface with large numbers of communications lines.

The communications processor makes it possible to remove most of the data communications overhead from the central or host computer by processing the communications in front of the host—hence the name front-end communications processor. A modern remote-access computer network is illustrated in Figure 2.6.3. Through the use of a front-end processor, the memory space and communications-instructions executions previously required for communications in the host computer were removed. This permits the host to concentrate its effectiveness on information processing.

FIGURE 2.6.2 Multiline controller

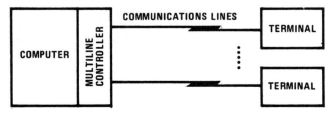

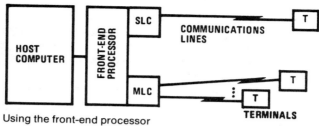

FIGURE 2.6.3   Using the front-end processor

2.7 SUMMARY

Although the first device used by man to perform calculations was the abacus, which was developed around 450 B.C., it was not until 1833, when Charles Babbage designed an "analytical engine," that the computer era dawned.

The modern history of digital computation commenced in 1939 at Harvard University and resulted in the development of the Mark I automatic sequence-controlled electromechanical calculator in 1944. In 1946, Dr. John von Neumann introduced the concept of the stored program, which is the basis of all modern computers. Four years later the world's first commercially produced electronic digital computer was used by the United States government to perform all the calculations of the 1950 national census. Computers' computation power and labor-saving attributes were recognized. The machines rapidly gained acceptance as a management tool as companies began to apply them to both scientific and business problems.

In spite of the rapid growth in the number of operating computers, their costs prevented every needful location within a company from having one. This resulted in the centralized location of computational equipment and the development of data communications networks with terminals at remote locations connected to the computer. In order to extend computational power to remote users, techniques and specialized devices were developed that permitted rapid data transfer to the computer for processing. The appropriate report and data were then sent to their designated receiving terminals.

Among the first places the computer pioneers turned to for developing networks were the common carriers—Western Union, the Bell System and associated telephone companies, and others, mainly because they already had large operating networks in place. Although few of these networks were designed to transmit data, they were available at almost all locations. Through the use of specialized components, they could be used for data transmission. Another advantage in turning to the common carriers was that they already had terminal devices available that sent messages between devices via their message- switching services.

These terminals were essentially a typewriter coupled or connected to a communications line and were a natural evolution from the original telegraph keys. The terminals, appropriately known as teletypewriters, were easily adapted for communicating with computers and formed the foundation of early data communications networks.

QUESTIONS

2.1 Discuss some of the similarities between Babbage's "analytical engine" and modern digital computers.

2.2 What were some of the disadvantages of vacuum tube technology employed in the first generation of computers?

2.3 What are the decimal equivalents of the following binary numbers?

> **A.** 10110110 **C.** 10110111
> **B.** 01101011 **D.** 11111111

2.4 Convert the following decimal numbers to their binary equivalents:

> **A.** 27 **C.** 410
> **B.** 186 **D.** 206

2.5 Convert the following binary numbers to their octal equivalents:

> **A.** 11111111 **C.** 11000101
> **B.** 10101011 **D.** 10001100

2.6 Convert the following binary numbers to their hexadecimal equivalents:

> **A.** 11111111 **C.** 11000101
> **B.** 10101011 **D.** 10001100

2.7 Construct a table from decimal 17 to 26 and their binary, octal, and hexadecimal equivalents.

2.8 Perform the following subtractions by using twos-complement addition:

> **A.** 101110 **C.** 100011
> −100111 −011010
> **B.** 1101110 **D.** 011111
> −1111001 −100000

2.9 How might data be represented octally in an 18-bit computer, 24-bit computer, and 32-bit computer?

2.10 What is the relationship between a procedure-oriented language, an assembly language, and machine language? Discuss ease of usage, machine transferability, documentation, and maintenance aspects.

2.11 Why is assembly language today the primary means of programming communications applications?

2.12 Why are bytes the preferred unit of information to be acted upon instead of bits?

2.13 What role do single-line and multiline controllers play in computer communications?

2.14 What are some of the advantages of employing a front-end processor to control computer communications?

CHAPTER 3

ROLE AND UTILIZATION OF TERMINALS IN DATA COMMUNICATIONS

3.1 INTRODUCTION

During the last decade a large number of terminals have been developed that can be attached to communications lines for transmitting data to a computer. These devices can be categorized into two specific types: terminals into which data is entered by human operators and terminals that perform the automatic collection of data from instruments. Prior to discussing the types, operation, and functions of terminals, let us first define what we mean by a terminal in the context of the data communications field.

A terminal is a device that permits information to enter or exit a data communications network where the network consists of one or more terminals linked via a communications line to computers. The terminal can be physically located anywhere communications facilities are available to link it to the computer: in the room next to the computer, on the opposite side of the continent from where the computer is located, or even, perhaps, on a different continent. Since any device that is used to input or output data can be classified as a terminal, the computer itself can be considered as a terminal device.

In normal practice, a user's input/output (I/O) device is called a terminal and it is considered to be communicating with a computer at the other end of the line. This arrangement forms a terminal-to-computer link or path. When a computer communicates with another computer, the link or path is referred to as a computer-to-computer link even though one or both computers may function as terminals. With the terminal-to- terminal link, these are the basic communications links (illustrated in Figure 3.1.1). Many computer peripherals can be removed from the computer room and attached to a communications line, thereby becom-

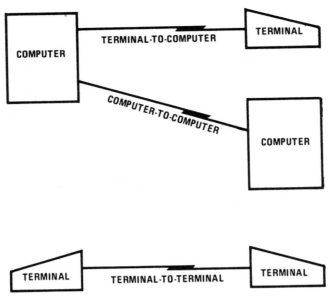

FIGURE 3.1.1   Basic communications links

ing terminal devices. Thus, such computer peripherals as card readers, card punches, and even the computer's control console can be considered terminal devices.

Types of Terminals

Some terminals can be used only to input data, some only to output (or receive) data, while some terminals permit data to be both inputted and outputted.

A keyboard-only device is generally used to transmit data to a data-collection device such as a computer. One example of a keyboard-only device is the push-button telephone that, after a call has been established, can be used to send data by the depression of the buttons, each of which transmits a different tone or frequency.

Quite similar to a normal typewriter, a keyboard-printer or teleprinter is a terminal that has a keyboard consisting of alphabetic, numeric, and function keys, as well as a printing mechanism. As a key is depressed, an internal signal generator transmits an electrical signal that defines that character. The signal is then transmitted over a communications channel to the computer, where the signal is interpreted and the character reproduced.

The transmit and receive capabilities of such terminals can be described as either keyboard send and receive (KSR), receive only (RO), or automatic send and receive (ASR). The KSR terminal has an alphanumeric keyboard for data entry at the operator's typing rate, and a character printer. As data is entered on the keyboard, a "hard" copy of each character is printed. Thus, data can be transmitted manually by keyboard and a local printed copy produced.

A receive-only terminal consists of a printer (and no keyboard). Here data is received as printed copy. This device is normally employed when there is no requirement at the terminal to transmit information to the computer. The RO can also be slaved to a video display to provide a local hard copy on an as-required basis (detailed later).

ASR machines employ local storage and have automatic send and receive capability. Data can be transmitted manually by keyboard or automatically via such storage devices as punched paper tape, magnetic tape, or cassettes. As data is transmitted or received, a local copy is printed for visual reference with or without employing the storage device. With the storage device employed, data can be batched off-line at the terminal operator's typing rate, then transmitted from storage at the communications line data rate in one continuous stream, to reduce communications costs. One of the earliest and most-utilized teleprinters is the Model 33 produced by the Teletype Corp., a subsidiary of AT&T.

Operating rates of keyboard terminals typically range from 10 to 120 characters per second. These data rates include both KSR and ASR terminals. Receive-only terminals have a much wider range of data rates, varying from 10 to 1,200 characters per second. This wider range is due to the greater variety of RO printers on the market. They range from simple teleprinter devices (without keyboards) to line printers specially adapted for data communications.

Although first used in telegraph networks, teleprinters have evolved dramatically to the point where today several million such devices are in use connecting users to timesharing networks via communications lines or directly to computers. The ASR-33 teleprinter has 63 printing characters plus the non-printing graphic, "space," and control characters formed by depressing the control key and the associated character key at the same time. This type of terminal can print up to 72 characters per line as well as respond to such control keys as carriage return, line feed, and signal bell.

The ASR-33 is one of many terminals that transmit and receive data encoded according to the American national standard code for information interchange (ASCII). Today, a family of terminals has evolved based upon the functional capability of the ASR-33. These devices, commonly referred to as TTY (Teletype)-type terminals, transmit and receive data encoded in ASCII, like the ASR-33. However, they usually operate at higher data rates, have more printing characters available, and can print more characters on a line than the ASR-33. Some of these devices include:

GE TermiNet 300

Computer Transceiver Execuport 300

Texas Instruments 700 Series.

One terminal still in use, but rapidly being phased out of existence due to advances in technology, is the punched-paper-tape type. This device consists of a transmitter and a receiver, and permits data recorded as holes punched in paper tape (one of the storage methods mentioned previously) to be transmitted and received over communications facilities. The transmission unit of the device consists of a paper-tape reader and a signal generator. As the paper tape passes through the reader, the holes previously punched in the tape are read by a sensing mechanism connected to the signal generator. The signal generator produces a signal according to the presence or absence of a hole on the paper tape, while at the receiver the operation is reversed with a paper-tape punch interfaced to a signal receiver. The presence of an electrical signal causes a hole to be punched, while in the absence of a signal no hole is punched. These terminals operate at speeds ranging from 10 to 300 characters per second.

One type of terminal that has gained widespread acceptance is the visual display or cathode ray tube (CRT) terminal. This terminal consists of a keyboard, a cathode ray tube for character display, a signal generator and interpreter, and a buffer area. These terminals are widely used in data communications applications where a hard-copy (printed) output is normally not required. (When a hard-copy output is required, an RO printer is normally slaved to the CRT so that the operator can depress a print button on the CRT's keyboard and have the current image on the tube transferred to the printer.)

When the CRT operator queries the computer by depressing the appropriate keys on the keyboard, coded signals are generated and an image of the character is reproduced on the screen. When there is a unit of information to be transmitted, the operator depresses a transmit or carriage-return key, and all of the entered information is transmitted to the computer.

Through the use of special keys, editing can be accomplished on CRTs. A cursor on the screen is used to indicate the position where the operator is to enter, delete, or change data previously entered. Normally, the cursor is a blinking small bar above, below, or at a character position that corresponds to a location of buffer storage. The terminal's buffer storage is designed to hold data for batching and editing until such time as the operator desires to transmit the information to the computer. When the operator keys data onto the CRT display, the data is placed in the terminal's buffer storage. The cursor automatically steps to the next position a character is to be displayed.

The position of the cursor can be altered rapidly by the use of cursor control keys. Once the operator has positioned the cursor, it can be homed to the first character position on the upper left-hand area of the display, spaced down, up, to the left, or right.

Other control keys can be used to clear the display, insert information onto a previously displayed line, erase lines previously entered, delete a character or group of characters, and so on. The operating data rates of CRTs vary considerably, normally ranging from 10 to 1,200 characters per second, with the operating speed usually limited by the type of communications facility employed.

Another type of terminal rapidly being connected to computer networks is the facsimile device. These terminals are basically duplicating devices that scan a document at a sending location and reproduce the document at a receiving location. Each facsimile terminal contains a transmitter and a receiver. The transmitter converts black and white spaces on a document into electrical signals while the receiver on the device it is "talking" to takes the electrical signal and reconverts it back into a series of black and white spaces. While some devices can transmit and reproduce only black and white, other terminals are capable of reproducing shades of gray, thus permitting half-tone pictures to be transmitted. Facsimile terminals currently permit one 8 1/2-×-11-inch page to be transmitted in about 10 seconds to 2 minutes, depending upon the type of machine used. When facsimile terminals are linked to a computer functioning as a message switch, documents may be routed to many users via a set of instructions. Or documents may be stored until the recipient is available to retrieve the message.

Some of the typical types of terminals that may be connected to computers or other terminals via appropriate communications facilities are illustrated in Figure 3.1.2.

3.2 FORMS AND USES OF DATA COMMUNICATIONS TERMINALS

As there are numerous types of data communications terminals, so are there uses for such terminals.

In addition to the telegraph, one of the earliest applications of data communications terminals was to connect two or more business locations via the use of teleprinters and communications lines provided by the telephone company. One

FIGURE 3.1.2   Typical terminals used in a computational network

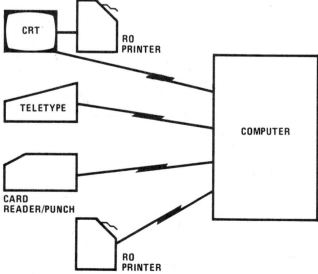

such elementary network may have utilized two teleprinters of the KSR type, for example. Here the operator at one location would transmit a message to the terminal connected on the opposite end of the line. The receiving teleprinter would receive and print out the message transmitted to it. After the message was completed, a response could be keyed back from the receiving end for verification.

Due to the slow operating speed of such devices, messages were usually short and it was tedious to transmit the same message to more than one location. Later developments resulted in a party line or multipoint circuit, as illustrated in Figure 3.2.1. Through this arrangement and special equipment, any one terminal could broadcast messages to one or more other terminals at the same time, or could selectively receive messages in some predefined sequence from each terminal on the line. Although this was a considerable improvement in customer capability, it did not permit one company to send messages to an office of another company. To do so would have required the other company's office to be on the same party line. Due to the number of companies some firms conducted business with, it was physically impossible to connect that large a number of teleprinters onto one party line.

These limitations resulted in the development of circuit and message switching by the common carriers. In circuit switching, a line physically connects each subscriber's terminal to the communications carrier's office, where circuits are physically switched to establish the required connections between the calling and called terminals. In message switching ("store and forward"), the message is first physically transmitted from a subscriber to the communications carrier, from where it is retransmitted to the intended recipient. One of the most common uses of

FIGURE 3.2.1   Multipoint or party-line network

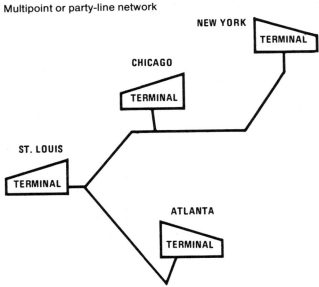

message switching is for the transmission of Mailgrams, where a person can go to selected post offices and have a message transmitted electronically to another post office, placed in an envelope, and hand delivered to its destination.

General Business Usage

Today and for the future, terminals will play an all-pervasive role in our lives. For the factory worker, badge and card readers record the employee's time of entry and exit. Such data is then processed by the computer to prepare the worker's paycheck. Also, management is provided with an immediate status of unmanned workstations at the start of the business day so that corrective actions might be taken.

In the area of order entry and inventory control, we do not have to think about big industrial plants but just have to drive to our nearest hamburger fast-food outlet to see how terminals are changing our lives. Here, when we place our order for a large hamburger, small french fries, and a medium Coke, the waitress depresses several buttons on a special keyboard of a terminal to indicate our selection. Immediately, selections are transmitted to a minicomputer or microprocessor, which can be located within the store or at a central location. A table lookup then takes place as prices are assigned to our selections, our order is subtotaled, appropriate sales tax is added, and a final total is computed. This information is then transmitted back to the terminal where it is listed on the printer. As we make our selections, the inventory in the store is automatically adjusted—so many ounces of soda, one cup and lid, etc.

When inventory reaches certain critical levels, reorders may then be generated automatically by the computer. As we pay for our purchase, the waitress keys in the amount rendered. The change due, if any, is automatically printed on the terminal and the printout is furnished to us as our receipt. During the day an automatic computation of sales from that terminal location and the amount received by the terminal operator may be computed, helping the owner's cash management.

Timesharing and Remote Computing

One of the most rapid growth areas for terminal applications has been in timesharing and remote computing. In a timesharing environment, the operator normally uses a TTY terminal to communicate with a computer, primarily by dialing the telephone number of the computer and using the switched telephone network as the communications link. After entering an appropriate identifier, which must be recognized as valid by the computer, the operator may execute, for example, an inventory analysis program. Here, the operator enters messages and data and the computer computes the number of units required to meet the company's obligations and the number of units that should be ordered from the manufacturer in order to receive a discount.

When larger amounts of data must be transmitted or received, remote batch terminals (RBTs) are normally employed. Some RBTs contain a small processor that enables local programs to be executed, while communications with the host or central computer occurs only when additional processing power is required. Other RBTs consist merely of a control unit and one or more peripheral units such as a line printer, card reader, or magnetic tape unit. Such a device is mainly used to effect a batch transfer of large quantities of data to the host computer, receive large amounts of processed data from the computer, or both.

Figure 3.2.2 shows two RBT configurations. In the top portion of the figure is a simple RBT configuration that consists of three peripheral devices: a line printer, a card reader, and an operator's console. The operator's console might be used to establish communications with the computer and inform it that a job will be transmitted for processing. Once the job is transmitted to the computer, the operator waits for its execution to be completed and directs the computer's output to the RBT line printer. Or the operator could disconnect the RBT from the communications facility and reconnect it at a later time to receive the completed job.

In the lower portion of Figure 3.2.2, a more complex RBT with local processing capability is illustrated. During the day, local programs could be executed on this

FIGURE 3.2.2   Remote batch terminals

SIMPLE RBT CONFIGURATION

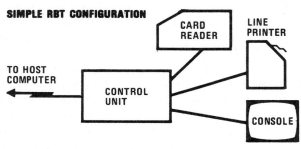

RBT WITH LOCAL PROCESSING CAPABILITY

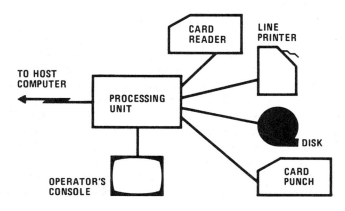

machine, while jobs that require the greater processing power of the host computer could be transmitted to and executed on that machine after normal working hours.

Inquiry/Response Applications

Two of the most common inquiry-and-response applications using terminals are airline reservation and stockbroker quotation networks. Each of these employs specially designed terminals with keyboards tailored for the particular application. In the stockbroker quotation application, keys are available to enter special symbols unique to that occupation. Thus, after the stockbroker enters the alphabetic symbol for a common stock, he may then enter one of several symbols to determine its current price, year-to-date earnings per share, last year's earnings per share, dividend paid this year, previously paid dividends, and other information of interest to investors.

For airline reservations, a different set of symbols is employed to denote unique information and changes. As an example, one key on the terminal keyboard might be used to denote a change or cancellation. Thus, once the terminal operator locates the flight a person is booked on, all that would be required is a depression of the cancellation key to remove the customer's reservation on that particular flight.

Future Trends

During the past decade our lives have become more and more dependent upon the utilization of terminals connected to computers.

Today, in many of the larger department stores, when the customer pays by credit card, the card is either read by the terminal, or the clerk enters the card number by means of a simple keyboard. Together with the amount of the purchase, this information is transmitted to the computer, which scans the customer's file to determine if the card has been reported lost or stolen, or if with this purchase the customer's allowable credit will be exceeded. In addition to performing credit verification, some terminals have additional connected devices to capture sales data in a more expedient manner than through the entry of information from a keyboard. Terminals of this type are usually referred to as point-of-sale devices and are rapidly replacing the conventional cash register in a variety of stores, shops, and offices where transactions between employees and customers take place. Usually one or more of these functions are performed by such devices: data capture, receipt issuance, credit verification, and local record maintenance.

One type of point-of-sale terminal that has great promise is an optical scanner attached to a terminal consisting of a printer, display, keyboard, and communications facilities. First used by the supermarket industry, many diverse operations— department stores, laboratories, warehouses, libraries and hospitals—are now using or planning to use such devices. The use of the scanner is based upon reading bar code symbols, which are a graphical representation of binary numbers.

Bar codes follow a variety of schemes, using the width, height, and distance between marks to express characters. The most commonly used bar code is the universal product code (UPC), which was adopted by the supermarket industry in 1973. Today almost 80% of all items in a supermarket carry the UPC label; and an increasing number of supermarket checkout counters have terminal devices capable of reading the code.

When the optical scanner is passed over the UPC label, the data represented by the bar code is read by the terminal and transmitted to a computer. The type of item is matched with its name and current price, which are then transmitted back to the terminal to illuminate the unit's display and print out on the customer's receipt. Since reading the bar code is faster, more accurate, and less costly than entering item prices on a conventional cash register, optical scanning point-of-sale terminals have a good potential for the future.

3.3 TERMINAL REQUIREMENTS AND CONSTRAINTS

Perhaps the key starting point in the design of a data communications network is the selection of the type of terminal to be utilized. Although this may at first appear to be a simple task, in many cases this may be a lengthy process due to the number of items that should be considered. In Table 3.3.1 the reader will find a list of terminal characteristics that should be reviewed prior to rendering a terminal selection decision. Note that the weight one gives to each of the items in the table is a function of the user's proposed or existing operating environment.

In examining the input/output (I/O) media, the type of peripherals that can be interfaced to the terminal as well as the terminal itself should be examined. Thus, the keyboard, plastic credit card reader, and optical scanner, for example, are just three of many methods of entering data. Concerning the output media, a decision of hard-copy printout vs. the "soft-copy" image on a CRT does not have to be an all or nothing situation today. Some CRTs can be clustered on a party-line arrangement and a group of such terminals may share a common printer at a particular location, as shown in Figure 3.3.1.

Another I/O media consideration is the type and amount of data to be displayed. If the terminal has a printing mechanism for output, there is no limit imposed on the length of print-out response. If the primary output mechanism is a display, one should limit responses to a full screen (or less) of information because

TABLE 3.3.1   TERMINAL CHARACTERISTICS TO BE EVALUATED

I/O media
Operating rate(s)
Off-line capability
Data codes and character set
Operator convenience
Cost
Security
Control of user errors
Error detection and correction

it is difficult to remember parts of information that are produced on one screen display as a new display continues the information received. Most CRTs display 80 characters per line on up to 24 lines of output for a maximum display of 1,920 characters. If graphical data is to be produced, a special graphical CRT display or graph-plotting printer attached to a terminal should be considered.

If the data to be transmitted can be batched together, then a mechanism for temporary storage prior to transmission should be considered. Such devices as paper tape reader/punch, magnetic tape unit, disk storage unit, or data cassette may interface the terminal. These devices may not only provide an off-line data entry capability but could also reduce communications costs by permitting data to be keyed at the terminal operator's typing speed and later transmitted to the computer at the higher data rate permitted by the communications facility.

Operating Rate

The operating rate of the terminal depends upon many factors, including the volume of traffic to be transmitted and received, the information transfer rate of the communications facilities, and the operating rate that the computer can support. Perhaps the most important factor, from a terminal user's viewpoint, is the psychological reaction to the operating rate. A device that receives at 10 characters per second may be too slow for applications where the operator awaits lengthy messages or reports. This situation might require a printer or display screen to operate at a higher data rate.

At the opposite extreme one may select an operating rate too rapid for the application. Consider, as an example, a CRT whose screen can be filled with information very rapidly, with the constraining factor on its operating rate normally being the communications line connecting it to the computer. If typical operator interaction requires the entry of, say, 20 characters and the display of 80 characters, then a data rate of 1,200 characters per second would in all probability be excessive. The 80-character response would only require 67 milliseconds to be displayed, far less time than the minimum required by humans to read such output. For most situations in which a CRT display is to be filled with data, an operating speed of 600 characters per second is sufficient.

FIGURE 3.3.1   Eliminating all-or-nothing decisions by sharing

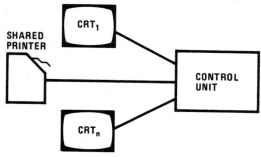

Data Code and Character Set

When a character is transmitted from a terminal, it is represented as a set of bit patterns according to the internal code of the device. In most cases the terminal's internal code and the transmission code are the same. Sometimes, the terminal code may differ from the transmission code or the computer's internal code. For these situations, code conversion must take place to make the terminal's code compatible with the code acceptable to the computer.

Code conversion can be accomplished by the computer or by certain terminals. Normally, remote batch terminals are the only ones that perform code conversion since buffer storage and the processing of instructions are required to perform the conversion. Interfacing code-conversion devices are also available commercially.

Two examples of code conversion are illustrated in Figure 3.3.2. In the top example an older model teleprinter designed for the 5-level Baudot code communicates with a computer whose internal code is ASCII. Here the computer converts data received from the terminal from Baudot to ASCII and data destined to the terminal from ASCII to Baudot. In the lower example the RBT's processor is used to convert data in the EBCDIC code into ASCII for transmission to the computer. Data from the computer is transmitted in ASCII and converted into EBCDIC at the RBT.

In addition to the data code supported by the terminal, its character set may be of equal importance. As an example, a terminal that supports the ASCII data code may only support a subset of the ASCII character set, eliminating, for example, all lower-case characters. For a text editing application where both upper- and lower-case characters are required, this type of terminal would probably be excluded from consideration.

Operator Convenience

This category can be most important, for if the terminal is difficult to operate, it may not be utilized. Items in this category include human factor considerations that ease operation of the terminal. An optical scanner or numeric keypad with no visual input display for verification are examples of inconvenience. Examples of convenience include an alert indicator such as a bell on a teleprinter or a blinking message on a display to attract the operator's attention to a certain situation.

Cost

Terminal lease costs vary dramatically, ranging from under $75 per month for teleprinters to many thousands of dollars per month for remote batch terminals. One should evaluate terminal costs in conjunction with the cost of communications facilities to link the device to the computer as well as any additional hardware or software costs necessary to make the terminal compatible with the computer. Thus, terminals that can be clustered to share one communications link may be less expensive than cheaper terminals that require individual communications channels to the computer, as illustrated in Figure 3.3.3.

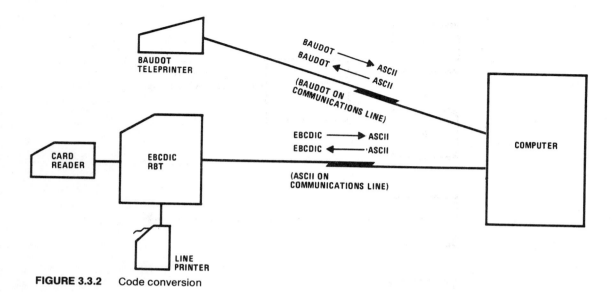

FIGURE 3.3.2   Code conversion

Security

To prevent unauthorized personnel from accessing a network and retrieving data with a terminal, a combination of hardware and software techniques can be employed. From appropriate software the terminal operator can be asked to enter a code or authorization number that is checked to ascertain if his use of the terminal is valid.

From a hardware standpoint there are a number of methods to maintain a level of security. One method is to have the terminal operable only upon the insertion of a key, card, or badge issued to authorized employees. Sometimes the terminal itself can be programmed to read an employee code keyed in by the terminal operator at the start of the business day and once again after each time the terminal is shut off.

Control of User Errors

Control of user errors is normally with a combination of hardware and software elements. A display screen that permits the user to move his cursor back to a previous position to change a character or characters that are in error or insert additional data is preferable to a terminal that does not permit these operations. Similarly, a keyboard without a display to let the operator verify data entered might cause operational problems.

Error Detection and Correction

In order for the terminal's receiver to stay in synchronization with the sender, the terminal may employ one of two methods for transferring data (covered in greater detail in Section 4.4).

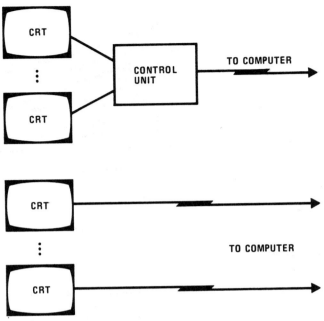

FIGURE 3.3.3   Evaluating configuration cost

The first method, known as asynchronous transmission, is also referred to as start-stop transmission. Teleprinters and similar devices employ this method where characters are transmitted one at a time on a character-by-character basis. Each character is identified by one start bit and one or more stop bits. Most asynchronous terminals also generate a parity bit for each transmitted character and contain

FIGURE 3.3.4   Vertical and horizontal parity checking

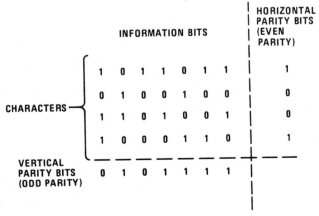

circuitry to verify the parity prior to transmitting the character. Parity is the addition of a bit to make the number of bits per character, excluding the start and stop bits, appear odd or even (as required). The two common parity methods include vertical and horizontal parity checking, as illustrated in Figure 3.3.4. The circuitry in asynchronous terminals normally provides a horizontal parity check, since the bits of a character are transmitted one at a time "horizontally." The bit configuration of an 8-level ASCII character code terminal—which transmits and receives an 11-unit code consisting of one start bit, seven information bits, a parity bit, and two stop bits—is illustrated in Figure 3.3.5.

The second method of transferring data is known as the block, or synchronous, mode. When this method of data transfer is employed, characters are blocked together for transmission as a group. Special synchronization characters are placed at the beginning and end of each block to denote the start and end of the block. The use of these special synchronization characters permits the start and stop bits used by the asynchronous terminals to be eliminated. Since a number of characters are blocked together prior to transfer, buffer storage must be available on the terminal.

Error control when terminals transfer data synchronously can be accomplished in a number of ways. One such method is by the generation of a block check character. Here, as each block of characters is transferred, the terminal's internal circuitry computes a check character which is physically placed at the end of the block. One simplistic example would be formation of a parity check character by grouping every seven parity bits into a character and transmitting it at the end of every seven characters transferred.

At the receiving end, the computer or terminal would perform an equivalent parity check character generation and compare the character it generated with the one that was transmitted. If the two match, the data is accepted; however, if they do not match, a message is sent to the terminal to retransmit the block of data.

A typical data block format for a synchronous terminal is illustrated in Figure 3.3.6. The number of characters used to form the block varies depending upon such factors as the type of data input (keyboard, card reader, etc.), the expected error rate and corresponding expected retransmission rate, as well as the terminal's buffer storage size.

Normally, terminals that transmit data synchronously are more expensive than asynchronous terminals since they require buffer storage and more complex circuitry. Although the use of parity was shown as one method to determine errors, it

FIGURE 3.3.5   Bit configuration of ASCII characters transmitted on an asynchronous terminal

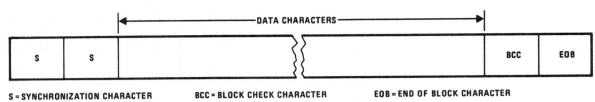

FIGURE 3.3.6   Typical data block format

should be recognized that a double bit error remains undetected by simple parity checking, and for synchronous terminals more advanced methods to include polynomial character generation are used as an error-checking tool.

3.4 JUSTIFICATION OF TERMINALS

The decision to employ terminals to communicate from remote distances to a computer is based on many of the same criteria employed for the procurement of any type of equipment. Such criteria include speed of information, operational efficiency, management control, and cost savings.

Speed of Information

For many organizations, the old adage "time is money" is especially true in today's era of rapid communications. A stockbroker who cannot rapidly quote a security price is in a position similar to a salesman who cannot quote delivery data for a product—he is without a customer. For some salesmen, a portable computer terminal is as important as a display case. By using a telephone, the salesman can use the direct-distance-dialing telephone network to connect his terminal to the company computer. He may then obtain such information as the current price of an item that may be especially important for products that drastically and rapidly vary in price, quantities on hand and ready for shipment, delivery schedules for equipment to be manufactured, and other data of importance to the customer.

Operational Efficiency

If an organization provides its workers with tools to reduce the time required to perform a function, the net result is to increase the operational efficiency of that firm. Terminals equipped with optical scanners to read the universal product code of items in a supermarket are one example of a terminal installation designed for increasing operational efficiency. Here one can expect the clerk to "optically ring up" more items in less time, more accurately. Similarly, terminals in a fast-food hamburger store may permit more customers to have their orders totaled by fewer clerks.

Management Control

Although terminals are usually first installed for applications that require speed of information or operational efficiency, management control usually results from an evolutionary maturing process. Thus, while the early terminals in fast-food stores were no more than electronic cash registers, through evolution they now are used to perform such varied tasks as inventory control and cash management, in addition to order entry. The data entered becomes part of a database for a Management Information System.

Cost Savings

Although cost savings normally are a result of the previously discussed criteria, one should also consider the possibilities terminals offer to increasing company profits. Labor is a large cost for a fast-food firm, a cost that can be reduced by electronic order entry. At the same time the data entered from the terminal can be used by a computer not only for inventory control but for the computation of optimum reorder levels to take advantage of supplier discounts. The result is additional cost savings to the organization.

In some firms, increasing sales and thus the organization's profit may be easier to obtain by the use of terminals than by cost reductions. The previously discussed example of the salesman would fall into this category. In another example, terminals used by new car dealers query a computer to find the nearest location of a car in a specific color requested by a customer. Here, the ability of a new-car dealer to locate and arrange for the prompt delivery of the desired car results in an additional sale and increased profits for the car dealer.

3.5 SUMMARY

The role of terminals in data communications is wide ranging and ever increasing. Although some terminals are used only to communicate with other terminals, the majority of such devices are used for transmitting and receiving data from a computer.

Many terminal types exist, and, in fact, a computer itself can be used as a terminal. However, terminals can generally be divided into three generic types—teleprinters, CRTs, and remote batch terminals. By the addition of specialized input/output units, such as an optical scanner, terminals can be utilized in a wide variety of ways.

Today, terminals are used not only for interactive timesharing applications but also in such diverse environments as libraries, hospitals, stockbroker offices, and supermarkets. In evaluating terminal characteristics, one must investigate the I/O media, required operating rate, off-line capability, data codes and character set supported, operator convenience, cost, security, control of user errors, and the method employed for error detection and correction.

QUESTIONS

3.1 In the context of the data communications field, define what we mean by a terminal.

3.2 Describe three basic communications links and their information flow.

3.3 Discuss the differences between a keyboard send and receive (KSR), receive only (RO), and automatic send and receive (ASR) terminal. What application is best suited for each type of terminal?

3.4 What function does the cursor on the CRT perform?

3.5 What are some of the advantages and disadvantages of multipoint circuits or party lines? What technological development reduced some of these disadvantages?

3.6 Cite some examples of the use of terminals for order-entry application. What special equipment might be required?

3.7 What are the similarities of, and differences between, teleprinters and remote batch terminals?

3.8 Describe some inquiry and response applications and denote some of the special features that may be required of terminals connected to such configurations.

3.9 What advantages result from connecting an optical scanner to a terminal?

3.10 Discuss some of the terminal characteristics that should be reviewed prior to selecting a specific device.

3.11 Where can code conversion take place?

3.12 What is parity?

3.13 What is the difference between synchronous and asynchronous data transfer?

3.14 Compute the odd parity bit for the following characters:

A. 1011101   C. 1110111
B. 1110100   D. 0111001

3.15 Why does a terminal that operates in a synchronous mode normally cost more than a terminal that operates in an asynchronous mode?

3.16 Cite a parity check problem that can occur.

3.17 Discuss some of the criteria involved in a terminal justification process.

CHAPTER 4

FUNDAMENTAL CONCEPTS OF TERMINAL-TO-COMPUTER COMMUNICATIONS

4.1 INTRODUCTION

In this chapter, the basic concepts and theory of terminal-to-computer communications will be examined. Starting at the lowest level of information, the bit, definitions and terminology will be developed to show the relationship to the type and structure of information that is transmitted.

Through an examination of the transmission modes and techniques available, as well as the basic types of terminal-to-computer linkages one can employ, the reader should be able to develop a firm foundation and understanding of terminal selection and connection options. Such information is of special value when one is not only considering the initial establishment of a network but may be examining the effect of changing the type of terminals connected to a computer.

4.2 TERMINOLOGY AND DEFINITION

Bits and Bauds

The fundamental building block of electronic information transfer is the binary digit, or bit. The bit is the lowest level of information representation and signifies the presence or absence of a state or condition. From the standpoint of a terminal or computer, the bit can be considered as being either in the 1 condition or the 0 condition, where the 1 state usually has a higher voltage than the 0 state. Bits can be represented by square waves, as illustrated in Figure 4.2.1.

Since bits are also used to represent a quantity of data transferred per unit of time, some confusion has occurred between bits/unit of time and the term baud. Bits/unit of time, usually expressed as bit/second or bps, defines the physical

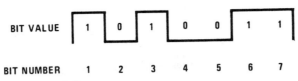

FIGURE 4.2.1 Bit representation

amount of data transferred during a certain time interval. Thus, 110 bit/s would signify that 110 bits of information are to be transferred in one second.

The term baud represents a unit of signaling speed equal to the number of discrete conditions or signal events per second. When one bit is used as a signal unit, baud speed and bps are equivalent, as shown in the top portion of Figure 4.2.2. If, through some technique, two bits are combined to form a signal unit, as shown in the middle portion of Figure 4.2.2., then the baud rate would be one half the bps rate. For this situation, the signal unit is called a dibit (double bit) and has four

FIGURE 4.2.2 Correspondence between bits and baud

TWO-STATE CODE, CODE UNITS 0 AND 1, BAUD EQUALS BIT/S

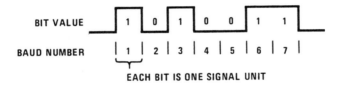

FOUR-STATE CODE, CODE UNITS 00, 01, 10, AND 11, BAUD IS HALF OF BIT/S

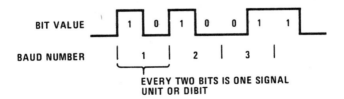

EIGHT-STATE CODE, CODE UNITS 000, 001, 010, 011, 100, 101, 110, AND 111, BAUD IS A THIRD OF BIT/S

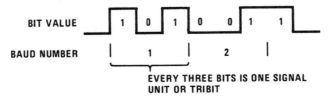

possible states or levels. If three bits are used to form one signal unit, as shown in the lower portion of Figure 4.2.2, eight possible states or levels can exist, and the signal unit is known as tribit or triple bit. How all this happens is a function of the modulation technique inside the modem, to be discussed in Section 4.12.

Bytes, Characters, and Words

When a sequence of bits is operated on as a unit by computer hardware, such a unit is normally referenced as a byte of information. A byte normally consists of the number of bits required to represent one character, where a character is a letter, figure, punctuation, or other symbol used to represent a higher level of information than the bit. The 6-bit byte was used by most computers designed before the mid-1960s, while the 8-bit byte is the most widely used byte size of computers on the market today.

Although a computer byte is of fixed size, it can contain different size characters as long as the number of bits grouped to represent the character does not exceed the size of the byte. This is illustrated in Figure 4.2.3, which shows the results of placing a 5-level Baudot character, a 7-level ASCII character, and an 8-level EBCDIC character into an 8-bit byte.

When referring to computers, a word is a fixed-length group of characters or bytes. In contrast to the definition of a bit or character, the definition of a word implies alignment of the data such that the word must have a certain address or it is not properly a word in the computer. In an 8-bit computer, the word size and byte size may be the same, with 8-bit bytes forming computer words of data or instructions. For this type of machine, if data is to be transmitted serially—that is, one

FIGURE 4.2.3   Many types of characters can be represented in a byte

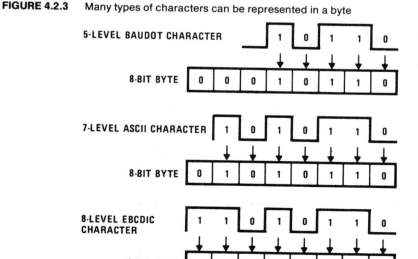

character at a time—then one word of information is transferred at a time via the computer's I/O unit. In a 16-bit computer, the word size and byte size normally differ, with two 8-bit bytes capable of being stored in one computer word to be operated upon internally at one time.

Here, when data is transmitted one character at a time, the first byte is transmitted and a byte shift operation is then performed so that the second character is now positioned where the first character was previously located. Next, the second character is transmitted. Data transfer by an 8-bit and 16-bit word-size computer are illustrated in Figure 4.2.4.

Blocks and Messages

In contrast to a message, which is an arbitrary amount of information whose beginning and end are defined, a block is a grouping of bits, transmitted as a unit over which some type of procedure is applied for error-control purposes.

From the lower portion of Figure 4.2.4, two characters of information are transmitted by the computer. If these characters are transmitted asynchronously, the start and ending positions of the character must be defined. To do so requires the addition of start and stop bits. In addition, a parity bit may be included to provide a limited form of error control. This technique was previously discussed in the Control of User Errors portion of Section 3.3.

FIGURE 4.2.4 Data transfer by 8- and 16-bit word-size computers

8-BIT COMPUTER

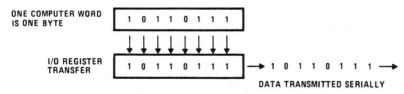

16-BIT COMPUTER

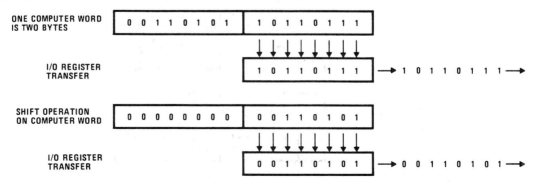

When data is transmitted in the block mode, the start and stop bits are not required to denote the beginning and end of each character. Instead, N characters are grouped together into a block of data for transmission. Special synchronization characters precede the block to insure that the information receiver is placed in step with the data transmitter. As the bits of each character are transmitted, some type of check character is developed based upon a predefined algorithm and appended to the end of the block.

At the receiver, a check character is generated by the terminal or computer using the same algorithm on the received data, and the two check characters are then compared. If the comparison is not equal, this signifies that an error has occurred during the transmission. This will normally require some type of error recovery procedure to be initiated. One error recovery procedure would be for the transmission to be repeated; that is, a block must be retransmitted. The tradeoffs between character-by-character and block-mode transmission will be examined later in the section on line protocol.

In the field of data communications, the terms block and message are frequently interchanged and may result in a degree of confusion. A message, as noted earlier, is an arbitrary amount of information whose beginning and end are defined. Thus, a message could consist of one block of information. In practice, however, a message usually contains many blocks of information. The message format will vary depending upon the management method of the data link employed. This management, known as line protocol, is discussed more fully later.

4.3 TRANSMISSION MODES

One method used to characterize terminals, communications lines, computer channels, and such communications components as acoustic couplers and modems, is by their transmission or communications mode. The three types of transmission modes available are simplex, half-duplex, and full-duplex.

Simplex

Transmission that occurs in one direction only is simplex, as illustrated in the top portion of Figure 4.3.1. In this mode of transmission, the receiver does not have a means of responding to the transmitted signal. An example of the simplex communications mode is a home radio, which can only receive signals transmitted from a radio station. In a data transmission environment, simplex transmission can be used to turn on or off specific devices at certain times of the day or when a certain event occurs.

Another example of simplex transmission is a computer-controlled environmental installation where a furnace is turned on or off depending upon the thermostat setting and the temperature in various parts of a building. Normally, simplex transmission is not utilized where man-machine interaction is required due to the inability of the receiver to reply to the originator.

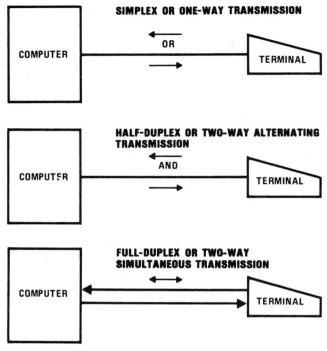

FIGURE 4.3.1 Transmission modes

Half-duplex

As illustrated in the middle portion of Figure 4.3.1, the half-duplex mode of transmission permits data transfer to occur in either direction, but not simultaneously. This is the most common mode of transmission employed in data communications today. Half-duplex transmission is used in citizen band (CB) radio transmission where the operator can either transmit or receive but cannot perform both operations at the same time on the same channel. After the operator has completed a transmission, the other party must be advised of this fact so he can now continue the conversation. This is accomplished by the operator saying the term "over," which tells the other operator to begin transmission.

When data is transmitted over a communications link, the transmitter and receiver of the transmission device must be appropriately turned on and off as the direction of the transmission varies. Since two wires are required to complete an electrical circuit, one for transmission and one for ground, the transmission flow on such a circuit must be halted each time the direction of travel is reversed. This halt is known as line or circuit "turnaround," and the time needed is a function of the circuit mileage on telephone lines.

Half-duplex transmission can occur on either a two-wire or four-wire circuit.

The switched direct-distance-dial telephone network is composed of two-wire circuits, whereas a circuit known as a leased line can be obtained as either a two-wire or four-wire facility. A four-wire circuit is essentially a pair of two-wire links that can be used for transmission in both directions simultaneously (full-duplex). Half-duplex communications can occur on either a two- or four-wire circuit. The turnaround time is minimized on a four-wire circuit.

Full-duplex

Transmission that occurs in both directions simultaneously is known as full-duplex. In this mode of transmission no turnaround time is required. Full-duplex transmission is often used when large amounts of alternating traffic must be transmitted and received within a fixed time period. Returning to the CB example, if one channel is used for transmission and another for reception, then two simultaneous transmissions can occur. While the elimination of turnaround time permits full-duplex transmission to provide more efficient throughput, this efficiency may be negated by the cost of two-way lines and more complex equipment required by this mode of transmission. Normally, a four-wire circuit is needed for full-duplex transmission. With the proper, higher-priced devices (modems), two-wire circuits may be used.

When referring only to terminal operations, the term full-duplex takes on a different meaning from the communications mode of the transmission medium. Here, the fact that the terminal is full-duplex may be used to denote that when the operator presses a key to transmit a character to the computer, it is echoed back to appear on the terminal's printer or display screen, as illustrated in Figure 4.3.2, as the operator continues to key in the data.

This mode of terminal transmission is known as echo-plex and is available with full-duplex opration only. When operating on half-duplex circuits, many terminals "copy" the transmitted signal back to the terminal for display to obtain a local copy or printout of characters as they are transmitted.

4.4 TRANSMISSION TECHNIQUES

Due to the necessity to synchronize a transmitting device with a receiving device, two techniques have been developed—asynchronous and synchronous transmission.

FIGURE 4.3.2   Echo-Plex

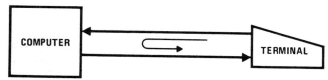

Asynchronous Transmission

Asynchronous transmission is commonly referred to as start-stop transmission, where one character at a time is transmitted or received. Start and stop bits are used to synchronize the receiver with the transmitter as well as to denote the beginning and end of the character transmitted. Most teleprinters, with the exception of some buffered terminals, employ this method of transmission.

In asynchronous transmission, each character to be transmitted is encoded into a series of pulses. The transmission of the character is initiated by a start bit equal in width to one pulse. The encoded character (series of pulses) is followed by a parity bit and one or more stop bits that may be equal to or longer than one pulse width, depending upon the transmission code used. The transmission of a 7-level ASCII character is illustrated in the top portion of Figure 4.4.1. If we assume two stop bits are used, then 11 bits must be sent to transmit the 7 information bits that represent the encoded character. Here the extra bits include one start bit, one parity bit and two stop bits.

By convention, the start bit is signified by a space, logic 0, or no current, while stop bits are signified by a mark, logic 1, or the presence of current. The start and stop elements are logically complements of each other, so that when a start signal is received, the transition clearly indicates the beginning of a character. Although the parity bit can be used for error control, it is not used on many teleprinters so that bit-position 8 may have no significance. Terminals that transmit data at 10 characters per second usually employ a stop element with a duration of two pulse widths. Thus, at that data rate the transmission of an 11-unit code would require a modulation rate of 110 baud.

For a typical 30-character-per-second teleprinter, a stop element of one pulse width is usually employed. Using one signal element for the stop element would

FIGURE 4.4.1 Asynchronous (start-stop) transmission

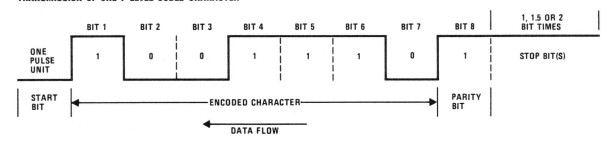

reduce the unit code per character to 10 signal elements. Thirty characters per second, each consisting of 10 signal elements or bits, would require a data rate of 300 bits per second. Since the bits are to be transmitted one at a time, a circuit with a modulation rate of 300 baud would be necessary for the transfer of information.

In the start-stop method of transmission, transmission begins anew on each character and stops after each character, as indicated in the lower portion of Figure 4.4.1. As each character is transmitted, idle time occurs between the transmission of characters. With synchronization starting anew with each character, any timing discrepancy is cleared at the end of the character and synchronization is maintained on a character-by-character basis.

Asynchronous transmission is normally employed at data rates under 2,000 bit/s. (See Table 4.4.1.) The "waste" of potential data-bit positions for the start and stop bits is the price one pays when using this type of transmission.

Synchronous Transmission

When a high data-transfer rate is required, the asynchronous method is inefficient due to the extra time required to transmit start and stop pulses. A second type of transmission, which involves sending a group of characters in a continuous bit stream, may then be employed to overcome the previously discussed asynchronous limitations. This type of transmission is known as synchronous or bit-stream synchronization.

In the synchronous transmission method, data transfer is controlled by a timing signal (clock) at the originating device. This timing signal may originate from the terminal itself or it may be provided by a communications component such as a modem, multiplexer, or front-end processor channel. At the receiving end, the communications component normally derives its timing from the line transitions, with a synchronized clock in the device used to control the sampling of the line conditions.

The receive clock must be kept in continuous step with the transmit clock to insure synchronization and avoid bits being gained or lost. In order to obtain and continue this synchronization, data transmission is blocked into a group of data bits preceded by the transmission of one or more special characters. These special synchronization or sync characters are at the same code level (number of bits per character) as the coded information to be transmitted. However, they have a unique bit configuration of zeros and ones that define the sync character. The receiver recognizes and synchronizes itself onto a stream of transmitted sync characters.

Once synchronization is achieved, the actual transmission of information can proceed, as illustrated in Figure 4.4.2. Since data is grouped or blocked into groups of characters for synchronous transmission, terminals transmitting and receiving data using this mode of data transfer must have a buffer for storing the character blocks.

In addition to the buffer, more complex circuitry is required by synchronous terminals since the receiving terminal must remain in step with the data originator

FIGURE 4.4.2   Synchronous transmission

for the duration of the transmitted information block. Synchronous transmission is normally employed when data rates in excess of 2,000 bit/s are required. The major characteristics of the two types of transmission covered in this section are listed in Table 4.4.1.

4.5 TYPES OF TRANSMISSION

The two types of data transmission that can be employed are serial and parallel. In serial transmission, the bits that compose a character are transmitted in sequence over one line. In parallel transmission, characters are transmitted serially, but all n bits that are used to represent the character are transmitted in parallel—that is, simultaneously over n channels. To examine the differences between these two methods, consider the transmission of an 8-bit character. To transmit this character via parallel transmission requires a minimum of eight lines with additional lines probably being required for control signals or for the transmission of a parity bit. Although parallel transmission is used extensively in computer-to-peripheral unit transmission, it is not normally employed other than when terminal devices are located in close proximity to a computer due to the high cost of the extra circuits required.

TABLE 4.4.1   CHARACTERISTICS OF TRANSMISSION TYPES

Asynchronous

- Each character is prefixed by a start bit and followed by one or more stop bits.
- A period of inactivity, idle time, can exist between transmitted characters.
- Bits within a character are transmitted at prescribed time intervals.
- Timing is established independently by terminals and computers.
- Transmission speeds normally do not exceed 1,800 bit/s over the switched telephone network or leased lines and 9,600 bit/s over direct terminal-to-computer connections.

Synchronous

- One or more sync characters prefix transmitted data.
- Sync characters are transmitted between blocks of data to maintain line synchronization.
- A number of characters are blocked together for transmission with no gaps existing between characters.
- Synchronized timing is established and maintained by the transmitting and receiving terminals, computers, or other devices.
- Terminals require storage (buffer) areas.
- Transmission speeds are normally in excess of 2,000 bit/s.

A typical use of parallel transmission is the in-plant connection of badge readers and similar devices to a computer located in that facility. One advantage of parallel transmission is that it can reduce the cost of terminal circuitry since the terminal does not have to convert the internal character representation into a serial data stream for transmission. Due to the increase in the number of conductors and connectors required by parallel transmission, the cost of the transmission medium and interface will increase, and these tradeoffs must be carefully examined. Since the total character can be transmitted at the same moment in time using parallel transmission, higher data transfer rates than that obtainable with serial transmission facilities are possible. For this reason, most local-facility terminal-to-computer communications is accomplished by the use of parallel transmission. The two types of transmission covered in this section are illustrated in Figure 4.5.1.

4.6 TYPES OF CIRCUITS

The three basic types of line connections or circuits available to connect terminals to computers or to other terminals are dedicated, leased, and switched.

A dedicated line is similar to a leased line in that the terminal and computer (or other terminal) are always connected to each other on these types of circuits, transmission always occurs on the same path, and, if required, the circuit can be readily tuned (conditioned) to improve transmission performance.

FIGURE 4.5.1   Types of data transmission

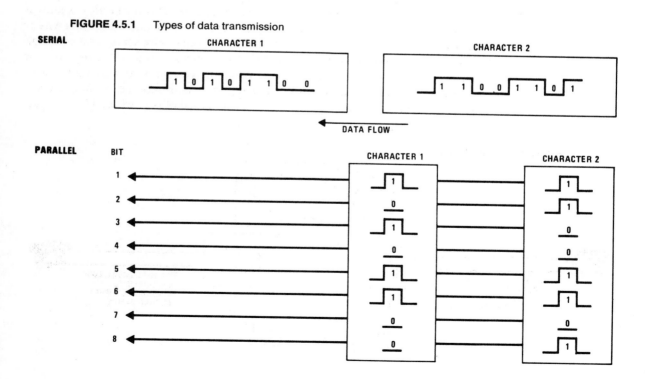

The key difference between a dedicated and a leased circuit or line is that a dedicated line refers to a transmission medium internal to a user's premises, where the customer has the right of way for cable laying. A leased line, however, provides a connection between separate sites where the customer has no right of way for cable laying. Another term for a dedicated circuit is a direct-connect line. This type of connection normally links a terminal or business machine on a direct path through the site to another terminal or business machine located at that site. The dedicated line can be a wire conductor installed by the employees of the company or by the computer manufacturer's personnel, or it can be a local telephone line installed by telephone company personnel.

The second type of circuit, the leased line, is commonly called a private line. It is obtained from a communications carrier to provide an exclusive-use transmission medium between two sites that could be in separate buildings in one city or in distant cities.

The third type of circuit, known as a switched line, is also often referred to as a dial-up connection, whose use permits contact with any party having access to the telephone network. The operator of a business machine accesses the computer by dialing the telephone number of a line connected to the computer. In using switched or dial-up transmission, telephone company switching centers (central offices) serve as intermediate connectors between the dialing party and the dialed party, as illustrated in Figure 4.6.1.

When the dialing party initiates the call, he is first connected to the telephone company central office serving his telephone exchange. This connection is known as a subscriber-loop connection and occurs over a two-wire line, where one wire is used for transmission in both directions while the other wire serves as a common ground. Next, based upon the number dialed, the call is routed through one or more switching centers to the telephone company central office serving the telephone exchange of the number dialed. The connection between telephone company central offices for long-distance calls is composed of four wires, with one pair

FIGURE 4.6.1   Switched network dialing

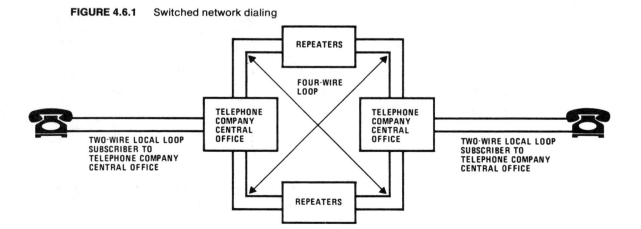

being used for each direction of transmission. When a full-duplex leased line is required, the subscriber loops are converted to four-wire circuits.

When wire terms are used in the context of data transmission, confusion may arise since the term four-wire was derived from the early days of telephone, and in some cases today it does not signify four physical wires. In such cases, two wires are used to form an equivalent four-wire circuit. Different frequencies are used to convey information back and forth on the channel. In this manner, simultaneous two-way transmission is possible without the frequencies' interfering with each other by using one frequency for transmission and another frequency for reception of data, all over the same pair of wires.

Once the telephone central office of the dialed party is reached, another local loop connection is established to finalize the connection between the dialing party and the dialed party. After the connection is established, the terminal and the computer conduct their communications. When communications is completed, the switching centers and central offices disconnect the path that was established for the connection and restore all paths used so they become available for other connections.

When using the switched telephone network for communications, routing is accomplished according to the telephone number of the dialed party. This routing takes place according to the network switching plan used by the telephone company.

Under the network numbering plan employed in the United States, which is the foundation of the network switching plan, subscriber stations are assigned 4-digit codes such as XXXX, where X is any number 0 through 9. The telephone company central office or exchange is assigned a 3-digit code such as NNX, where N is any number 2 through 9. One or more central offices or exchanges are used to form an area code or numbering plan area (NPA) with the assignment of a 3-digit code to prefix the central office and subscriber station numbers.

The middle digit in the area code is always a one or zero. Within an area code or numbering plan area, central office codes are never duplicated. Also, one physical switching machine at a central office may serve subscribers with different central office codes. As an example, a switching machine could serve subscribers with the 444, 445, and 446 prefixes.

One variation of the area code is the international dialing access code. To dial a telephone in a foreign country from certain areas of the U.S. requires first dialing the international access code, 011, followed by a two-digit country code, a city code, and the local number.

Cost, speed of transmission, and degradation of service are the primary factors used in the selection process between leased and switched facilities. In general, if data communications requirements to a computer involve occasional random contact from a number of terminals at different locations, and if each call is of short duration, dial-up service is normally employed. Switched circuits are commonly used for data transmission at speeds up to 4,800 bit/s.

If a large amount of transmission traffic occurs between a computer and a few terminals, leased lines are usually installed. Since a leased line is fixed as to its routing, it can be tuned or conditioned to reduce errors in transmission as well as permit ease in determining the location of errors, since its routing is known. Different categories of leased lines can be selected that permit transmission from under 100 bit/s to many hundreds of thousands of bits per second. Additional information concerning the different categories of leased lines is discussed in the section entitled "Transmission Rates." In Table 4.6.1, the reader will find a list of some of the limiting factors involved in determining the type of line to use for transmission between business machines and computers.

4.7 LINE STRUCTURE

Both the geographical distribution of terminals and computers as well as the distance between each terminal and the computer it will transfer data to are important parameters that must be considered in developing a network configuration. The methods employed to connect terminals to computers or other terminals result in one or more line structures that produce a data communications network configuration. The two types of line structures basic to any network are point to point and multipoint, the latter also commonly referred to as multidrop.

Point-to-Point Link

When a direct connection is established between two points in a network, the line structure is known as a point-to-point link. Here the two points that are connected can be two terminals, a terminal and computer, or two computers. This type of line structure can be established using a dedicated, switched, or leased circuit as illustrated in the top portion of Figure 4.7.1. Each terminal transmits and receives information to and from the computer via an individual connection that links a specific terminal to the computer.

TABLE 4.6.1 LINE SELECTION GUIDE

Line Type	Distance Between Transmission Points	Speed of Transmission	Use for Transmission
Dedicated (Direct connect)	Local	Limited by the conductor	Short or long duration
Switched (Dial-Up)	Limited by telephone-access availability	Normally up to 4,800 bit/s	Short Duration transmission
Leased	Limited by communications company availability	Limited by type of facility selected	Long-duration or frequent short-duration calls

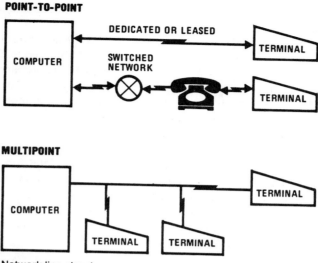

FIGURE 4.7.1   Network line structures

Multipoint Link

In the early period of telephone development, and to some extent even today in several areas, a number of subscribers would be connected to a single-wire pair. This type of connection was known as a party line, and communications problems would arise if two subscribers wished to place a call at the same time. The advantage of this type of circuit arrangement was that individual lines from each subscriber to the telephone company office were eliminated and replaced by one line linking all subscribers on the party line to the telephone company central office.

Today we can construct a line structure equivalent to the party line, for data communications applications, which we call a multipoint or multidrop circuit. The primary advantage of such a structure is to permit terminals to share a common line and thereby reduce the cost of the transmission medium, as illustrated in the lower portion of Figure 4.7.1.

For a multipoint line structure to be effective, one location must be designated as the master or controlling location while the remaining locations are called tributaries or slaves. Normally, each location has a unique digital address. In a data communications environment, the computer is normally the master while the connected terminals are the slaves. To regulate traffic on the circuit, the control location will use one of two methods, known as polling and selecting, detailed in the next section, 4.8. These methods are designed to prevent data transmitted from one terminal from interfering with data transmitted from another terminal, and are also known as line discipline. Although no two terminals on a multipoint line may transmit data at the same time, two or more terminals may receive messages at the same time. The number of terminals receiving such a message is dependent upon the addresses assigned to the message. In some networks, a "broadcast" address permits all terminals connected to the same multidrop line to receive a message at the same time.

One variation of a point-to-point line to permit multiple terminals to communicate via a common line to a computer is obtained through the utilization of special control units, as illustrated in Figure 4.7.2. These control units are known as modem-sharing units, line-sharing units, message interface units, and other such terms. They permit terminals to be clustered at a common geographical location and share a common circuit for communications to a computer. Again, each terminal may have a unique address.

Both point-to-point and multidrop lines may be intermixed in developing a network. Factors that must be considered in the selection of a line structure are numerous and include communications line costs, terminal support of a multipoint line discipline, computer support of that discipline, access and response times, the computer processing time, transmission delays caused by the transfer of data through various communications components, transmission speeds and distances, and the volume of traffic to be tranferred.

4.8 LINE DISCIPLINE

In order for several devices to share the use of a common, multipoint communications line, without the devices interfering with one another, a line discipline must be put into effect. The line discipline for multipoint circuits prevents transmission by more than one terminal at any time, although one or more devices may receive information simultaneously. This line discipline combines polling and selecting, and requires that each terminal on the line have a unique address of one or more characters, as well as circuitry to respond to a message sent to that address.

Polling and Selecting

When the computer polls a line, in effect it samples each terminal in a predefined sequence (polling list) to determine if the terminal has data to transmit. If the terminal has no data to transmit, the computer is informed of this fact and continues its polling sequence in accordance with its polling list until it encounters a terminal on the line that has data to send. At this point the computer will stop polling and permit the terminal to transmit its data. When the message transmitted by the terminal is completed the computer will poll the next terminal on the line.

FIGURE 4.7.2   Point-to-point line using control units

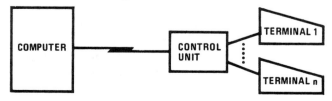

As the computer polls each terminal, the other terminals on the line must wait until they are polled before they can be serviced. Conversely, transmission of data from the computer to each terminal on a multidrop line is accomplished by the computer selecting the terminal address to which the data is to be transferred, informing the terminal that data is to be transferred to that terminal, and then transmitting data to the selected terminal.

Polling and selecting can be used to service both asynchronous and synchronous terminals that are connected to independent, multidrop lines. With polling, a considerable amount of time is utilized by the computer addressing each terminal to determine if the terminal has data to transmit. Due to the control overhead, synchronous, high-speed transmission is normally used for polling although asynchronous transmission has been successfully employed when terminals have short messages.

In the synchronous environment, terminals have a buffer. For a CRT terminal that is normally employed on a multidrop circuit, the buffer area is usually equal to the number of characters that can be displayed on the screen. Thus, when the CRT operator depresses the transmit key on the terminal, no data is actually transmitted to the computer until the terminal is polled. Then the data in the buffer is transmitted and the computer polls the next terminal.

In an asynchronous environment, once the computer selects a terminal, the computer locks out all other terminals on the line until the message is completed. Asynchronous multipoint lines are usually employed to connect a number of receive-only terminals, or terminals with limited transmission requirements, to a central computer. An example of this type of environment would be a state weather news distribution service that connects a number of state offices to the central prediction bureau. Here the central location may prepare forecasts for each area and address and transmit the forecasts to each terminal via a multipoint circuit used to connect all terminals to the central computer.

By the use of signals and procedures, polling and selecting line control insures the orderly and efficient utilization of multidrop lines. An example of a computer polling the third terminal on a multipoint line and then receiving data from that terminal is shown in the top portion of Figure 4.8.1. At the bottom of that illustration, the computer first selects terminal number 2 on the line and then transfers a block of data to that terminal.

When terminals transmit data on a point-to-point line to another terminal or computer, the transmission of that data is under the control of the terminal operator. This method of line control is known as non-poll-and-select or free-wheeling transmission.

Additional information concerning multipoint line efficiency and turnaround times is provided in Chapter 5.

4.9 TRANSMISSION CODES AND CONTROL CHARACTERS

Within a computer, data is structured according to the architecture of the machine. This internal representation of data is seldom suitable for transmission to devices

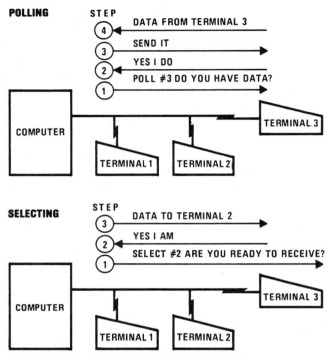

FIGURE 4.8.1   Polling and selecting

other than the peripheral units attached locally to the computer. In most cases, in order to transmit data, the internal information of the computer must be reformatted or translated into a suitable transmission code. This transmission code then creates a correspondence between the bit encoding of data for transmission or internal device representation and printed symbols. Although code conversion can be performed by the computer or by terminals with internal processing capability, the transmission code used is usually dictated by the character code that the remote terminals are designed to accept. Current terminal codes include Baudot, which is a 5-level (5 bits per character) code; binary coded decimal (BCD), which is a 6-level code; the American standard code for information interchange (ASCII), which is normally a 7-level code; and the extended binary coded decimal interchange code (EBCDIC), which is an 8-level code.

In addition to information being encoded into a certain number of bits based upon the transmission code used, the unique configuration of those bits to represent certain control characters can also be considered as a code that may be used to control the line discipline employed. These control characters indicate the start of header (SOH), the end of a message (EOM), and so on, with the number of permissible control characters standardized according to the code employed.

In computer-to-computer data transfers, a large amount of processing time otherwise involved in converting internal data into data coded for transmission can be avoided by sending the data in the format used by the computer for internal processing. This type of transmission is known as binary-mode transmission, transparent data transfer, code-independent transmission, and, most commonly, as native-mode transmission.

Morse Code

One of the most common codes, the Morse or International code, consists of a series of one, two, three, or four dots and dashes. The letter V, for example, consists of three dots and a dash. Although this code is written as a series of dots and dashes, the actual transmission consists of long and short signals with pauses between each character, as illustrated in Figure 4.9.1. By the use of long and short signals inter-mixed with pauses to denote character separations, a unique character configuration is developed that can be recognized by an experienced operator.

In the early development of mechanized telegraph equipment, Morse code was not used since the characters varied in length between pauses. Even today, this code is not practical for a computer communications environment. To overcome the variable-length problems associated with Morse code, a five-bit code, Baudot, named after its inventor, was developed.

Baudot Code

The 5-level Baudot code was devised by a Frenchman, Emil Baudot, and provides a mechanism for encoding characters by an equal number of bits, in this case five. Through the work of an American, Howard Krum, a method was developed to permit the synchronization of transmitted characters to a receiver, thus permitting the development of automatic transmission and reception equipment.

Since the number of different characters that can be derived from a code having two different (binary) states is 2^m, where m is the number of positions in the code, the 5-level Baudot code permits 32 unique character bit combinations.

Due to the necessity to transmit not only the 26 letters of the alphabet but also digits, punctuation marks, and special symbols, the sum of which exceeds 32, it became necessary to devise a mechanism to extend the capacity of the Baudot code to include additional character representations. This extension was accomplished

FIGURE 4.9.1   Morse code transmission of letter "V"

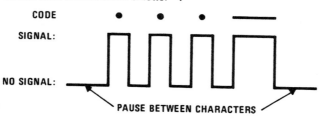

by the incorporation of two "shift" characters into the code: "letters shift" and "figures shift." Here the transmission of a shift character is used to inform the receiver that the characters that will follow the shift character should be interpreted from a symbol and numeric set or from the alphabetic set of characters. In Table 4.9.1, the 5-level Baudot code is listed for one particular terminal pallet arrangement. A transmission of all ones (11111) in bit positions 1 through 5 is used to indicate a letters shift, and the characters that follow the transmission of that shift character are interpreted as letters. Similarly, the transmission of ones in bit

TABLE 4.9.1 5-LEVEL BAUDOT CODE

Letters	Figures	Bit Selection				
		1	2	3	4	5
Characters						
A	—	1	1			
B	?	1			1	1
C	:		1	1	1	
D	$	1			1	
E	3	1				
F	!	1		1	1	
G	&		1		1	1
H	—			1		1
I	8		1	1		
J	'	1	1		1	
K	(	1	1	1	1	
L	)		1			1
M	.			1	1	1
N	,			1	1	
O	9				1	1
P	0		1	1		1
Q	1	1	1	1		1
R	4		1		1	
S	'	1		1		
T	5				1	
U	7	1	1	1		
V	;		1	1	1	1
W	2	1	1			1
X	/	1		1	1	1
Y	6	1		1		1
Z	"	1				1
Functions						
Carriage return	<				1	
Line feed	=		1			
Space				1		
Letters shift		1	1	1	1	1
Figures shift		1	1		1	1

positions 1, 2, 4, and 5 (11011) is used to indicate a figures shift, and the following characters are now interpreted as numerals or symbols based upon their code structure.

BCD Code

Corresponding to the development of computers was the implementation of coding to convert alphanumeric characters into binary notation and the binary notation of computers into alphanumeric characters. One of the earliest codes used to convert data from alphanumeric characters into a computer-acceptable format uses the binary coded decimal code.

The BCD coding technique permits decimal numeric information to be represented by 4 binary bits and permits an alphanumeric character set to be represented through the use of 6 bits of information, as shown in Table 4.9.2. One advantage of this code is that two decimal digits can be stored in an 8-bit computer word and manipulated with appropriate computer instructions. Although only 36 characters are listed in Table 4.9.2, a BCD code is capable of representing a set of 2^6 or 64 different characters.

In addition to the transmission of letters, numerals, and punctuation marks, a considerable number of control characters may be required to insure line discipline is maintained. These control characters may be used to switch on and off devices that are connected to the communications line, control the actual transmission of data, manipulate message formats, and perform such additional functions as acknowledge messages received correctly and request retransmission of messages received in error.

EBCDIC Format

To accommodate these control characters, an extended character set is usually required. One such character set is the extended binary coded decimal interchange code (EBCDIC), which is an extension of the BCD code and employs eight bits instead of six to represent characters. This code permits 2^8 or 256 unique characters to be represented, although only 109 are currently assigned meanings. This code is primarily used for transmission by byte-oriented computers, where a byte is a grouping of eight consecutive binary digits operated on as a unit by the computer. The use of this code in many instances may relieve the byte-oriented computer from performing code conversion when both the computer and connected terminals operate with the same character set. The EBCDIC character set is listed in Table 4.9.3.

ASCII Format

As a result of the proliferation of data transmission codes, attempts to develop a standardized code for data transmission were initiated. One result was the Amer-

TABLE 4.9.2   BINARY-CODED DECIMAL CHARACTER SET

Bit Position

b_6	b_5	b_4	b_3	b_2	b_1	Character
0	0	0	0	0	1	A
0	0	0	0	1	0	B
0	0	0	0	1	1	C
0	0	0	1	0	0	D
0	0	0	1	0	1	E
0	0	0	1	1	0	F
0	0	0	1	1	1	G
0	0	1	0	0	0	H
0	0	1	0	0	1	I
0	1	0	0	0	1	J
0	1	0	0	1	0	K
0	1	0	0	1	1	L
0	1	0	1	0	0	M
0	1	0	1	0	1	N
0	1	0	1	1	0	O
0	1	0	1	1	1	P
0	1	1	0	0	0	Q
0	1	1	0	0	1	R
1	0	0	0	1	0	S
1	0	0	0	1	1	T
1	0	0	1	0	0	U
1	0	0	1	0	1	V
1	0	0	1	1	0	W
1	0	0	1	1	1	X
1	0	1	0	0	0	Y
1	0	1	0	0	1	Z
1	1	0	0	0	0	Ø
1	1	0	0	0	1	1
1	1	0	0	1	0	2
1	1	0	0	1	1	3
1	1	0	1	0	0	4
1	1	0	1	0	1	5
1	1	0	1	1	0	6
1	1	0	1	1	1	7
1	1	1	0	0	0	8
1	1	1	0	0	1	9

ican Standard Code for Information Interchange (ASCII). This 7-level code, listed in Table 4.9.4, is based upon a seven-bit code developed by the International Organization for Standardization (ISO).

ASCII characters are encoded in seven bits, while an eighth bit is available for use as a parity bit. The use of the parity bit is optional and can be odd or even. Today, most terminal devices are built to conform to the ASCII code, which permits a large degree of code compatibility between different manufacturers of such devices. Although the EBCDIC character set was developed by IBM and is

TABLE 4.9.3   EBCDIC CHARACTER SET

Bit positions 0,1 → `00` (hex 0–3), `01` (hex 4–7), `10` (hex 8–B), `11` (hex C–F)
Bit positions 2,3 → `00`, `01`, `10`, `11` within each group
First hexadecimal digit → 0 1 2 3 4 5 6 7 8 9 A B C D E F

Bit positions 4,5,6,7	Second hexadecimal digit	0	1	2	3	4	5	6	7	8	9	A	B	C	D	E	F
0000	0	NUL	DLE	DS		SP	&	−									0
0001	1	SOH	DC1	SOS				/		a	j			A	J		1
0010	2	STX	DC2	FS	SYN					b	k	s		B	K	S	2
0011	3	ETX	TM							c	l	t		C	L	T	3
0100	4	PF	RES	BYP	PN					d	m	u		D	M	U	4
0101	5	HT	NL	LF	RS					e	n	v		E	N	V	5
0110	6	LC	BS	ETB	UC					f	o	w		F	O	W	6
0111	7	DEL	IL	ESC	EOT					g	p	x		G	P	X	7
1000	8		CAN							h	q	y		H	Q	Y	8
1001	9		EM							i	r	z		I	R	Z	9
1010	A	SMM	CC	SM		¢	!		:								
1011	B	VT	CU1	CU2	CU3	.	$	,	#								
1100	C	FF	IFS		DC4	<	*	%	@								
1101	D	CR	IGS	ENQ	NAK	(	)	_	'								
1110	E	SO	IRS	ACK		+	;	>	=								
1111	F	SI	IUS	REL	SUB	|	¬	?	"								

CONTROL CHARACTER REPRESENTATIONS

ACK	Acknowledge	IGS	Interchange group separator	ETX	End of text
BEL	Bell	IL	Idle	FF	Form feed
BS	Backspace	IPS	Interchange record separator	FS	Field separator
BYP	Bypass	IUS	Interchange unit separator	HT	Horizontal tab
CAN	Cancel	LC	Lower case	IFS	Interchange file separator
CC	Cursor control	LF	Line feed		
CR	Carriage return	NAK	Negative acknowledge	SUB	Substitute
CU1	Customer use 1	NL	New line	SYN	Synchronous idle
CU2	Customer use 2	NUL	Null	TM	Tape mark
CU3	Customer use 3	PF	Punch off	UC	Upper case
DC1	Device control 1	PN	Punch on	VT	Vertical tab
DC2	Device control 2	RES	Restore		
DC4	Device control 4	RS	Reader stop		
DEL	Delete	SI	Shift in		
DLE	Data link escape	SM	Set mode		
DS	Digit select	SMM	Start of manual message		
EM	End of medium	SO	Shift out		
ENQ	Enquiry	SOH	Start of heading		
EOT	End of transmission	SOS	Start of significance		
ESC	Escape	SP	Space		
ETB	End of transmission block	STX	Start of text		

SPECIAL GRAPHIC CHARACTERS

¢	Cent sign	−	Minus sign, hyphen
.	Period, decimal point	/	slash
<	Less-than sign	,	Comma
(	Left parenthesis	%	Percent
+	Plus sign	—	Underscore
|	Logical OR	>	Greater-than sign
&	Ampersand	?	Question mark
!	Exclamation point	:	Colon
$	Dollar sign	#	Number sign
*	Asterisk	@	At sign
)	Right parenthesis	'	Prime, apostrophe
;	Semicolon	=	Equal sign
¬	Logical NOT	"	Quotation mark

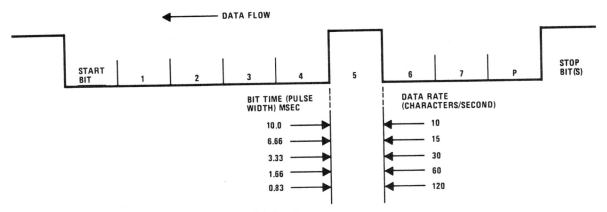

FIGURE 4.9.2   ASCII code bit time and data rate

still employed by most of that firm's computers, an ASCII character set is also available for some computers produced by that manufacturer.

Character Timings

The time required to generate a character varies according to the operating speed of the terminal. In Figure 4.9.2, the ASCII time intervals are illustrated for the character bit periods (unit intervals) at terminal operating speeds ranging from 10 characters per second to 120 characters per second. Thus, at 30 characters per second each bit requires 3.33 msec for transmission. In order to determine the time required for a character to be transmitted, multiply the number of bits used to construct the character by the bit width in milliseconds. (A total of 10 bits—including parity and control bits—is assumed.)

Code Conversion

One frequent problem in data communications is that of code conversion. This can be recognized when we consider what must be accomplished to enable a computer with an EBCDIC character set to communicate with a terminal that has an ASCII character set. When the terminal transmits a character, it is encoded according to the ASCII character code in Table 4.9.4. Thus, the letter A would be transmitted as 1000001, ignoring parity, start, and stop bits if we are employing asynchronous transmission. Upon receipt of that character, the computer must convert the bits of information of the ASCII character into an equivalent EBCDIC character, in this case 11000001. Conversely, when data is to be transmitted to the terminal, it must be converted from EBCDIC to ASCII. This character translation requires computer processing time, which could be used for other activities if both the computer and terminal codes were identical.

Code Efficiency

The efficiency of any two-condition (binary-based) code can be expressed by the formula:

$$E = \frac{\log_2 CS}{BC}$$

where E = the efficiency of the code
CS = number of characters or symbols required
BC = number of bits in the code

Let us assume that for a particular application, 32 different characters are required and a 6-bit code is to be used. By applying the formula we obtain

$$E = \frac{\log_2 32}{6} = \frac{5}{6} = 83.3 \text{ percent}$$

If an 8-bit code were used, then the code efficiency would be reduced to 5/8 or 62.5 percent.

Based upon the above methodology, the Baudot code, when employing letter and figure shift to extend the character set, becomes extremely efficient. As listed in Table 4.9.1, this 5-level code can be used to represent 55 different characters. If we require 32 characters, the code has an efficiency of $\log_2 32/5$ or 5/5, which is 100 percent. If we assume that all 55 characters are required, the coding efficiency is approximately 116 percent.

Control Characters

Within the transmission code, two sets of control characters may be encountered: those for terminal control and those for transmission control.

The terminal control character, as its name implies, is used to control functions on the terminal. These functions can include a line feed, ringing the bell to obtain the operator's attention, and so on.

In the area of transmission control, characters were assigned meanings to overcome the problems associated with message control, error detection and correction, and other problems associated with data transmission. A list of some of these transmission control characters and their assigned meanings will be found in Table 4.9.5.

4.10 PROTOCOLS

A protocol is the management method of the data link to include the attached terminal. In a data communications environment, both the terminal protocol and the data link protocol must be considered.

TABLE 4.9.4 THE ASCII CHARACTER SET

This coded character set is to be used for the general interchange of information among information processing systems, communications systems, and associated equipment.

b4 b3 b2 b1	COLUMN / ROW	0	1	2	3	4	5	6	7
0 0 0 0	0	NUL	DLE	SP	0	@	P	`	p
0 0 0 1	1	SOH	DC1	!	1	A	Q	a	q
0 0 1 0	2	STX	DC2	"	2	B	R	b	r
0 0 1 1	3	ETX	DC3	#	3	C	S	c	s
0 1 0 0	4	EOT	DC4	$	4	D	T	d	t
0 1 0 1	5	ENQ	NAK	%	5	E	U	e	u
0 1 1 0	6	ACK	SYN	&	6	F	V	f	v
0 1 1 1	7	BEL	ETB	'	7	G	W	g	w
1 0 0 0	8	BS	CAN	(	8	H	X	h	x
1 0 0 1	9	HT	EM	)	9	I	Y	i	y
1 0 1 0	10	LF	SUB	*	:	J	Z	j	z
1 0 1 1	11	VT	ESC	+	;	K	[	k	{
1 1 0 0	12	FF	FS	,	<	L	\	l		
1 1 0 1	13	CR	GS	−	=	M	]	m	}
1 1 1 0	14	SO	RS	.	>	N	^	n	~
1 1 1 1	15	SI	US	/	?	O	__	o	DEL

Character Representation and Code Identification

The standard 7-bit character representation, with b_7 the high-order bit and b_1 the low-order bit, is shown below.

Example:

The bit representation for the character "K," positioned in column 4, row 11, is

b_7	b_6	b_5	b_4	b_3	b_2	b_1
1	0	0	1	0	1	1

The code table for the character "K" may also be represented by the notation "column 4, row 11" or alternatively as "4/11." The decimal equivalent of the binary number formed by bits b_7, b_6, and b_5, collectively, forms the column number, and the decimal equivalent of the binary number formed by bits b_4, b_3, b_2, and b_1, collectively, forms the row number.

The standard code may be identified by the use of the notation ASCII.

The notation ASCII (pronounced "as-key") should ordinarily be taken to mean the code prescribed by the latest edition of this standard. To explicitly designate a particular (perhaps prior) edition, the last two digits of the year of issue may be appended, as "ASCII 68" or "ASCII 77."

TABLE 4.9.4   Continued

Control Characters

Col/Row	Mnemonic and Meaning[1]	Col/Row	Mnemonic and Meaning[1]
0/0	NUL Null	1/0	DLE Data Link Escape (CC)
0/1	SOH Start of Heading (CC)	1/1	DC1 Device Control 1
0/2	STX Start of Text (CC)	1/2	DC2 Device Control 2
0/3	ETX End of Text (CC)	1/3	DC3 Device Control 3
0/4	EOT End of Transmission (CC)	1/4	DC4 Device Control 4
0/5	ENQ Enquiry (CC)	1/5	NAK Negative Acknowledge (CC)
0/6	ACK Acknowledge (CC)	1/6	SYN Synchronous Idle (CC)
0/7	BEL Bell	1/7	ETB End of Transmission Block (CC)
0/8	BS Backspace (FE)	1/8	CAN Cancel
0/9	HT Horizontal Tabulation (FE)	1/9	EM End of Medium
0/10	LF Line Feed (FE)	1/10	SUB Substitute
0/11	VT Vertical Tabulation (FE)	1/11	ESC Escape
0/12	FF Form Feed (FE)	1/12	FS File Separator (IS)
0/13	CR Carriage Return (FE)	1/13	GS Group Separator (IS)
0/14	SO Shift Out	1/14	RS Record Separator (IS)
0/15	SI Shift In	1/15	US Unit Separator (IS)
		7/15	DEL Delete

[1](CC) Communications control; (FE) Format effector; (IS) Information separator

TABLE 4.9.5   TRANSMISSION CONTROL CHARACTERS

SYN	— Synchronous Idle	— Used by synchronous transmission systems to provide message and character framing and synchronization.
SOH	— Start of Header	— Used at the beginning of a sequence of characters to indicate address or routing information. Such a term is referred to as a Heading. A STX character terminates a heading.
STX	— Start of Text	— Used at the beginning of a sequence of characters that is to be treated as an entity to reach the ultimate destination.
ETX	— End of Text	— Used to terminate a sequence of characters started with STX.
ETB	— End of Transmission Block	— Used to indicate the end of a sequence of characters started with SOH or STX.
EOT	— End of Transmission	— Used to indicate a termination of transmission. A transmission may include one or more records and their associated headings.
ACK	— Acknowledge	— A character sent by the receiving station to the transmitting station to indicate successful reception of a message.
NAK	— Negative Acknowledge	— A character sent by the receiving station to the transmitting station to indicate unsuccessful reception of a message.
ENQ	— Enquiry	— A character used to request a response from a remote station. The response that a remote station generates is predefined.

The terminal protocol—another name for terminal control characters—can include such control characters as the bell, line feed, and carriage return for teleprinter terminals, cursor positioning characters for a display terminal, and form control characters for the line printer attached to a remote batch terminal. The data link protocol is used to define the control characteristics of a particular link and is a set of conventions to be followed to govern the transmission of data and control information. Further, a terminal can have a predefined control character or set of control characters that are unique to the terminal and are not interpreted by the line protocol.

Poll and select is often considered to be a type of line discipline or control, with the control character configuration to perform poll and select considered the line protocol.

In general, the line protocol permits the exchange of information according to an order or sequence by establishing a series of rules for the interpretation of control characters that are employed to govern the exchange of information. These characters control the execution of a number of tasks that are essential for the exchange of information in a data communications environment. Some of these information control tasks are listed in Table 4.10.1.

Although these tasks are important, only some of them may be required for the data transmission since the series of tasks required is a function of the total data communications environment. An example of this situation is the connection of a single terminal to a computer. Here, the establishment and verification of the connection may not be required. Conversely, when several terminals are connected to a computer via a multipoint or multidrop link, verification of the terminal's identification would be required to insure that the data transmitted from the computer would be received by the proper terminal. In addition, once a terminal session is completed, this fact must be recognized to enable the computer's resources to be made available to other terminal users. Thus, connection disengagements of terminals other than those connected directly on a point-to-point circuit must be conducted to permit the channel on a front-end processor to become available to service other users.

Another important information control task is the transmission sequence that is employed to establish the precedence and order of transmission, to include both data and control information. One example involves a number of terminals connected via a multipoint circuit to a computer. Here, this task defines the rules for when such terminals may transmit and receive information.

TABLE 4.10.1   INFORMATION CONTROL TASKS

Connection establishment
Connection verification
Connection disengagement
Transmission sequence
Data sequence
Error control procedures

In addition to the transmission of control information following a sequence, the data itself may be placed into sequence. Data sequencing is normally employed in synchronous transmission where a long block of data may be broken into smaller blocks for transmission, with the size of the data blocks being a function of the error control procedure employed. When divided into smaller blocks, the amount of data that must be retransmitted in the event that an error in transmission is detected is reduced. Although error-checking techniques currently employed are more efficient when short blocks of data are transmitted, the efficiency of the transmission will correspondingly decrease since either a positive or negative acknowledgment is returned to the transmitting device after each block is received and checked. For communications between synchronous buffered terminals and computers, block lengths of up to several thousand characters can be transmitted. Normally, block lengths from 80 to 512 characters are the most common block sizes transmitted. Although some protocols specify block length, most protocols permit the user to set the size of the block.

In the area of error control procedures, the most commonly employed method to correct errors in transmission is to inform the transmitting device to retransmit the block of data. To correct by retransmission requires the coordination of the transmitting and receiving devices, with the receiving device continuously informing the transmitting device of the status of each of the previously transmitted data blocks. If the block previously transmitted contained no detected errors, the receiving device will transmit a positive acknowledgment to the transmitting device and the sender will then transmit the next block of information.

If the receiving check character fails to match the transmitted block-check character, the receiver will transmit a negative acknowledgment and discard the block since it is in error. The transmitting station will then retransmit the previously sent block and, depending upon the protocol employed, several retransmissions may be attempted for continuous appearing error conditions.

This continuous sequence of retransmissions may continue until a default limit is reached. Or, garbled data due to a bad circuit or other problems will result in a limit to the number of retransmissions that can occur. Once this limit is reached, the computer may then terminate the terminal's session and the terminal operator will have to reestablish the connection.

Line Control Example

Consider the transmission of information contained on a reel of magnetic tape to a computer for processing. Here the magnetic tape unit would normally be a peripheral unit of a remote batch terminal. Let us additionally assume that transmission is via a leased line, synchronous modems are employed at both ends of the circuit, and that the transmission of data from the terminal to the computer will be in blocks of fixed size with a longitudinal parity check. To reduce this example to a manageable magnitude, assume that only two blocks of data will be transferred. If transmission is half-duplex, then the flow of data is as illustrated in Figure 4.10.1.

Prior to information on the magnetic tape being transmitted to the computer,

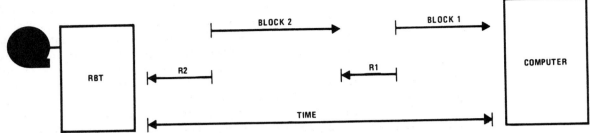

FIGURE 4.10.1   Typical half-duplex synchronous transmission

synchronization must be established between the terminal and the computer. With the use of synchronous modems, the bit timing for the transmitter and receiver can be provided by those devices. When the terminal begins to transmit the first block of data, two sync characters will be used as a prefix to provide block framing; thus the terminal's software will add these characters to the block while the block is in the terminal's memory being prepared for transmission. At the computer, these transmitted sync characters will be used for synchronization and then stripped from the received block.

After bit and character timing has been established, the start of the text must be indicated. This is accomplished by the use of the STX (start of text) control character, which again is added to the block by the software in the terminal and removed from the block by the computer's software.

Next, the actual text will follow. Here the block size will be a function of the size of the terminal's buffer area as well as other factors, such as line conditioning and error rates. To indicate the end of the block, another control character, ETB (end of transmission block), is used. Next, for error control a block check character is added to the end of the block as shown in Figure 4.10.2. Since we assume a longitudinal redundancy check is used to form the block check character, this character is then made up of the sum of all the even parity bits in the text.

If the first block has been received by the computer and the computation of the BCC character matches the BCC character at the end of the block, we can assume no transmission errors have occurred. To indicate this, the computer will assemble a suitable reply to be transmitted to the terminal. If transmission was asynchronous, the reply could be simply an ACK (acknowledge) control character with suitable start and stop bits for synchronization. In the synchronous mode, we must send a reply message suitably framed with control characters as shown in

FIGURE 4.10.2   Primary block transmission

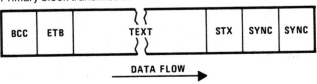

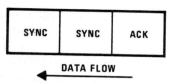

FIGURE 4.10.3   Message acknowledgment

Figure 4.10.3. In Figure 4.10.1 R1 indicates the transmission of this acknowledgment.

The next and final block to be transmitted from the terminal to the computer must be framed. The starting point and end of the text must be indicated. Since the second block is the final block to be transmitted, that no additional messages will follow will be indicated by the use of the EOT (end of transmission) control character. The second block to be transmitted is shown in Figure 4.10.4.

Assuming again that the second block was received without any indicated errors, the computer's response would be as shown in Figure 4.10.3 and also indicated as R2 in Figure 4.10.1. This simplistic example illustrates the extent to which a protocol and control characters are required to insure that a data link transfer of information is properly managed. Now let us examine two specific methods used to govern synchronous data transfer.

Bisync (BSC) and HDLC Overview

Due to the variety of facilities that can be employed for communications, as well as the number of network configurations and line structures available, many complex line protocols have been developed to effectively utilize them. Among current protocols, one of the most frequently employed for synchronous transmission is IBM's binary synchronous communications (BSC or bisync), which was first introduced in 1966. This protocol is employed for data transfer by many medium- and high-speed devices and provides a set of rules that carry out the synchronous transmission of binary-coded data. This protocol can be used with a variety of transmission codes. However, BSC is limited to the half-duplex transmission mode. Another limitation is that it requires receipt acknowledgement of every data block transmitted. Due to the success of BSC, of which there are several versions, a number of other protocols have been developed. Whereas BSC is a character-oriented protocol, newer protocols have been developed that are bit oriented and

FIGURE 4.10.4   Last block transmission

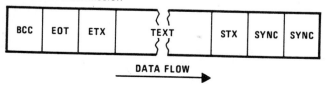

permit full-duplex transmission. These new protocols permit a greater volume of information to be transmitted in a given time period and thus are more efficient than BSC. One such protocol, high-level data link control (HDLC), was developed by the International Organization for Standardization (ISO) to reduce the frequent acknowledgment-negative acknowledgment series of transmissions required by the BSC protocol.

BSC Examination

As mentioned previously, BSC is a procedure used to control the transmission of digital data on a half-duplex line connecting two or more devices.

The BSC protocol specifies the communications control characters used for the formatting of text, status indicators, synchronization functions, and error control. This protocol may be used on point-to-point and multipoint circuits, via dedicated, switched, or leased facilities.

Block Size

The basic foundation of BSC communications is the message block illustrated in Figure 4.10.5. Each block may contain an optional header, text, and a trailer. To identify these elements, several control characters are used, including SOH (start of header), STX (start of text), and ETX (end of text). As previously discussed, sync (synchronization) characters must be employed to establish timing coordination between the transmitter and receiver. The number of such characters used varies with the type of application, and the two such characters shown in Figure 4.10.5 are a commonly used pattern where the message block follows the sync characters.

A message may consist of one or more blocks of information, where each block

FIGURE 4.10.5   Basic BSC message block

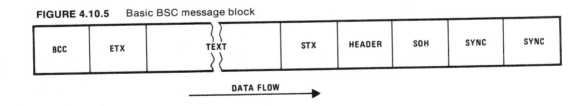

| BCC | ETX | TEXT | STX | HEADER | SOH | SYNC | SYNC |

DATA FLOW ⟶

CONTROL CHARACTERS USED TO IDENTIFY HEADER, TEXT, AND TRAILER INCLUDE:

SOH = START OF HEADER, TRANSMITTED BEFORE
     THE HEADER CHARACTERS

STX = START OF TEXT, TRANSMITTED BEFORE
     THE FIRST DATA CHARACTERS

ETX = END OF TEXT, TERMINATES A MESSAGE
     BLOCK STARTING WITH SOH OR STX

BCC = BLOCK CHECK CHARACTER

contains text and a trailer, while only the first block is required to contain the header. In Figure 4.10.6, a two-block message is illustrated. Here, the ETX character of a one-block message is replaced by an ITB (end of intermediate transmission block) character for all blocks except the last block.

For purposes that become obvious, the header is also known as an address, since this information field contains a character or characters that identify the originating and/or receiving location. For a multipoint circuit, a separate control message may be used for addressing in place of the header. The SOH character indicates that the following character or characters are the header.

The next portion of the message block is the text, which is identified by a preceding STX character. Whereas a short message may be just a single block followed by an ETX, some messages may consist of a multiblock where only the last block of text is followed by an ETX character.

The last portion of the message block is the trailer, which consists of a block check character (BCC). This contains a count for error-checking in one of several ways, depending on the code employed. One method is based upon a cyclic redundancy check (CRC). Within BSC, two modes of CRC are employed: CRC-12, which is used for 6-bit transmission codes, and CRC-16, which is used for 8-bit EBCDIC transmission codes. The CRC is a division performed by both the transmitting and receiving stations using the numeric binary value of the message as a dividend, which is divided by a constant. The quotient is discarded, and the remainder serves as the check character, which is then transmitted as the BCC.

The other method of obtaining a block check character is through a vertical redundancy check (VRC) and longitudinal redundancy check (LRC). The VRC is an odd-parity check performed on a per-character basis when the transmission code employed is the 7-level ASCII code. Whereas the VRC checks characters for odd parity, the LRC checks an entire horizontal line, bit position by bit position, within a block for odd parity. The LRC becomes the BCC character and is transmitted to the receiving station.

As the block is received by the destination station, that receiver computes a BCC in the same manner the transmitting station generated its BCC. At the end of the block, the receiver compares its block count with the sender's BCC character. If the two are not equal, a negative acknowledgment (NAK) character is sent to the transmitter, requiring the block to be retransmitted. If the error continues due to some type of abnormal condition, such as line noise, and a preset number of attempts is reached in trying to transmit an error-free block, the transmitter will abort and a new connection must be established.

FIGURE 4.10.6   Multiblock message

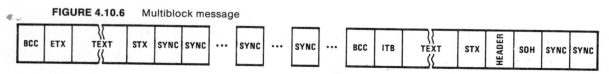

ITB = END OF INTERMEDIATE TRANSMISSION BLOCK

Synchronization and Transmission Sequence

Prior to the transmission of a message block, the sending location will transmit synchronizing (SYN) characters to synchronize the receiver with the transmitter. Next, a message exchange is initiated when one location transmits an inquiry (ENQ) control character to the other location. The ENQ character, in effect, bids for the line in both a point-to-point and multipoint circuit. If the other location can accept the message, it will acknowledge the inquiry by sending an ACK control character in response. Throughout the synchronization and transmission sequence, each acknowledgment is alternately numbered one and zero.

As illustrated in Figure 4.10.7, initially a terminal is idle. Assume that the terminal operator has entered enough data to fill the CRT display, corrected it, and wishes to transmit that data to the computer. The operator depresses the transmit key on the CRT, which in turn sends an enquiry (ENQ) control character to the computer preceded by two SYN characters. The computer responds by transmitting two SYN characters and an even, positive acknowledgment (ACK0) to the terminal.

Next, the terminal transmits two SYN characters followed by the message block, which contains the data keyed on the CRT. Now assume that the computer receiving the message block detects an error, since the computed BCC does not

FIGURE 4.10.7   Synchronization and transmission sequence

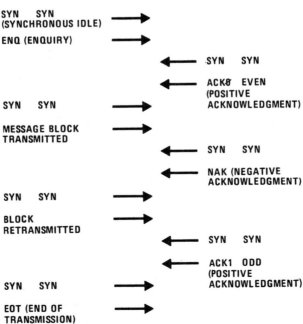

match the transmitted BCC character. Then, the computer will respond with two SYN characters and a negative acknowledgment (NAK). This NAK causes the terminal to retransmit the message block, preceded again by two SYN characters.

Now assume that the block was received error free so that the computer responds with an odd positive acknowledgment (ACK1) again preceded by two SYN characters. Since one screen was transmitted, and we have assumed that only one message block was required, to conclude the transmission, the terminal will send an end of transmission (EOT) control character. This character will reset all stations (here the terminal and computer) to what is known as the control mode, in which they are neither the transmitter nor the receiver.

Acknowledgment Sequence

Through the utilization of even and odd acknowledgments (ACK0 and ACK1), a sequential check of a series of replies to the state of transmitted message blocks can be accomplished. An ACK0 is the first affirmative reply to a polling-selection (multipoint) or a connection (point-to-point) line bid. Thereafter, the ACK0 alternates with ACK1 to inform the device transmitting message blocks that the previous block was accepted without error and that the receiver is ready to accept the transmission of the next block of information. In Figure 4.10.8, an acknowledgment sequence is illustrated that eliminates the SYN characters.

During the sequence illustrated in Figure 4.10.8, if for some reason an ACK is not received, the transmitter will send an ENQ to the receiver. An example of this type of situation is illustrated in Figure 4.10.9, where the transmitter has not received an ACK1 after the second message block was transmitted. After waiting a period of time, which is known as the timeout period, the sender will transmit an ENQ. If the receiver responds to the ENQ with an ACK0, then the message was lost, since the receiver is still acknowledging the first message block. Conversely, if the receiver responds with an ACK1 to the ENQ, then the message was received but the resulting acknowledgment was lost. To compensate for the lost message block, the data originator would retransmit the second message block. For the other case, where the acknowledgment was lost, when the data originator finally receives the ACK1 as a result of the transmission of an ENQ, it would then continue its transmission.

Timeouts

In the previous example, a timeout period was mentioned as time that would elapse until the data originator would transmit an ENQ to determine the status of its previously transmitted message block. Within the BSC protocol, several timeout situations are normally employed: transmit, receive, disconnect, and continue.

Transmit timeout

On a periodic basis during transmission, usually once per second, one or two SYN characters are automatically inserted into a message. These SYN insertion char-

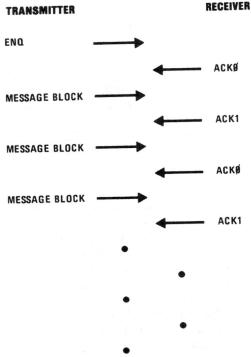

FIGURE 4.10.8   Alternating acknowledgment sequence

acters are for timing purposes, to maintain synchronization between the transmitting and receiving devices. Also, they serve as a "timefill" in the absence of a message, so that the circuit remains operational and the receiver knows that transmission is still in progress. These SYN insertion characters are deleted from the message by the receiver; hence they have no effect on the message content.

Receive Timeout

The receive timeout period is normally three seconds and is used to limit the waiting time for a transmitting station to receive a reply. The receive timeout also allows any receiving or monitoring station to check the circuit for SYN-idle characters. These SYN-idle characters indicate that the transmission is continuing; thus this timeout is reset and restarted each time a SYN-idle is detected.

Disconnect Timeout

This timeout is normally an option that may be used on switched-network data links. It is normally set at 20 seconds to prevent a station from holding a connection

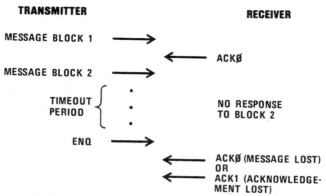

FIGURE 4.10.9   Use of ENQ when a message is nonresponsive

for prolonged periods of inactivity. When a station has been inactive for that period of time, it will disconnect itself from the network.

Continue Timeout

This timeout, normally set at two seconds, is used to prevent a three-second timeout, such as a receive time-out, from occurring. This timeout is employed by stations where the speed of the input or output devices affect buffer availability and cause transmission delays. This timeout indicates that transmission or reception is delayed, but will continue, and that the link should be maintained. This is accomplished by sending a temporary text delay (TTD) two-character sequence within two seconds of receiving acknowledgment of the previous block. In response to the TTD, the receiving station will transmit a character sequence known as a WACK (wait before transmit positive acknowledgment). It is used to prevent further transmission until it is ready to receive again.

Transparency

In the discussion of control characters so far, no text could contain sequences that include control characters, since the receiver would detect them as control characters and perform the expected transmission control operation. BSC transparent mode allows control characters to be inserted in text, and thus permits the transmission of many types of raw data within the standard BSC message format, without worrying about the effect such data will have on line or message control.

Since some type of line protocol control is necessary, control characters must still be employed under the transparency mode of operation. To use control characters, but reduce the probability of raw data being interpreted as such, a data link escape (DLE) character is prefixed to the control characters. Now, only when a two-character sequence of the DLE character and a normal control character is received, will the receiver recognize it as a control character.

HDLC

In order to alleviate some of the limitations of BSC, especially its design for half-duplex operations, a series of high-level data link control (HDLC) type protocols have been developed. Three of these HDLC protocols include IBM's synchronous data link control (SDLC), Burrough's data link control (BDLC), and Honeywell's data link control (HDLC).

The key difference between HDLC protocols and previous data link protocols is that they are bit oriented rather than character oriented. Another significant difference is that HDLCs are naturally transparent: a data bit's significance is determined by its position in the bit stream. An examination of bit patterns to determine if a control character is present is the method employed by BSC. In HDLC, transparency permits unrestricted bit patterns to appear in the data since the bit patterns of control functions reside at fixed locations.

When a transmission follows a BSC protocol, large messages are broken into a series of smaller blocks of fixed size. In comparison, the HDLC protocol permits variable length messages in what is called a frame. There can be any number of frames in a single transmission.

Frame Format

In HDLC, the same frame format is used to serve lengthy transmissions, such as remote batch, and short messages, such as inquiry and conversational transmissions.

An HDLC frame is illustrated in Figure 4.10.10. The frame itself is delimited by the flag fields, one at the beginning of the frame and one at the end of the frame. Both flags consist of the specific 8-bit sequence 01111110. Between frames, any number of flag fields may be transmitted to keep the link active and synchronized. In addition, the flag serves to alert the receiving station to the possibility that a frame is beginning. Upon the detection of an 8-bit nonflag field immediately after the flag, the receiving device knows that a new frame is being transmitted. To prevent a flag bit pattern from appearing between flags within a frame, zeros are inserted and deleted as required. When five 1s appear, a 0 is inserted in the bit

FIGURE 4.10.10   HDLC frame

ENDING FLAG	FRAME CHECK SEQUENCE	INFORMATION	CONTROL	ADDRESS	BEGINNING FLAG
8	16	VARIABLE	8	8	8

DATA FLOW →

BIT LENGTH

stream after the last 1. The receiver, after detecting five 1s followed by a 0, deletes the zero.

The 8-bit field following the beginning flag is the address field. This field defines the station for which the frame is intended if the frame was originated by a primary station. The primary station is normally a computer and the secondary station a remote terminal. In a frame sent by a secondary station, the address field identifies the sending station.

Following the address field is an 8-bit control field. The functions of this field include conveying counts of frames transmitted or received, so that frames do not have to be received in sequence but only have to be reassembled into sequence after receipt.

After the control field, the beginning of the information field is encountered. As noted, this field is of any length and can contain text that includes control characters. Upon conclusion of the information field, a frame-check sequence field follows. This 16-bit field functions as a block check, similar to the block check character of BSC, to detect transmission errors. Finally, the frame is concluded by the 8-bit ending flag, which contains the flag bit sequence 01111110.

HDLC Operations

In addition to point-to-point and multipoint operations, HDLC can be used for network looping as illustrated in Figure 4.10.11. When used in looping, all transmissions flow in the same direction around the loop and each frame passes through the secondary stations, where they are inspected to determine the frame's address. If the station address equals the frame address, the station acts on the data for its own use.

Secondary stations can transmit only when permitted to do so by the primary station. Once each station completes its transmission, the next station in the loop can begin transmission. The primary station can also poll individual secondary stations, in which case a response is transmitted by that secondary station to the specific poll.

4.11 TYPES OF SERVICE

When the distance between the terminal and the computer is relatively short, the transmission of digital information between those two devices may be accomplished simply by cabling the terminal directly to the computer. As the distance between the two devices increases, the pulses of the digital data transmitted will start to distort, until a point is reached where they become unrecognizable by the receiver. There are two methods or types of service for the transmission of data: analog and digital. For each type of service, specialized communications equipment is necessary when transmission exceeds a short distance.

Since telephone lines were originally developed to carry voice (analog) signals, the digital signals to be transmitted between a computer and terminal over this type of medium must first be converted into a signal that is acceptable for trans-

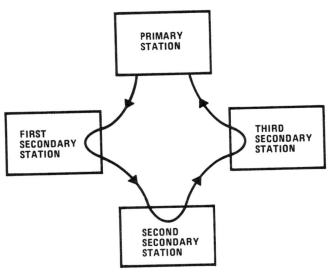

FIGURE 4.10.11 HDLC network looping

mission over the telephone line. To convert these digital signals into suitable analog signals, a modem is employed. The term modem is a contraction of the terms modulation and demodulation, and denotes the basic functions performed by that device. The modem is an electronic device that converts the digital signals generated by computers and business machines into analog tones that are suitable for transmission over the telephone network's analog facilities.

At the receiving end of the circuit, a similar device samples the transmitted tones, converts them back to the original digital signals that were transmitted, and delivers these digital signals to the connected digital device. An example of the signal conversion performed by modems is illustrated in Figure 4.11.1. This illustration shows the interrelationship between terminals, computers, and a transmission line when an analog transmission medium is used for the transfer of digital data. (Modulation techniques are discussed in Section 5.3.)

In the telephone network, both switched and leased lines are available that provide analog service. Therefore, modems or similar devices can be used for data transmission over both of these types of analog network facilities. Modems can be used on direct-connect, leased, or switched line facilities; they are hard-wired to direct-connect and leased lines, whereas they may be either directly connected or interfaced to a switched facility. Due to this type of connection, a terminal user can only communicate with the distant location at the other end of a leased line but can communicate with many devices when the modem is connected to a switched line.

Most low-speed terminals utilize a device called an acoustic coupler, which is a modem whose connection to the switched telephone line is obtained by acoustically coupling the telephone headset to the coupler. The primary advantage of this device is that no hard-wired connection to the switched telephone network is

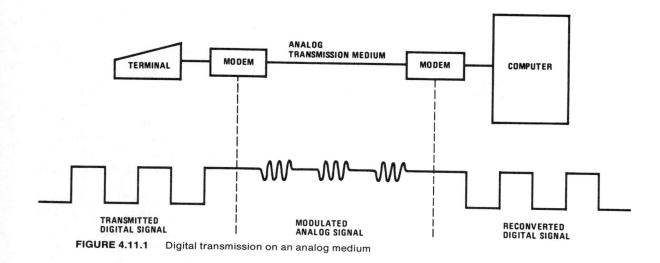

FIGURE 4.11.1   Digital transmission on an analog medium

required, and a terminal interfaced to such a device may be portable and can be moved with the acoustic coupler from location to location. The interrelationship of modems, acoustic couplers, terminals and the analog transmission medium is illustrated in Figure 4.11.2.

Analog Facilities

Currently, several categories of analog switched facilities are offered by communications carriers. Each type of facility has its own rate structure and set of operating characteristics. Normally, prior to determining which category or categories of service should be employed for an optimum cost-effective means of communications, an analytic study of the number of calls, quantity of transmitted data, and other parameters is conducted. The common types of analog switched facilities include direct distance dialing (DDD) and wide area telecommunications

FIGURE 4.11.2   Interrelationship of modems, acoustic couplers, terminals, computers, and analog transmission medium.

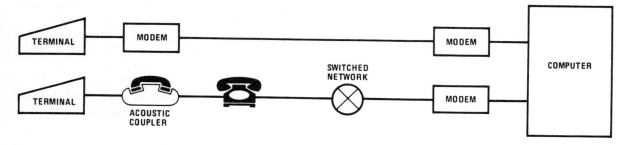

service (WATS). Foreign exchange (FX) can be considered a hybrid type of service since it is a combination of switched and leased analog facilities.

The first type of switched service to be discussed, direct distance dialing, permits the user to dial directly any telephone connected to the public switched telephone network. In turn, the dialed telephone number may be connected to another terminal, a computer, or some type of business machine or data communications component. In addition to installation costs, the charge for this service may be a fixed monthly fee if no long-distance calls are made, on a message unit basis based upon the number and duration of local calls, or a fixed fee plus any long-distance charges incurred. Depending upon the day of the week and time of day, discounts from normal long-distance rates are available for selected calls made without operator assistance.

The second category of switched service to be discussed, WATS, may be obtained in two different forms, known as OutWATS and InWATS. Each form is designed for a particular type of communications requirement common to a large number of telephone company subscribers. OutWATS may be used when a specific location has a requirement to place a large number of telephone calls to geographically distributed locations. Providing the reverse capability, InWATS permits a number of geographically distributed locations to communicate with a common facility.

Although calls initiated on WATS are similar to calls placed on the regular public switched telephone network, charges for usage can vary considerably between the two facilities. Instead of being charged on an individual call basis as on the switched network, the WATS facility user is charged a flat sum per block of hours used per month for communications. Usage in excess of that block is then billed on an overtime basis.

In order to use a WATS line, a voice-band trunk called an access line is installed between the telephone company central office and the subscriber's facility. Other than certain geographical calling restrictions, which are a function of the service area of the WATS line and of cost considerations, the user may place as many calls as desired on this trunk if the service is OutWATS. If the user has InWATS service, he may then receive as many calls as users dialing his telephone number.

InWATS, the well-known "800" area code, permits remotely located personnel to initiate calls to a central facilities telephone number, toll free, so long as the call originator is within the service area provided by the particular InWATS type of service selected. The charge for both types of WATS services is a function of the service area as well as the total call durations within a month. The service area can be intrastate, a group of states bordering the user's state where the telephone connected to the WATS access line is located, or a grouping of distant states. In 1978, WATS service was extended from the continental United States to Alaska, Hawaii, Puerto Rico, and the Virgin Islands. Additional detail on WATS is included in Section 8.2.

One hybrid type of switched service that can be used advantageously under certain conditions to include geographical dispersion of terminals and period access requirements is a foreign exchange (FX) line. This circuit combines the public switched network with a leased line. It may result in communications from one or more terminals to a computer at substantially less cost than the price of equivalent direct distance dialing.

The foreign exchange line is similar to a standard telephone in that when the phone is placed off hook, a dial tone is received. Instead of a local subscriber area dial tone, however, the foreign-exchange-line user receives the dial tone of a distant or foreign exchange as illustrated in Figure 4.11.3. In this manner, the user can dial long-distance calls within the foreign exchange area with the cost of such calls limited to the leased-line cost and perhaps a foreign exchange call toll. The total cost normally is considerably less than the cost of equivalent long-distance calls.

For terminal-to-computer communications, the use of the line illustrated in Figure 4.11.3 is effective when a terminal remotely located from the computer is only required to access that computer or another device within the same foreign exchange area. Here the initiation of communications is one way, with the terminal the originator. The user of the FX line is restricted to dialing the telephone numbers of a particular exchange.

An FX line can be employed to service many terminals that require communications with a computer, as illustrated in Figure 4.11.4. Here, each terminal user within a geographical area (telephone exchange) dials a local number, which is answered if the FX line is not in use.

From the foreign exchange, information is transmitted via a dedicated (leased) voice line to a permanent connection in the central (local) office of a communications carrier near the computer's location. A line from the central office is then extended to the customer's computer location to complete the connection. Since only one terminal at a time may use the FX line, normally only groups of terminals whose usage can be prescheduled or whose operational effectiveness is not reduced by contending for the line are suitable for using this method of communications.

The major difference between using an FX line and a leased line is that any terminal dialing the foreign exchange line provides the second modem required for the transmission of data over the facility; whereas a leased line used for data transfer normally has a fixed modem and terminal attached to one end of the circuit and a fixed modem and computer or terminal at the other end of the line.

FIGURE 4.11.3   Foreign exchange line

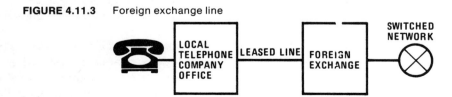

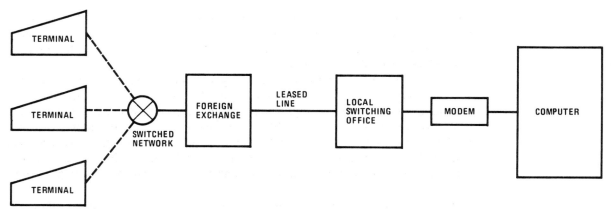

FIGURE 4.11.4 FX line used to support many terminals

Digital Facilities

The second type of communications service available for user consideration, digital service, has been offered comparatively recently to interconnect large geographical areas.

Using digital service, data is transmitted from its source to its destination in its original digital form. Digital service avoids the conversion of signals into an analog form for transmission and reconversion back into a digital form, as is the case when modems or acoustic couplers are used to transmit data over analog facilities.

In the place of modems and couplers, users can select one of two basic arrangements to connect their terminals or computers to a digital medium. A digital service unit (DSU) provides a standard interface to a user's terminal that is compatible with modems and conducts such functions as signal translation, data regeneration, reformatting, and timing. In place of modems that are designed to operate at numerous data rates, the DSU is designed to operate at one of four speeds: 2,400, 4,800, 9,600 and 56,000 bit/s. In operation, the transmitting portion of the DSU processes the user's signal into bipolar pulses suitable for transmission over the digital medium. At the destination, the receiving portion of the DSU extracts timing information, and regenerates mark and space data from the received bipolar signal.

The second device that can be employed for communications on a digital medium is a channel service unit (CSU). It is provided by the communications carrier to those customers who desire to perform the signal processing to and from the bipolar line themselves, as well as to retime and regenerate the incoming signal through their own equipment.

When data is transmitted over a digital medium, the signal is regenerated by the communications carrier numerous times prior to its arrival at its destination. In general, digital service gives data communications users an improved level of performance and reliability when compared to data transmission over an analog medium. (Also refer to Section 5.5.)

Hybrid Digital Service

Although digital service is offered at many locations throughout the United States and at several international locations, for those user locations outside the serving area of a digital facility, an analog extension is often required to connect to the service. In Figure 4.11.5, the utilization of digital service via an analog extension is illustrated. As shown, if the closest city to the terminal located at city 2 that offers digital service is city 1, then to use digital service to communicate with the computer, an analog extension must be installed between city 1 and city 2. In such cases, the performance, reliability, and possible cost advantages of using digital service may suffer. Digital service is currently available for leased service where the leased digital line, like the leased analog line, is dedicated for full-time use to a particular customer.

4.12 TRANSMISSION RATE

A number of different methods exist to define the rate of data transmission. The most common method employed, the data signaling rate, is usually expressed in bits per second, or bit/s. Another method is the modulation rate, which is a term most frequently used by a communications engineer and is expressed in terms of baud units. (Also refer to Section 4.2.)

Data Signaling Rate

The data signaling rate, expressed in bit/s, defines the rate at which information can be transmitted. Examine the 8-level, 11-unit coded character illustrated in Figure 4.12.1.

The data signaling rate for serial transmission is defined as:

$$R = \frac{1}{(T)} \log_2 N \text{ bit/s}$$

where T = duration of the unit signal element in seconds and N = the number of signaling conditions.

FIGURE 4.11.5   Analog extension to digital service

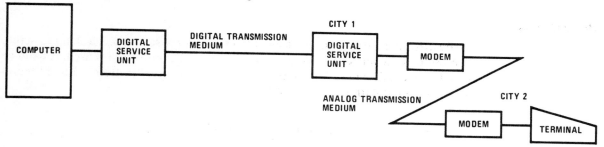

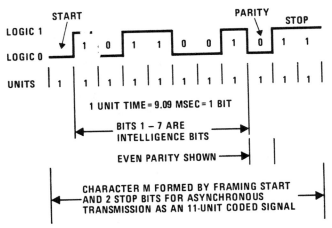

FIGURE 4.12.1   8-level, 11-unit coded character representation

Since the transmission of the character M requires 11 units to be transferred, with each unit time equal to 9.09 msec, and two signaling conditions can occur, with the presence of logic level 0 or 1, the data signaling rate becomes:

$$R = \frac{1}{(.00909)} \log_2 2 = 110 \text{ bit/s}$$

Sometimes the data signaling rate may be expressed in characters per second, or words per minute. In order to compare line speeds, these alternative expressions must be converted to a common denominator such as bits per second. To do this conversion, one must know the number of bits in a character for the code used as well as the meaning of a "word." In data transmission, a word is considered to be six characters in length, normally five letters and a space. For conversion, the following formula can be used:

$$R = \frac{\text{words/min.} \times \text{chars./word} \times \text{bits/char.}}{60 \text{ seconds}}$$

Modulation Rate

To describe the performance of a circuit in terms of the rate at which changes in the condition of the line can be made in a given time, the term baud is used. A baud is equal to one unit signal element per second. Returning to the illustration of Figure 4.12.1, the modulation rate is therefore

$$\text{Rate} = \frac{1}{0.00909} = 110 \text{ baud}$$

Based upon the above, it is wrong to conclude that a baud is the same as one bit per second, since if more than two signaling states are used, the answers would be completely different. This becomes apparent when we examine a new type of data signaling obtained by using four logic levels, as illustrated in Figure 4.12.2. Using four logic levels produces four different ways of combining two binary digits, and thus the number of signals necessary to transmit the information is only one-half that necessary with two-state signaling. For the situation illustrated in Figure 4.12.2, the data signaling rate would be

$$\text{Rate} = \frac{1}{0.00909} \log_2 4 = 110 \times 2 = 220 \text{ bit/s}$$

While the data signaling rate has doubled, the modulation rate is still 1/.00909 or 110 baud.

Factors Affecting Data Rates

While the types of terminals, modems, or acoustic couplers, as well as the line discipline and type of computer interfaced via a transmission medium, all play roles that affect transmission rates, the transmission medium itself is the most important factor.

The services offered by communications carriers such as American Telephone and Telegraph Co. (AT&T) and Western Union (WU) for data transmission are based upon their available facilities. Analog transmission is most readily available and can be employed on in-plant dedicated lines or switched or leased telephone circuits. Available mainly in large cities and surrounding areas, digital transmission can be used from nondigital service locations by the use of an analog extension as illustrated in Figure 4.11.5. Within analog and digital service, several grades of transmission are available for customer consideration.

In general, three grades of transmission can be obtained on analog service: narrow band, voice band, and wideband. (Ref. Sec. 8.2.) The data signaling rate

FIGURE 4.12.2   Data signaling using four logic levels

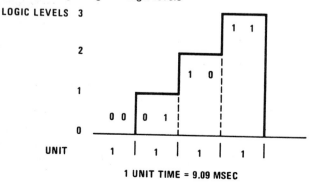

1 UNIT TIME = 9.09 MSEC

that can be obtained on each is dependent upon the bandwidth and electrical properties of each type of circuit offered within each grade of service. Summing up a very complex subject, it can be stated that transmission speed is a function of the bandwidth of the communications circuit, and the greater the bandwidth, the higher the possible speed of transmission.

When a communications carrier divides a voice-band circuit, or groups a number of transmissions from different users onto a single portion of a circuit, a narrow-band circuit is obtained. Typical transmission rates on narrow-band facilities range between 45 and 300 bit/s. One example of narrow-band usage is Teletype terminals that are connected to message-switching networks over such facilities.

In comparison to narrow-band facilities that have a bandwidth in the range of 200 to 400 Hertz, voice-band facilities have a bandwidth of approximately 3,000 Hertz. When using voice-band facilities for data, speeds obtainable are based upon the type of voice-band facility used: dial-up transmission on the public switched telephone network, or transmission via a leased line.

For the public switched telephone network, maximum data rates are between 4,800 and 7,200 bit/s, with 9,600 bit/s possible on occasion. Since leased lines can be tuned or conditioned, a data rate of up to 9,600 bit/s can be employed on such a facility. (Recent modem developments have made rates on the order of 14,400 bit/s attainable.) Although low data rates can be used on both narrow-band and voice-band circuits, one should not confuse the two since a low data rate on a voice circuit is transmission at a speed far less than the maximum permitted by that type of circuit; whereas a low data rate on a narrow-band facility is at or near the maximum transmission rate permitted by that type of line.

When the bandwidth of several voice-band circuits are grouped together to provide a wider bandwidth than available on a single voice circuit, the result is known as a wideband or group-band facility. Wideband facilities can only be obtained when employing leased lines and are used for transmission at rates in excess of 9,600 bit/s. Transmission rates on wideband facilities vary with the type of offerings of different communications carriers. Data rates normally available include 19.2, 40.8, 50, and 230.4 kbit/s.

For the situation where terminals are directly connected to a computer, transmission rates are a function of the distance between the terminal and the computer as well as the gauge of the conductor used to connect the two devices together.

In digital transmission, present offerings by AT&T's Dataphone digital service (DDS) provide interstate, full-duplex, point-to-point, and multipoint leased line, synchronous digital transmission at data rates of 2.4, 4.8, 9.6, and 56 kbit/s, as well as data rates of 1.344 and 1.544 Mbit/s between the servicing areas of digital cities.

Recently a new high-speed digital switched communications service was proposed by AT&T. This service is designed to offer customers full-duplex, synchronous transmission over a common switched digital network at a data rate of 56 kbit/s. In Table 4.12.1, the main types of analog and digital facilities as well as the data rates and general use of such facilities are listed.

TABLE 4.12.1   TRANSMISSION FACILITIES

Facility	Transmission Speed	Use
Analog		
Narrowband	45-300 bit/s	Message switching
Voice band	Less than 4,800 to 7,200 bit/s	Timesharing; remote job entry
Switched	Up to 9,600 bit/s	Remote job entry; computer-to-computer
Leased		
Wideband	9,600 bit/s and up	Computer-to-computer; remote job entry; tape-to-tape transmission; high-speed terminal to high-speed terminal
Digital		
Leased line	2.4, 4.8, 9.6, 56 kbit/s	Remote job entry; computer-to-computer; high-speed facsimile
Switched		
(proposed)	56,000 bit/s	Terminal-to-terminal; computer-to-computer; high-speed terminal to computer

4.13 LINK TERMINOLOGY [Refer to Section 3.1]

When more than one terminal transmits data over a common circuit, such as a multipoint line, this line is known as a multiterminal-to-computer link.

Although terminals may be configured with appropriate communications facilities to communicate directly to a computer over individual computer-to-terminal links, economics may justify the utilization of a device to combine the data from many low-to-medium-speed terminals onto one or more high-speed paths for retransmission to a computer. Many such devices that can be used to combine data transmitted from many terminals are now offered by various manufacturers.

Two of the more commonly employed devices are concentrators and multiplexers. Circuits used to connect the terminals to a concentrator are known as concentrator-to-terminal links while those that connect terminals to multiplexers are known as multiplexer-to-terminal links. The high-speed line that connects the concentrator to a computer or host processor is known as a concentrator-to-host link while for multiplexers such connections are called multiplexer-to-host links. When one concentrator transmits data to another concentrator, this type of circuit is known as a concentrator-to-concentrator link, whereas the circuit used to connect multiplexers is known as a multiplexer-to-multiplexer link. Finally, the transmission path between computers is known as a host-to-host link to indicate the source and receiver of information. In Figure 4.13.1, some of the typical types of data links are illustrated.

FIGURE 4.13.1 Link terminology

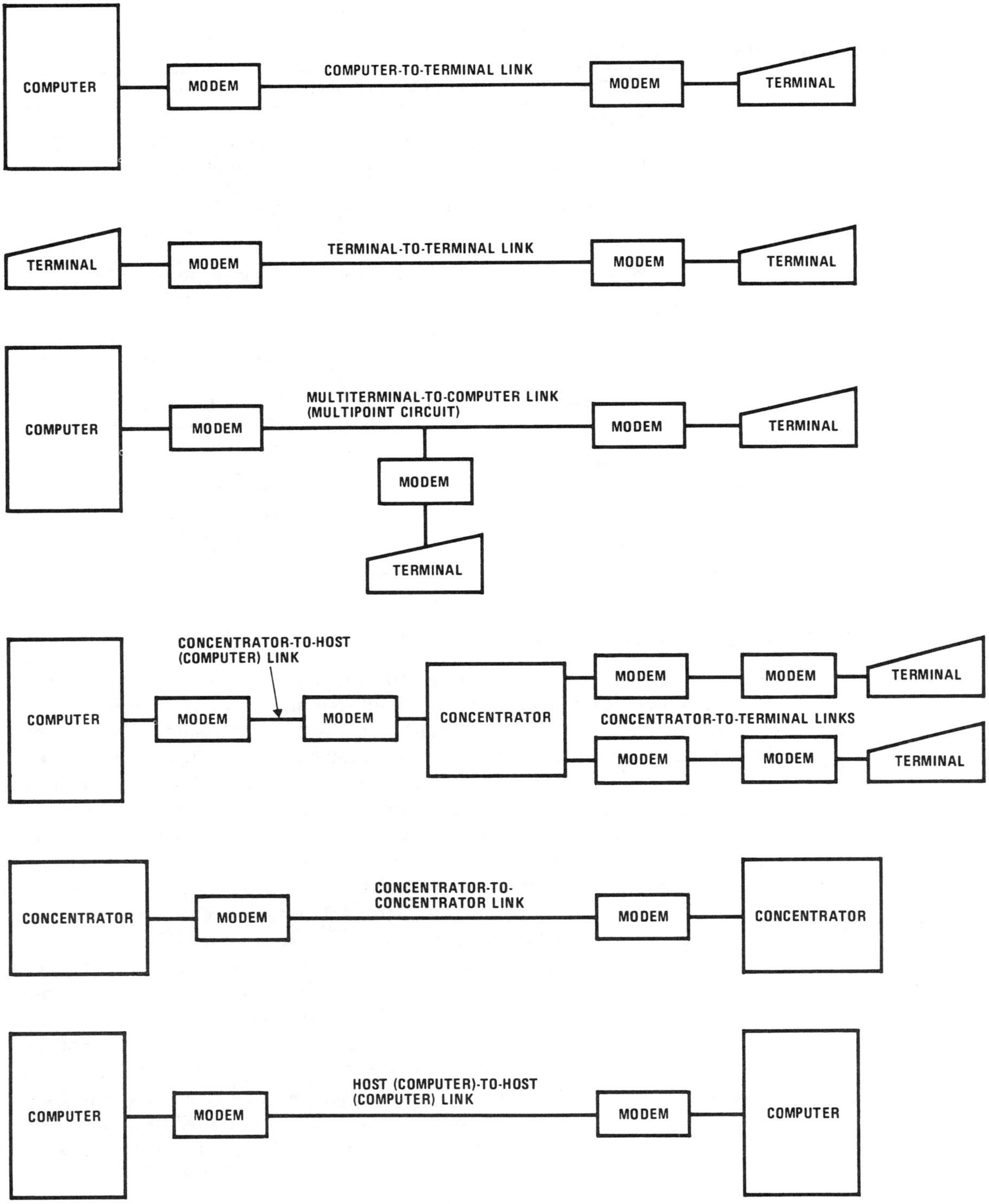

COMPUTER — MODEM — COMPUTER-TO-TERMINAL LINK — MODEM — TERMINAL

TERMINAL — MODEM — TERMINAL-TO-TERMINAL LINK — MODEM — TERMINAL

COMPUTER — MODEM — MULTITERMINAL-TO-COMPUTER LINK (MULTIPOINT CIRCUIT) — MODEM — TERMINAL
MODEM — TERMINAL

COMPUTER — MODEM — CONCENTRATOR-TO-HOST (COMPUTER) LINK — MODEM — CONCENTRATOR — MODEM — MODEM — TERMINAL
CONCENTRATOR-TO-TERMINAL LINKS
MODEM — MODEM — TERMINAL

CONCENTRATOR — MODEM — CONCENTRATOR-TO-CONCENTRATOR LINK — MODEM — CONCENTRATOR

COMPUTER — MODEM — HOST (COMPUTER)-TO-HOST (COMPUTER) LINK — MODEM — COMPUTER

96

QUESTIONS

4.1 What is the difference between a bit and a baud?

4.2 What is the difference between a character and a computer word? What is the relationship between a character and a computer-word size?

4.3 What are the three modes of transmission? Explain how communications operates in each mode.

4.4 Contrast asynchronous and synchronous transmission. What are the advantages and disadvantages of each transmission technique?

4.5 Contrast serial and parallel transmission. Which one requires less transmission time? Explain.

4.6 Define the normal utilization of the three basic types of line connections.

4.7 Define the two basic types of line structures and the advantages and disadvantages of each.

4.8 What are some of the functions control characters perform? Cite five examples of control characters and their utilization.

4.9 Define the function of a transmission code.

4.10 Why is Morse code not suited for automatic data transmission?

4.11 How many different characters can be represented by a 10-bit code?

4.12 How long would it take to transmit one bit of a 12-bit character at 120 characters per second? How long would it take to transmit the entire character?

4.13 What does a protocol perform? Discuss several protocol control tasks.

4.14 Discuss the differences between BSC and HDLC type protocols.

4.15 Why is a transparency mode of operation for data transfer important? Contrast BSC and HDLC transparency methods.

4.16 What are the key differences between analog and digital service?

4.17 Discuss the difference between a leased line, WATS line, and foreign exchange line.

4.18 What is an analog extension and why is it used?

CHAPTER 5

BASIC TRANSMISSION DEVICES

5.1 INTRODUCTION

The function of a data communications network is to transfer information from one location to another. This transfer is accomplished by two types of communications signals—digital and analog.

In this chapter, the basic methods of transferring information, starting with a terminal directly connected to a computer, will be examined. Next, the problems, limitations, and techniques associated with transmission over the most frequently used medium, the telephone network, will be covered as well as transmission with the more recently introduced digital services.

To transmit and receive information over a medium requires a variety of devices. The two basic devices used for data transmission on analog media are acoustic couplers and modems. Their transmission compatibility, frequency-band limitations, and noise problems, as well as the service unit used on digital networks, will be examined in detail. In covering these components, the interrelationship of data transmission equipment, terminals, and computers will then be presented to develop an understanding of how networks can be developed, and altered.

5.2 TRANSMITTING DIGITAL SIGNALS

The basic element found in most networks, a terminal directly connected to a computer, can be examined to develop an understanding of the capacity of a communications channel.

If the direct connection is of limited distance and the electrical properties of the line have no abnormalities, then the received digital pulses will be equal in shape to the digital pulses transmitted from the other end of the line—top portion of Figure 5.2.1. Unfortunately, this ideal situation seldom occurs in real life since every circuit has a degree of resistance, inductance, and capacitance associated with it that causes signal distortion.

Due to these electrical properties, the square-edged digital pulses become distorted as they travel over the communications lines, as illustrated in the middle portion of Figure 5.2.1.

In addition to distortion, a factor known as signal attenuation must be considered. Attenuation results from a loss of signal strength as the distance between transmitter and receiver increases, as shown in the lower portion of Figure 5.2.1. The net effect is that the transmitted pulses may not be recognizable at the receiver.

Two additional factors can also have a bearing on the quality of the received pulses. The first factor, transmission speed, is easy to visualize since the higher the data rate, the more pulses per unit time; and the more pulses per unit time, the narrower the pulses. It is easier to distort a narrower pulse than a wide one, to the point where a receiver cannot recognize it. The second factor is random noise, commonly referred to as thermal noise, caused by the molecular vibrations within electronic circuitry. This produces a very-low-level mixture of electromagnetic waves at different frequencies—similar to the hiss one may hear when an FM radio is tuned between stations. Thus, if the transmitted signal power falls too far, the thermal noise level can swamp the data-transmission level and thus cause errors.

FIGURE 5.2.1

TRANSMITTED DIGITAL PULSES   **RECEIVED DIGITAL PULSES**

NO DISTORTION

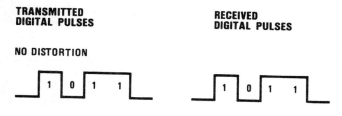

DISTORTION DUE TO ELECTRICAL PROPERTIES OF LINE

ATTENUATION EFFECT

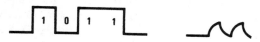

Additional sources of noise include static from the atmosphere, interference from electrical equipment, and noise produced from the components of electrical circuits, including telephone company switching centers, cables, and switches.

One method used to characterize the quality of a circuit is by determining its signal-to-noise ratio. This ratio is simply the signal power divided by the noise power, and it can be increased by increasing the signal strength, decreasing noise, or both. A high signal-to-noise ratio is desirable since it maximizes the capacity of a channel.

Another method to categorize the quality of transmission over a circuit is by stating the ratio of the power transmitted to power received. In a telephone circuit environment, rather than try to determine the loss of power due to transmission through such components as telephone instruments, switchboard connections, and the circuit, the total loss can be determined by end-to-end measurements. When measuring for the overall loss, a test frequency of approximately 1,000 Hz is used by convention. The loss or gain for the entire circuit is given by the equation

$$N = \log_{10} \frac{P1}{P2} \text{ bels}$$

where N = power ratio in bels
P1 = power transmitted
P2 = power received

Since the bel is a large unit, the decibel (dB), or one-tenth of a bel, is used so that the loss or gain becomes:

$$P = 10 \log_{10} \frac{P1}{P2}$$

where P = power ratio in dB.

If an amplifier produces a stronger signal at the receiver, then the received signal, P2, will be greater than P1 and the logarithm of P1 over P2 will be negative. If the power transmitted (P1) is greater than the power received (P2), the logarithm will be positive. As an example, consider a circuit where the power received was measured to be only a hundredth of the power transmitted. Then, the power ratio would be

$$P = 10 \log_{10} \frac{P1}{P2} = 10 \log_{10} \frac{100}{1} = +20 \text{dB}.$$

On a telephone circuit, losses due to the line and equipment will always arise. However, one is able to obtain a zero-loss circuit when the gains from the amplifiers in the circuit are adjusted to counterbalance exactly the losses due to the circuit and component attenuation. It is important to note that the decibel is not an absolute unit but the logarithmic expression of a ratio that defines over-all loss in terms of the power sent and power received over a circuit.

Similarly, the decibel can be used to express the ratio between the signal and noise on a circuit. The correspondence between various decibel losses and power ratios is listed in Table 5.2.1. Note that a reference point is required to define the relationships. In this case, 0 dB is equivalent to 1:1 ratio and serves as the reference point.

For the user who wishes to extend the physical distance between his terminal and the computer, the problems of distortion, attenuation, and noise may be insurmountable when transmission is over an ordinary pair of telephone-type wires, unless special equipment is installed to enhance the level of transmission. One such device is a line driver, which can be used to extend the distance that a digital signal can be transmitted down a line and still be recognized properly at the receiver.

A line driver is basically a digital repeater that amplifies and reshapes digital signals. The line driver is normally employed on direct connect lines of in-plant facilities where power source and shelter are available. This device can be inserted at any point in the direct-connect line. It operates by sampling bits being transmitted, then retransmitting such bits after amplifying and regenerating them so that their structure is reformatted back into the original shape. This regeneration process is illustrated in Figure 5.2.2.

As terminal locations increase in distance from the computer, a point is reached where it becomes impractical to continue the utilization of a direct connection between the terminal and the computer. When such a distance is reached, an

TABLE 5.2.1   DECIBEL RELATED TO POWER RATIO

dB	Power Ratio Signal-to-Noise Ratios
0	1:1
+3	2:1
+6	4:1
+9	8:1
+10	10:1
+13	20:1
+16	40:1
+19	80:1
+20	100:1
+23	200:1
+26	400:1
+29	800:1
+30	1,000:1
+33	2,000:1
+36	4,000:1
+39	8,000:1
+40	10,000:1

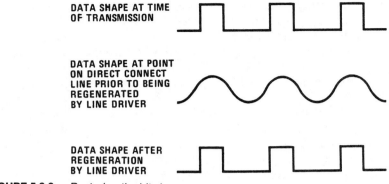

DATA SHAPE AT TIME
OF TRANSMISSION

DATA SHAPE AT POINT
ON DIRECT CONNECT
LINE PRIOR TO BEING
REGENERATED
BY LINE DRIVER

DATA SHAPE AFTER
REGENERATION
BY LINE DRIVER

FIGURE 5.2.2   Restoring the bit shape

alternative medium must be employed. One such medium is the analog telephone network.

5.3 SIGNAL MODULATION AND DEMODULATION

Designed for the transmission of voice signals, the analog telephone network does not employ digital repeaters. Instead, analog amplifiers rebuild the level of a voice signal when it becomes faint. Unfortunately, amplifers also amplify noise and distortion that are present on the circuit. To better understand analog transmission, let us first investigate the frequency spectrum and its application to both voice and data transmission.

When a person speaks, he or she is transmitting a continuous range of frequencies that travels through the air. Light waves and electromagnetic waves on a wire conductor can also be described in terms of their frequencies. That is, the amplitude of the signal at a given point in time is oscillating. The rate of oscillation is referred to as the frequency, which is described in terms of Hertz (cycles per second). Although the human ear can hear sounds of frequencies ranging from about 30 up to 20,000 Hertz, telephone circuits transmit only between approximately 300 and 3,300 Hertz. This collection of frequencies, or band, that is passed is sufficient to understand speech and to recognize the speaker. When voice telephone signals travel between telephone company central offices, many of these signals may be packed together (multiplexed) electronically to enable one wideband channel to carry many conversations simultaneously. To do so requires a considerable engineering effort, since this involves assigning 3-kiloHertz bands for each voice signal, raising the signal to a higher frequency for transmission, and then separating (filtering) them back to individual voice channels at the receiving end.

When attention was focused on telephone circuits for their use in transmitting digital data, a significant problem had to be overcome. The telephone circuit was designed for analog transmission: a continuous wave shape such as the human voice's. If we wish to transmit digital data (discrete square-shaped pulses) over such a medium, a device would be required to convert the digital bit stream into an analog signal, and back again.

As mentioned in Section 4.11, one such device developed to perform this function is a modem, and the process it uses is called modulation. At the other end of the telephone line, a similar device must be employed to reverse the process, converting the analog signal back into digital pulses. This process is called demodulation, and the device at each end of the line is built to perform modulation and demodulation. The utilization of such a device to permit a remote terminal to communicate with a computer over a telephone circuit is illustrated in Figure 5.3.1.

Modems incorporate components that protect the circuits from many signals that could cause interference with other users or with the telephone network's signals.

Modulation Techniques

In designing a modem, a variety of modulation techniques can be used. Each has a different set of characteristics and a different level of circuit complexity. Some designs permit transfer at a high data rate and are expensive, while other less-costly designs are used for low-speed digital signaling. The majority of modems operate by transmitting a continuous sine wave and then modulating it in accordance with the data that is to be transferred.

As illustrated in Figure 5.3.2, a sine wave is a spectral line that relates to transmission at a given frequency. Here, current or voltage is applied to produce an amplitude. In addition to the amplitude, the frequency and phase of the wave may be varied to carry information. Expressed as a function of time, the sine wave may be represented by the following equation:

$$a = A \text{ sine } (2\pi \text{ ft} + \Theta)$$

where a = instantaneous amplitude of voltage or current at time t
     A = maximum amplitude of voltage or current
     f = frequency in Hertz
     Θ = phase in degrees (zero in Fig. 5.3.2)

To make the sine wave carry information (that is, to modulate the sine wave), the values of A, f, or Θ may be varied. The varying of these parameters produces the

FIGURE 5.3.1   Modem operation

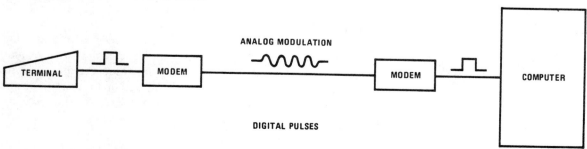

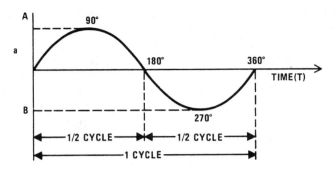

a = INSTANTANEOUS AMPLITUDE AT TIME T
T = TIME
A = MAXIMUM POSITIVE AMPLITUDE
B = MAXIMUM NEGATIVE AMPLITUDE

FIGURE 5.3.2   Sine wave

three basic types of modulation: amplitude modulation, frequency modulation, and phase modulation. Figure 5.3.3 illustrates the three types. Assume that a sine wave centered in the telephone voice band at approximately 1,500 Hertz is modulated to transmit the digital signal. The amplitude can be varied with the bit pattern as illustrated in the top portion of Figure 5.3.3.

The middle portion of the illustration shows frequency modulation; and the lower portion of that illustration shows phase modulation. It should be noted that the simple presence or absence of a signal on the circuit can be used to convey information that would be equivalent to the presence or absence of a signal of a fixed amplitude.

Bandwidth

One of the most important terms in the communications field is bandwidth. This term refers to the width of the range of frequencies that a channel can transmit, and not the frequencies themselves. If the lowest frequency a channel can transmit is f_1 and the highest f_2, then the bandwidth is the difference between the highest and lowest frequencies $f_2 - f_1$. Since a telephone line can transmit frequencies from approximately 300 to 3,300 Hertz, its bandwidth is 3 kiloHertz.

Normally, f_1 and f_2 are the frequencies at which amplitude is 3 dB down from the maximum amplitude within the band. Thus, frequencies less than f_1 or greater than f_2 can be transmitted but the amplitude will be seriously attenuated.

The capacity of a channel for information transfer is proportional to its bandwidth. A channel with a 15 kiloHertz bandwidth can transfer five times as many bits per second as a channel with a 3 kiloHertz bandwidth. As the maximum transfer rate of a channel is reached, the signals transmitted on that circuit become uninterpretable, since they are received in too distorted a shape for the receiver to be able to recreate them.

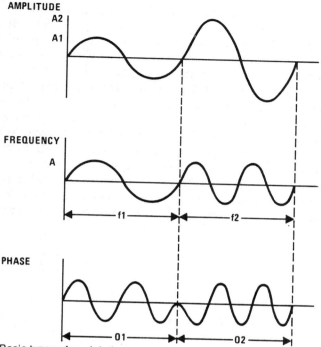

FIGURE 5.3.3 Basic types of modulation

In 1928, Nyquist developed the relationship between bandwidth and the baud rate on a circuit as

$$B = 2W$$

where B = baud rate
W = bandwidth in Hertz

That is, in Nyquist's relationship, the rate at which data can be transmitted without incurring intersymbol interference must be less than or equal to twice the bandwidth in Hertz. For a typical voice circuit with a bandwidth of about 3,000 Hz, data transmission can only be supported at baud rates lower than 6,000 symbols or signaling elements per second. Today, only the most expensive and efficiently designed modems approach the Nyquist baud rate limit of 2W.

Since any oscillating modulation technique, such as amplitude modulation, frequency modulation, or phase modulation, immediately halves the achievable signaling rate, most modems operate at one-half to one-quarter of the Nyquist limit. Since this limit applies only to the signaling, or baud rate, and not to the actual data rate in bits per second, increasing the amount of information each pulse or signal carries (by coding) will correspondingly increase the number of bits per second transmitted.

Although this technique would appear to remove data transfer limitation, increasing the amount of information per pulse through the use of multilevel coding, as illustrated in Figure 4.2.2, introduces new problems. In a 2-level code, the difference between each level is large when compared to higher-level codes. This relationship is illustrated in Figure 5.3.4, where the pulse height of a 2-level code is eight times the height of an 8-level tribit code. Thus, as the height of the pulse is reduced, it becomes more susceptible to distortion. Another problem with multilevel coding is the circuitry required to distinguish each level transmitted. Presently, 8-level coding, representing 3 bits per baud, is the upper range used before error rates begin to rise to an unacceptable level. Error rates increase because as the levels are reduced in size, they become more susceptible to noise.

In 1948, C. Shannon presented a paper concerning encoding and decoding methods that could be employed to transmit data, and the relationship of coding to noise. In this paper, Shannon calculated the theoretical maximum bit-rate capacity of a channel of bandwidth W Hertz as

$$C = W \log_2\left(1 + \frac{S}{N}\right)$$

where W = bandwidth, in Hertz
     S = power of the transmitter
     N = power of the thermal noise

Using a signal-to-noise ratio of 30 dB and the bandwidth of a typical telephone line, Shannon's capacity would be approximately 15,000 bit/s. This value can be considered the ultimate design goal for modems on voice-grade lines. Present devices attain data rates of 14,400 bit/s on leased lines and normally 9,600 bit/s or less on the switched network. Thus, the highest data transfer rates in use today are slightly less than the theoretical maximum.

The relationship between Shannon's law of data transfer in bits per second and Nyquist's relationship between bandwidth and baud is discussed next. Shannon's formula defines the maximum bit rate (C), which, when divided by the baud rate (B), indicates the number of bits that must be represented by one signal element. Thus,

$$N = \frac{C}{B}$$

where N = number of bits/signal element.

Once the number of bits per signal element is computed, then the number of code levels required, L, becomes

$$L = 2^N$$

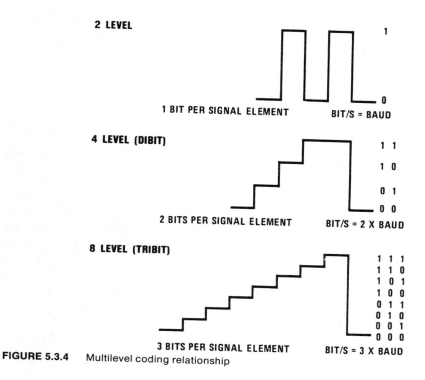

2 LEVEL

1 BIT PER SIGNAL ELEMENT   BIT/S = BAUD

4 LEVEL (DIBIT)

2 BITS PER SIGNAL ELEMENT   BIT/S = 2 X BAUD

8 LEVEL (TRIBIT)

3 BITS PER SIGNAL ELEMENT   BIT/S = 3 X BAUD

FIGURE 5.3.4   Multilevel coding relationship

Additional Modulation Techniques

When modems employ frequency modulation, a number of problems can occur. First, as the modulation rate increases, the spread between frequencies used must be increased. This can create a problem when transmission is to occur over the public switched telephone network, since different frequencies are employed for such supervisory functions as circuit switching and call termination. If these frequencies are not avoided as the modem modulates the frequency in response to changing data rates, false operations could be initiated. One method employed to avoid this problem is frequency-shift keying (FSK), in which just two frequencies are used, one to represent a 1 bit and another a 0 bit, as shown in Figure 5.3.5.

Normally, FSK modulation is employed to transfer information at low data rates.

Although multilevel signaling can be conducted using frequency modulation, such a technique is seldom employed. The increase in the number of separate frequencies that have to be transmitted causes a corresponding increase in bandwidth requirements.

A second technique widely employed in modem design actually consists of a number of variations of phase modulation. One method to better understand the principles of phase modulation is to think of a modem having two sine-wave

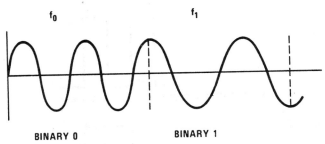

FIGURE 5.3.5 Frequency-shift keying

generators, as illustrated in the top portion of Figure 5.3.6, with each sine wave of the same frequency but out of phase—in this case by 180 degrees.

If the output of the modem is switched between each of these sine waves as the digital pulses entering the modem vary between 0 and 1, then the phase shift can be used to represent different information states. The result of this phase shifting is shown in the lower portion of Figure 5.3.6, where a phase change of 180 degrees is used to represent a binary 0, while the normal in-phase sine wave represents binary 1.

Currently, two types of phase modulation are employed in the design of modems and the circuitry required to detect the phase information. The first

FIGURE 5.3.6 Using phase change to represent different information states

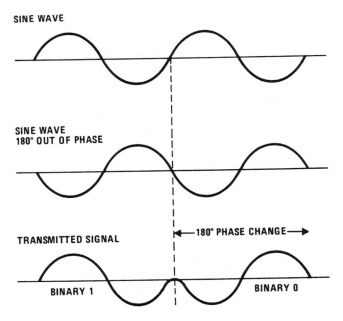

method, known as fixed-reference phase modulation, assigns a meaning to each phase position as in the previous example. Here, a reference wave of the same frequency as the modulation signal, but of constant phase, must be generated at the demodulator to detect the phase of the incoming modulated signal.

The second method, known as differential phase modulation, assigns meanings to each change in phase and not to the phase conditions. This method does not require a separate reference wave and thus reduces to a degree the circuitry required in the modem. Here, one change in phase would be interpreted as a binary 0 if the preceding phase was interpreted as a binary 1, and so on. One of the primary reasons for the design of a number of modems that employ phase modulation is that multiphase-generating modem circuitry is less complex than modems designed for other modulation techniques. The multiphase signals permit multiple bits of information to be represented by one phase change.

As an example, consider the multilevel coding relationships illustrated in Figure 5.3.4. By using 8 different phases, three bits of information (tribits) can be represented by each discrete phase change. In Table 5.3.1, the relationships between several modulation rates and the number of bits per second of data that can be theoretically transmitted by the employment of different levels of phase modulation are listed. While the data transfer rate can substantially increase as the corresponding number of phases employed increase, the small changes in phase required to differentiate between states will drive up the cost of circuitry. In addition, as the number of phases increases, the degrees separating each phase decrease, increasing the probability of errors in reception.

Currently, two methods are primarily employed in the design of four-phase modulation modems. The first method, as illustrated in Figure 5.3.7, uses 0-, 90-, 180-, and 270-degree phase shifts, while the second method employes 45-, 135-, 225-, and 315-degree phase shifts. In the first method, a long string of repetitive dibits, such as 00 00 00 00 or 11 11 11 11, could cause synchronization problems, since phase changes could be delayed for a considerable time, and most modems of this type rely on periodic phase changes to resynchronize timing. This problem can

TABLE 5.3.1   MODULATION RATES AND DATA RATES

Modulation Rate (Baud)	Bits per Signal Element	Number of Phases	Data Transfer Rate (Bit/s)
1,200	1	2	1,200
1,200	2	4	2,400
1,200	3	8	3,600
1,200	4	16	4,800
1,200	5	32	6,000
2,400	1	2	2,400
2,400	2	4	4,800
2,400	3	8	7,200
2,400	4	16	9,600
2,400	5	32	12,000

be resolved by the second method shown in Figure 5.3.7. Since no zero-degree phase is present as in the previous method, there is always a continuous phase transmitted.

Quadrature Amplitude Modulation

The quadrature amplitude modulation (QAM) technique combines both phase and amplitude modulation to obtain data rates in the range of 4,800 to 9,600 bit/s. In a QAM modem, two signals at the same frequency, but 90 degrees out of phase with each other, are employed, hence the term quadrature. Figure 5.3.8 contains a vector diagram of the QAM technique. For each signal, four possible levels of amplitude can be applied: A1, A2, A3, and A4.

The combination of the signals P and Q, which are 90 degrees out of phase, can be used to generate 16 different conditions, each signifying four bits of information.

Pulse Modulation Techniques

Unlike previously discussed modulation techniques, pulse modulation is not employed in modems. Instead, this technique is employed by devices designed to transmit data over digital media. Some pulse modulation techniques are also used to multiplex, or group, a number of voice connections for transmission over a common circuit. In Table 5.3.2, the four basic methods of pulse modulation techniques are listed.

In pulse amplitude modulation, a signal is sampled at successive intervals in time and converted into a series of similar-width pulses from which the original analog signal can readily be reconstructed, as illustrated in Figure 5.3.9. When the pulse duration technique is employed, the width of the pulse is varied in accordance with the sampled signal, while the amplitude and leading-edge position remain constant.

Using the pulse position technique, the leading edge of the pulse shifts back and forth in accordance with the sampled signal while the width and amplitude of the pulses remain constant. In the pulse code technique, the amplitude of the sampled signal is quantized into discrete pulses at a certain amplitude level. This level is maintained until there is a significant change in the sampled signal, with the number of levels a function of the rate of change of the signal. If the sampled signal

FIGURE 5.3.7   Different four-phase modulation techniques

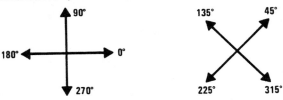

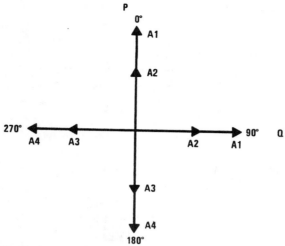

FIGURE 5.3.8   Quadrature amplitude modulation

varies rapidly, many levels will be required. A slow-changing signal would require fewer levels.

5.4 MODEMS AND COUPLERS

One method that can be employed to categorize data communications components is to examine the functions they are designed to perform. In this section, the characteristics, operation, and utilization of components designed primarily to effect data transmission over analog media will be covered.

Analog Media Employment

Today, despite the fact that several communications carriers have introduced all-digital transmission facilites that are more efficient than analog media, the analog telephone network remains the primary facility employed for data transmission. Business machines, including terminals and computers, transmit digital pulses. Telephone circuits are designed to transmit analog signals such as the human voice. Therefore, a device to convert the digital pulses into analog tones capable of being transferred on telephone circuits becomes necessary when one

TABLE 5.3.2   BASIC PULSE MODULATION TECHNIQUES

Pulse code modulation (PCM)
Pulse amplitude modulation (PAM)
Pulse duration modulation (PDM)
Pulse position modulation (PPM)

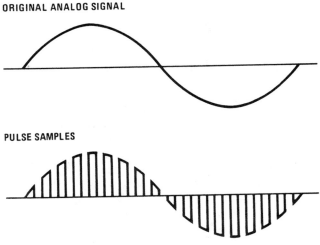

ORIGINAL ANALOG SIGNAL

PULSE SAMPLES

FIGURE 5.3.9   Pulse amplitude modulation

wishes to transmit digital data over these facilities. Two such devices that can be used to convert and reconvert signals are modems and acoustic couplers.

Modem Components

In its most basic form, a modem consists of a power supply, a transmitter, and a receiver. The power supply usually takes 120 or 220 VAC, and transforms it into a DC voltage necessary to operate the modem's circuitry. In the transmitter, a modulator, amplifier, filtering, wave-shaping, and signal-level control circuitry convert the digital pulses of the business machine into a modulated, wave-shaped signal that can be transmitted over a telephone circuit.

The complexity of the modulator and its circuitry varies depending upon the modulation technique employed. Normally, modems employing FSK modulation at low data rates have circuitry much less complex than modems that employ QAM modulation to transfer data at rates up to 9,600 bit/s. The modem's receiver consists of a demodulator and associated circuitry that reverse the modulation process. They convert the analog telephone signal back into a series of digital pulses that is acceptable to the digital device at the other end of the circuit.

If the operations of the transmitter and receiver are combined to enable the device to transmit and receive data alternately, the modem is said to be capable of half-duplex operation. In this mode, the transmitter must be turned off at the opposite end of the line when the other modem's transmitter is turned on, as illustrated in Figure 5.4.1. Conversely, the receiver of one modem is enabled while the receiver of the second device is disabled before each change in the direction of data flow. The time interval required for these operations is called the modem turnaround time. This factor can have a large effect on the quantity of data

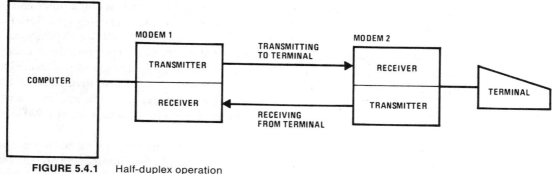

FIGURE 5.4.1 Half-duplex operation

transmitted (throughput) when a line is frequently turned around to transmit acknowledgments concerning the validity of previously received data blocks.

If the modem's transmitter and receiver are capable of operating simultaneously, the modem is said to operate in the full-duplex mode. This simultaneous transmission and reception of data can be accomplished by either splitting the telephone line's bandwidth into two distinct channels on two-wire circuits, or by using two two-wire pairs such as obtainable on a four-wire leased line.

For the former, the transmitter of the modem on one side of the line operates at the same frequency as the receiver at the other end of the line, while the receiver of one modem operates at the same frequency as the transmitter of the other modem. Tying the transmitter to the receiver and vice versa establishes two transmission paths over one pair of wires, permitting full-duplex data transfer to take place. In the four-wire case, separate signal paths are formed over each of the two two-wire circuits.

Transmission Technique

Currently, modems are designed for either asynchronous or synchronous data transmission. In the asynchronous mode of operation, also called start-stop transmission, the timing necessary for the receiving modem to synchronize itself with the transmitting modem is supplied by the transmitted character. This type of transmission is usually generated by unbuffered terminals where the time between character generation and transmission occurs randomly. Here, the character being transmitted is initialized by the character's start bit as a mark-to-space transition on the line, and is terminated by the character's stop bit (or bits), which is converted into a "space 1 marking" signal on the line. Between the start and stop bits, the digital pulses represent the encoded data that defines the character that was transmitted. (Refer to Section 4.4.)

As characters are transmitted, the asynchronous modem places the circuit in the "marking" condition between the stop bit of one character and the start bit of the next character. Upon receipt of the start bit from the next character, the modem switches the line to a mark-to-space transition and the modem at the other end of the line recognizes this transition as a signal to sample the data being sent. Both the marking and spacing conditions are audio tones produced by the modem's modulator to denote the equivalent binary data levels representing these conditions. The two tones are generated at predefined frequencies, and the transition between the two states, as each bit of the character is transmitted, defines the character. Usually employed with low-speed teleprinter terminals and equivalent devices, asynchronous transmission normally is used for data transfer at 1,800 bit/s or less.

When data is transmitted synchronously, more efficient line utilization is normally obtained, since the bits of one character are followed immediately by the bits of the next transmitted character, with no start and stop bits required to delimit each character. Instead, synchronous transmission groups a number of characters into a block for transmission, with the length of the data block constrained by such factors as the terminal's buffer area and the expected line error rate.

Quite often, block length in data transmission is a function of the terminal's physical characteristics, which, in effect, is the buffer size of the device. As an example, when data is to be transmitted to represent punched-card images, it is often convenient to transmit 80 characters of one card as a block because users want compatibility with the 80-column card deck used in data processing. If punched cards are being read by a remote batch terminal for transmission to a computer, and the data is such that every three cards contain information about one employee, then the block size might be increased to 240 characters. In order to transmit data synchronously, the individual characters in each data block must be identified as they occur in time. To do so, a timing signal, which is usually provided by the modem, places each character into a unique time period, as illustrated in Figure 5.4.2.

Modem Classification (Table 5.4.1)

Modems can be classified by many categories to include the mode of transmission and transmission technique as well as by the application features they contain and the type of lines they are built to service. Generally, modems can be classified in four line-servicing groups: subvoice or narrow-band lines, voice-grade lines, wide-band lines, and dedicated lines. Subvoice-band modems require only a portion of the voice-grade channel's available bandwidth and are commonly used with equipment operating at speeds up to 300 bit/s. On narrow-band facilities, modems can operate in the full-duplex mode by using one-half of the available bandwidth for transmission in each direction, and an asynchronous transmission technique.

Modems designed to operate on voice-grade facilities may be asynchronous or synchronous, half-duplex or full-duplex. Asynchronous transmission is normally employed at speeds up to and including 1,800 bit/s. Although a leased, four-wire line will permit full-duplex transmission at higher speeds, transmission via the switched telephone network normally occurs in the full-duplex mode at data rates up to 1,200 bit/s.

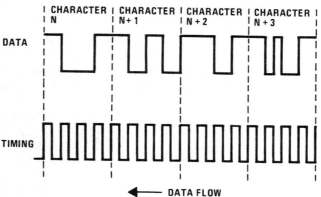

FIGURE 5.4.2   Synchronous timing signals

Voice-grade modems currently transfer data at rates up to 9,600 bit/s, and usually require leased facilities for transmission at speeds above 7,200 bit/s.

Wideband modems—which are also referred to as group-band modems since a wideband circuit is a grouping of lower-speed lines—permits users to transmit synchronous data at speeds above 9,600 bit/s. Although wideband modems are primarily used for computer-to-computer transmission applications, they are also used to service multiplexers that combine the transmission of many low- or medium-speed terminals to produce a composite of higher transmission speed. The uses of group-band modems and multiplexers are explained later.

Dedicated or limited-distance modems, which are also known by such names as short-haul modems and modem bypass units, operate on dedicated solid conductor, twisted-pair wires, or on coaxial cables, permitting data transmission at distances ranging up to 15 to 20 miles depending upon the modem's operating speed and the resistance of the conductor.

Limited-Distance Modems

These modems can operate at speeds ranging up to 1.5 million bits per second and are particularly well suited for in-plant usage where the user desires to install his own communications lines between terminals and a computer located in the same facility or complex. Also, compared to voice-band and wideband modems, these modems are relatively inexpensive since they are designed to operate only for limited distances. In addition, by using this type of modem and stringing his own in-plant line, the user can eliminate a monthly telephone charge that would occur if the telephone company furnished the facilities. Limited-distance modems are explained in greater detail in Section 13.

In Table 5.4.1, the common applications of limited-distance modems are denoted by the types of lines they can be connected to.

TABLE 5.4.1 COMMON MODEM FEATURES

FEATURES	SUB VOICE	VOICE GRADE			WIDEBAND	DEDICATED
LINE TYPE	UP TO 300 BIT/S	LOW SPEED UP TO 1,800 BIT/S	MEDIUM 2,000 TO 4,800 BIT/S	HIGH SPEED 7,200 TO 9,600 BIT/S	19,200 BIT/S AND UP	UP TO 1.5 MEGABIT/S
ASYNCHRONOUS	●	●				
SYNCHRONOUS			●	●	●	●
SWITCHED NETWORK	●	●	●			
LEASED ONLY				●	●	●
HALF-DUPLEX	●	●	●	●		●
FULL-DUPLEX	●	●	●	●	●	●
FAST TURNAROUND FOR DIAL-UP USE				●		
REVERSE/SECONDARY CHANNEL	●	●	●			
MANUAL EQUALIZATION			●			
AUTOMATIC EQUALIZATION		●	●	●		
MULTIPORT CAPABILITY			●	●		
VOICE/DATA			●	●		●

Line Type Operations

Most modems with a rated transmission speed of up to 4,800 bit/s and some that transmit data at 7,200 bit/s can operate over the switched, dial-up telephone network. Since a circuit obtained from a dial-up telephone connection is a two-wire line, when this line is used to carry traffic in both directions alternately, the line and the modem operate in the half-duplex mode. The turnaround time varies by device and can become a considerable overhead factor if short bursts of data are transmitted, with each burst requiring a short acknowledgment.

To visualize some of the overhead problems associated with line turnaround, a short examination of an error-control procedure for synchronous transmission follows.

One common error-control procedure used in synchronous transmission is obtained by the use of an acknowledgment-negative acknowledgement (ACK-NAK) sequence. When this sequence is used, the terminal or computer transmits a block of data to the receiving station. Appended to the end of the block is a block check character that is computed based upon a predefined algorithm. At the receiving device, the block of data is examined and a new block check character is developed using the same algorithm, which is then compared to the transmitted block check character. If both block check characters are equal, the receiving device sends a positive acknowledgment (ACK) signal.

If the block check characters do not match, then an error in transmission has occurred and the receiving device transmits a negative acknowledgment (NAK). This informs the transmitting device that the block should be retransmitted.

This procedure is also referred to as automatic request for repeat (ARQ) and requires that the line upon which transmission occurs be turned around twice for each block. Returning to the 80-character punched card image block, transmitting this data as a 960 bit block with control characters appended, at 9,600 bit/s, would take just 100 milliseconds, whereas if the modem turnaround time were 150 milliseconds, 300 milliseconds would be necessary to turn the line around twice. Although recently developed modem features have reduced modem turnaround time, this problem can be avoided or eliminated by using a modem with a reverse channel for acknowledgment signal or by establishing full-duplex transmission such as over a leased four-wire circuit.

Reverse and Secondary Channels

To eliminate turnaround time when transmission is over the two-wire switched network, or to relieve the primary channel of the burden of carrying acknowledgment signals on four-wire dedicated lines, modem manufacturers have developed a reverse channel that is used to provide a path for the acknowledgment of transmitted data, at a slower speed than the primary channel. This reverse channel can provide a simultaneous transmission path for the acknowledgment of data blocks (transmitted over the higher-speed primary channel) at up to 150 bits/s.

A secondary channel, similar to a reverse channel, can be used in a variety of applications, including providing a path for a high-speed terminal and a low-speed terminal simultaneously. When a secondary channel is used as a reverse channel, it is held at one state until an error is detected in the high-speed data transmission. It is then shifted to the other state as a signal for retransmission. Another application where a secondary channel can be utilized is when a location contains a high-speed synchronous terminal and a slow-speed asynchronous terminal. If both devices are required to communicate with a similar distant location, one way to alleviate dual line requirements as well as the cost of extra modems to service both devices is by using a pair of modems that have secondary-channel capacity, as shown in Figure 5.4.3. Although a reverse channel is usable on both two-wire and four-wire telephone lines, the secondary-channel technique is usable only on a four-wire circuit. A secondary-channel modem derives two channels from the same line; a wide one to carry synchronous data at speeds of 2,000, 2,400, 3,600, or 4,800 bit/s, and a narrow channel to carry slower asynchronous data. Some modems with the secondary-channel option can actually provide two slow-speed channels as well as one high-speed channel, with the two slow-speed channels being capable of transmitting asynchronous data up to a composite speed of 150 bits per second.

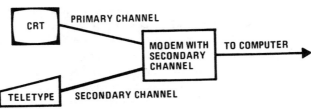

FIGURE 5.4.3   Secondary channel operation

Error Conditions and Compensation

Data signals transmitted over a medium that was designed for voice conversations are often received with a degree of distortion. This distortion may be caused by several factors, including the circuit's characteristics as well as interference from other signals on other lines in the network. In general, while a large degree of distortion may not affect voice communications, a small amount of distortion can be very detrimental to data transferred by a modulated signal. As we speak on a telephone circuit, our ear and brain can effectively neutralize and compensate for any distortions present in the audible signal range since the speed of voice signal transfer is relatively slow when compared to data transmission rates.

For a modulated digital signal, even a slight degree of distortion can cause a bit position or signal level to be completely misinterpreted and thereby cause an error in the reception of the data. As data rates increase, the number of signals per unit time (baud) or the number of levels per baud, or a combination of both, must increase. Thus, reducing the signal time or reducing the differences in amplitude, frequency, or phase in a modulated signal to encode more data makes that signal more susceptible to error, to the point where even small distortions in the received signal may alter the meaning of the data.

Distortion

Signal distortion is a rather general term for an effect produced by many and various conditions. In general, as a current travels through a circuit, it encounters opposition, technically called impedance, which acts as a partial barrier to its flow. Some of the factors that contribute to this impedance include the circuit's resistance, capacitance, and inductance. Two of the primary causes of distortion are signal attenuation and delay.

Attenuation is the ratio of the power of a transmitted signal to its received strength, measured in decibels as follows:

$$10 \log_{10} \frac{\text{Power sent}}{\text{Power received}}$$

as detailed in Section 5.2.

In order to have a valid comparison of attenuation on different circuits, a reference frequency is employed for the measurements of power sent and power received. Normally, a 1,000-Hz reference frequency is employed for attenuation measurements. This reference frequency is most important since higher frequencies are subject to greater attenuation than lower frequencies. Without such a reference, comparisons would not be meaningful.

A second common cause of signal distortion is due to the time it takes a signal to propagate to the receiver. This delay time, as expected, is known as propagation delay. Since different frequencies have different delay times, a term known as envelope delay is used as a measurement. This delay is a measurement of the differences in propagation delays of the several frequencies present in a modulated signal. As with attenuation measurements, envelope delay measurements employ a reference frequency, typically between 1,500 and 1,900 Hz. Delay is measured in milliseconds (msec) or microseconds (usec) based upon the employed reference frequency.

While attenuation and delay are the two main causes of distortion, other factors such as noise, phase jitter, amplitude jitter, phase hits, gain hits, and dropouts can cause short-term transient effects and incidental phase and amplitude modulation. Amplitude and phase jitter are terms that denote a change in amplitude and phase with respect to frequency that occurs at random.

Line Conditioning and Equalization

In order to increase the data-handling capacity of a telephone circuit, a reduction in amplitude attenuation and envelope delay distortion of received signals must be accomplished by techniques known as line conditioning and equalization.

Line conditioning can be obtained on leased lines by having the communications carrier add special equipment to the circuit. Such equipment includes attenuation and delay equalizers and amplifiers.

The attenuation equalizer adds a degree of signal loss to the lower frequencies of a modulated signal so that the loss throughout the transmitted band is nearly the same for all transmitted frequencies. Next, an amplifier is used to restore the signal back to its original level. Since the loss is made nearly uniform by the attenuation equalizer, the amplification process becomes much easier to accomplish.

To compensate for envelope delay, delay equalizers are employed. These devices introduce an element of delay to some of the transmitted signals in order to adjust a uniform delay element that makes the entire signal reach the receiver at the same time. This delay equalizer is necessary since without it the higher frequencies would arrive at the receiver ahead of the lower frequencies.

Based upon AT&T network standards, several grades of conditioning are available for selection by users of private lines. Such conditioning is only available on that type of circuit, since the path is fixed and adjustments can be made to its characteristics as previously explained. A monthly charge is assessed for line conditioning.

With the public switched network, different paths are employed to establish every dialed call depending on which circuits are busy. Thus, the routing is, in effect, random and no fixed adjustment can be made to such a path.

Even when transmission is on a leased, conditioned circuit, some degree of amplitude attenuation and envelope delay distortion will be present. This is because the conditioning only assures that these distortions do not exceed certain limits. It does not remove them entirely. Due to this fact as well as the unavailability of conditioning over the public switched network, most modems that operate at bit rates of 2,400 bit/s and above are equipped with equalizers. These line equalizers can be either fixed, manually adjustable, or automatic and adaptive.

An equalizer is basically an inverse filter that corrects amplitude and delay distortions, which if uncorrected could lead to intersymbol interference during transmission. A well-designed equalizer matches line conditions by maintaining some of the modem's electrical parameters at the widest range of marginal limits in order to take advantage of the data rate capability of the line while eliminating intersymbol interference. The design of the equalizer is critical since if the modem operates too near or outside of these marginal limits, the transmission error rate will increase.

The faster the modem's operating speed, the greater the need for the modem to employ equalizers. In addition, as the data rate of the modem increases, so does the complexity of its equalizer. Today, many modems with rated speeds up to 4,800 bit/s designed for the dial-up network employ nonadjustable, fixed equalizers that have been made to match the average line conditions that have been found to occur on that type of facility. Thus, most modems with fixed or nonadjustable equalizers are designed for a normal, randomly routed call between two locations over the dial-up network.

If the modem is equipped with a signal-quality light that will indicate an unacceptable error rate, or if there is difficulty with the connection, the operator can alleviate the problem by simply terminating the call and dialing again. This should route the connection through different points on the dial-up network.

Manually adjustable equalization is an old technique that is rapidly being replaced by fixed and automatic equalization. Manual adjustment is still employed on some 4,800 bit/s modems used for data transfer over leased lines, with the parameters being tuned or preset at installation time, and re-equalization usually not required unless the lines are reconfigured.

At first used by 7,200- and 9,600-bit/s modems designed for leased-line use, automatic equalization is now employed on 4,800 and 2,400 bit/s modems designed for operation over the public switched telephone network. With automatic equalization, a certain initialization time is required to adapt the modem to existing line conditions. This initialization time becomes important both during and after line outages, since long initial equalization times can extend otherwise short dropouts unnecessarily.

Recent modem developments have shortened the initial equalization time to under 30 milliseconds, whereas only several years ago a much longer time of up to 275 milliseconds was commonly required. After the initial equalization, the modem continuously monitors and compensates for changing line conditions by an adaptive process. This process allows the equalizer to "track" the frequently occurring line variations during data transmission without interrupting the traffic flow. On one 9,600-bit/s modem, this adaptive process occurs 2,400 times a second, permitting the rapid recognition of variations as they occur.

Many modem manufacturers describe their equipment in terms of compatibility or equivalency with modems manufactured by Western Electric for the Bell System. Numerous modem manufacturers produce devices compatible with Bell's that operate at speeds up to 2,400 bit/s. A few vendors manufacture equipment compatible with Bell's that transmit at speeds up to 4,800 bit/s. Some vendors make modems at capacities and performance for which Bell has no equivalent.

Bell System 103/113 Series Modems

Bell 103/113 series modems operate in the lowest speed category. The terminology used to describe the functions of these and compatible modems can lead to confusion. This confusion is a result of the terminology used in the designation of "originate" and "answer-only" operation. In this case, the terminology should not be confused with the terms to describe simplex operation since here both the originate-only and answer-only modems each have and utilize both a transmitter and receiver. This designation is used to describe the reversing of the transmit and receive functions between two channels at opposite ends of the telephone line. This reversal of the transmit and receive functions is accomplished within the 3,000-Hz bandwidth of the telephone circuit by assigning the two channels used to different frequencies, providing filtering circuitry in the modems to separate these channels into discrete bands, and establishing design criteria. Thus, a modem that transmits in one band and receives in a second band is designated as an originate modem or an answer modem, depending upon the bands used.

Bell System 103 and 113 series modems, operating at 300 bit/s, are designed so that one channel is assigned to the 1,070- to 1,270-Hz frequency band, while the second channel is assigned to the 2,025- to 2,225-Hz band. Modems that transmit in the 1,070- to 1,270-Hz band, but receive in the 2,025- to 2,225-Hz band, are designated as an originate modem, while a modem that transmits in the 2,025- to 2,225-Hz band, but receives in the 1,070- to 1,270-Hz band, is designated as an answer modem. When using such modems, their correct pairing is important, since two originate modems cannot communicate with each other.

Bell System 113A modems are originate only devices that should be normally used when calls are to be placed in one direction. This type of modem is mainly used to enable Teletype-compatible terminals to communicate with timesharing services where such terminals only originate calls. Bell System 113B modems are answer only and are primarily used at computer sites where users dial in to establish communications. Since these modems transmit and receive on a single set of frequencies, their circuitry requirements are less rigorous than other modems and their costs are thus lower. Figure 5.4.4 shows the frequency assignment for modems in this series.

Modems in the 103 series, which includes the 103A, E, F, G, and J, transmit and receive in either the low or the high band. This ability to switch modes is denoted as

	ORIGINATING END	**ANSWERING END**
TRANSMIT	1,070 Hz SPACE 1,270 Hz MARK	2,025 Hz SPACE 2,225 Hz MARK
RECEIVE	2,025 Hz SPACE 2,225 Hz MARK	1070 Hz SPACE 1,270 Hz MARK

FIGURE 5.4.4   Frequency assignment of Bell System 103/113 modems

"originate and answer" in comparison to the Bell 113A, which operates only in the originate mode, and the Bell 113B, which operates only in the answer mode.

Bell System 201 Series Modems

The Bell 201 series modems are designed for synchronous bit-serial transmission at data rates of 2,000 and 2,400 bit/s. The 201A modem is an obsolete device and is being phased out of use. The 201A is designed to operate over the switched network at 2,000 bit/s. The 201B modem is designed for 2,400 bit/s transmission over leased lines. The 201C modem is designed to operate at 2,400 bit/s over the switched network or leased lines and its introduction made both the 201A and 201B obsolete. It provides increased data transfer rates over the 201A and can operate on either switched or leased lines, whereas the prior models did not have this flexibility.

Bell System 202 Series Modems

Bell System 202 series modems are designed for speeds up to 1,200 or 1,800 bit/s. The 202C modem can operate on either the switched network or on leased lines, in the half-duplex mode on the former and either the half- or full-duplex mode on the latter. This series of modems uses frequency-shift-keyed (FSK) modulation and the frequency assignments are such that a mark is at 1,200 Hz and space at 2,200 Hz. When either modem is used for transmission over a leased four-wire circuit in the full-duplex mode, modem control is identical to the 103 series modem in that both transmitters can be "strapped" on continuously, which eliminates the line turnaround delays.

Since the 202 series modems do not have separate bands, half-duplex operation is required for switched network utilization. This means that both transmitters (one on each modem) must be alternately turned on and off to provide two-way communications.

The Bell 202 series modems have a 5-bit/s reverse channel for switched network use. Due to the slowness of this reverse channel, its use is limited to status and control-function transmission. Status information such as "ready to receive data" or "device out of paper" can be transmitted on this channel. Due to the low transmission rate, error detection of received messages and an associated negative acknowlegment (NAK) and request for retransmission are normally accomplished by the regular turnaround, which can be completed at almost the same rate that one obtains in using the reverse channel for that purpose. Non-Bell 202 equivalent modems produced by many manufacturers provide reverse channels of 75 to 150 bit/s, which can be utilized to enhance overall system performance. Reverse keyboard-entered data as well as error detection information can be practically transmitted over such a channel.

While a data rate of up to 1,800 bit/s can be obtained with the 202D modem, transmission at this speed requires that the leased line be conditioned for transmission by the telephone company. The 202S and 202T modems are recent additions to the 202 series and are designed for transmission at 1,200 bit/s and 1,800 bit/s over the switched network and leased line, respectively. At speeds in excess of 1,400 bit/s, the 202T requires line conditioning when interfaced to either 2- or 4-wire circuits, whereas for a 2-wire circuit, conditioning is required at speeds in excess of 1,200 bit/s when an optional reverse channel is used.

Bell System 203 Series Modems

This series of obsolete modems permits transmission of data at up to 3,600 bit/s on the switched network and up to 10,800 bit/s when leased lines are used. This series of modems was made obsolete by the introduction of the 208 and 209 Bell modems.

Bell System 208 Series Modems

The Bell System 208 series modems are of recent design and use a quadrature amplitude modulation technique. The 208A modem is designed for either half-duplex or full-duplex operation at 4,800 bit/s over leased lines. The 208B modem is designed for half-duplex operation at 4,800 bit/s on the switched network.

Bell System 209 Series Modem

The 209A modem is designed for single-channel transmission at 9,600 bit/s over leased lines or for selective data rates depending upon the number of channels in increments of 2,400 bit/s. The 209A modem has a built-in synchronous multiplexer that combines up to four data rate combinations for transmission at 9,600 bit/s. The multiplexer combinations are shown in Figure 5.4.5.

FIGURE 5.4.5 Bell 209 A multiplexer combinations

2,400–2,400–2,400–2,400 BIT/S

4,800–2,400–2,400

4,800–4,800

7,200–2,400

9,600

Bell System 212A Modem

This dual-speed modem permits either asynchronous or synchronous transmission over the switched network. The 212A contains a 103-type modem for asynchronous transmission at speeds up to 300 bit/s. Frequency-shift-keyed modulation is used for 300-bit/s transmission and dibit phase-shift-keyed modulation for 1,200 bit/s transmission, which permits the modem to operate either asynchronously or synchronously at this speed. The key advantage in the use of this modem is that it permits reception of two different transmission speeds. Before the terminal operator initiates a call, he selects the operating speed at the originating set. When the call is made, the answering 212A modem automatically switches to that operating speed.

During data transmission, both modems remain in the same speed mode until the call is terminated, when the answering 212A can be set to the other speed by a new call. The dual-speed 212A permits both terminals connected to Bell System 100 series modems operating at up to 300 bit/s, or terminals connected to other 212A modems operating at 1,200 bit/s, to share the use of one modem at a computer site, and thus may reduce equipment requirements.

Modem Interface and Handshaking

In data communications, the term interface is often used to denote the type of electrical connection between the business machine and its associated data communications equipment. The business machine, which may be a computer or terminal, is called data terminal equipment (DTE), while its associated data circuit-terminating equipment (DCE) can include such devices as modems and acoustic couplers. Two typical DTE-DCE interfaces are illustrated in Figure 5.4.6. Currently, three types of interfaces are used: voltage, contact closure, and current loop.

FIGURE 5.4.6   Typical DTE-DCE interfaces

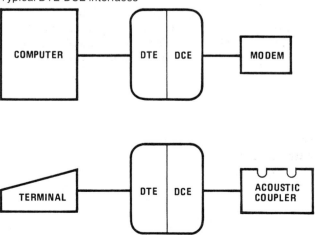

Voltage interfaces are the type most frequently employed in DTE-DCE connections. Most voltage interfaces conform to the Electronic Industries Association (EIA) standard RS-232-C. This interface standard specifies a 25-pin connector attachment between DTE and DCE, with specified pin assignments for ground, data, control, and timing circuits. In addition, this interface standard specifies the electrical and mechanical requirements of the interface and has an operating range up to 20,000 bit/s in bit-serial operation for both the asynchronous and synchronous modes of data transfer.

Through the utilization of this interface, standard interaction between many types of equipment produced by many different vendors becomes possible, which permits users a high degree of flexibility in selecting equipment for their specific requirements.

In the RS-232-C interface, two types of connectors are required to effect a DTE-DCE connection. In conforming to the standard, a female connector is connected to the DCE, while a male connector is employed with the DTE.

This standard also specifies a cable length of 50 feet or less between devices, regardless of the data transfer rate. When employing this interface, the pin assignments listed in Table 5.4.2 must be used. However, unassigned pins may be used for additional functions if required for operation.

Another voltage interface that closely resembles the RS-232-C interface and is employed as a European standard is the International Consultative Committee for Telegraphy and Telephony (CCITT) V.24 interface. Table 5.4.2 also shows numbered CCITT V. 24 circuits. A more recently adopted standard, EIA RS-449 (and its associated standards), provides capabilities beyond those of RS-232-C. These include higher data rates and longer cable lengths.

The contact closure interface is a mechanical relay type that is employed with bit-parallel data transmission. This interface, due to its electromechanical nature, operates at a low speed, usually under 100 characters per second. Presently, no standard exists that covers this type of interface. However, voltage and current limits are specified by the communications carrier when this interface is used. Within these limits the user can determine his own electrical requirements.

A current loop interface permits the direct connection of two DTE devices at extended distances within a facility. As an example, a terminal may be connected to a computer at a distance in excess of the 50-foot RS-232-C standard when a current loop interface is employed. Presently, military interface standard MIL 188C defines one type of current loop connection.

Modem Handshaking

Modem handshaking is the exchange of control signals necessary to establish a connection between a modem and a business machine at one end of a line and another modem and business machine at the other end of the circuit. The signals required to set up and terminate calls as well as the signals used for the transmission of information are predetermined according to the standard the devices are designed to follow and the circuits the devices are designed to operate with.

TABLE 5.4.2 EIA RS-232-C AND CCITT V. 24 EQUIVALENT INTERFACE PIN ASSIGNMENT

Pin Number	Signal Direction (DTE → DCE)	EIA RS-232-C Circuit	CCITT V.24 Equivalent	Description
1		AA	101	Protective ground
2	→	BA	103	Transmitted data
3	←	BB	104	Received data
4	→	CA	105	Request to send
5	←	CB	106	Clear to send
6	←	CC	107	Data set ready
7		AB	102	Signal ground (Common Return)
8	←	CF	109	Received line signal (detector)
9		–		Reserved for data set testing
10		–		Reserved for data set testing
11		–		Unassigned
12	←	SCF	122	Secondary received line signal detector
13	←	SCB	121	Secondary clear to send
14	→	SBA	118	Secondary transmitted data
15	←	DB	114	Transmission signal element timing (DCE)
16	←	SBB	119	Secondary received data
17	←	DD	115	Receiver signal element timing (DCE)
18				Unassigned
19	→	SCA	120	Secondary request to send
20	→	CD	108.2	Data terminal ready
21	←	CG		Signal quality detector
22	←	CE		Ring indicator
23	→	CH/CI	111/112	Data signal rate selector (DTE/DCE)
24	→	DA	113	Transmit signal element timing (DTE)
25				Unassigned

As an example, let us examine the operation of a Bell 113-type data set as illustrated in Figure 5.4.7. The handshaking routine commences when an operator at a remote terminal dials the telephone number of a similar modem connected to a computer. At the computer site the telephone rings and this activates a ring indicator signal (circuit CE), which is set on by the answering modem and passed to the computer. This signal informs the computer that the associated data set has received a ringing signal.

In response the computer will send a data terminal ready (circuit CD) to its modem to enter and remain in the data mode. When set, it permits the modem to automatically answer the incoming call; when reset, it commands the modem to disconnect the line at the end of the call. When the computer sends the data-terminal-ready signal to its modem, the modem then transmits a tone signal, which to the human ear sounds like a high-pitched beep. The operator at the other end, upon hearing this tone, will depress the data button on his modem.

Once this data button is depressed, the originating modem will transmit a data-set-ready (circuit CC) signal to the terminal and the answering modem will send the same signal to the computer it is interfaced to. At this point in time, both modems are placed in the data mode of operation.

In a timesharing environment, the computer normally transmits a request for user identification to the terminal operator. To do this, the computer sets request-to-send (circuit CA), which informs the terminal's modem that it wishes to transmit data. The terminal's modem will then respond with a clear-to-send (circuit CB) signal and will transmit a carrier signal. The computer's modem detects the clear-to-send and carrier-on signals and begins its data transmission to the terminal.

FIGURE 5.4.7   Bell type 113 data set interface

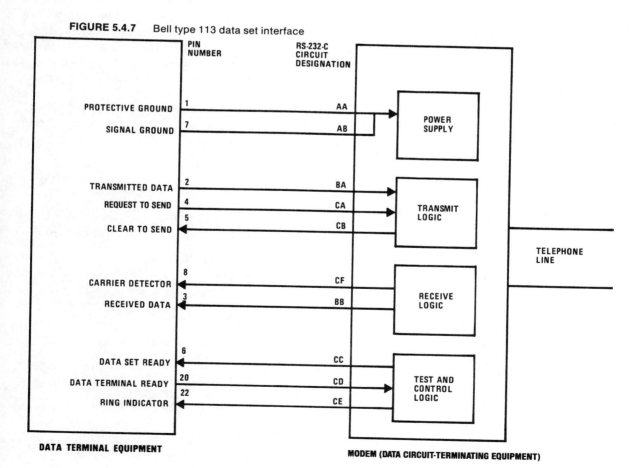

When the computer completes its transmission, it drops the request-to-send signal and the terminal's modem then terminates its carrier signal.

Depending upon the type of circuit that transmission occurs over, some of these signals may not be required. For example, on a switched-network two-wire line, the request-to-send signal determines whether a terminal is to send or receive data, whereas on a leased four-wire circuit this signal can be permanently raised. For further information, the reader should refer to specific vendor literature or appropriate Bell System technical reference publications. A list of some of the modem-handshaking control signals and their functions is presented in Table 5.4.3.

Modem Features

Over the last several years a number of features have been incorporated into modems that have increased their operational flexibility. Among these features are multiport capability, multiple-speed selection, and voice/data capability. Modems with a multiport capability offer a function similar to that provided by a multiplexer, which is a device that combines several data streams into one composite (higher-speed) data stream for economies in transmission. At the receiving end, another multiplexer then breaks out the composite data stream into its original parts. In fact, multiport modems contain a limited-function multiplexer that provides the user with the capability to transmit more than one synchronous data stream over a single transmission line, as illustrated in Figure 5.4.8.

In comparison with conventional multiplexers, the limited-function multiplexer used in a multiport modem combines only a few high-speed synchronous data streams, whereas multiplexers can normally concentrate a mixture of asynchronous and synchronous, high- and low-speed data streams.

Multiple Speed Selection

For data communications networks that require the full-time service of dedicated lines, but also require access to the switched network if the dedicated circuit should

TABLE 5.4.3   MODEM HANDSHAKING SINGNALS AND THEIR FUNCTIONS

Control Signal	Function
Transmit data	Serial data sent from device to modem
Receive data	Serial data received by device
Request to send	Set by device when user program wishes to transmit
Clear to send	Set by modem when transmission may commence
Data set ready	Set by modem when it is powered on and ready to transfer data. Set in response to data terminal ready
Carrier detect	Set by modem when signal present
Data terminal ready	Set by device to enable modem to answer an incoming call on a switched line. Reset by device to disconnect call
Ring indicator	Set by modem when telephone rings

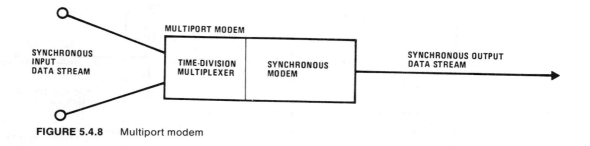

FIGURE 5.4.8   Multiport modem

fail or degrade to the point where it cannot be used, dial backup capability for the modems becomes necessary. Since transmission over dedicated lines usually occurs at a higher data rate than one can obtain over the switched network, one method to facilitate dial backup is through switching down the speed of the modem. Thus a multiple-speed modem that is designed to operate at 9,600 bit/s over dedicated lines may be switched down to 7,200 or 4,800 bit/s for operation over the dialup network until the dedicated lines are restored.

Voice/Data Capability

Many high-speed modems can be obtained with a voice/data option that permits a specially designed telephone set, commonly called a voice adapter, to provide the user with a voice communications capability over the same line that is used for data transmission. Depending on the modem, this voice capability can be either alternate voice/data or simultaneous voice/data. Thus, the user may communicate with a distant location at the same time data transmission is occurring or he may transmit data during certain times of the day and use the line for voice communications at other times. Voice/data capability can also be used to minimize normal telephone charges when data transmission sequences require voice coordination.

Self-testing Features

Many low-speed and most high-speed modems have a series of test switches that may be used for local and remote testing of the modem and line.

In the local, or analog, test mode, the transmitter output of the modem is connected to the receiver input, disconnecting the customer interface from the modem. A built-in word generator is used to produce a stream of bits, which is checked for accuracy by a word comparator circuit, and errors are displayed on an error lamp as they occur. The local test is illustrated in Figure 5.4.9.

To check the modems at both ends as well as the transmission medium, a digital loop-back self-test may be employed. To conduct this test, personnel must normally be at each modem to push the appropriate test buttons, although a number of vendors have introduced modems that can be automatically placed into the test mode at the distant end when the central-site modem is switched.

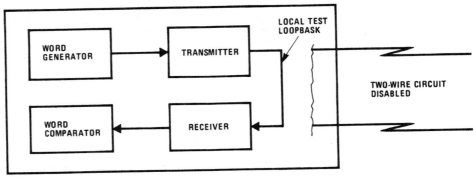

FIGURE 5.4.9   Local (analog) testing

In the digital loop-back test, the modem at the distant end has its receiver connected to its transmitter, as shown in Figure 5.4.10. At the other end, the local modem transmits a test bit stream from its word generator and this bit stream is looped back from the distant end to the receiver of the central-site modem, where it is checked by the comparator circuitry. Error lamps indicate that either the modems or the line may be at fault.

The analog loop-back self-test should normally be used to verify the internal operation of the modem; the digital loopback test will check both modems and the carrier. While analog and digital tests are the main self-tests built into modems, several vendors offer additional diagnostic capabilities that may warrant attention.

Acoustic Couplers

Unlike conventional modems, which may require a permanent or semipermanent connection to a telephone line, an acoustic coupler permits data transmission to occur through the handset of an ordinary telephone. Similar in function

FIGURE 5.4.10   Digital loopback self-test

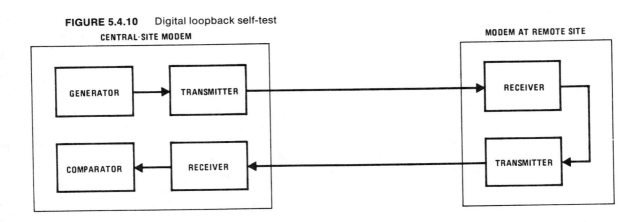

to a modem, an acoustic coupler is a device that accepts a serial asynchronous data stream from data terminals, modulates that data stream into the audio spectrum, and then transmits the audio tones over a switched or dial-up telephone connection.

Acoustic couplers are equipped with built-in cups into which a conventional telephone handset is placed. Through the process of acoustic coupling, the modulated tones produced by the acoustic coupler are directly picked up by the attached telephone handset. Likewise, the audible tones transmitted over a telephone line are picked up by the telephone earpiece and demodulated by the acoustic coupler into a serial data stream that is acceptable to the attached data terminal.

Acoustic couplers use two distinct frequencies to transmit information, while two other frequencies are employed for data reception. One of the frequencies from each pair is used to create a mark tone, which represents an encoded binary one from the digital data stream; another from each pair of frequencies generates a space tone, which represents a binary zero. This utilization of frequencies permits full-duplex transmission to occur over the two-wire switched telephone network.

Since acoustic couplers enable any conventional telephone to be used for data transmission purposes, the coupler does not have to be physically wired to the line and thus permits considerable flexibility in choosing a terminal working area, which can be anywhere a telephone handset and standard electrical outlet is located. Acoustic couplers are manufactured as both separate units and as built-in units to data terminals, as shown in Figure 5.4.11.

Since acoustic couplers are normally employed to permit portable terminals to communicate with data processing facilities, and since many low-speed modems at such facilities are furnished by Bell, most manufacturers of acoustic couplers have designed them to be compatible with low-speed Bell modems. Acoustic couplers that transmit and receive marks and spaces per the indicated frequencies shown in Figure 5.4.12 are compatible with Bell System 103- and 113-type modems. Other acoustic couplers transmit and receive data at speeds up to 1,200 bit/s and are compatible with Bell System 202 series modems.

Operations

When a terminal is attached to or has a built-in acoustic coupler, and the operator wishes to send data to a computer, he merely dials the computer's telephone access number and, upon establishing the proper connection (hearing a high-pitched tone), places the telephone headset into the coupler.

FIGURE 5.4.11

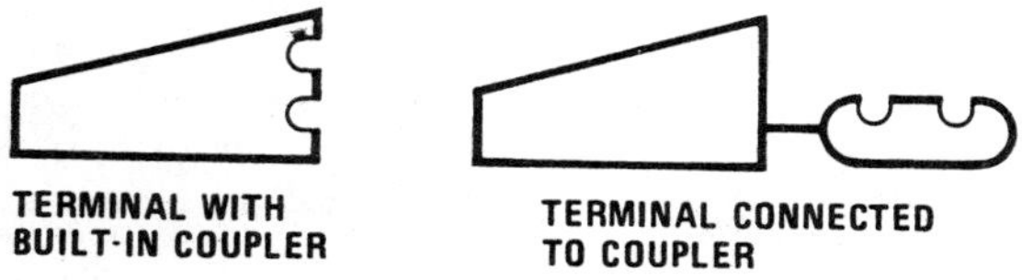

TERMINAL WITH
BUILT-IN COUPLER

TERMINAL CONNECTED
TO COUPLER

COUPLER FREQUENCY	TRANSMISSION SPEED	BELL SYSTEM MODEM COMPATIBILITY
TRANSMIT		
1,070 AND 1,270 Hz (ORIGINATE MODE)	0—450 BIT/S	103 AND 113 TYPE MODEMS (DATA SETS)
2,025 AND 2,225 Hz (ANSWER MODE)		
RECEIVE		
2,025 AND 2,225 Hz (ORIGINATE MODE)		
1,070 AND 1,270 Hz (ANSWER MODE)		

FIGURE 5.4.12   Acoustic coupler modem compatibility

Although terminal usage varies by the numerous applications they are used for, the prevalent utilization of acoustic couplers is for obtaining access to timesharing networks. In a timesharing network, a group of dial-in computer telephone access numbers may be interfaced to a rotary switch that enables users to dial the lowest telephone number of the group and automatically "step" past or bypass busy numbers. Each telephone line is then connected to a modem on a permanent basis, and the modem in turn is connected to a computer port or channel. An answering device in each modem automatically answers the incoming call, establishing a connection from the user who dialed the number to the computer port, as shown in Figure 5.4.13.

In contrast to the modems that are permanently connected to telephone lines, the telephone can be used for conventional voice communications when not connected via the acoustic coupler. To obtain the use of a line for voice communications when that line is connected to modems, a device known as a voice adapter must be installed.

FIGURE 5.4.13   Network access in a timesharing environment

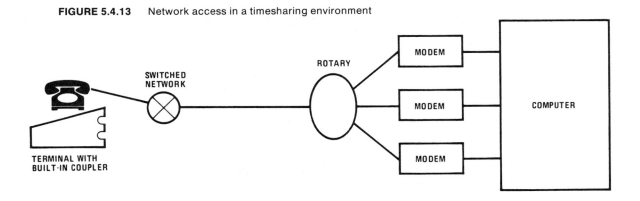

One disadvantage associated with the use of acoustic couplers is a reduction of transmission rates when compared to rates that can be obtained by using regular modems. Due to the properties of carbon microphones in telephone headsets, the frequency band that can be passed is not as wide as the band that modems can pass. Although typical data rates of acoustic couplers vary between 110 and 300 bit/s, some units do permit transmission at 450, 600, and even 1,200 bit/s. For usage with low-speed terminals, the acoustic coupler can be viewed as a low-cost alternative to a modem, while increasing user-transmission-location flexibility.

Problems in Usage

One possible cause of errors in the transmission of data can be ambient noise leaking into the acoustic coupler. The coupler should be kept far away from the terminals to reduce noise levels. Similarly, if the terminal is not in use, one should remove the telephone from the coupler, since the continuous placement of the headset in that device can cause crystallization of the speaker and receiver elements of the telephone. This will act to reduce the level of signal strength. Another item that may warrant user attention is the placement of a piece of cotton inside the earpiece, behind the receiver of the telephone. Although the placement of cotton at this location is normally done by most telephone companies, this should be checked since the cotton keeps speaker and receiver noise from interfering with each other and acts to prevent transmitted data from interfering with received data.

One easily resolved problem is the poor placement of the telephone handset into the coupler. On many occasions users have hastily placed the handset only partially into the coupler, a situation that reduces signal level.

5.5 DIGITAL TRANSMISSION AND SERVICE UNITS

In the early 1970s carriers began offering communications networks designed exclusively for the transmission of digital data. Specialized carriers, including the now defunct Datran, performed a considerable service to the information processing community through their pioneering efforts in developing digital networks. Without their advancements, major communications carriers may have delayed the introduction of all-digital service media.

In December 1974, the FCC approved the Bell System's Dataphone digital service (DDS), which was shortly thereafter established between five major cities. Since then the service has been rapidly expanded to the point where more than 100 cities have been added to the DDS network. Western Union International set another milestone in February 1975 by applying to the FCC for authority to offer its international digital data service (IDDS) from New York to Austria, France, Italy, and Spain. Although IDDS has not been implemented, digital data transmission by major carriers has become a reality.

Comparison of Facilities

When analog, or voice-grade, transmission facilities are utilized, the data stream may be modulated into two distinct amplitudes, frequencies, or phases, each representing marks and spaces, or binary ones and zeros, respectively. In so-called voice-grade telephone circuits, the usable bandwidth is approximately 3,000 Hertz and the power transmitted at the higher frequency is significantly lower than the power transmitted at the lower one. This bandwidth limitation not only causes a loss of distinction between the vocal "s" and "f" sounds, but also limits the amount of information that can be transmitted via modulated analog signals.

In the switched telephone network, the characteristics of a data path cannot be exactly determined because each new call may take a different set of links. Over long distances, multiple voice-grade lines are often combined into 3,600 channels of 4,000 Hz each and sent by microwave transmission. In this combining, or multiplexing process, an original 2,225-Hz signal may be shifted to 19,225-Hz for transmission, and end up as a 2,220-Hz or 2,230-Hz signal at the receiver. This transmission over the switched network normally occurs at data rates up to 4,800 bit/s. By obtaining a leased line, employing automatic equalization, and conditioning the line, data rates of 9,600 bit/s can be readily achieved.

With voice-grade type of analog transmission, the data is easily amplified, although any noise or distortion along the path is also amplified. In addition, the data signals become highly attenuated, or weakened, by the telephone characteristics originally geared to voice transmission. For the analog transmission of data, expensive and complex modems must be employed at both ends of the link to shape (modulate) and reconstruct (demodulate) the digital signals.

When digital transmission facilities are used, the data travels from end to end in its original form with the digital pulses regenerated at regular intervals as simple values of one and zero. Inexpensive digital service units are employed at both ends of the link to condition the digital signals for digital transmission. (Ref. Section 4.11.)

DDS is strictly a synchronous facility providing full-duplex, point-to-point and multipoint service limited to speeds of 2.4, 4.8, 9.6, and 56 kbit/s.

Terminal access to the DDS network is accomplished by means of a digital service unit, which alters serial unipolar signals into a form of modified bipolar signals for transmission, and returns them to serial unipolar signals at the receiving end. The various types of service units will be discussed in detail later in this section.

Digital Signaling

It is important to understand what modified bipolar signaling is and why it is necessary, since this form of signaling is the foundation of digital data transmission. Using the top portion of Figure 5.5.1, let us first examine a serial, unipolar signal commonly produced by such devices as teleprinters and other data terminals. In normal return-to-zero bipolar signaling, a binary zero is transmitted as zero volts and a binary one as either a positive or negative pulse, opposite in polarity to the previous binary one. This alternation of positive and negative pulses produces an alternating polarity, which returns the voltage sum to zero and avoids any undesirable direct current buildup, as illustrated in the middle portion of Figure 5.5.1.

Since DDS incorporates its own network codes to include such information as zero suppression, idle, and out-of-service data, the original bipolar format will be violated when such network control information is transmitted. Such a bipolar violation occurs when the alternate polarity rule previously discussed is violated. An example of this violation is when the last pulse transmitted is sent as a positive pulse and the next pulse is transmitted in a similar manner. In the lower portion of Figure 5.5.1 a bipolar sequence containing bipolar violations is illustrated. Here the letter B in a pulse indicates that the polarity was determined by the bipolar rule while the letter V indicates that the polarity was formed in violation of the bipolar rule.

One of the key aspects of the insertion of DDS network control codes that modifiy and violate the bipolar signal is the use of a zero suppression code. Since a long succession of binary zeros would not provide the necessary transitions to maintain proper timing recovery, strings of more than six zeros are replaced with zero suppression codes to maintain synchronization. Since the unrestricted inser-

FIGURE 5.5.1   Developing bipolar signaling

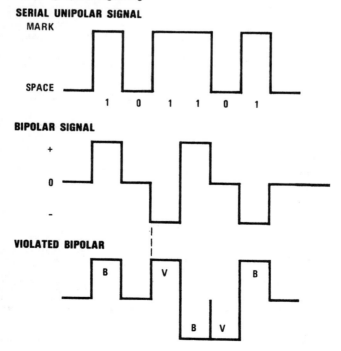

tion of violations in the DDS pulse stream would be meaningless, time slots are reserved prior to a violation for application of a binary pulse or no-pulse in such a way that successive violations alternate in polarity.

Figure 5.5.2 shows how a bipolar signal undergoes violation insertion. In this example, a zero suppression sequence is inserted into the binary channel signal. The resultant signal, as shown, returns the voltage sum to zero.

For digital transmission, precise synchronization is the key to success of an all-digital network. It is essential that the data bits be generated at precise intervals, interleaved in time, and read out at the receiving end at the same interval to prevent loss or garbling of data sequences. To accomplish the necessary clock synchronization on the Bell digital network, a master reference clock is used to supply a hierarchy of timing in the network. Should a link to the master clock fail, the nodal timing can operate independently and retain synchronization for up to two weeks without excessive slippage during outages.

Service Units and Network Integration

In discussing the characteristics of service units that interface terminals to digital networks, it is important to understand the functional differences between channel service units (CSU) and data service units (DSU). Figure 5.5.3 contains a simplified schematic diagram of the Bell System 500A-type DSU and the 550A-type CSU. When a channel service unit is installed, the customer must supply all of the transmit logic, receive logic, and timing recovery in order to use that device, whereas the DSU performs these functions.

The CSU is devoid of circuitry necessary to provide timing recovery and detect, or generate, DDS network control codes, which becomes the customer's responsibility when this device is used. Nominal 50% duty cycle bipolar pulses are

FIGURE 5.5.2   Modified bipolar signaling

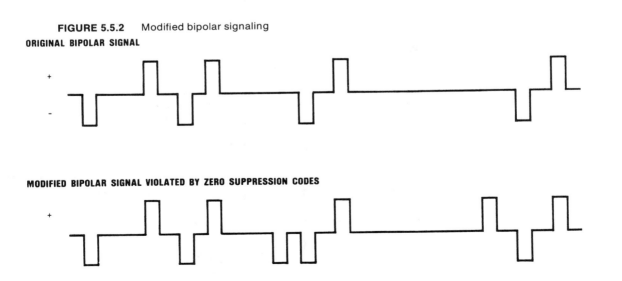

ORIGINAL BIPOLAR SIGNAL

MODIFIED BIPOLAR SIGNAL VIOLATED BY ZERO SUPPRESSION CODES

accepted from the customer on the transmit and receive data leads. The pulses, synchronized with the DDS, are amplified, filtered, and passed on to the 2-wire metallic-pair telephone company cable. The signals on the receive pair are amplified and equalized by the line receiver. The resultant bipolar pulses are then passed to the customer, who must recover the synchronous clock used for timing the transmitted data and sampling the received data. The customer must further detect the DDS network codes, enter appropriate control states, and remove bipolar "violations" from the data stream.

CSU interfacing is accomplished by use of a 15-pin female connector that utilizes the first six pins: the four previously described plus a status indicator and ground lead. In addition to the communications carriers, several vendors offer compatible channel service units for customer connection to digital networks.

In comparison to channel service units, digital service units incorporate all the circuitry necessary to make the device plug compatible with existing modems and terminals. The unit includes an analog circuit, similar to that described in the CSU, plus a digital circuit that handles all timing-recovery and network-control codes.

FIGURE 5.5.3   Service units for digital transmission

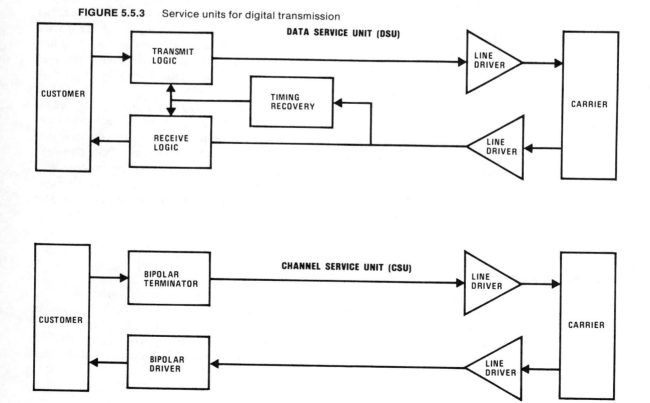

TABLE 5.5.1   DATAPHONE DIGITAL SERVICE INTERFACE UNITS

	Speed	List Code
Bell 500A-Type DSUs	2.4 kbit/s	500A-L1/2
	4.8 kbit/s	500A-L1/3
	9.6 kbit/s	500A-L1/4
	56 kbit/s	500A-L1/5
Bell 550A-Type CSUs	2.4 kbit/s	550A-L1/2
	4.8 kbit/s	550A-L1/3
	9.6 kbit/s	550A-L1/4
	56 kbit/s	550A-L1/5

DSU interfacing is accomplished by use of a standard 25-pin EIA RS-232-C female connector on the 2.4- through 9.6-kbit/s units, using ten pins for signaling. The wideband 56-kbit/s unit utilizes a 34-pin CCITT, V.35 (Winchester-type) connector using fourteen pins for signaling. Several independent suppliers also manufacture DSU-type units, which offer even more flexibility in the form of multiport options. Present Bell System 550A channel service units and 500A digital service units are listed in Table 5.5.1. Both the DSU and CSU devices incorporate properly balanced and equalized terminations for the 4-wire loop as well as circuitry to permit rapid remote testing of the channel. The signals on the 4-wire loop are the same for both devices and are terminated in the serving central office of the communications carrier into a complementary unit called an office channel unit or OCU. From here, the time-division multiplexing hierarchy begins as illustrated in Figure 5.5.4.

Signals from the OCUs are fed into the first stage of multiplexing, which combines up to twenty 2.4-, ten 4.8- or five 9.6-kbit/s signals into a single 64-kbit/s channel, which is the digital capacity of a voice channel in T1 digital transmission. A second stage of multiplexing takes the 64-kbit/s bit streams and efficiently packs them into a T1 bit stream operating at 1.544 Mbit/s, which may carry voice as well as data signals over existing long-line facilities. Using this scheme, future expansion of DDS may be accomplished at a very rapid pace. This could at a later date relegate analog transmission of data to history.

Analog Extensions to DDS

The Bell System provides an 831A data auxiliary set that allows analog access to DDS for customers located outside the DDS servicing areas. The 831A connects the EIA RS-232-C interfaces between a data service unit (500A type) and a voice-band data set. The 831A contains an eight-bit store, control, timing, and test circuits that allow loopback tests toward the digital network. Figure 5.5.5 illustrates a typical analog extension to a DDS servicing area.

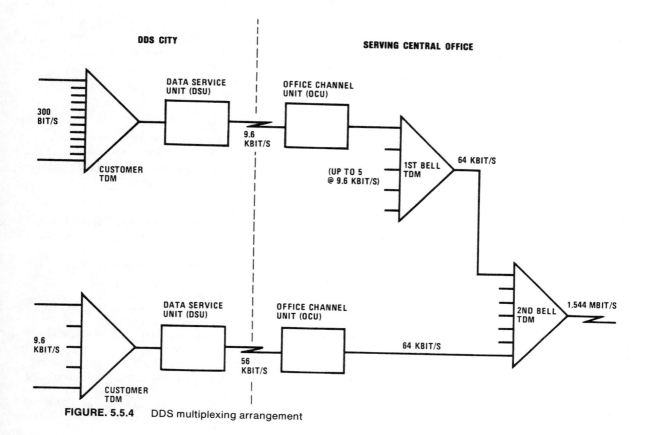

FIGURE. 5.5.4 DDS multiplexing arrangement

FIGURE 5.5.5 Analog extension to DDS

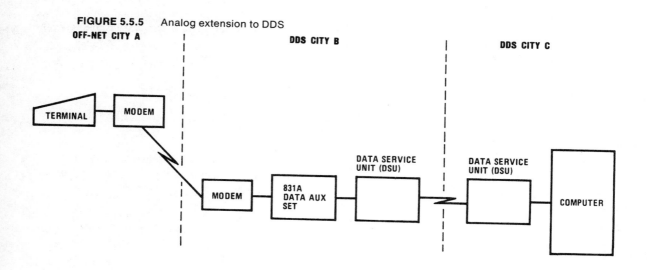

QUESTIONS

5.1 What factors affect the shape of digital signals transmitted in their digital form?

5.2 What is a signal-to-noise ratio and how is it used?

5.3 What power ratios result from the following circuit measurements?

  a. Power transmitted 1 watt; Power received .1 watt.

  b. Power transmitted .2 watt; Power received .005 watt.

  c. Power transmitted .05 watt; Power received .00025 watt.

5.4 Where would a line driver be employed and how does it function?

5.5 Discuss the differences between amplitude, frequency, and phase modulation.

5.6 What is the relationship between a channel's bandwidth and its signaling capacity?

5.7 How can an increase in the amount of information a signal pulse represents lead to an increase in the number of bits per second transmitted?

5.8 Discuss some of the problems associated with multilevel coding.

5.9 What is the relationship between Nyquist's baud limitation law and Shannon's formula that defines the maximum bit rate that can be transmitted over a channel?

5.10 What basic functions does a modem perform?

5.11 What timing differences exist between asynchronous and synchronous modems?

5.12 What are the four line-servicing groups modems can be classified into? What are the differences in operating speeds between these groups?

5.13 What are the two key causes of circuit distortion and in what units are they measured?

5.14 Why is a reference frequency important for attenuation measurement?

5.15 What devices can be employed by a communications carrier to condition a leased line? How do these devices operate?

5.16 Why is line conditioning available only on leased lines? What devices do modems designed to operate on the switched network employ due to the unavailability of conditioning on that facility?

5.17 Why is the RS-232-C interface standard an important consideration when obtaining communications equipment?

5.18 What function does modem handshaking perform?

5.19 What key advantages are obtained from using acoustic couplers instead of modems?

5.20 What is the difference between serial unipolar signals, bipolar signals, and modified bipolar signals such as the violated bipolar signal used for digital transmission of the Bell System's Dataphone digital service (DDS)?

5.21 Convert the following serial unipolar signal into a bipolar signal:

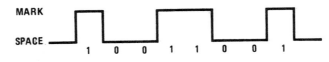

5.22 What is the difference between a digital service unit and a channel service unit?

5.23 What devices and facilities are required to obtain an analog extension to the Bell System's DDS?

CHAPTER 6

REGULATION AGENCIES AND COMMUNICATIONS VENDORS

6.1 INTRODUCTION

Any company has the right to develop its own data transmission facilities as long as such facilities are for its own exclusive use and do not interfere with other existing or potential public or private transmission services. As an example, lines connecting several terminals to a computer in an organization's building can be strung as long as those lines do not use portions of existing telephone company circuits. The communications carrier may agree to the use of its facilities in return for a prescribed payment. When a terminal and a computer are located in different buildings, it may be possible for the company to run a very long cable between the two locations. However, the company not only has to construct the transmission medium but may also have to obtain property rights from numerous companies and individuals to install its lines over alien property. Due to both the high cost of constructing facilities for individual use as well as the complexity and costs involved in obtaining property rights and then maintaining such constructed facilities, private transmission facilities are mostly impractical and not commonly encountered. Due to the preceding problems, most data transmission networks, therefore, use transmission facilities provided by communications common carriers.

In the United States, about 3,000 companies are currently recognized as communications carriers. They provide a wide range of services, including facilities for voice, data, facsimile, printed messages, and packet switching, as well as appropriate communications channels for television transmission, over such media as switched and leased lines and satellite channels.

Communications common carriers furnish communications services to the public. These carriers are regulated by one or more federal, state, and international agencies and organizations. In the United States, the early growth of communications was by telegraph, which generally followed railroad company rights-of-way. Until 1934, both telephone and telegraph services were regulated by the Interstate Commerce Commission (ICC). Due to congressional dissatisfaction with the ICC's inability to regulate communications effectively, the Communications Act of 1934 was passed. This legislation created the Federal Communications Commission (FCC).

6.2 REGULATION AGENCIES AND TARIFFS

The FCC is an independent Federal agency whose role is to regulate interstate and international communications originating in the United States. This regulation applies to communications by radio, telephone, telegraph, facsimile, and other transmissions by wire, cable, or radio.

Under the provisions of the 1934 Communications Act, all communications common carriers are required to furnish services at reasonable charges upon reasonable request. No carrier may construct, acquire, or operate interstate or foreign facilities originating in the United States without the approval of the FCC.

Tariffs

Under the provisions of the Communications Act, every common carrier must file schedules with the FCC that show all charges, practices, classifications, regulations, and other pertinent data for interstate communications services offered to the public. These schedules are known as tariffs and are normally filed several months before their terms are to become effective. Once a tariff is filed, it will automatically become effective, having the force of law, unless it is suspended or disapproved by the FCC.

In addition to a tariff being a schedule of rates, practices, and regulations, it should also be viewed as a contract between the communications common carrier and the service subscriber. Thus, tariffs form a significant portion of the machinery by which the FCC enforces the duties and prohibitions imposed on common carriers. Not all communications common carriers have to file tariffs of their own for a particular type of service. If these carriers concur with the tariffs filed by other common carriers, they may apply to use that tariff. However since in many cases jurisdiction over common carriers is divided between FCC and state or municipal regulatory agencies, there is frequently a variation in tariff rates for the same service in different locations.

One example of a tariff with a high degree of concurrence among a large number of communications common carriers is tariff 245, which was filed with the FCC by the American Telephone and Telegraph Company. This tariff covers the V-H measuring plan which establishes the basis for determining the cost of a telephone call by providing a uniform method for calculating the distance between an originating station and a receiving station. In this tariff, areas in the United

States and Canada are assigned a mathematical coordinate on a vertical (V) and a horizontal (H) basis. By dividing each area into a series of small squares, each with equivalent latitude and longitude, the distances between any two points in airline miles can be calculated from the coordinates by the Pythagorean theorem. Since the cost of telephone circuits and calls are a function of distance, this tariff provides a foundation for determining the cost of telephone calls on the switched network and for private leased lines.

FCC and State Regulation

Interstate services cross state lines; intrastate services do not cross state lines and are normally regulated by state or municipal agencies. Due to this division of jurisdiction over communications common carriers by Federal, state, and perhaps municipal regulatory agencies, there is frequently a variation in tariff rates for the same service in different locations. In addition, carriers may operate under separate tariff regulations. This can result in minor variations of a generally available basic service.

International Regulations

As many companies in different nations began to construct telegraph and telephone facilities, network incompatibilities resulted in subscribers of one country not being able to communicate with subscribers of communications common carriers in a second country. These incompatibilities and the difficulties they caused made the development of an international engineering and standards organization a necessity. In 1863, the International Telecommunications Union (ITU) was founded to promote cooperation and compatibility.

The ITU is an administrative international organization that is responsible for the allocation, registration, and utilization of the radio frequency spectrum; it studies and makes recommendations on technical, operating, and tariff questions in regard to international telephone and telegraph communications; performs such other functions as the coordination and publication of telecommunications service data required for the international operation of such services; and plans and manages technical cooperation programs for developing countries.

TABLE 6.2.1   CCITT STUDY GROUPS

Designation	Study Group
II	Telephone operators and tariffs
III	Lease of telecommunications circuits
IV	Transmission maintenance of international lines
V	Protection against dangers and disturbances of electromagnetic origin
VII	New networks for data transmission
XI	Telephone switching and signaling
XVII	Data transmission
XVIII	Digital networks

Included within the ITU organization are two very important committees, the Consultative Committee on International Telephony and Telegrapy (CCITT) and the Consultative Committee on International Radio (CCIR). Within the CCITT are specialized study groups that are periodically formed to conduct technical and administrative conferences in order to develop international operating practices, pricing, policy arrangements, and technical specifications. A few of the current CCITT study groups are listed in Table 6.2.1.

Thus, the foreign counterpart of the RS-232-C interface standard, the CCITT V.24 standard, was developed by Study Group V.

Intelsat

During the early years of the space age, the feasibility of using satellites for communications was proven to be economically and technically practical. In the early 1960s, the U.S. Communications Satellite Corporation (Comsat) was established by an Act of Congress to construct and operate a global public communications satellite network.

Due to the growth in communications between countries via satellite, an international regulatory agency, the International Telecommunications Satellite Consortium (Intelsat), was established in 1964. From an initial membership of eleven countries, Intelsat has grown to about 100 members today. Representing the United States in Intelsat, Comsat acts as the manager of the consortium and is responsible for the design of the Intelsat series satellites that were built by Hughes Aircraft and launched by the National Aeronautics and Space Administration (NASA). In the United States, Comsat owns and operates a number of earth stations, while most such stations overseas are owned and operated by the local, government-owned Postal Telephone and Telegraph (PTT) organizations.

The Intelsat network consists of a number of satellites positioned over the Atlantic, Pacific, and Indian oceans as well as earth stations located throughout the world. This satellite network permits direct connections between any two operating members, and is designed to permit voice, data, and television transmission.

6.3 CHANGES IN U.S. REGULATORY ENVIRONMENT

Until the early 1950s, telephone companies in the United States in general prohibited their subscribers from attaching subscriber-provided equipment to a telephone company circuit. In 1956, a U.S. Circuit Court of Appeals overturned the Federal Communications Commission in a legal case where the FCC had ruled that the Bell Telephone System could prevent a subscriber from attaching a foreign device to his telephone. The device was called a Hush-A-Phone and was a mechanical attachment that snapped on to the handset of a telephone.

Following the guidelines set by the Circuit Court of Appeals, the FCC issued its now-famous Carterfone decision in June 1968. The FCC ruled that the Bell System could not prevent subscribers from using their telephones in conjunction with a device known as a Carterfone, which acoustically coupled the telephone handset to a two-way radio. The Carterfone was designed to permit conversations between private mobile radio units and telephone subscribers without the intervention and cost of special telephone equipment.

One of the key impacts of the Carterfone decision was to liberate the growth of data communications applications from tariff restraints imposed by the telephone industry that had previously prohibited the attachment of foreign equipment to telephone company circuits.

The Carterfone decision was the most significant of several moves made by the FCC that spurred the utilization of data communications. Others were the specialized carrier decision, the "Open Skies" decision that fostered communications satellites, the approval of packet-switching networks as value-added carriers, and the certification of Satellite Business Systems as a voice, data, and image carrier. As a result of these decisions, the number of vendors manufacturing data communications devices, offering data communications services, as well as the general use of data communications for information transfer, has grown in leaps and bounds.

Data Access Arrangements

Shortly after the Carterfone decision, the FCC ruled (1969) that independent-manufactured (non-Bell) modems could be connected to the switched public telephone network. Such connections, however, had to be made through telephone company supplied protective devices called data access arrangements or data couplers. These devices were required to act as a protective interface between the telephone circuit and the subscriber-provided modem, and performed such functions as ring detection, DC isolation, and surge protection to protect the circuit from being disturbed by a modem malfunction.

There are three types of data access arrangements in use today. Such access arrangements can be obtained from the various telephone companies that lease these devices to the subscriber, or they may be purchased from several independent manufacturers. The cost of the device depends upon the type of access arrangement required and the tariff schedule of the particular telephone company (if a subscriber leases from the telephone company). Typical cost of such access arrangements ranges between $4 and $8 per month from various local telephone companies.

FCC Registration Program

In 1976, the Federal Communications Commission created an equipment registration program to permit devices produced by non-telephone company manufacturers to access the public switched telephone network. This access was to be accomplished without the requirement of installing a data access arrangement, on the condition that such equipment was built to conform to certain interconnection specifications established by the FCC.

On October 1, 1976, the FCC equipment registration program rules were finalized and resulted in the elimination of access arrangements when the user obtained certified equipment. This enabled subscribers to reduce costs and ease the installation of non-telephone company equipment to telephone company lines.

Under the FCC interconnect registration program, customer-provided equipment that is registered—as a result of meeting a series of operational characteristics—can be interfaced via a plug to a telephone-company-supplied jack for connection to the public switched telephone network. Equipment manufactured prior to the program or equipment that does not meet the series of FCC operational characteristics can still be used. But such equipment must interface the telephone company jack through a registered data access arrangement provided either by the telephone company or by an independent manufacturer.

In Figure 6.3.1, the effect of the FCC registration program is illustrated for the interconnection of various types of transmitting and receiving equipment to telephone company facilities.

If the subscriber desires to transmit data over a leased telephone company circuit (Fig. 6.3.1A), no data access arrangement is required regardless of the type of modem used. This is because the leased line is for the exclusive use of that subscriber and any interference caused by nontelephone company equipment on that circuit will only affect that user. For the subscriber who obtains telephone company equipment (Fig. 6.3.1B), no access arrangement is required since the telephone company equipment is registered. A similar interface arrangement oc-

FIGURE 6.3.1 Interconnection under the FCC registration program

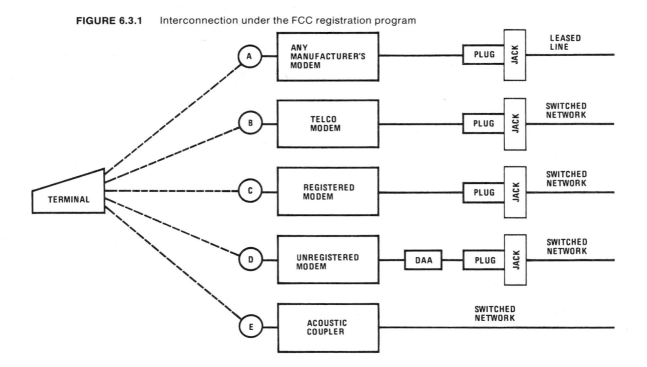

curs when any vendor-manufactured modem that is certified under the FCC registration program (Fig. 6.3.1C) is connected to the switched network. When an unregistered modem (Fig. 6.3.1D) is connected, a data access arrangement must be obtained to interface the telephone company jack. For users who install devices that are acoustically coupled to a telephone circuit, such as a terminal with a built-in acoustic coupler (Fig. 6.3.1E), neither an access arrangement nor a plug-jack connection is required, since the interface to the telephone line is via the telephone headset and the coupler's power supply is thus segregated from the telephone company line (no hard-wired connection).

The intent of recent deregulatory actions regarding AT&T and IBM is to free both firms to pursue just about any data communications endeavors. Many vendor announcements—including those of IBM and AT&T—will be keyed to these actions.

QUESTIONS

6.1 What is a tariff and why is it important?

6.2 Discuss the division of jurisdiction in the United States with respect to communications common carriers.

6.3 What is the purpose of the International Telecommunications Union?

6.4 How has the Federal Communications Commission's equipment registration program affected the connection of equipment to telephone company facilities?

6.5 What type of subscriber equipment can be connected to the public switched telephone network via a plug-jack connection?

CHAPTER 7

THE COMMUNICATIONS INDUSTRY

7.1 INTRODUCTION

To place in perspective a discussion of carrier offerings, operation, and cost, which will be covered in Chapter 8, let us first consider the organization and structure of the communications common carrier industry in the United States and several foreign countries.

As discussed in Chapter 6, communications common carriers are companies that are licensed by one or more international, federal, state, and municipal agencies to provide service to the public at reasonable rates upon reasonable request. In the United States, the communications industry consists of the telephone companies, specialized carriers, Western Union, satellite carriers, and a number of international record carriers. Each of these communications groups consists of a number of companies and subsidiaries, ranging from over 2,000 telephone companies to several international record carriers. Each of these groups is licensed to provide a variety of services to include the transmission of voice, data, data by packets, printed messages, video, facsimile, telemetry, and television.

7.2 THE U.S. TELEPHONE INDUSTRY

Although there are over 2,000 telephone companies in the United States, this industry is dominated by five large companies that generate over 95 percent of all telephone company revenues. The largest and most important of these large companies is AT&T, which is the undisputed leader in the field.

AT&T

AT&T provides a wide range of products and services to satisfy a variety of communications needs, ranging from basic telephone service for the public switched telephone network subscribers to Dataphone service. The latter is designed to enable certain types of business machines to transfer data to other business machines and computers over the telephone network or a specialized digital network.

AT&T was incorporated in 1885. Today, AT&T provides telephone service to over 70 percent of the population of the United States and handles over 90 percent of the long-distance calls placed in the nation. Through various degrees of control, ranging from ownership of all to a large majority of stock, AT&T controls 22 associated telephone companies and the Western Electric Co., which is the manufacturing arm. Together with Western Electric, AT&T owns the Bell Telephone Laboratories, which performs research and development functions. The Bell Telephone Laboratories performs centralized research and it was here that the transistor and solar battery were invented. A subsidiary of Western Electric, the Teletype Corp., manufactures a specialized line of teleprinters of which the most famous is the Teletype ASR-33. There are over one-half million ASR-33 terminals performing such diverse functions as message switching, computer console controller, data entry applications, and general timesharing use.

Figure 7.2.1 is a diagram of the AT&T structure. The Long Lines Department (now AT&T Communications) provides service to both the 22 AT&T associated companies and independent telephone companies under license contracts. It also operates long-distance lines that provide the connections between the associated companies and the independent telephone companies.

One of the most important factors that influences the business activities of AT&T results from a 1956 consent decree between it and the U.S. Department of Justice. This consent decree resulted from a Justice Department antitrust suit that asked the court to sever Western Electric from AT&T. This was resolved by a consent decree. AT&T retained ownership of Western Electric but agreed not to

FIGURE 7.2.1   Bell telephone system structure

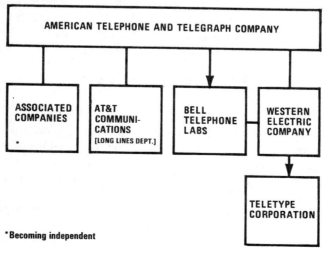

*Becoming independent

engage in any business activities other than providing common carrier communications services. In addition, Western Electric agreed not to manufacture any equipment that was not sold or leased to Bell operating companies for utilization in providing common carrier communications services.

At this writing, AT&T is divesting itself of its 22 "associated companies" (Figure 7.2.1.)—called Bell operating companies (BOCs). The BOCs intend to regroup into seven independent regional blocks. And AT&T's newest division, AT&T Information Systems (ATTIS), formerly American Bell Inc. (ABI), is free to compete with other data communications vendors of products and services. One ATTIS offering is Net/1000, a packet network that will compete with the GTE Telenet and Tyment services. ATTIS is AT&T's means of dissociating itself from the 1956 consent decree.

Independent Telephone Companies

The independent telephone companies, in general, offer the same facilities as the Bell operating companies, and are compatible with and also interconnect to them. These independent telephone companies range in size from small local companies that may provide service to a few hundred subscribers to General Telephone and Electronics (GT&E), which is usually considered the leader of the independents.

GT&E is a highly diversified communications and manufacturing company with operations throughout the United States and abroad. GT&E operates a network quite similar to AT&T's. Its structure includes a number of operating companies in the United States, and several international subsidiaries. It recently acquired Telenet, which specializes in packet-switched data communications.

Automatic Electric Company, a subsidiary of GT&E, is similar to Western Electric in that it produces communications equipment for the independent telephone industry. Another GT&E subsidiary, Lenkurt Electric Co., manufactures modems, microwave radios, and other commercial and military communications equipment.

Today, there are about 200 telephone companies that have more than 10,000 subscribers, and approximately another 100 have more than 5,000 subscribers. To represent these independent companies, the United States Independent Telephone Association (USITA) was formed, with headquarters in Washington, D.C. USITA coordinates their operations through committees dealing with such subjects as technical practices, accounting standards, and legal matters.

7.3 WESTERN UNION

Incorporated in 1851, soon after the development of telegraphy, Western Union has played a vital role in the development of communications in the United States. Beginning with the offering of public message telegraph service, Western Union now provides a number of computer-controlled store-and-forward message-switching services that will be discussed in Chapter 8.

Although the telegram for a long time provided the largest portion of Western

Union's revenue, it has substantially declined over the last few years. Custom-built private-wire networks, facsimile service, and message-switching services (such as Telex, TWX, and Mailgram) now generate a substantial portion of Western Union's revenue.

Western Union operates communications facilities throughout the United States, offering a variety of services for industry and government. It obtains a substantial portion of such facilities from the AT&T and independent telephone companies. Although Western Union has been historically known for its low-speed message-switching operations, it has constructed microwave facilities across the United States that permit transmission at data rates up to 48,000 bit/s, and has entered the satellite communications arena.

TWX and Telex

Today, Western Union offers two fully automatic teletypewriter message-switching networks. Telex is a message-oriented, 66 word-per-minute service; TWX is a message- and data-oriented, 100 word-per-minute service.

Telex service was introduced to the United States in 1958 by Western Union while the older TWX service was purchased from the Bell System in 1971. After the purchase of TWX, Western Union integrated the two services so that any Telex operator could reach any TWX station, and vice versa.

Today, over 150,000 terminals in the United States and approximately 500,000 such devices overseas are connected to these two networks.

Other Services

Other Western Union services include Data Com, Info Com, Hot/Line, and Mailgram.

Data Com is a channel-derivation service available on a private interstate basis between selected city pairs. Here Western Union uses discrete channel subdivision equipment to derive data channels at 150, 300, 600 and 1,200 bit/s for subscriber use.

Info Com is a computer-controlled, store-and-forward, message switch that provides each subscriber with a pseudo-private network that is configured by Western Union to a particular client requirement. Users share a national network of interconnected computers that provide store-and-forward message switching. However, software provides the privacy and integrity of each user network. Through Info Com, Western Union permits subscribers access to all of its major record communications services. As an example, Info Com subscribers can transmit messages to Telex or TWX subscribers or to a Mailgram address.

Hot/Line Telephone Service permits subscribers instant, no-dial, point-to-point metered service within and between certain cities. This service may be over terrestrial or satellite links.

As a joint offering of Western Union and the United States Postal Service, Mailgram service permits messages to be sent electronically to any location in the

United States for delivery with the next business day's mail. It is similar in concept to the Postal Service's own E-Com service.

7.4 SPECIALIZED CARRIERS

The birth of the specialized carrier industry occurred in 1969 when the Federal Communications Commission approved the application of Microwave Communications Inc. (MCI) to offer shared private microwave service as a common carrier.

Initially, such service was offered between Chicago and St. Louis and nine intermediate locations. This service permitted up to five subscribers to share a single channel of 2,000-Hz bandwidth for the transmission of voice, facsimile, and data. Since the bandwidth per channel was well below customary telephone company channel bandwidths, MCI's rates were substantially lower than rates charged by existing communications carriers. During the early years of MCI's development, its growth was restricted due to problems it had in linking its microwave network with subscribers through local facilities leased from telephone companies—which were not anxious to assist a competitor in the removal of revenue from their organizations. In the early 1970s, a series of legal rulings required the telephone companies to provide interconnections with specialized common carriers. Thus, several such carriers were able to compete with AT&T Long Lines Department for a small but growing percentage of the interstate private-line market.

MCI has widened its data communications offerings, and has acquired WUI, one of the major original international record carriers.

Southern Pacific

Headquartered in Burlingame, Calif., Southern Pacific Communications Company (SPCC) is one of just two survivors among 19 companies that previously challenged the American Telephone and Telegraph Company in the long-distance communications market.

This company is a specialized common carrier that provides coast-to-coast private-line communications services via microwave, cable, and satellite facilities for business, institutional, and governmental customers.

Among SPCC's offerings are three separate types of communications services: Sprint for voice transmission, Speedfax for facsimile service, and Datadial for data transmission. The bulk of usage on the SPCC network is for long-distance calls through its Sprint service, which is very similar to competing services such as Execunet (offered by MCI). An SPCC subscriber in San Diego, as an example, picks up the standard telephone company handset, and by dialing a code, is routed through the SPCC network, which is a series of microwave relays within line-of-sight of each other (or via satellite), to, say, Atlanta. From Atlanta, the call is routed through regular telephone company lines, like any other local call, to its destination in the Atlanta area.

One of the key advantages of the SPCC network, in addition to reduced rates, is its ability to furnish subscribers with call records to help them control their telephone costs.

Founded in 1970 during a diversification effort of its parent, Southern Pacific Co., SPCC initially built its network along the railroad right-of-way, linking major California cities and the Southwest. Since then it has rapidly expanded to the East and North, purchasing the voice and data portions of United Video in Missouri, Oklahoma and Texas in 1974, and the assets of Data Transmission Company (Datran) in 1976. By 1979, SPCC linked 72 cities throughout the United States and had over 30,000 customers. The network has been purchased by GT&E.

7.5 VALUE-ADDED CARRIERS

A value-added carrier uses transmission facilities leased from the communications common carriers, such as AT&T and the independent telephone companies. However, these facilities are connected through the use of computers (switches) and other specialized equipment that produce a new method of transferring data, by adding (compared to raw transmission) such functions as error control and code conversion.

Traditionally, charges for the use of the public switched telephone network have been based upon the duration of the connection and the distance between the originator and the receiver. When data transmission requirements increased to the point that a leased line connecting a remote terminal to a computer at a fixed monthly rate was more economical than the use of the switched network, most users still only used the leased-line facility a fraction of the available time for data transmission.

The Federal Communications Commission's rulings over the last few years have sought to encourage competition in the transmission of information. Several approaches to user requirements have emerged. One particular type of value-added network designed to meet the needs of certain types of data communications is based upon what is known as packet-switching technology. Packet switching is a form of store-and-forward message switching in which the information to be transmitted is grouped into packets. Each packet receives a destination address, so that packets from many subscribers can be routed over common facilities so long as they can be interrogated at certain locations in the network and then routed to their appropriate destinations.

In general, public packet-switching networks offer subscribers an in-place network that one cannot usually cost-effectively develop for himself by establishing his own private network. This is because a public network spreads the cost of the service and resources among many subscribers through the use of the technology. Two value-added carriers in this country employing packet-switching are GTE Telenet and Tymnet. In addition to providing packet-switching service at hundreds of locations throughout the United States, these companies provide transmission service to Europe, Asia, and the Middle East.

As mentioned earlier, AT&T plans to introduce a packet-switching network called Net/1000, to be provided by its Information Systems division.

Other public packet-switching networks include ADP Autonet, Graphnet, and Uninet.

7.6 SATELLITE CARRIERS

Over the last few years, satellite communications has rapidly become a reality. The growth in satellite communications has been especially large for long-distance communications, especially transoceanic communications where laying cable is a long and tedious process when compared to a satellite launching.

In 1963, the Communications Satellite Corp. (Comsat) was incorporated to design, launch, and operate communications satellites as well as to sell circuit capacity to other communications common carriers. Comsat is a privately owned U.S. corporation formed by Congress under the Communications Satellite Act of 1962. Under the provisions of the Act, Comsat was directed to establish a global commercial communications satellite system in cooperation with other countries as quickly as possible. Currently, Comsat derives most of its revenues from the assorted satellite services it provides to a number of U.S. communications common carriers serving the public between the U.S. and foreign locations. These services are offered through the satellites of the International Telecommunications Satellite Organization (Intelsat), which was discussed in Chapter 6. Because the cost of transmission via a satellite is independent of distance, satellite transmission has distinctively different cost characteristics when compared to terrestrial communications circuits.

In 1974, Western Union became the first company in the United States to operate domestic satellite communications using its own satellite. In that year its Westar I and II satellites were launched. Each of these satellites contains 12 transponders, each capable of relaying 1,200 one-way voice channels, or 24,000 telegraph channels, or 50 million bits per second of data—or some combination of these. By 1976, Western Union obtained revenues of almost $20 million from Westar services, including almost $9.5 million for facilities leased for fixed terms to three other communications common carriers that were providing communications services in competition with Western Union. In 1976, RCA discontinued its use of Westar service when it launched its own satellite. In 1974, RCA inaugurated its Phase I domestic satellite service known as RCA Satcom, employing Telesat Canada's Anik II Satellite and four RCA-operated earth stations near New York City, San Francisco, and Juneau and Anchorage, Alaska. RCA's Phase II satellite service was established in 1976 when RCA-owned satellites were launched into orbit, and several additional earth stations were established.

Whereas traditional satellite communications, such as the Intelsat network, rely on service interconnections with terrestrial telephone company facilities, American Satellite Corp., which commenced operation in July 1974, now offers subscribers a new type of service that removes many of the constraints of telephone company interconnections. Formerly, subscribers were limited not so much by the physical capacity of the satellite channel but mainly by the limitations of the interconnecting telephone company facilities, as illustrated in the top portion of Figure 7.6.1. In addition to this public-access type of service, American Satellite also provides its subscribers with a direct-access (private) service by installing an antenna and assorted equipment necessary to comprise an earth station at the customer's site. This station is usually mounted on the customer's roof or parking lot and connected by a short cable to the subscriber's equipment in the building. (See Fig. 7.6.1, bottom.)

Among the offerings competing with the ones mentioned are those of RCA Cylix.

7.7 INTERNATIONAL RECORD CARRIERS (IRCS)

Communications between the United States mainland and international overseas locations are normally provided within the U.S. by six communications common carrier organizations. These organizations include International Telephone and

FIGURE 7.6.1

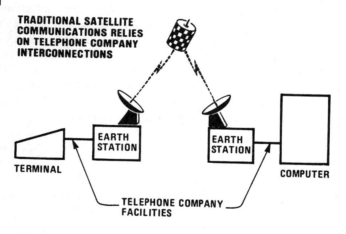

TRADITIONAL SATELLITE
COMMUNICATIONS RELIES
ON TELEPHONE COMPANY
INTERCONNECTIONS

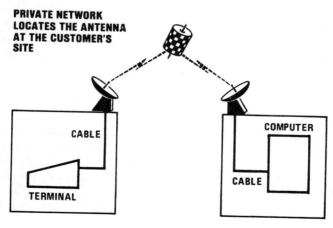

PRIVATE NETWORK
LOCATES THE ANTENNA
AT THE CUSTOMER'S
SITE

Telegraph (ITT) World Communications, Western Union International, Inc. (not related to Western Union), TRT Telecommunications Corp., RCA Global Communications, Inc., FTC Communications Inc., and AT&T Long Lines.

In determining national and international locations, the Communications Act of 1934 has caused a degree of confusion because the Act defines Canada and Mexico as domestic points, and Alaska and Hawaii international locations.

United States value-added carriers, such as Telenet and Tymnet, extend their U.S. facilities overseas through contractual arrangements with various international record carriers. Communications from the United States to Canadian locations is provided by AT&T and Western Union.

RCA Global Communications Inc.

In 1919, the Radio Corporation of America was created to provide international communications facilities. Today, RCA Global Communications (Globcom) provides leased telegraph, telegram, and Telex, and facsimile, data, television, and message-switching services. Globcom is the largest international record carrier operating in the United States. Through its subsidiary, RCA Alascom Inc., it provides telephone service from the U.S. mainland to Alaska via a separate RCA Satcom satellite. Initially, RCA Globcom had five international "gateway" cities in the United States: New York, San Francisco, Washington, D.C., Miami, and New Orleans. Gateways are cities from which messages and data are sent from the continental United States to numerous overseas locations—and vice versa. Recently, gateway cities have proliferated extensively.

ITT World Communications

Originally formed as the American Cable & Radio Corp. (AC&R), this subsidiary of International Telephone and Telegraph is now the second largest international record carrier in the United States. ITT World Communications (Worldcom) operates many gateway cities in the continental United States and maintains and staffs more than 100 overseas traffic locations. It also provides service in Hawaii and Puerto Rico. Unlike RCA, which maintains switching centers at many of its gateway locations, ITT transmits all of its international traffic to New York City, where the data is then routed overseas via a large centralized message-switching computer.

Western Union International

Originally operated as a division of Western Union, Western Union International became a separate company with no affiliation to its former parent. In 1963, when Western Union acquired monopoly rights (since removed) to U.S. domestic Telex and telegraph traffic, Congress forced the company to divest itself of its international operations.

Today Western Union International is a division of MCI, and provides a variety of services, including international Telex, leased lines, cablegrams, and provides subscribers with a measured-use leased-line digital facility for U.S.-to-European transmission.

TRT Telecommunications

This small international record carrier was founded as a subsidiary of United Fruit (now United Brands). TRT operates Telex services to many Central American countries from gateway cities in the United States as well as provides Telex service to selected European cities.

FTC Communications Inc.

Smallest of the international record carriers, this company is an operating subsidiary of the French Telephone and Telegraph Co. Presently it offers limited leased-line and Telex services from a gateway in New York City. Like its competitors, it is completely interconnected with the Western Union Telex and TWX message-switching network that delivers overseas transmission directly to domestic "hinterlands" cities.

FCC rulings have blurred the distinction between domestic carriers and IRCs. For example, Western Union is no longer restricted to domestic operations. Correspondingly, the IRCs now offer their services within the continental United States. Competition appears to be the keynote.

7.8 COMMON CARRIERS IN FOREIGN COUNTRIES

In place of independent companies, public telecommunications facilities in most foreign countries are provided by national organizations that are a part of the government. Most such organizations fall under the cognizance of the Minister for Posts and Telecommunications.

In the United Kingdom, public telecommunications facilities are provided by British Telecom. Although this organization maintains all the equipment that it installs and has some manufacturing facilities, it places orders for new equipment with several private telephone equipment manufacturers in Britain as well as a number of overseas firms.

In France, all public telecommunications facilities are provided by the Telecommunications Division of the State Secretariat for Posts and Telecommunications, commonly abbreviated as the PTT. Unlike its British counterpart, the French PTT owns no manufacturing facilities and orders necessary customer equipment primarily from four French telephone equipment manufacturers.

In most western European countries, a large variety of services are offered for data transmission. As an example, the German Federal Post Office offers switched data communications services at 50 bit/s on the Telex network and at up to 4,800 bit/s on the public switched network, with private line channels available for subscribers to transfer data at rates over 48,000 bit/s. One difference between common carriers in foreign countries and in the United States is that whereas equipment from many different vendors can be considered by a subscriber in the U.S., in most foreign countries only one device or at best a few devices manufactured by different vendors are available for consideration.

QUESTIONS

7.1 Discuss the structure of AT&T and its relationship with the 2,000 independent telephone companies in the United States.

7.2 What function does the Bell Telephone Laboratories perform for AT&T? (May be part of answer to 7.1.)

7.3 What effect did the 1956 consent decree have on AT&T's business activities?

7.4 What interconnect problems restricted the growth of MCI and other specialized carriers? How were these problems resolved?

7.5 Explain the origin of the term value-added.

7.6 What are the differences in structure and equipment utilization between common carriers in foreign countries and carriers in the United States?

CHAPTER 8

COMMON CARRIER OFFERINGS: COST AND SELECTION CONSIDERATIONS

8.1 INTRODUCTION

Today, a number of communications carriers have facilities designed for the transmission of data. These facilities range from the public switched telephone network, which was designed for analog-voice-type transmission, to more recently introduced digital facilities designed expressly for the transmission of digital data. In between these extremes are a number of hybrid services that, through the utilization of computers and the combination of various transmission media, provide specialized offerings. Examples of these offerings include specialized common carriers, value-added carriers, and satellite carriers.

In this chapter, carrier offerings will first be examined as they apply to data communications. Starting with the public switched telephone network, a number of telephone company facilities will be examined to include their operational limitations, cost considerations, and flexibility and ease of utilization. Next, the concepts, interface requirements, and financial considerations of a few specialized offerings will be examined.

Note that all costs and means of establishing them, such as those detailed in the rate tables included herein, should be considered as typical, not necessarily current, and to be used primarily for the examples and exercise questions. If readers have actual current applications, they are urged to refer to the latest figures, obtainable from the appropriate vendors or government organizations.

Finally, a number of general guidelines will be developed based upon the comparison of several facilities, assuming predetermined or expected traffic volumes.

8.2 TELEPHONE COMPANY ANALOG SERVICE

Today, the most common method of data communications occurs over the public switched telephone network. Since this network was designed for the transmission of analog signals, modems (data sets) are employed at the transmitting stations to modulate the digital pulses of computers and business machines. The signals are then suitable for transmission over the analog medium. At the receiving station, the modem reconverts (demodulates) that signal back into its original digital format.

Within the category of switched network transmission, several types of services are available for subscriber consideration. The most common service is direct distance dialing (DDD) over the switched network, in which the originator dials the number of the called party. This technique is known as station-to-station dialing, in contrast to operator station-to-station and person-to-person switched network calls, where operator intervention is required.

A second category of service is wide area telecommunications service (WATS), in which calls are made over the switched network. But the economics and geographical areas that can be called may differ from general public switched telephone network usage.

A third type of switched network facility is a foreign exchange (FX) line, really a hybrid combination of a leased line and the switched telephone network. WATS and FX service will be discussed later in this chapter.

Switched Network Utilization

Although the last ten years have witnessed an increase in the number of specialized communications carriers and their data transmission offerings, today the bulk of data transmission traffic is still carried by the switched telephone network. In this network, a telephone call is switched through to its destination once dialing has been completed.

Once a telephone number is dialed, the number wanted is passed from the subscriber's telephone to the local telephone company central office serving that subscriber, as illustrated in Figure 8.2.1. At that central office, the requested number is examined and circuits are switched to provide the subscriber with a connection to a distant central office, where the number is examined again, and more circuits switched, until the dialing party is connected to the dialed party. Although only two central offices are shown in Figure 8.2.1, it should be realized that a call placed on the switched network can travel through many such offices, with the routing being a function of existing traffic on the network. Thus, a call from New York to Atlanta could conceivably be routed through Boston, Los Angeles, and Kansas City.

Because a different path is likely to be selected each time a call is placed, telephone connections established on the switched network cannot be conditioned for the transmission of data. Normally, data rates up to 4,800 bit/s can be achieved on the switched network with acceptable error rates, while some organizations

FIGURE 8.2.1   Switched network circuit path

have achieved minimal error conditions at 7,200 and 9,600 bit/s for short periods. Up to 14,400 bit/s has been reached on leased lines.

The key advantage to using the switched telephone network is that it is universally available. Also, it is less expensive than other types of service when usage is low and the number of users in a geographical area is not large. The primary data use of the switched network today is for timesharing applications at rates ranging from 110 to 1,200 bit/s. Here, a terminal operator dials the telephone number of a modem (connected to a computer) that has an automatic answer feature. At the terminal, the operator has either an acoustic coupler or another modem, as illustrated in Figure 8.2.2. While only one modem is shown at the computer site, in general that location has many such devices connected to a rotary switch. The rotary permits a user to dial any one of a block of telephone numbers assigned to the modems and have the call automatically "stepped" to the next available line if the dialed number is busy. One advantage to using the switched network is that, once a subscriber completes his transmission, the modem at the computer site becomes available to service another user. If for some reason the quality of the switched connection leaves something to be desired, say is too noisy, the terminal operator only has to terminate the call and redial the number to obtain a new routing over the switched network.

While timesharing applications over the switched network mainly employ asynchronous terminals, synchronous devices can also use that network for data transmission. One example of the latter is remote batch terminals, which

FIGURE 8.2.2   The switched network can be used for computer timesharing

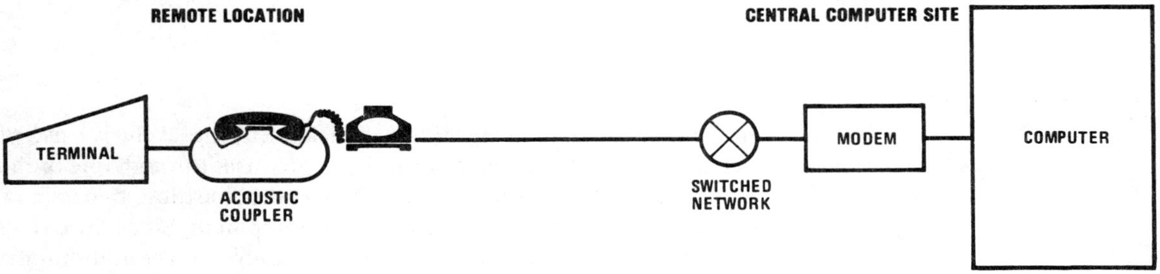

REMOTE LOCATION   CENTRAL COMPUTER SITE

TERMINAL — ACOUSTIC COUPLER — SWITCHED NETWORK — MODEM — COMPUTER frequently use the switched network at 2,400 and 4,800 bit/s to transmit and receive large volumes of data.

Switched Network Cost

The cost of a telephone call on the switched network depends upon such factors as the time of day that the call is originated, the day the call is originated, whether the call is interstate or intrastate, the distance between the called and calling parties, and the duration of the call. For example, the cost of a 20-minute transmission from a terminal 2,000 miles away from the computer at the day rate, when dialed, can be computed as follows (see Table 8.2.1):

First minute	$ 0.74
Additional minutes	
at $0.49 × 19	9.31
Total cost	$10.05

Since switched telephone network utilization is normally economical compared with leased line service (which is charged on a flat-fee monthly basis), one common procedure is to estimate the monthly communications cost of a terminal via the switched network. This can be done in several ways. First, if usage varies from day to day, a log can be kept for the month of total transmission minutes per day, and a monthly cost developed, through the use of Table 8.2.1. If an estimate of daily average transmission length is available, then simply multiplying that number by 22 working days per month may suffice.

Returning to our original daily cost of $10.05, if transmissions average 20 minutes per day, then an accurate monthly cost of $10.05 × 22 or $221.10 would be spent transmitting data over the switched telephone network.

Also, in a switched network several seconds may elapse for call completion, during which period no data can be transmitted.

When telephone calls are placed within certain geographical areas surrounding the subscriber, a number of different types of rates may be available. Some telephone companies offer a category of service that permits the subscriber to dial an unlimited number of local calls for one monthly fixed rate. Or the subscriber can select a lower monthly fixed rate that permits less calls, and then must pay an additional amount for each call dialed in excess of the base number permitted.

Private Leased Lines

A private leased line is a permanent circuit dedicated to the exclusive use of a subscriber. Such a line is routed from a subscriber's premises through one or more telephone company central offices to the subscriber's other location, bypassing the public switched telephone network and its signaling equipment. Since the circuit is permanent, the same line is always used for each tranmission, and conditioning can be applied to the path to improve its transmission quality.

TABLE 8.2.1 RATE TABLE

**Intra—U.S.—Mainland Message Telephone
Mileages and Corresponding Rates**

FCC TARIFF NUMBER 263

DIAL STATION-TO-STATION
Operator Station-to-Station and Person-to-Person

Rate Mileage	Initial Period			Additional Minutes
	Day	All Days, All Hours		Day
	Dial Station-to-Station	Operator Station-to-Station	Person-to-Person	All Classes of Service
	Initial 1 minute	Initial 3 minutes	Initial 3 minutes	Each Additional minute
1–10	.32	1.24	3.64	.16
11–22	.40	1.84	3.84	.22
23–55	.48	2.44	4.04	.28
56–124	.57	3.16	4.31	.37
125–292	.58	3.21	4.36	.39
293–430	.59	3.28	4.43	.42
431–925	.62	3.33	4.48	.43
926–1910	.64	3.37	4.52	.44
1911–3000	.74	3.57	4.72	.49

Discounts — Discounts apply to total charges for Dial Station-to-Station messages and to total Additional Minute Charges # only for Operator Station-to-station and Person-to-Person messages with total fractional amounts rounded down to the lower cent.

Rates Effective 3-3-82

**RATE DISCOUNTS APPLICABLE TO
INTERSTATE LONG DISTANCE CALLS**

	MON.	TUES.	WED.	THUR.	FRI.	SAT.	SUN.
8:00 A.M. to *5:00 P.M.	Day Rate Period FULL RATE						
5:00 P.M. to *11:00 P.M.	Evening Rate Period 40% Discount						EVE 40%
11:00 P.M. to *8:00 A.M.	Night and Weekend Rate Period 60% Discount						

*to but not including

One advantage of a leased line for many applications is that higher data rates are possible than one can obtain on the switched network. Another advantage of a leased line is that no setup time is required to dial the other party, have the call routed, and have a device on the other end answer the call. Since this line is used exclusively by the subscriber, there is no possibility that he will encounter a busy-line signal, as when calls are placed over the switched network.

Another advantage of leased lines is that a subscriber can obtain a four-wire circuit, enabling full-duplex transmission at high data rates. On the switched two-wire network, full-duplex transmission is only possible when the frequency band is split to separate transmission and reception of data, thereby lowering the data transmission rate—or by placing two calls between the same locations, for higher data rates. Lastly, the monthly cost of a leased line is fixed, regardless of its usage, whereas the cost of transmitting data on the switched network normally increases as the transmission time increases.

Types of Circuits

Presently, communications common carriers offer three types of private circuits that are defined by their bandwidth: subvoice-band (narrow band), voice band, and wideband.

A subvoice-band channel is a private line, for the exclusive use of a subscriber, that has a bandwidth of less than 300 Hz. This type of circuit permits transmission at data rates up to about 150 bit/s, has the narrowest bandwidth, and permits the lowest rate of data transfer of the three types of circuits offered. Since this type of circuit is frequently used by slow teleprinters and similar devices, it is sometimes referred to as a telegraph circuit.

A voice circuit has a bandwidth of approximately 3,000 Hertz. This is the most-frequently used leased line and permits data transfer at speeds up to 14,400 bit/s (Ref. Sec. 4.12).

Finally, the bandwidth of a number of voice-grade lines can be combined into a wideband (broadband) circuit. Such a circuit has a bandwidth well over 3,000 Hertz, which supports data at about 500,000 bit/s or more.

As mentioned previously, the most frequently used leased line for data transmission is a voice-grade circuit with a bandwidth of about 3,000 Hertz. AT&T refers to this type of line used for data transmission as a Type 3002 circuit, and the economics involved in using such a facility will be examined. The user should contact his telephone company representative to obtain current pricing information because tariffs change quite frequently. In addition, one can ask for specific pricing information from his telephone company representatives for narrow-band and wideband leased lines, as indicated in Table 8.2.2.

Type 3002 Cost Considerations

When the quantity of transmitted data increases, faster terminals and higher-speed modems may be employed to maintain or reduce the transmission time over the switched network. At a certain volume of transmission, the cost of telephone calls made over the switched network will equal or exceed the cost of a private leased line. This crossover point between leased and switched-network facilities varies due to a number of leased-line factors. These factors can best be explained by first examining the structure of a two-point Type 3002 line, as illustrated in Figure 8.2.3. Here, the components of a two-point leased line include two station terminals, one

TABLE 8.2.2   LEASED LINE CHANNELS AVAILABLE FOR DATA TRANSMISSION

Series 1000	Narrow band
Type 1001	Narrow up to 30 bit/s
Type 1002	Up to 55 bit/s
Type 1005	Up to 75 bit/s
Type 1006	Up to 150 bit/s
Type 1007, 1008, 1012 1024, 1048	Overseas channels (San Francisco to Honolulu)
Series 3000	Voice band
Type 3002	Up to 14,400 bit/s
Series 5000	Wideband data channels
Type 5700	Maximum equivalent voice grade channels, 60
Type 5800	Maximum equivalent voice grade channels, 240
Series 8000	Wideband data channels
Type 8800	Channels of approximately 48 kHz for use as a wideband data channel

at each of the customer's sites; two channel terminals, each located at a telephone company central office; and the interexchange channel, which connects the subscriber through two or more telephone company central offices between sites. The station terminal charge is a monthly cost that includes a local loop from the channel terminal (at the nearest telephone company central office) to the customer location. The station terminal may include a standard telephone termination or connection to a private branch exchange (PBX) or other equipment.

Between telephone company central offices, the interexchange channel cost includes the cost of the central office channel terminals and the channel itself, based upon the category of the locations connected and the distance between those locations. Currently, cities in the United States are divided into two categories or rate centers: A and B. Category A rate centers are listed in Tariff FCC No. 260, while category B rate centers are listed in Tariff FCC No. 264. Currently, there are three rate schedules (I, II and III) that apply between each pair of customer service locations on an airline mileage basis, as listed in Table 8.2.3.

Each rate schedule lists the interexchange monthly charges for service 7 days a week, 24 hours a day. In Tables 8.2.4 and 8.2.5 the interexchange mileage charges are listed for leased lines between two category A rate centers, A and B rate centers, and two category B rate centers. The first station terminal per user location costs $36.05 per month. With the exception of a one-time installation charge of $78.05

TABLE 8.2.3   LEASED LINE INTEREXCHANGE RATE SCHEDULES

Schedule	Rate Application
I	Chann el between 2 category A rate centers
II	Channel between a category A and a category B rate center
III	Channel between 2 category B rate centers

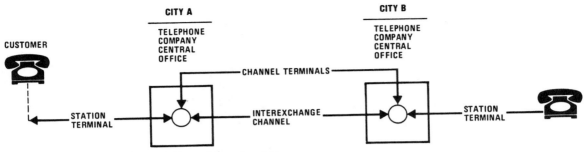

FIGURE 8.2.3   Two-point leased-line structure

for either half- or full-duplex service, all charges are monthly and permit either asynchronous or synchronous data transfer at data rates up to 9,600 bit/s. Usually, data transfers over 4,800 bit/s require circuit conditioning at a monthly cost of about $21.15 (Type D1).

As an example of leased-line cost, consider a circuit connecting a category A rate center location with a category B rate center location, and the distance between these two locations is 1,050 miles. From Table 8.2.4, the monthly charge for the 1,050 miles interexchange circuit is $1,221.83. To this cost add the station terminal charge of $36.05 per month for each end of the line, resulting in a total monthly cost of $1,293.93.

For a multipoint leased line, the cost computation is similar to that of a two-point circuit, with the exception that an additional station terminal is required at each point on the multipoint circuit and the interexchange mileage charge between each point is based on the rate centers that are connected. Then, the total mileage costs and station terminal charges are accumulated to obtain the total monthly cost.

Intrastate Leased Lines

Intrastate rates vary from state to state, and charges can be obtained from the local telephone company servicing that particular state. These rates are generally higher than interstate rates; however, when one portion of a circuit crosses a state line, then the entire circuit is charged at the interstate rate.

Foreign Exchange Service (Ref. Sec. 4.11)

A foreign exchange (FX) line is a hybrid combination of a leased line and public switched telephone network access, as illustrated in Figure 8.2.4. A foreign exchange line can be used in a variety of ways for economical data transmission. As illustrated in Figure 8.2.4, when the subscriber in city A picks up his telephone, he will be connected via a leased line to the switched network at city B. Therefore, he can have "toll-free" access to other telephone numbers in that city. In a data communications environment, city B usually has an automatically answering

TABLE 8.2.4   SCHEDULE I INTEREXCHANGE RATES (Between two Category A rate centers)

Mileage	Charge	
1	$ 73.56	
2–14	$ 73.56 + $2.59 for each mile over	1 mile
15	$109.82	
16–24	$109.82 + $2.16 for each mile over	15 miles
25	$131.42	
26–39	$131.42 + $1.62 for each mile over	25 miles
40	$155.72	
41–59	$155.72 + $1.62 for each mile over	40 miles
60	$188.12	
61–79	$188.12 + $1.62 for each mile over	60 miles
80	$220.52	
81–99	$220.52 + $1.62 for each mile over	80 miles
100	$252.92	
101–999	$252.92 + $ .94 for each mile over	100 miles
1,000	$1,098.92	
over 1,000	$1,098.92 + $ .58 for each mile over	1,000 miles

Where one rate center is an international boundary point, charge is as determined above minus $36.05.

SCHEDULE II INTEREXCHANGE RATES (Between Category A and Category B rate centers)

Mileage	Charge	
1	$ 75.00	
2–14	$ 75.00 + $4.77 for each mile over	1 mile
15	$141.78	
16–24	$141.78 + $4.47 for each mile over	15 miles
25	$186.48	
26–39	$186.48 + $2.89 for each mile over	25 miles
40	$229.83	
41–59	$229.83 + $1.95 for each mile over	40 miles
60	$268.83	
61–79	$268.83 + $1.95 for each mile over	60 miles
80	$370.83	
81–99	$370.83 + $1.95 for each mile over	80 miles
100	$346.83	
101–999	$346.83 + $ .94 for each mile over	100 miles
1,000	$1,192.83	
over 1,000	$1,192.83 + $ .58 for each mile over	1,000 miles

Where one rate center is an international boundary point, charge is as determined above minus $36.05

modem and thereby permits an unlimited number of terminals within that area to communicate one at a time with a computer located in city A. In addition to an interexchange-channel monthly bill, which is computed similarly to the previously discussed private leased-line charge, several additional costs may be incurred when

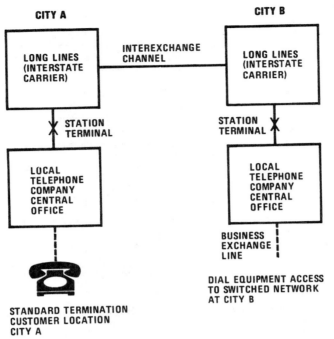

FIGURE 8.2.4   Two-point foreign exchange service

employing foreign exchange service. First, a monthly business exchange line charge, which varies by city, is provided and billed by the local telephone company in city B. Next, the connection from the customer's location in city A to the local telephone company central office is provided and billed by the telephone company serving that area. In certain large population areas, such as New York City, in addition to a monthly business exchange line charge, a charge per call made over a base number per month is added to the monthly charge.

Wide Area Telecommunications Service (WATS)

WATS is a packaged discount telecommunications plan arranged for subscribers who either make many outgoing long-distance calls to many geographical areas or who receive many such calls from certain geographical areas. WATS provides the subscriber with dial switched network access between a station connected to a WATS access line and other stations in designated service areas.

Under the WATS arrangement, customers have a choice of five service areas (Zones 1 through 5) for service within the contiguous United States and one service area (Zone 6) for service to Alaska and Hawaii. Zone 1 consists of all of the subscriber's adjacent states while the higher zones progressively expand the area of service. For example, a user in Georgia with a band 1 WATS can receive toll-free

TABLE 8.2.5   SCHEDULE III INTEREXCHANGE RATES   (Between two Category B rate centers)

Mileage	Charge	
1	$ 76.43	
2–14	$ 76.43 + $6.35 for each mile over	1 mile
15	$165.33	
16–24	$165.33 + $5.48 for each mile over	15 miles
25	$220.13	
26–39	$220.13 + $4.03 for each mile over	25 miles
40	$280.58	
41–59	$280.58 + $3.03 for each mile over	40 miles
60	$341.18	
61–79	$341.18 + $2.31 for each mile over	60 miles
80	$387.38	
81–99	$387.38 + $1.95 for each mile over	80 miles
100	$426.38	
101–999	$426.38 + $ .97 for each mile over	100 miles
1,000	$1,299.38	
over 1,000	$1,299.38 + $ .58 for each mile over	1,000 miles

Where one rate center is an international boundary point, charge is as determined above minus $35.05.

calls from the states of Alabama, Florida, Kentucky, Mississippi, North Carolina, South Carolina, and Tennessee. Service to a higher number zone includes service to all lower numbered zones.

Two categories of WATS service can be selected by subscribers—Outward service known as Outwats and Inward service, Inwats. Outwats service provides for the origination of calls from a subscriber with an outward WATS access line to all telephones in a designated zone of service. Similarly, Inwats service provides for the termination of calls to an Inwats access line from all telephones in a designated zone of service. Inwats is the commonly known toll-free "800" number.

Both Inwats and Outwats, when obtained as interstate offerings, do not permit calls to or from points within the same state in which the access line terminates. Such services are considered intrastate and are provided by local operating companies in the subscriber's state.

WATS Cost

Both Inwats and Outwats charges are based upon the zone or service area selected and the total monthly communications time. There are also several miscellaneous charges, including access line, installation, and so on.

Tables 8.2.6 and 8.2.7 detail the AT&T Outwats and Inwats rates. Six rate steps are associated with each state (or portion), and charges for the 22 rate steps are given. As an example of Wats costs, suppose a computer is located in Georgia, and the firm has a number of terminals that must communicate with the computer from the states surrounding Georgia. From Table 8.2.7, the cost of a Band 1 WATS is $18.38/hour for the first 15 hours of usage, $16.78/hour for the next 25 hours, $15.20/hour for each hour over 40, and $13.46/hour for each over 80. The cost for 90 hours of usage would be $1,437.80. This is added to the $31.65 charge for the access line.

8.3 TELEPHONE COMPANY DIGITAL SERVICE

As filed in Tariff FCC No. 267, Dataphone digital service (DDS) offered by AT&T provides subscribers with interstate private leased-line digital communications between about 100 major metropolitan areas in the United States.

In comparison to leased private voice-grade lines, in which digital data must first be modulated into an analog signal for transmission, DDS is designed exclusively for the transmission of digital data in digital format, without the need for modems or other modulation equipment. DDS offers users full-duplex transmission of digital signals at synchronous speeds of 2.4, 4.8, 9.6, and 56 kbit/s, employing end-to-end digital technology. Both point-to-point and multipoint digital service are available.

The primary advantage of DDS is that noise and distortion are not amplified on that facility as they are in analog transmissions. Instead of amplifying the digital signal, the signal is regenerated at regular intervals as it travels through the DDS network, thus reconstructing new, clean pulses that minimize the possibility of bits being received in error. Because of all-digital technology, DDS is guaranteed to provide the subscriber with an average performance in excess of 99.5-percent error-free seconds for operation at all data rates. If the error performance level should drop below that figure, the period of substandard performance is considered by the telephone company as a circuit interruption, and the subscriber receives a credit allowance for that period of time.

In place of modems that are required on analog circuits, users of DDS can select one of two types of interface devices (Ref. Sec. 4.11). The first device, known as a data service unit (DSU), performs such functions as signal regeneration, timing recovery, signal reformatting, proper coding and decoding of signals, formatting, and the generation and recognition of control signals. If the subscriber decides to provide his own equipment to perform the functions of the DSU, the telephone company will furnish the user a device known as a channel service unit (CSU) as part of a digital access line to provide network protection and remote loopback testing capability.

The components of a digital data channel are quite similar to those of the previously discussed analog type 3002 leased line. Instead of a station terminal, the digital service subscriber receives a digital station terminal, which provides a path for digital transmission within the serving area of a digital city, between the subscriber's premises and the telephone company central office. The monthly charge per station terminal depends upon the transmission speed selected and whether or not the subscriber or the telephone company furnishes the digital service unit. Table 8.3.1 lists the monthly cost of digital station terminals.

TABLE 8.2.6   WIDE AREA TELECOMMUNICATIONS SERVICE

Monthly Charges
Outward WATS

(A) Access line charge
    A monthly charge of $31.65 applies to each Outward WATS access line.

(B) Rate Step Table

Home Rate State	SA1	SA2	SA3	SA4	SA5	SA6	Home Rate State	SA1	SA2	SA3	SA4	SA5	SA6
ALABAMA	4	7	9	11	17	22	NEVADA	5	8	13	16	18	20
ARIZONA	6	9	12	15	18	20	NEW HAMPSHIRE	2	7	11	15	18	22
ARKANSAS	4	7	9	11	15	21	NEW JERSEY	1	5	9	13	18	22
CALIFORNIA-N	8	12	15	17	18	20	NEW MEXICO	6	8	10	13	17	21
CALIFORNIA-S	7	11	15	17	18	20	NEW YORK-NE	3	7	10	14	18	22
COLORADO	7	8	10	12	16	21	NEW YORK-SE	1	7	10	14	18	22
CONNECTICUT	1	7	10	14	18	22	NEW YORK-W	3	5	10	14	18	22
DELAWARE	1	5	9	13	18	22	NORTH CAROLINA	4	7	8	12	18	22
DIST. OF COLUMBIA	1	4	8	12	18	22	NORTH DAKOTA	6	9	11	14	15	21
FLORIDA	7	10	12	13	18	22	OHIO-N	3	5	7	10	17	22
GEORGIA	4	7	10	12	18	22	OHIO-S	3	5	8	10	17	22
IDAHO	5	9	13	15	18	19	OKLAHOMA	5	7	9	12	15	21
ILLINOIS-N	3	6	8	10	15	21	OREGON	5	9	15	17	18	19
ILLINOIS-S	3	6	8	10	15	21	PENNSYLVANIA-E	1	5	8	12	18	22
INDIANA	3	6	8	10	16	21	PENNSYLVANIA-W	3	5	8	12	18	22
IOWA	4	7	9	11	14	21	RHODE ISLAND	1	6	11	14	13	22
KANSAS	5	7	9	12	14	21	SOUTH CAROLINA	4	7	9	12	18	22
KENTUCKY	3	5	8	10	17	22	SOUTH DAKOTA	5	8	10	12	15	21
LOUISIANA	5	8	10	13	16	21	TENNESSEE	5	6	8	10	17	22
MAINE	6	9	12	16	18	22	TEXAS-E	6	9	11	14	16	21
MARYLAND	2	5	9	12	18	22	TEXAS-S	8	11	12	14	16	21
MASSACHUSETTS	2	7	11	14	18	22	TEXAS-W	7	9	11	14	16	21
MICHIGAN-N	5	8	9	12	17	21	UTAH	6	7	11	14	18	20
MICHIGAN-S	4	7	9	12	17	21	VERMONT	2	7	11	14	18	22
MINNESOTA	6	8	10	12	15	21	VIRGINIA	3	5	8	11	18	22
MISSISSIPPI	5	7	9	11	16	22	WASHINGTON	8	11	15	17	18	19
MISSOURI	5	7	8	10	5	21	WEST VIRGINIA	2	5	7	11	18	22
MONTANA	7	10	12	14	17	20	WISCONSIN	3	7	9	11	16	21
NEBRASKA	5	8	9	12	14	21	WYOMING	5	9	10	13	16	21

(C) Monthly Usage Rate Table
    The hourly rates apply to the average use for each rate period, rounded to the nearest tenth of an hour, for each access line within a service group.

PER HOUR OF USE PER RATE PERIOD PER ACCESS LINE

Rate Steps	First 15 Hours Business Day	Evening	Next 25 Hours Business Day	Evening	Next 40 Hours Business Day	Evening	Over 80 Hours Business Day	Evening	All Hours Night/Weekend
1	$17.41	$11.31	$15.48	$10.07	$13.56	$8.81	$11.68	$7.45	$6.05
2	$18.29	$11.90	$16.29	$10.59	$14.27	$9.29	$12.08	$7.86	$6.36
3	$18.72	$12.17	$16.67	$10.84	$14.61	$9.50	$12.35	$8.02	$6.51
4	$19.06	$12.39	$16.97	$11.03	$14.88	$9.66	$12.58	$8.17	$6.62
5	$19.35	$12.58	$17.22	$11.19	$15.09	$9.82	$12.77	$8.31	$6.71
6	$19.60	$12.74	$17.45	$11.35	$15.30	$9.95	$12.94	$8.41	$6.81
7	$19.92	$12.95	$17.74	$11.52	$15.55	$10.11	$13.15	$8.55	$6.92
8	$20.29	$13.19	$18.05	$11.73	$15.82	$10.29	$13.39	$8.70	$7.05
9	$20.59	$13.39	$18.33	$11.92	$16.07	$10.44	$13.60	$8.84	$7.15
10	$20.86	$13.56	$18.58	$12.08	$16.28	$10.59	$13.77	$8.95	$7.26
11	$21.10	$13.71	$18.78	$12.20	$16.47	$10.71	$13.93	$9.06	$7.33
12	$21.32	$13.85	$18.97	$12.34	$16.62	$10.81	$14.06	$9.14	$7.40
13	$21.51	$13.99	$19.14	$12.45	$16.78	$10.91	$14.20	$9.22	$7.47
14	$21.73	$14.13	$19.34	$12.58	$16.96	$11.02	$14.34	$9.33	$7.55
15	$21.95	$14.27	$19.56	$12.71	$17.13	$11.15	$14.49	$9.42	$7.63
16	$22.21	$14.44	$19.77	$12.85	$17.32	$11.26	$14.66	$9.53	$7.71
17	$22.46	$14.59	$19.99	$13.00	$17.52	$11.39	$14.82	$9.64	$7.80
18	$22.90	$14.89	$20.37	$13.24	$17.86	$11.61	$15.10	$9.82	$7.96
19	$23.96	$15.57	$21.32	$13.86	$18.69	$12.15	$15.81	$10.28	$8.39
20	$25.82	$16.78	$22.98	$14.94	$20.14	$13.09	$17.04	$11.08	$9.04
21	$26.96	$17.52	$23.99	$15.59	$21.03	$13.67	$17.79	$11.56	$9.44
22	$29.04	$18.88	$25.85	$16.80	$22.65	$14.72	$19.17	$12.46	$10.16

(D) Uniform Service Order Code
    USOC WT1 Service Area 1   USOC WT3 Service Area 3   USOC WT5 Service Area 5
    USOC WT2 Service Area 2   USOC WT4 Service Area 4   USOC WT6 Service Area 6

TABLE 8.2.7 WIDE AREA TELECOMMUNICATIONS SERVICE

Monthly Charges

800 Service (Inward WATS)

(A) Access line charge
A monthly charge of $36.80 applies to each 800 Service access line.

(B) Rate Step Table

Home Rate State	SA1	SA2	SA3	SA4	SA5	SA6	Home Rate State	SA1	SA2	SA3	SA4	SA5	SA6
ALABAMA	4	7	9	11	17	22	NEVADA	5	8	13	16	18	20
ARIZONA	6	9	12	15	18	20	NEW HAMPSHIRE	2	7	11	15	18	22
ARKANSAS	4	7	9	11	15	21	NEW JERSEY	1	5	9	13	18	22
CALIFORNIA-N	8	12	15	17	18	20	NEW MEXICO	6	8	10	13	17	21
CALIFORNIA-S	7	11	15	17	18	20	NEW YORK-NE	3	7	10	14	18	22
COLORADO	7	8	10	12	16	21	NEW YORK-SE	1	7	10	14	18	22
CONNECTICUT	1	7	10	14	18	22	NEW YORK-W	3	5	10	14	18	22
DELAWARE	1	5	9	13	18	22	NORTH CAROLINA	4	7	8	12	18	22
DIST. OF COLUMBIA	1	4	8	12	18	22	NORTH DAKOTA	6	9	11	14	15	21
FLORIDA	7	10	12	13	18	22	OHIO-N	3	5	7	10	17	22
GEORGIA	4	7	10	12	18	22	OHIO-S	3	5	8	10	17	22
IDAHO	5	9	13	15	18	19	OKLAHOMA	5	7	9	12	15	21
ILLINOIS-N	3	6	8	10	15	21	OREGON	5	9	15	17	18	19
ILLINOIS-S	3	6	8	10	15	21	PENNSYLVANIA-E	1	5	8	12	18	22
INDIANA	3	6	8	10	16	21	PENNSYLVANIA-W	3	5	8	12	18	22
IOWA	4	7	9	11	14	21	RHODE ISLAND	1	6	11	14	18	22
KANSAS	5	7	9	12	14	21	SOUTH CAROLINA	4	7	9	12	18	22
KENTUCKY	3	5	8	10	17	22	SOUTH DAKOTA	5	8	10	12	15	21
LOUISIANA	5	8	10	13	16	21	TENNESSEE	5	6	8	10	17	22
MAINE	6	9	12	16	18	22	TEXAS-E	6	9	11	14	16	21
MARYLAND	2	5	9	12	18	22	TEXAS-S	8	11	12	14	16	21
MASSACHUSETTS	2	7	11	14	18	22	TEXAS-W	7	9	11	14	16	21
MICHIGAN-N	5	8	9	12	17	21	UTAH	6	7	11	14	18	20
MICHIGAN-S	4	7	9	12	17	21	VERMONT	2	7	11	14	18	22
MINNESOTA	6	8	10	12	15	21	VIRGINIA	3	5	8	11	18	22
MISSISSIPPI	5	7	9	11	16	22	WASHINGTON	8	11	15	17	18	19
MISSOURI	5	7	8	10	5	21	WEST VIRGINIA	2	5	7	11	18	22
MONTANA	7	10	12	14	17	20	WISCONSIN	3	7	9	11	16	21
NEBRASKA	5	8	9	12	14	21	WYOMING	5	9	10	13	16	21

(C) Monthly Usage Rate Table
The hourly rates apply to the average use for each rate period, rounded to the nearest tenth of an hour, for each access line within a service group.

PER HOUR OF USE PER RATE PERIOD PER ACCESS LINE

Rate Steps	First 15 Hours Business Day	Evening	Next 25 Hours Business Day	Evening	Next 40 Hours Business Day	Evening	Over 80 Hours Business Day	Evening	All Hours Night/Weekend
1	$17.38	$12.51	$15.86	$11.42	$14.37	$10.34	$12.72	$9.16	$8.29
2	$17.93	$12.91	$16.36	$11.79	$14.82	$10.67	$13.13	$9.45	$8.54
3	$18.18	$13.09	$16.60	$11.95	$15.03	$10.83	$13.30	$9.58	$8.66
4	$18.38	$13.24	$16.78	$12.08	$15.20	$10.94	$13.46	$9.68	$8.75
5	$18.55	$13.36	$16.95	$12.20	$15.34	$11.05	$13.57	$9.77	$8.84
6	$18.71	$13.47	$17.08	$12.29	$15.46	$11.24	$13.69	$9.86	$8.91
7	$18.58	$13.60	$17.26	$12.42	$15.63	$11.25	$13.83	$9.96	$8.99
8	$19.10	$13.76	$17.45	$12.56	$15.80	$11.38	$13.99	$10.08	$9.11
9	$19.29	$13.89	$17.62	$12.69	$15.96	$11.49	$14.13	$10.17	$9.19
10	$19.44	$14.00	$17.75	$12.78	$16.07	$11.58	$14.23	$10.25	$9.26
11	$19.58	$14.10	$17.88	$12.89	$16.20	$11.66	$14.33	$10.32	$9.32
12	$19.70	$14.18	$17.99	$12.95	$16.29	$11.73	$14.43	$10.39	$9.39
13	$19.81	$14.26	$18.09	$13.03	$16.39	$11.79	$14.49	$10.43	$9.43
14	$19.92	$14.34	$18.21	$13.12	$16.48	$11.87	$14.59	$10.51	$9.49
15	$20.06	$14.45	$18.33	$13.21	$16.58	$11.94	$14.69	$10.57	$9.56
16	$20.21	$14.55	$18.45	$13.28	$16.72	$12.03	$14.79	$10.65	$9.63
17	$20.35	$14.66	$18.59	$13.39	$16.82	$12.12	$14.90	$10.72	$9.70
18	$20.59	$14.82	$18.81	$13.54	$17.02	$12.26	$15.08	$10.86	$9.82
19	$21.56	$15.52	$19.62	$14.13	$17.89	$12.58	$15.74	$11.33	$10.35
20	$23.24	$16.73	$21.15	$15.23	$19.29	$13.89	$16.97	$12.22	$11.16
21	$24.26	$17.47	$22.08	$15.90	$20.14	$14.50	$17.71	$12.75	$11.65
22	$26.14	$18.82	$23.79	$17.13	$21.70	$15.62	$19.08	$13.74	$12.55

(D) Uniform Service Order Code

USOC 8L1 Service Area 1   USOC 8L3 Service Area 3   USOC 8L5 Service Area 5

USOC 8L2 Service Area 2   USOC 8L4 Service Area 4   USOC 8L6 Service Area 6

The next element in the cost of DDS transmission is the channel cost. This cost depends upon the transmission speed selected and the interexchange mileage between telephone company central offices in the cities served. Current channel rates between digital cities are listed in Table 8.3.2

As an example of the cost involved in digital transmission, assume that a company has a remote batch terminal and wishes to transmit data over a digital medium at 9.6 kbit/s to its central computer complex located 1,000 miles from the terminal. If the telephone company will supply the required digital service units, and assuming both the terminal and the computer are located in digital city serving areas, then the monthly cost of digital transmission is

	Monthly Cost
Digital station terminal	
2 at $428.00	$856.00
Channel mileage	1,098.92
Total cost	$1,954.92

TABLE 8.3.1   DIGITAL STATION TERMINALS IN DIGITAL CITIES

The following rates apply for each Digital Station Terminal where the DSU is furnished by the telephone company.

For Transmission Speeds of:	Monthly Charge	Non-Recurring Charge	USOC
2.4kbit/s	$144.65	$248.00	DF1
4.8 kbit/s	$253.00	$248.00	DF5
9.6 kbit/s	$428.00	$248.00	DF8
56 kbit/s	$953.00	$324.00	DF9

The following rates apply for each Digital Station where the DSU or equivalent is furnished by the customer or user.

For Transmission Speeds of:	Monthly Charge	Non-Recurring Charge	USOC
2.4kbit/s	$ 99.65	$148.00	DJC
4.8 kbit/s	$208.00	$148.00	DJF
9.6 kbit/s	$383.00	$148.00	DJG
56 kbit/s	$908.00	$224.00	DJH

The following rates apply for each Digital Station Terminal which is terminated at a Principal Telephone Company Central Office for the purpose of connecting to an analog/digital adapter furnished under Tariff FCC No. 260.

For Transmission Speeds of:	Monthly Charge	Non-Recurring Charge	USOC
2.4kbit/s	$ 36.05	$148.00	DFF
4.8 kbit/s	$ 36.05	$148.00	DFG
9.6 kbit/s	$ 46.65	$148.00	DFM
56 kbit/s	$180.00	$224.00	DFP

TABLE 8.3.2   CHANNEL COST BETWEEN DIGITAL CITIES

For transmission speed of 2.4, 4.8, or 9.6 kbit/s Per Airline Mile, Per Month		
Mileage	**Charge**	
1	$ 73.56	
2–14	$ 73.56 + $2.59 for each mile over	1 mile
15	$109.82	
16–24	$109.82 + $2.16 for each mile over	15 miles
25	$131.42	
26–99	$131.42 + $1.62 for each mile over	25 miles
100	$252.92	
101–999	$252.92 + $ .94 for each mile over	100 miles
1,000	$1,098.92	
over 1,000	$1,098.92 + $ .58 for each mile over	1,000 miles

For Transmission Speed of 56 kbit/s Per Airline Mile, Per Month		
Mileage	**Charge**	
1	$ 367.80	
2–14	$ 367.80 + $12.95 for each mile over	1 mile
15	$549.10	
16–24	$549.10 + $10.80 for each mile over	15 miles
25	$657.60	
26–99	$657.60 + $ 8.10 for each mile over	25 miles
100	$1,264.60	
101–999	$1,264.60 + $ 4.70 for each mile over	100 miles
1,000	$5,494.60	
over 1,000	$5,494.60 + $ 2.90 for each mile over	1,000 miles

If one wishes to compare the cost of digital leased-line transmission with data transfers over a type 3002 voice-grade circuit at data rates up to 9,600 bit/s, the cost of analog modems must be added to the cost of the analog circuit for a proper comparison. This is because the DSU or CSU used acts as a data transmitter and receiver, except it does not modulate the digital signal as a modem does.

Analog/Digital Connections

Through the utilization of a device known as an analog/digital adaptor, two separate services, analog leased line and a DDS circuit, can be combined. This device provides interface compatibility for control signals and retiming for data signals. It is furnished by the telephone company at its central office for the connection of private-line service and a Dataphone digital service operating at 2.4, 4.8, or 9.6 kbit/s. This device permits an analog extension with modems on both ends of the circuit to be used to link a subscriber outside of a digital serving area to the DDS network. The cost of the analog/digital adaptor is listed in Table 8.3.3.

TABLE 8.3.3   ANALOG/DIGITAL ADAPTER COST

Data Rate	Monthly Cost
2.4 kbit/s	$216.00
4.8 kbit/s	274.00
9.6 kbit/s	432.00

8.4 VALUE-ADDED CARRIERS

Value-added carriers began operation in the United States during 1975, interconnecting a handful of cities via a new technological approach. These carriers link over 150 cities in the United States as well as sites in over 250 cities worldwide.

The value-added carriers are different from previously discussed data transmission services and private data networks in both the enhanced and extensive offerings to users and the sophisticated technology they employ. The technology, called packet switching, makes it possible for the value-added carrier to provide any user, large or small, with the kind of fast-response, error-free, low-cost-per-transaction data transmissions now available only to companies that have invested in their own private networks.

In essence, the value-added carrier takes advantage of the substantial economies of scale resulting from one very large network—fully utilizing such expensive resources as transmission lines and concentration equipment by sharing the network among the subscribers. These carriers pass on a portion of the consequent savings to the individual subscriber through tariff charges based mainly on connect time and characters transmitted.

Beyond the economics, leasing existing communications facilities allows the carrier to obtain just as much transmission capacity for each location as is required by the traffic load. This provides the flexibility to adapt quickly to subscriber traffic and geographical demands, and permits the incorporation of new transmission offerings—such as satellite services—as they become available.

In a value-added network, data is transmitted in units called packets, with each packet containing a specified number of characters. These packets are then routed through the carrier's network by minicomputers placed in the carrier's switching centers. Other minicomputers in the carrier's network are used as terminal interface processors, connecting computers and terminals to the network so that such devices become compatible with one another for transmission and reception of data. Here, the interface processors build portions of transmissions into packets, and transmit the packets to the carrier's switching centers via common carrier facilities, where they are retransmitted to the packet destination.

History

Conceptually and technologically, value-added carriers had their origin in Arpanet (Advance Research Project Agency Network), a nationwide consortium of computers at numerous research centers tied together over a packet-switching network. However, Arpanet is operated on behalf of the U.S. Government to support research activities of various Federal agencies and not as a communications common carrier.

In 1973 the Federal Communications Commission approved the concept of value-added networks and determined that they should be regulated as common carriers, permitting potential public network operators to propose a value-added network as long as they applied for FCC approval. On April 16, 1974, Telenet Communications Corp. (now part of GT&E) received FCC authorization as a value-added carrier. Beginning service in 1975 between 16 cities, by 1976 Telenet's service was extended to 30 cities and by 1980 approximately 80 cities were linked.

Carrier Use

To use a value-added carrier's service, users do not have to be located in a service city since a switched or leased line can be used to access the carrier's nearest facility. In addition to transmitting user data, value-added carriers program their computer interfaces to provide such services for customers as code conversion, speed conversion, and error detection and control. In addition, the computers at the carrier's monitoring centers gather data for user traffic statistics and billings, and provide other network-related services.

Carrier Office Interface and Routing

Figure 8.4.1 illustrates typical subscriber connections to a value-added carrier's central office. The criteria for choosing either a dial-up line via the switched network or a leased line to access the carrier's central office are substantially the same as those employed in configuring private data communications networks. In short, such factors as transmission speed, acceptable busy-signal incidence, response time, volume of traffic, length of individual transmissions or transactions, and whether line use is substantially continuous or mostly occasional must be considered. In addition, multipoint circuits may be used to connect many terminals on a common line, or individual terminals may be connected on point-to-point leased lines.

As an example of the packet-switching technology, let us examine a subscriber located in Seattle who wants to transmit a message via a value-added carrier to his computer center in Houston. To initiate a connection to the carrier, the subscriber may dial a Seattle access number or he may have a leased line to the carrier's central office if volume of transmission is high. Once the subscriber connects to the carrier, he enters the computer center's code to inform the carrier where he desires to be routed to. The carrier then makes a virtual connection for the subscriber to be routed to the computer.

As the subscriber transmits messages to the computer, the carrier's equipment formats the messages into prescribed data packets. After each packet is formed, it is transmitted to and through a number of carrier central offices to Houston. While

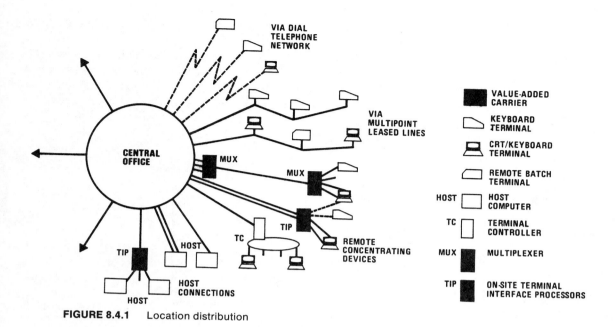

FIGURE 8.4.1   Location distribution

the first packet may travel via San Francisco, Los Angeles, and Dallas to Houston, other packets could travel different routes, with all packets being error checked over each hop of the journey and buffered at Houston to await the arrival of the other packets.

As packets arrive at the carrier's Houston central office without error, they are released from the central office and passed to the subscriber's computer via a leased line connecting the computer facility to the carrier's central office. The computer receives the packets in the same order as they were sent, since the carrier's equipment rearranges the packets into proper sequence. Although the original message may have started out at a low data rate, say, at 300 bit/s, once it enters the carrier's network it will be transmitted at 9,600, 50,000 or 56,000 bit/s. Even including electrical propagation, queuing, and acknowledgment delays, a packet will proceed from any source office to any destination office in, on average, one-half second.

Carrier Differences

Telenet and Tymnet, two of the leading value-added carriers, use markedly different approaches to packet switching. These differences significantly influence the performance and cost of the services offered. While one carrier is less expensive in certain cases, the other provides better response times in different situations. When both provide equivalent performance, the costs become more competitive. Both carriers offer similar benefits for new users, including immediate nationwide service, high reliability, flexibility, network management, and reduced costs, especially in start-up situations.

Looking at Telenet first, it supports dial-in asynchronous, dedicated, and TWX connections to the network. Asynchronous connections support transmissions at 110 to 300 bit/s (10 to 30 characters per second), and 1.2 kbit/s (120 characters per second). Figure 8.4.2 shows one of the ways a remote user can be connected to his host computer via Telenet. Here, the interfaces to the terminal and to the host computer are the same. Telenet also supports the CCITT X.25 host-computer packet-switching interface standard.

FIGURE 8.4.2 Connecting to user's host

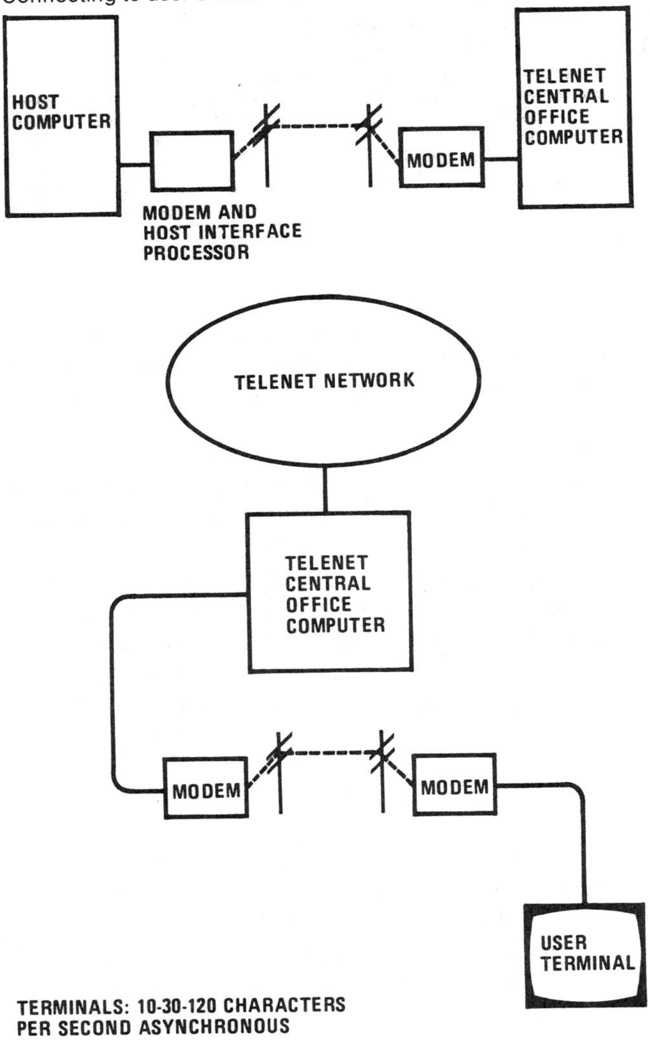

TERMINALS: 10-30-120 CHARACTERS
PER SECOND ASYNCHRONOUS

In addition to providing packet switching, Telenet provides dynamic or adaptive routing of packetized data between its major network nodes, as illustrated in Figure 8.4.3. As shown, consecutive packets from a source may follow different routes to the destination node. This dynamic routing permits the network to distribute the intra-network data transmission workload evenly over all the nodes, thereby attaining high line utilization.

Also offered is automatic network recovery from failure or congestion on any node or link. The dynamic alternate routing feature is the main reason for Telenet's high data transmission reliability. Also, in every transmission between a terminal and a host computer, there are two nodes that must operate—the node directly connected to the terminal and the node directly connected to the host computer. Since most Telenet nodes are equipped with "hot standby" hardware, total node failures are extremely rare.

FIGURE 8.4.3 Dynamic routing

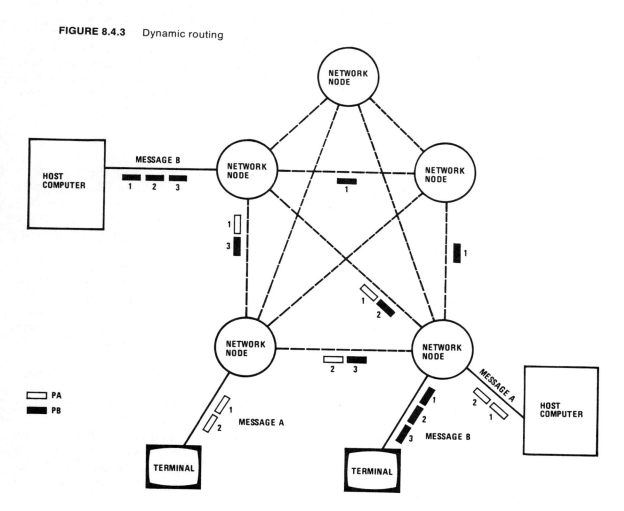

Another network feature is software-controlled timers at each end of each virtual connection. Instead of waiting until enough data for a complete packet is received, Telenet uses a packetizing algorithm to forward a partially filled packet when either a special control character is received (for example, a carriage-return or a page-reject), or after a certain amount of time has passed. The timer option provides for better response times for sending data from the user while he's keying in the last part of a message, thus giving the network a "head start" on the message transmission. These software-controlled timers are table driven—meaning that Telenet can set them to customer specifications for each virtual connection. In this way, each terminal or host can have the response-time performance optimized.

Proximity to Telenet's service cities is important for dial-in users because such users must pay a distance-dependent telephone charge to connect terminals to Telenet. For subscribers that anticipate large volumes of traffic, Telenet provides a leased line and modems to connect a subscriber's terminal or computer to a Telenet central office, with the charge dependent upon the proximity of the host computer and terminals to Telenet central offices. For the connection to a customer's computer site, leased access charges vary with the type of computer interface, the number of computer ports to be accessed, and the transmission rate. These leased-line fees can vary from a few hundred dollars per month to thousands of dollars per month. In addition, Telenet charges subscribers a monthly account fee of $140.

Interfacing the Host

Two types of host interfaces are available from Telenet. With the first type of interface, Telenet connects a network access processor—called a Telenet processor (TP)—at the customer's computer, through multiple low- and high-speed asynchronous ports. It appears to the customer computer as a rotary of dial-in modems. No hardware or software changes to the customer computer are required. TPs are available with up to 480 network access ports.

A typical configuration of a customer host utilizing a TP-1000 supporting up to seven simultaneously active asynchronous low-speed remote terminals would cost $600 per month. A configuration utilizing a TP-2200 equipped with 32 network access ports would cost $1,900 per month. In both cases, any number of terminals can attempt to access the host, but only seven (or 32) can be connected at any time.

The second type of host-to-network interface available from Telenet is the packet-mode interface: X.25. This interface is available to Telenet customers throughout the United States at a flat monthly charge (detailed later) independent of customer location. The X.25 interface is also available on public packet networks in other countries, including Bell Canada's Datapac network, the French Transpac network, and the British International Packet Switching Service.

The X.25 network interface requires special communications software resident in the customer's computer or front end. Such network access software is presently furnished by Telenet for several computers, including IBM 360s and 370s, Univac 110Xs, DEC PDP-11s, and Burroughs 6700/7700/7800s. In a growing number of cases, the computer manufacturers themselves are furnishing X.25 network access software as an integral and supported part of the manufacturer's standard communications software.

A typical interface configuraticn of a customer host utilizing the X.25 network interface protocol, supporting up to 225 simultaneously active remote asynchronous terminals (110 to 1.2K bit/s), could cost $1,000 to $1,500 for access line speeds of 2.4-9.6 kbit/s.

In addition to the basic connection and account fees, Telenet charges for monthly usage. Usage is measured both for dial-in hours on line and number of packets used. For customers with more than several hundred terminal hours per month in any given city, Telenet offers a service called private packet exchange or PPX, which reduces the hourly dial-in rate in these cities to less than a dollar per hour.

These charges, while dependent on traffic volume, also depend on how efficiently this traffic is packed into hours and packets. When a terminal transmits data at its rated speed (such as 30 characters per second), and when Telenet's variable length packets (maximum of 128 user characters per packet) are filled with data, then transmission is 100 percent efficient. The 100 percent data transmission and product usage efficiency yields the lowest possible cost.

However, in the real world, this rarely occurs. Very few 30-and 120-character-per-second terminals operate at 100 percent data transmission efficiency. (There are 108,000 characters per hour at 30 characters per second.) More typical usage is 16,000 to 40,000 characters per hour for 30-character-per-second terminals, and 30,000 to 75,000 characters per hour for 120-character-per-second terminals. Packet efficiency is dependent upon several factors, including transmission speed, message size, and response-time performance considerations. Consequently, efficiency typically falls in the 5 to 30 percent range.

While it appears that packet costs are almost negligible because they are 3 percent of the total monthly cost in a 100 percent efficiency situation, as packets are used less efficiently, these costs rise significantly. Packet costs are determined by the user's total monthly load, the number of input-output transactions in the load, the number of characters in a transaction, the relative sizes of the typical two messages that make up each transaction, the transmission speed, and network packetizing algorithms.

A transaction occurs when a message is sent from a terminal to a host computer, and then a response message is returned to the terminal (or vice versa).

Since the charges are based on 128-character packets, sending a 129-character message costs twice as much as sending a 128-character message. Clearly, the closer each of the two messages in a transaction is to a multiple of 128, the more efficient the data transmission over the Telenet network. As indicated later, the efficiency is also dependent on the network packetizing algorithm when it is applied.

The packet charges on the Telenet network can be calculated for an application using the transaction concept. The fixed monthly data transmission load (in millions of characters) for any application can be expressed in packets by assuming that data transmission occurs as transactions—a message is sent from a source to a destination, and, at a later time, a response message is received at the original source from that destination; that all message sizes can be expressed as ratios of sent to received—1:1, 1:2, 1:3, 1:4, 1:5, etc.; and that protocol handshaking characters are not transmitted over the network. Based upon these assumptions, the minimum number of packets in a transaction are determined:

$$\text{Packets per transaction} = \frac{\text{smaller message size}}{128} + \frac{\text{larger message size}}{128}$$

Note that each message-size division must be rounded to the next higher whole number—there are no fractional packets.

The number of characters in a transaction is determined by simply summing the message sizes:

Characters per transaction =
(smaller message size) + (larger message size)

The number of transactions in a fixed monthly load is calculated by dividing the characters per transaction into the total characters per month:

Transactions per month =
(Total characters per month)/(Characters per transaction)

Finally, the monthly packet transmission costs for Telenet can be calculated using the formula:

Monthly packet costs =
(60¢/1,000 packets) × (packets/transaction) × (transactions/month)

To illustrate this formula, consider the following two cases. In the first, the smaller outgoing message is 25 characters and the larger return message is 125 characters (a 1:5 ratio), yielding a minimum of two packets per transaction. In the second case, the smaller message is increased by one character (26 characters) and the 1:5 ratio maintained, making the large message 130 characters. The larger message now exceeds 128 characters. As a result, a minimum of three packets is now required for each complete transaction. The packet transmission costs for a 10-million-character monthly load are $133 in the first case and $192 in the second. This is a 44 percent difference for the six extra characters per transaction. When the $192 cost is compared to a 100-percent-packet-transmission efficiency cost of $78, we see that it is more than 2.4 times the 100 percent case.

The smaller message-size ratios (such as 1:1) are almost always more expensive, and a sharp increase in cost occurs as the messages get smaller and packet usage becomes more inefficient. The network packetizing algorithm may also introduce more inefficiency in order to decrease response time (discussed later).

In typical interactive transaction applications, average output messages—which are computer generated—are greater in length than input messages—which are people generated. Thus, message-size ratios are generally 1:5 or larger. Telenet reports that its typical users operate in a 1:10 ratio.

The monthly costs are inversely proportional to both the data transmission and packet efficiency. Thus, a $1,400 monthly charge for 10 million characters based on 100 percent efficiency is a very conservative estimate of monthly usage charges for Telenet service.

Telenet's performance also varies with the application. The major factors to consider are reliability and response time. With dynamic routing, node failure affects only the terminals and hosts connected at that node. Most Telenet central offices are not network nodes. There are many "intelligent" offices, each such office having several nodal computers.

Response Time

The response time is defined as the time between the end of the operator input and the beginning of his receipt of computer output—that is, the time he's waiting for a reply to begin. The response-time length has three components: access-line transmission time, network transition time, and host computer time.

Delays introduced by Telenet's network as well as the overall message transmission time can be estimated. Host time depends on the user application.

Tymnet's Character

In contrast to Telenet's message orientation, Tymnet is character oriented. While it uses packet switching within the network, the packets may contain data from multiple users. The packets (64 characters each) transfer data between nodes. Because they can contain data from many users, they are almost always full.

In this way, the transmission bandwidth between nodes is efficiently used. Tymnet does not use a dynamic routing algorithm for each packet, but rather dynamically establishes a path that remains fixed for the duration of the logical connection.

To understand how the shared-packets/fixed-routing technology works, let's walk through a terminal transaction of 25 characters to the host, 125 characters back to the terminal, noting the time required for each step to execute:

Step 1. Terminal logs onto the network. As soon as the network validates the user account, a path to the host computer is established. This path is based on the most cost-effective routing at the time of the log-in (not included in response-time calculation).

Step 2. Terminal enters characters. The network passes each character along to the host, assembling and disassembling packets along the way (see Fig. 8.4.4) until the message reaches the host.

Step 3. The terminal enters the last character. (1 character @ 30 characters per second = 0.03 sec.)

Step 4. The network inserts this character into the first available packet, and passes it along to the host computer. The packets consist of 512 bits (8 bits/character), and are assumed to pass through three intermediate nodes. (512 bits @ 9.6 kbit/s = 0.053 sec. × 4 = 0.21 sec.)

Step 5. The host computer processes the message and then returns the first character of the response message to its network node. (1 character @ 30 characters per second = 0.03 sec.)

Step 6. The first character passes through the network to the terminal's network node as soon as the net receives it—Tymnet does not wait for the rest of the message. (512 bits @ 9.6 kbit/s = 0.053 sec × 4 = 0.21 sec.)

Step 7. The terminal's network node sends the first character to the terminal. (1 character @ 30 characters per second = 0.03 sec.)

Step 8. The host sends more characters. Each is passed to the terminal as the network receives it (not included in response-time calculation).

Step 9. Steps 2 to 8 continue, each character being transmitted over the same established path, one at a time, until the logical connection is terminated (not included in response-time calculation).

Total response time equals 0.51 sec.

This character-at-a-time method yields a similar response time to that of Telenet. The time required for transmission is kept to about 0.51 seconds, assuming a 30-character-per-second line into the host computer. Tymnet's published response time, less than 0.75 seconds, includes additional delays within the network.

Tymnet's charges are not based on the number of packets (since these are shared by many users), but rather on characters transmitted. This algorithm is more representative of actual transmission volumes.

City Nodes

Tymnet has nodes in over 130 cities, which are divided into high- and low-density and overseas categories. Because of economies of scale, the higher-density cities have reduced rates. Tymnet's character charges are a substantial portion of the monthly costs. These charges can be reduced by almost one-third if a 1.2-kbit/s line is used, although, typically, terminals used with telecommunications networks do not support speeds above 300 bit/s.

Tymnet has service available in over 15 cities outside the U.S. In addition, Tymnet interfaces with Telenet (in New York City) and Bell Canada's Datapac. Although Tymnet does not use an X.25 interface with any of its customers, X.25 is used for the Datapac interface with Tymnet, and is planned for the Telenet-Tymnet interface. Tymnet considered making X.25 available to its synchronous-interface customers, but decided to continue using the Tymnet bisync-like interface.

For a direct comparison between packet-switched network vendors, potential customers must make several assumptions and pick a specific network configuration. As an example, one might consider terminal access at 30 characters per second from five geographical areas for four hours of transmission per day via public dial-in service provided by each vendor. Next, one may estimate the total

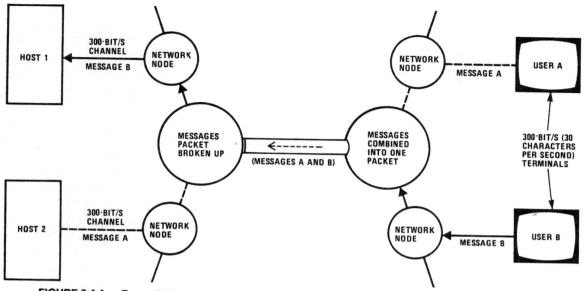

FIGURE 8.4.4   Tymnet's routing with shared packets

monthly data transmission character load, and obtain the interconnection cost for the subscriber's central computer to be connected to the vendor's nearest central office facility.

When such a specific configuration is examined and costed out, the differences in tariffs for interfacing a host computer may offer significant savings between vendors. A second factor that becomes readily visible from an actual configuration is the terminal access cost. While one vendor currently offers service in more cities, the cost of accessing that network may be more expensive than that of the other vendor at certain locations. In the final analysis, each network user must evaluate network charges using characteristics of his own application.

Other value-added carriers (Ref. Sec. 7.5) compete with Telenet and Tymnet, including AT&T Information Systems Net/1000. A functional comparison of the Telenet and Tymnet operational characteristics is shown in Table 8.4.1 The key point that all data communications users must remember is that if they want a variety of cost-effective communications service offerings, they must—on a periodic basis—evaluate their networks and the latest offerings.

This evaluation should include the consideration of non-telephone company communications services where cost effective, or where unique and highly desired user benefits are provided. In Section 8.6 an economic comparison of the charges incurred for transmission via a value-added carrier versus transmission over several types of telephone company circuits will be made. These comparisons are based upon tariffs in effect at the time this book was written and thus the reader is advised to obtain the latest filed tariff information to avoid inaccuracies due to tariff or service changes.

TABLE 8.4.1   FUNCTIONAL COMPARISON OF TELENET AND TYMNET

Feature	Telenet	Tymnet
Virtual Call Service		
• High priority (interactive users, minimum transit delay)	Now	Now
• Low priority (noninteractive, longer packets transferred)	Planned	?
• Past select (inquiry transactions)	Planned	?
• Receive collect calls	Now	Now
Network Message Switching Services		
• Message delivery		
A. Upon demand	Planned	Now
B. Automatic delivery	Planned	Planned
• Message storage	Planned	Now
• Multidestination (Broadcast) messages	Planned	Now
• Delivery acknowledgment	Planned	Now
• Message text editing	Planned	?
• Data entry formatting	?	?
Private Network Systems		
• Under tariff	Now	Now
• Lease/purchase	Now	Now
• Custom protocols by request	Now	Now
Network Management		
• Network control center	Now	Now
• Customer network control console	Now	?
• Detailed call accounting	Now	Now
• Logical subnetworks	Now	Now
• User authorization IDs/passwords	Now	Now
• Network command language	Now	?
• Data entry language	?	?
Host Interfaces		
• Emulation		
TTY	Now	Now
IBM 3271 BSC	Planned	Planned
IBM 2780/3780 BSC	Now	Now
IBM HASP multileaving	Now	Now
• Message level	?	?
• X.25 Packet mode	Now	Now
Terminal Interfaces		
• Asynchronous contention (unbuffered terminals)	Now	Now
• Asynchronous contention (buffered terminals)	Now	Now
• Asynchronous polled	Planned	?
• Synchronous polled	Planned	?
• Synchronous contention		
A. IBM 2780 BSC	Now	Now
B. IBM HASP multileaving	Now	Now
Geographic Coverage		
• 1979	Over 150 cities in U.S.	Over 150 cities in U.S.
• 1980	Over 300 cities in U.S.	Over 200 cities in U.S.

8.5 SATELLITE SERVICES

Over the last decade, satellite comunications has captured the interest of diverse users in business, government, and international agencies. The interconnections provided by satellite networks permit the economical and reliable transmission of voice, television, and data.

Due to technological advances in developing both launch vehicles and satellites, it has become possible to place into orbit larger satellites with expanded capacities for data transfer to and from earth stations. In addition, the size and cost of earth stations have decreased to the point where user-owned stations are now a practical consideration for a number of organizations.

Compared to conventional communications methods, satellite transmission offers a number of unique advantages. First, the cost of transmission is distance insensitive. Conventional communications methods have a cost proportional to distance. Next, satellites have a low-cost point-to-multipoint (broadcast) capability that is most expensive to duplicate with conventional techniques. Broadcasting means transmission from an earth station to a satellite will be relayed back to earth, addressed so that many earth stations can receive the transmitted message at the same time. On a terrestrial link, a message-switching service, or other computer-based services, interfacing to many land lines, would be required to duplicate this feature.

United States Services

After numerous delays to resolve complicated legal and technical problems, the Federal Communications Commission authorized U.S. domestic satellite services in 1972. After this landmark ruling, a rapid development of U.S. domestic satellite networks took place.

The first domestic satellite, Westar 1, was launched for Western Union Telegraph Co. in 1974 (see Sec. 7.6). This satellite was built by Hughes Aircraft and launched by the National Aeronautics and Space Administration. Westar 2 followed in the same year. With excess capacity, Western Union leases bulk channel capacity to other communications common carriers as well as to military and commercial customers. Currently, American Satellite Corp. leases a number of transponders from Western Union for use in its resale satellite network. Comsat General, a subsidiary of Comsat, has leased the entire capacity of three Comstar satellites to AT&T. This satellite system, in turn, is jointly used by AT&T and GTE for long-distance telephone transmission.

As mentioned in Chapter 7, the first U.S. domestic satellite communications network actually placed into operation was done so by RCA using the Canadian ANIK A2 satellite. Today, RCA's series of manufactured satellites (Satcom) are owned and operated by RCA American Communications. In addition to acting as a communications common carrier, RCA leases satellite capacity to other organizations, including RCA Alaska Communications and other common carriers.

Typical Satellite Charges

One of several domestic communications satellite common carriers authorized by the FCC to provide satellite communications services within the United States, American Satellite Corp.'s circuits are used to transmit voice, data, facsimile, and video. As an example of the cost of satellite channels, American Satellite's end-to-end rates for 30 routes per channel on an individual basis, and per channel when a large grouping is obtained by a subscriber, are listed in Table 8.5.1.

In addition to the circuit charges listed in Table 8.5.1, a cost of $28 per month per termination is billed to the subscriber. To eliminate the effects of propagation delay in data transmission via satellite, ASC has developed a device known as a satellite delay compensation unit (SDCU). This device negates the effect of the approximately 45,000-mile round trip that signals travel to the satellite and back, which normally takes between 0.5 and 0.6 seconds, depending upon the location of earth stations. Since most synchronous protocols, such as IBM's BSC, use a stop-and-wait technique to determine if previously transmitted data blocks were received correctly, a positive acknowledgment causes a wait of at least one-half a second for each block transmitted. When propagation time is high, this time waiting for acknowledgment seriously impairs the overall efficiency of the channel. The SDCU is designed to overcome this delay, and its cost to subscribers is listed in Table 8.5.2.

In addition, American Satellite offers subscribers a private satellite network via the installation of rooftop antennas on a customer's premises that will directly bounce signals off an ASC satellite to another customer location. In addition to a one-time installation charge of $10,000 for each earth station, ASC charges $10,000 for the first circuit and $2,500/month for each additional circuit. These circuits are 56-kbit/s digital channels that can carry a mixture of voice, facsimile, and data through the use of multiplexers and other devices.

TABLE 8.5.1 AMERICAN SATELLITE END-TO-END RATES

	Route	Single Channel		Route	Single Channel
1.	ATL-DCA	820	16.	DAL-SFO	895
2.	ATL-CHI	820	17.	HOU-SFO	895
3.	ATL-HOU	820	18.	CHI-LAX	895
4.	CHI-NYC	820	19.	CHI-SFO	895
5.	ATL-DAL	820	20.	ATL-LAX	1,095
6.	ATL-NYC	820	21.	LAX-PGH	1,095
7.	CHI-DAL	820	22.	ATL-SFO	1,095
8.	CHI-HOU	820	23.	SFO-PGH	1,095
9.	DAL-PGH	820 +	24.	LAX-DCA	1,095
10.	DAL-DCA	895	25.	SEA-PHI	1,095
11.	HOU-DCA	895	26.	LAX-PHI	1,095
12.	DAL-LAX	895	27.	SEA-NYC	1,095
13.	DAL-NYC	895	28.	SFO-DCA	1,095
14.	HOU-LAX	895	29.	NYC-LAX	1,095
15.	HOU-NYC	895	30.	NYC-SFO	1,095

TABLE 8.5.2 ASC CIRCUIT WITH SATELLITE DELAY COMPENSATION TERMINATING EQUIPMENT:

- Such circuits will be available to customers at normal circuit rates plus the termination charges listed below.
- The tariffed rates for Satellite Delay Compensation Termination packages are in lieu of—not in addition to—the existing $28.00 termination charge per end.

	Monthly Rate
• Satellite Delay Compensation Termination packages with 9,600-bit/s modem	$339.00
• Satellite Delay Compensation Termination packages with 4,800-bit/s modem	$264.00
• Satellite Delay Compensation Termination packages with 2,400-bit/s modem	$189.00
• Satellite Delay Compensation Termination packages with customer provided modem	$114.00

In addition, there will be an installation charge in connection with the SDCU.

- The Satellite Delay Compensation Termination packages will be subject to a six-month cancellation notice during the first year of the service period and a three-month cancellation notice thereafter.

SDCU Lease Arrangements

The SDCUs will be offered to any entity on a one-year lease basis at a unit cost of $250 per month. For orders involving quantities of three or more, the lease price for the first three units will be $700 per month and $200 per month for each additional unit.

Southern Pacific also offers communications satellite services. As an example, a San Francisco-to-New York circuit would cost a subscriber $2,760 (9,600 bit/s Digital Data Service) per month plus $39.44 per circuit in end-termination charges, or a total of $2,838.88 per month for one such circuit. On volume, other city pairs can be as low as $400/month. Also, one must add the interconnect costs between the SPC earth station and the subscriber's facilities.

8.6 SERVICE SELECTION CONSIDERATIONS

Although this section primarily examines service or facility selection from an economic standpoint, the reader should note that other factors may govern a final decision. These factors include installation cost, which should be amortized over the expected life of the transmission method selected; the time between placing an order and having service operational; the anticipated error rate on each medium; and the expansion potential of both the medium and the subscriber's requirements.

Leased Line vs. Dial-Up

In comparing leased line with dial-up telephone calls made over the public switched telephone network, several factors must be considered, including flexibility, operating data rates, reliability, expansion, and economy of usage.

With a leased line, the subscriber has his business machine at one end of the line permanently connected to the business machine at the other end of the circuit. Thus, unless special devices such as a fallback switch are employed, the terminal and its associated modem cannot be used for communications to another business machine. When the public switched telephone network is employed, the business machine operator merely dials the telephone number of the modem connected to the business machine he wishes to communicate with. When his transmission is completed, the operator hangs up his telephone and then can receive a new dial tone and initiate a call to another business machine. Thus, in a terminal-computer communications environment, the terminal and its associated data communications equipment (such as a modem or acoustic coupler) become multifunctional.

Concerning operating data rates, both leased lines and the public switched network generally permit transmissions at minimal error (1 bit in error per 100,000 transmitted) at data rates of 4,800 bit/s and below. Since a leased line has a fixed routing, it can be conditioned to permit higher data transfer rates on that medium than over the switched network. Thus, data transfer rates over 4,800 bit/s for relatively long periods of time (usually an hour or more per day) normally employ a leased line as the transmission medium. This is because, economics aside, transmission on the switched network at such a data rate would cause too many errors in received data blocks, resulting in many retransmissions that would extend the transmission time. On the switched network, under extremely noisy conditions, there would be so many retransmissions that the session would, for all practical purposes, never be accepted at the receiving terminal.

As for reliability, when a leased line experiences an outage, the subscriber must wait until the circuit is repaired before transmission can restart. For transmission over the public switched network, however, the telephone company equipment will automatically switch the subscriber around faulty equipment and lines. Thus, unless the local loop from the subscriber to the telephone company central office is affected, the user can normally redial when his switched circuit becomes inoperative and be routed around the impairment.

Requirements

To examine the economic tradeoffs between using the public switched telephone network and leased lines, let us first develop a set of requirements to be examined.

TABLE 8.6.1

Average number of calls to computer per day—2
Average call duration—50 minutes

Number of characters transmitted and received per call—5,000
Working days/month—22
Distance Kansas City to Atlanta—676 miles

Suppose our firm's branch office in Atlanta is to receive one 300 bit/s computer terminal next month and that the terminal will be used to run timesharing programs by being connected to our Kansas City computer center, a distance of 676 miles. From a previously conducted study, the following information was estimated, as listed in Table 8.6.1. Based upon this information, we can examine the economics of leased vs. switched service.

Switched vs. Leased-Line Cost

If we assume that the terminal operator dials station-to-station during normal daytime hours, we can use columns 1 and 4 from Table 8.2.1 to determine the cost of an average telephone call of 50 minutes between two points 676 miles apart. From column 1, the initial 1 minute cost is 62 cents and from column 4, the cost per additional minute is 43 cents. Thus, the cost of an average call is $(.62 + 49 \times .43) = \$21.69$. Using the provided figures of 2 calls per day on the average and 22 working days per month, total communications cost, exclusive of modems and the telephone company business line that connects the subscriber's telephone to the switched network, will be:

$$\$21.69 \text{ call} \times 2 \text{ calls/day} \times 22 \text{ days/month} = \$954.36/\text{ month}$$

It should be noted that the computed $954.36 monthly cost is an average. Some months the cost will be over that amount and some months less. However, if the subscriber's computer utilization should increase, perhaps due to new applications or a growth in business at the Atlanta office that requires additional processing power, then the cost of utilizing the public switched telephone network will similarly increase.

Since both Atlanta and Kansas City are category A rate centers, Table 8.2.4 can be used to compute the cost of the interexchange channel between those two cities. Thus, from that table the mileage cost is $252.92 plus 94 cents per mile for each mile over 100 miles, resulting in a total mileage cost of $794.36 per month. To this cost, the charge for two station terminals, one at the Atlanta office and one at the computer site in Kansas City are required, each costing $36.05 per month. Thus, the total leased line cost becomes $866.46 per month, excluding the cost of modems. No conditioning would be required since the terminal is to operate at 300 bit/s.

In comparing the cost of using leased lines vs. using the switched network, it appears the subscriber can save approximately $88 per month by installing the leased line. Since this is a fixed monthly cost, one must determine that call estimates are fairly accurate or the analysis could result in a wrong decision. Suppose only one call per day actually transpires; however, the estimate of an average call duration of 50 minutes is correct. Then the cost of using the switched network would be $477.18/month, substantially below the cost of a leased line. Note that in this comparison, the number of characters transmitted and received per call given in Table 8.6.1 has not been used. This information is only relevant for costing transmission via a value-added carrier where one part of the charge element is based upon the number of characters or packets transmitted.

Leased vs. Foreign Exchange

In this comparison we are actually comparing the use of two leased lines, one of which is connected to the public switched network. The normal employment of a foreign exchange line is to place the "open end" of the circuit in a city where several terminals requiring contention or scheduled access to a computer are located. The "closed end" of the circuit is located at the computer site. Thus, terminal operators in the open-end city dial the telephone number of that line and are then connected to the modem at the computer site, as shown in the top portion of Figure 8.6.1.

One alternative configuration to service several terminals located in a distant city (from where the computer is located) can be accomplished by the installation of a multipoint leased line as shown in the lower portion of Figure 8.6.1.

FIGURE 8.6.1   Foreign exchange vs. multipoint line

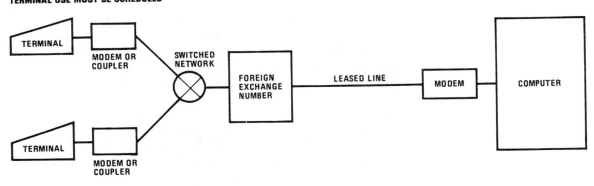

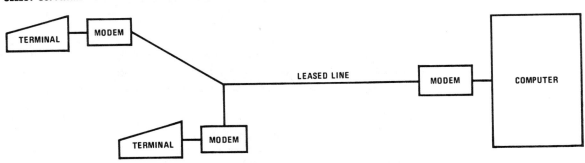

For this type of operating environment, poll and select software must be available for use by the computer, and buffered terminals capable of recognition of their address must be installed.

If we assume all terminals are near each other, then the leased-line cost for each circuit is approximately equivalent. Other cost differences between the two circuits may result from the modems employed and local telephone company costs. For the FX line, terminals could use low-cost acoustic couplers or asynchronous low-speed, low-cost modems.

For a multipoint environment, synchronous transmission, normally employed, results in more expensive terminals and modems. For access to the FX line, each dialed call may incur a local toll charge, perhaps 10 cents, depending upon the local operating telephone company. For the multipoint leased line, no such toll charge will be incurred. While the terminals that access the computer via the FX line can also access other business machines through the use of the switched network, terminals on the multipoint circuit can only access the computer inter-faced to that line.

Although poll-and-select permits all terminals to communicate with the computer at the same time, terminals using the FX line can do so only one at a time and must therefore either contend for access to the FX line or have their usage scheduled.

Switched vs. WATS

Normally, an Inwats access is used to link a number of terminals scattered throughout a geographical area (or areas) to a central computer via the public switched telephone network. Usually, the connect time per terminal is such that on an individual basis transmission via the switched network is less expensive than installing leased lines from each terminal location to the computer center. When this situation arises, the subscriber may then want to determine the cost of Inwats service in order to see if savings can be obtained by the use of such a facility.

As an example of switched network vs. WATS cost, suppose a user has six terminals scattered in the states surrounding the state in which the computer is located. Assume that each terminal will transmit 20 minutes per day to the computer, and the average distance from each terminal to the computer center is 350 miles. Then, from Table 8.2.1, the average cost, assuming calls are made station-to-station during normal business hours, is 59 cents for the first minute plus 42 cents for each additional minute, for a total of $8.57 per call. If the firm has 22 working days per month, then the cost of 20-minute-per-day transmission from 6 terminals would be 6 × $8.57 × 22, or $1,131.24 per month for a total of 2 hours per day or 44 hours per month transmission, which is equivalent to a cost of $25.71 ($1,131.24/44 hours) per hour.

From Table 8.2.7, the cost of an Inwats line for any state is $36.80 plus a maximum of $19.29 per hour for each additional hour. Based upon these figures, it is more economical for a subscriber to select a measured-time Inwats service.

Switched vs. WATS vs. Value-Added Carrier

When the services of a value-added carrier are to be considered, one of the first items to be determined is the service areas of that carrier. Today, value-added carriers service several hundred cities in the United States, providing subscribers with dial-in connections via the public switched telephone network at data rates up to 4,800 bit/s. In comparison, switched network service is available at every location throughout the United States.

Currently there are three basic components in the cost of using a value-added carrier that are billed to subscribers. These components include a terminal-connect-time charge, a character or packet transmission charge, and a host computer interconnection charge. The latter is the charge to link the central office of the value-added carrier to the subscriber's computer and to permit a certain number of terminals to simutaneously dial and connect to the value-added carrier's network and then be connected via the network to the computer.

For a cost comparison, assume that six terminals now require one hour of transmission per day and the previously discussed parameters remain constant. Thus, communications over the switched network would cost $3,393.72 per month if that medium were employed.

In trying to estimate the cost of a value-added carrier, one must estimate the number of characters or packets to be transmitted and received, depending on which method the carrier employs for billing pupposes. Let us assume that the carrier under consideration bills by characters, and its cost components are as listed in Table 8.6.2.

Let us further assume that each terminal on the average will transmit and receive 40,000 characters per hour. Thus, all six terminals would result in 240,000 characters per day or 5,280,000 characters per month. While this may appear to be a large number, as we will see, character or packet costs represent only a small portion of a value-added carrier's total cost. Thus, 5,280,000 characters per month at 60 cents per 100,000 characters would cost the subscriber $31.68 per month.

Next, the six terminals will require a total of 132 connect-hours per month at a cost of $3.50 per hour or a total of $462 for the connect-time charge component.

Lastly, the carrier's fixed charge of $800 per month will provide the subscriber with a leased line from the carrier's central office to the user's computer, and equipment to permit up to eight 110- to 300-bit/s terminals to simultaneously access the computer from any entry point in the network.

TABLE 8.6.2. HYPOTHETICAL VALUE-ADDED-CARRIER COST COMPONENTS

A. Character charge.
  $.60 per 100,000 characters
B. Connect time charge
  $3.50 per terminal hour, 110 to 300 kbit/s
C. Central office to subscriber host computer line and equipment
  $800.00 per month for eight 110 to 300-kbit/s connections

Adding the three components produces a total monthly charge of $1,293.68, which in this example is substantially less than the cost of transmission via the public switched network. If we divide the computed cost by the total monthly terminal connect time of 132 hours (6 hours per day times 22 working days per month), the cost per hour is $9.80. From Tables 8.2.6 or 8.2.7, both WATS services result in a cost per hour exceeding $9.80. Therefore a value-added carrier would be the most economical under the circumstances cited in this situation.

Terrestrial vs. Satellite

Let us examine the transmission of data both via satellite and over conventional land facilities. For the latter, numerous possibilities exist. To narrow our choices, let us assume the requirement is to transmit data from a remote batch terminal located in San Francisco to a computer located in New York City at 9,600 bit/s, 10 hours per day, seven days per week. Due to these operating times as well as the high operating data rate, use of the public switched telephone network is excluded.

We could estimate the cost of a leased Type 3002 analog circuit or 9.6-kbit/s Dataphone digital service and compare those rates to the cost of transmitting by satellite.

Satellite Considerations

Since we are only to transmit data at 9.6 kbit/s, the physical installation of a satellite ground station at the San Francisco terminal location and the New York City computer site would not be cost-effective, since these stations are designed to transmit data at 56 kbit/s and rent for approximately $10,000 per month.

From Table 8.5.1, the cost of a New York City to San Francisco channel (route 30) is $1,095 per month plus termination and special equipment charges. From Table 8.5.2, a satellite delay compensation termination, which includes a satellite delay compensation unit with customer-provided modems and a channel termination, is $114 per month per end, resulting in a total earth-station-to-earth-station cost of $1,323. To this cost add the interconnect charges to link the facilities in each city to the earth station. If we assume that the distance between the subscriber's facility and the carrier's earth station in each city is one mile and intrastate leased line interexchange charge is $51 for the first mile plus $25 for each station termination, then the total cost for satellite transmission is $1,525 per month. These cost components are illustrated in Figure 8.6.2.

In comparison, let us now examine the cost of a telephone company type 3002 interexchange channel (terrestrial) between San Francisco and New York City. These two cities are category A rate centers, hence the rates listed in Table 8.2.4 apply for costing the interexchange channel charge. The airline distance between these two cities is 2,571 miles. Thus the circuit cost would be $1,098.92 per month for the first 1,000 miles plus 58 cents per month for each mile over 1,000 miles, resulting in a monthly expenditure of $2,010.10. Adding the cost of two station terminals at $25 apiece per month results in a monthly cost of $2,060.10, which is $535.10 more than the cost of equivalent satellite service in this example.

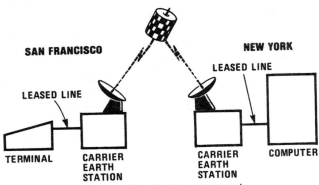

FIGURE 8.6.2   Communications via satellite: charge components

It should be noted that under present tariffs, telephone companies do not offer discounts for users requiring multiple channels, whereas satellite carriers offer substantially reduced rates when multiple channels are required by a subscriber between two common points.

QUESTIONS

8.1 Discuss the differences between using the public switched telephone network, leased lines, foreign exchange line, and WATS service. Under what condition might each service be used for data transmission?

8.2 What would the monthly cost of data transmission over the public switched telephone network be under the following circumstances:

	A	B	C
Working days/month	22	20	21
Distance, calling to called party	575	400	485
Average call duration (min.)	20	17	19

8.3 Determine the monthly cost of a type 3002 leased line based upon the following situations:

	A	B	C
Rate centers connected	A-A	A-B	B-B
Distance between centers (miles)	851	426	1,357

8.4 Determine the monthly cost of Inwats service under the following circumstances:

	A	B	C
Access line location	New Jersey	Oregon	Virginia
Monthly transmission time (hrs.)	11	250	28
Service band	5	2	3

8.5 Discuss some of the advantages obtained in using Dataphone digital service in comparison to Type 3002 leased lines.

8.6 Determine the monthly cost of Dataphone digital service under the following circumstances:

	A	B	C
Transmission rate	2.4 kbit/s	4.8 kbit/s	9.6 kbit/s
Mileage of circuit	860	2,050	1,000
Station terminal furnished by	Telephone Co.	Customer	Telephone Co.

8.7 Given the following value-added carrier cost components:

Connect time cost, $3.50/hour
Character transmission cost, $1.00/100,000 characters
Monthly central office to computer cost, $1,000.00

Determine the cost for using a value-added carrier, the public switched telephone network, and type 3002 leased lines for data transmission under the following circumstances. Assume each terminal will use an individual leased line for its connection to the computer.

	A	B	C
Number of terminals	2	3	2
Calls/day/terminal	2	3	4
Average call duration (min.)	30	20	25
Transmitted characters/call	5K	10K	20K
Working days/month	22	21	22
Avg. called to calling party distance (miles)	850	1,000	2,000
Rate center categories			
A-A	1	1	1
A-B	-	1	1
B-B	1	1	-

CHAPTER 9

INTERFACING DATA TRANSMISSION DEVICES

Chapter 5 covered the methods and problems associated with modulation of analog signals. Next, two basic transmission devices, acoustic couplers and modems, were examined with respect to their transmission characteristics and compatibility, frequency-band limitations, and noise and distortion problems. In that chapter, elementary modem interfacing and handshaking via data terminal equipment (DTE) to data circuit-terminating equipment (DCE) interface was covered. Table 5.4.2 listed EIA RS-232-C and CCITT V.24 equivalent interface pin assignments, and some of the control signals for the operation of a Bell Type 113 modem were explained.

Using the information presented in Chapter 5 as a foundation, this chapter concentrates on the interfacing of DCE to DTE over different types of transmission media. The basic circuits of the RS-232-C interface will be examined in detail, and several problems and limitations of the interface and transmission method employed are covered. Also, the Electronic Industries Association (EIA) recommended standard RS-449, which replaced the widely used RS-232-C interface for Federal government equipment connections on June 1, 1980, is discussed.

9.1 RS-232-C MODEM INTERFACE

The 25-pin interface listed in Table 5.4.2 can be rearranged into four basic groupings, based upon the function the circuit is designed to perform. This rearrangement is shown in Table 9.1.1, in which the circuits have been categorized into ground, data, control and timing, and secondary operation.

Ground Circuits

The two ground circuits included on the RS-232-C standard are protective ground and signal or common ground. Protective ground, circuit AA, pin 1, must be

TABLE 9.1.1   RS-232-C CIRCUIT ASSIGNMENTS BY OPERATION

CIRCUIT OPERATION	CIRCUIT	PIN NUMBER	DESCRIPTION	GND	DATA		CONTROL		TIMING	
					FROM DCE	TO DCE	FROM DCE	TO DCE	FROM DCE	TO DCE
GROUND	AA	1	PROTECTIVE GND	X						
	AB	7	SIGNAL GND	X						
DATA	BA	2	TRANSMITTED DATA			X				
	BB	3	RECEIVED DATA		X					
CONTROL	CA	4	REQUEST TO SEND					X		
	CB	5	CLEAR TO SEND				X			
	CC	6	DATA SET READY				X			
	CD	20	DATA TERMINAL READY					X		
	CE	22	RING INDICATOR				X			
	CF	8	RECEIVED LINE SIGNAL DETECTOR				X			
	CG	21	SIGNAL QUALITY DETECTOR				X			
	CH	23	DATA SIGNAL RATE SELECTOR (DTE)					X		
	CI	23	DATA SIGNAL RATE SELECTOR (DCE)				X			
TIMING	DA	24	TRANSMITTER SIGNAL ELEMENT TIMING (DTE)							X
	DB	15	TRANSMITTER SIGNAL ELEMENT TIMING (DCE)						X	
	DD	17	RECEIVER SIGNAL ELEMENT TIMING (DCE)						X	
SECONDARY DATA	SBA	14	SECONDARY TRANSMITTED DATA			X				
	SBB	16	SECONDARY RECEIVED DATA		X					
SECONDARY CONTROL	SCA	19	SECONDARY REQUEST TO SEND					X		
	SCB	13	SECONDARY CLEAR TO SEND				X			
	SCF	12	SECONDARY REC'D LINE SIGNAL DETECTOR				X			
		9	RESERVED DATA SET TESTING (POWER FOR							
		10	RESERVED DATA SET TESTING TEST SETS)							
		11	UNASSIGNED							
		18	UNASSIGNED							
		25	UNASSIGNED							

electrically bonded to the device or the frame of the equipment, or to an external ground. The purpose of this circuit is to ground any voltage leak and thus protect the user from being shocked if he touches the device.

Signal ground, or common ground, is circuit AB on pin 7. This circuit establishes a common ground reference potential for all interchange circuits except protective ground. Hence it is also referred to as common or return ground. Circuit AB is normally connected to the protective ground circuit via an internal wire strap. In certain situations, frame noise may be introduced by this strapping and the removal of the strap will normally alleviate this situation.

Data Circuits

The data circuits are the paths through which data is transmitted and received. The two data circuits are transmit data (circuit BA on pin 2) and receive data (circuit BB on pin 3).

The direction of data flow on circuit BA is from the data terminal to the associated communications equipment: DTE to DCE. The signals for this circuit are thus generated by the data terminal. When the terminal is not sending data or is

	INTERCHANGE VOLTAGE	
	-3 TO -25V	+3 TO +25V
BINARY STATE	1	0
SIGNAL CONDITION	MARKING	SPACING
FUNCTION	OFF	ON

FIGURE 9.1.1   Interchange voltage and conditions on interface leads

between transmitting characters, a negative voltage is applied to this interface lead to denote a marking or binary 1 signal condition. The interchange voltages that represent the mark and space signaling conditions are denoted in Figure 9.1.1.

Although data is transmitted on the BA circuit, certain control signals must be activated or set to the ON condition before data transfer can occur. The hand-shaking routine illustrated by the control signals in Figure 9.1.2 must first occur. As illustrated, the data terminal equipment initiates a request-to-send signal. If the data circuit-terminating equipment has control of the telephone circuit, it will send a clear-to-send signal back, as well as a data-set-ready signal. In response, the terminal will transmit a data terminal ready signal to the DCE. These control circuits will be discussed in more detail later.

The received data lead (circuit BB, pin 3) passes signals from the DCE to the DTE. For data to flow over this circuit, the DCE obtains a signal from the transmitting device via the connecting line. The DCE converts or demodulates that signal for transmission via circuit BB to the receiving business machine. This received-data circuit can have its state varied by the received line signal detector (circuit CF, pin 8) control circuit. When circuit CF is OFF, this condition forces circuit BB to a marking condition.

FIGURE 9.1.2   Handshaking prior to transmitting data

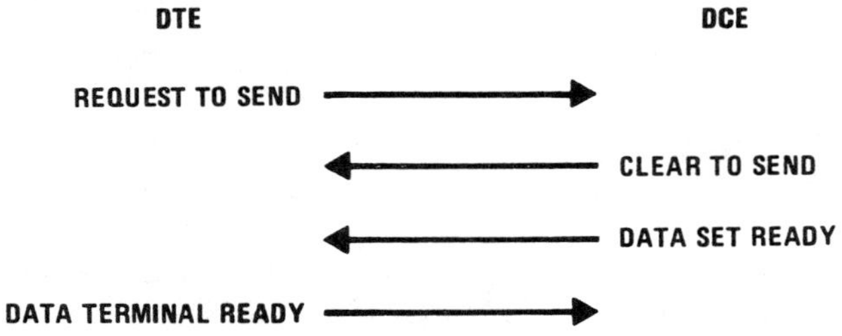

DTE   DCE

REQUEST TO SEND ────────────▶

                              ◀──────────── CLEAR TO SEND

                              ◀──────────── DATA SET READY

DATA TERMINAL READY ────────────▶

SIGNAL STATE	TRANSMISSION MODE	
	HALF-DUPLEX	FULL-DUPLEX
ON	INHIBITS RECEIVING OF DATA	MAINTAINS DCE IN RECEIVE MODE
OFF	INHIBITS TRANSMISSION OF DATA	MAINTAINS DCE IN TRANSMIT MODE

FIGURE 9.1.3   Effect of request-to-send signal on transmission

If transmission is half-duplex, the received-data circuit is in an inactive or marking state whenever the attached DCE has its request-to-send lead in ON. This is because, in half-duplex transmission, a device can either transmit or receive data at one time, but not perform both operations at the same time. To permit a transmission to be completed prior to turning the line around—in a half-duplex mode—for data reception, the received data lead is held in a marking condition for a short time after the request-to-send signal is turned OFF.

Control Circuits

Of the nine RS-232-C control circuits, request to send, clear to send, data set ready, received line signal detector, data terminal ready, and ring indicator are considered the basic control circuits.

Request to send (circuit CA, pin 4) is transmitted from the DTE and functions as a signal to prepare the local DCE, such as a modem, for transmission when half-duplex transmission is employed. This signal controls the transmission direction of the local DCE. The effect of the request-to-send signal on half-and full-duplex transmission is illustrated in Figure 9.1.3. Here, changing the condition of the circuit from OFF to ON places the DCE in the transmit mode.

This signal can be turned ON at any time as long as the clear-to-send circuit is in the OFF condition. Once the request-to-send signal is activated, if the associated DCE is ready to transmit, it will turn on the clear-to-send circuit. Conversely, when the request-to-send signal changes states from ON to OFF, this change informs the DCE to complete its transmission, then places the equipment in a nontransmit or receive mode, depending upon the device's operation.

Clear to send (circuit CB, pin 5) is transmitted from the DCE to the DTE. When this circuit becomes active, it informs the terminal equipment that the DCE is ready to transmit data. The clear-to-send signal occurs in response to data-set-ready and request-to-send ON conditions and is combined with those two signals and a data-terminal-ready signal to indicate that data is ready to be transmitted. When the clear-to-send signal is OFF, its absence indicates to the terminal that a data transfer via the transmit data circuit should not occur since the communications equipment is not ready.

The data-set-ready signal (circuit CC, pin 6) is passed from the DCE to the terminal device and indicates to the terminal the status of the local communications equipment. When in the ON condition, this circuit indicates that the local DCE is connected to a communications channel, that any timing functions required by the transmission medium have been completed, and that the local DCE is not in a talk, test, or dial mode of operation. When the data-set-ready circuit is in an OFF condition, this status informs the local DTE to ignore all circuit signals with the exception of a ring indicator "signal." If the data-set-ready signal should switch to an OFF condition during a call prior to the data-terminal-ready signal turning OFF, the data terminal equipment will interpret this situation as a lost or broken connection and terminate the call. For those modems that have voice adapters, interrupting a data call by transferring to voice coordination causes the data set ready signal to go OFF and remain OFF while voice is present.

The received-line-signal-detector signal (circuit CF, pin 8) indicates whether or not the signal being received falls within the frequency range associated with the DCE-to-DTE transmission. An ON condition signifies that the data being received is a signal suitable for acceptance by the DCE.

As an example, the ON condition on circuit CF could indicate that a 4,800-bit/s modem connected to a transmission line is receiving a signal that can be demodulated by that modem. Conversely, an OFF condition indicates that either an unsuitable signal or no signal is being received by the modem from the transmission line. In addition, an OFF condition on the CF circuit will put the received data circuit (BB) in a marking or OFF condition.

For operation in the half-duplex mode, RS-232-C places the CF circuit in the OFF condition whenever request-to-send is ON, and for a brief time after that signal goes OFF. Thus, appropriate delay times are built into DCE to prevent the loss of a line signal by insuring that a signal is turned ON in response to one going OFF. Also, sufficient time elapses between the two to prevent misinterpretation of the signals.

The data-terminal-ready signal (circuit CD, pin 20) is transmitted from the DTE to the DCE. This signal may be ON at any time and controls the switching of the DCE to the telephone line. Here, an ON condition prepares the DCE for connection to the telephone line and then helps to maintain that connection. When the signal returns to an OFF state, it removes the DCE from the line. When transmission is over the switched network, the data-terminal-ready signal cannot be turned ON again until the data-set-ready signal is turned OFF.

The ring indicator signal (circuit CE, pin 22) is transmitted from the DCE to the DTE and denotes that a ringing signal is being received from a remote station. This signal is normally used only when transmission is over the switched telephone network. All modems designed for operation over the switched network have a ring indicator circuit. For manual answering, this circuit is disabled.

To see the interaction of the previously discussed signals, let us examine the operation of these circuits when transmission is accomplished over one particular medium using a specific type of modem.

9.2 CIRCUIT OPERATION, SECONDARY AND TIMING CHANNELS

The operation of the circuits in an EIA RS-232-C modem-to-terminal interface depends upon many factors, including the transmission mode, the type of modems employed, and the transmission medium.

For an example, we will investigate the circuit operations between a 113D-type modem and a data terminal when transmission is over the switched network. The 113D modem is "answer only," single mode. Its transmitter and receiver are tuned to specific frequencies so that, by convention, an "originate only" modem's transmitter operates at the same frequency as the 113D's receiver, and the "originate only" receiver operates at the same frequency as the 113D's transmitter.

Assuming that the 113D modem has the automatic-answer feature set, when a terminal operator at a remote site dials the 113D telephone number at the computer, a ringing voltage is placed on the connected line. In response to this, indicator circuit CE is turned ON while the ringing voltage is present. If the data-terminal-ready circuit CD is then turned ON by the computer, the modem will be connected to the line after the end of the ringing interval. When connected, the data-set-ready circuit CC is turned on by the modem.

In response to the data-set-ready signal, the computer, if ready, will raise its request-to-send CA circuit, and the modem will transmit a mark frequency at 2,225 Hz. After the receipt of this tone, the originating station will transmit a 1,270 Hz tone.

If this signal is not received after 14 ± 4 seconds from the beginning of the connection attempt, an abort timer will automatically disconnect the 113D modem from the line. If the 113D receives a continuous 1,270-Hz mark tone, however, the modem turns on the received line signal detector CF and clear-to-send CB circuits, which in turn enable the transmit data BA circuit. At this time the computer can send and receive data.

This sequence of circuit operations is illustrated in Figure 9.2.1. In this illustration, time starts at the top of the Time axis, and the elapsed time increases as one goes down this axis.

Secondary Channel Circuits

Also known as auxiliary circuits, secondary circuits are equivalent in operation to their primary circuits. The transmission direction of secondary channels is independent of the primary channel and is controlled by the set of secondary control interchange circuits.

In comparison to a primary channel, transmission speed on a secondary channel is considerably slower since that channel has a much narrower band than the primary channel.

Several types of asynchronous and a few synchronous modems incorporate secondary and reverse channels. In comparison to a secondary channel, whose data flow can be either direction, transmission on a reverse channel is always opposite the transmission direction of the primary channel. For synchronous transmission the reverse channel may be used to acknowledge data blocks received without

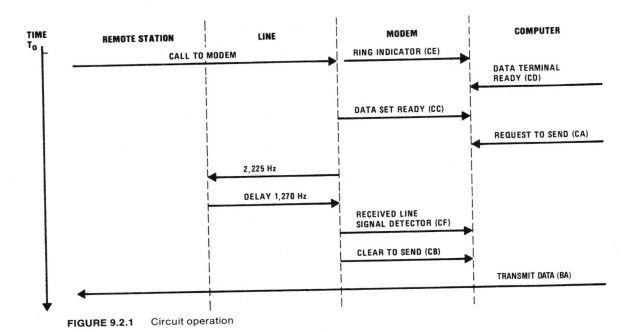

FIGURE 9.2.1 Circuit operation

having to turn around the direction of primary transmission. Secondary and reverse channels are illustrated in Figure 9.2.2.

Secondary channel operating speeds normally range up to 300 bit/s. Their incorporation into modems permits a low-speed terminal, such as a teleprinter, to share a circuit with a higher-operating-speed terminal. Figure 9.2.3 shows a modem with a secondary channel serving a remote batch terminal and a teleprinter.

FIGURE 9.2.2 Secondary and reverse channels

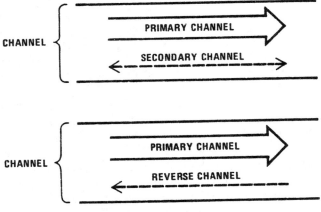

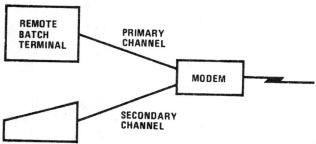

FIGURE 9.2.3   Secondary channel permits two terminals to share the line

If the secondary channel is used as a reverse channel for circuit assurance, or to interrupt condition. As an example, as data blocks are received correctly, the carrier secondary channel ON and OFF. Since the direction of the secondary channel is opposite that of the primary channel, an ON condition on circuit CA (primary request-to-send) will inhibit that condition from occurring on circuit SCA at the same time. Data is normally not transmitted when the secondary channel is used as a reverse channel. Instead, the presence or absence of carrier is used to denote an interrupt condition. As an example, as data blocks are received correctly, the carrier signal remains ON (ACK). However, if a data block is received in error and a retransmission is thus required, carrier is turned OFF (NAK) to provide the same function as transmitting a negative acknowledgment. Since a reverse channel only requires the presence or absence of carrier, secondary clear to send, transmitted data, and received data do not perform any functions in a reverse channel role.

Timing Circuits

In the EIA RS-232-C circuit assignments, three circuits are used for timing. Transmit signal element timing (circuit DA, pin 24) is transmitted from the DTE to the DCE; transmit signal element timing (circuit DB, pin 15) is transmitted from the DCE to the DTE; and receiver signal element timing (circuit DD, pin 17) is transmitted from the DCE to the DTE.

Timing signals are supplied either by the modem or by the business machine to synchronize the modem with the terminal device. This timing signal is only required for synchronous transmission, since in asynchronous transmission each start-stop bit sequence in a character synchronizes the transmission. Thus pins 15, 17, and 24 are normally unassigned when asynchronous modems are employed.

For synchronous modems, the timing source may be internal or external, so long as the frequency of the connected clock is an appropriate multiple of the baud rate to obtain the desired data transfer rate. Circuit DB is used for internal clocking, while circuit DA provides the modem with external clocking. The third timing circuit, DD, provides the local terminal with received signal element timing information. Whenever the receiver line signal detector is ON, this circuit is ON and stays ON for a short time after the receiver line signal detector signal goes OFF. The DD circuit is active whenever its voltage is positive, and turns OFF when negative.

9.3 RS-449 GENERAL-PURPOSE INTERFACE STANDARD

This standard, together with EIA standards RS-422 and RS-423, is intended as a replacement for EIA RS-232-C for the interface between data terminal equipment (DTE) and data circuit-terminating equipment (DCE) employing serial binary data interchange. This standard is intended primarily for data applications using analog networks.

EIA Standard RS-232-C is in need of replacement in order to specify new electrical characteristics and to define several new interchange circuits. New electrical characteristics are needed to accommodate advances in integrated-circuit design, to reduce crosstalk between interchange circuits, to permit greater distances between equipment, and to permit higher data rates.

With the expected increase in use of standard electrical interface features between many different kinds of equipment, it is appropriate to publish the electrical interface characteristics in separate standards. Two electrical interface standards have been published for voltage digital interface circuits:

EIA Standard RS-422,
Electrical Characteristics of Balanced Voltage Digital Interface Circuits

EIA Standard RS-423,
Electrical Characteristics of Unbalanced Voltage Digital Interface Circuits

With the adoption of RS-422 and RS-423, it became necessary to create a new standard that specifies the remaining characteristics (i.e., the functional and mechanical characteristics) of the interface between data terminal equipment and data circuit-terminating equipment. That is the purpose of the RS-449 standard.

The basic interchange circuit function definitions of RS-232-C have been retained in this standard. However, there are a number of significant differences:

1. Application of this standard has been expanded to include signaling rates in excess of 2,000,000 bits per second.

2. Ten circuit functions have been defined in this standard that were not part of RS-232-C. These include three circuits for control and status of testing functions in the DCE (circuit LL, local loopback; circuit RL, remote loopback; and circuit TM, test mode), two circuits for control and status of the transfer of the DCE to a standby channel (circuit SS, select standby; and circuit SB, standby indicator), a circuit to provide an out-of-service function under control of the DTE (circuit IS, terminal in service), a circuit to provide a new signal function (circuit NS, new signal), and a circuit for DCE frequency selection (circuit SF, select frequency).

In addition, two circuits have been defined to provide a common reference for each direction of transmission across the interface (circuit SC, send common; and circuit RC, receive common).

3. Three interchange circuits defined in RS-232-C have not been included in this standard. Protective ground (RS-232-C, circuit AA) is not included as part of the interface, to permit bonding of equipment frames, when necessary, to be done in a manner in compliance with national and local electrical codes. However, a contact on the interface connector is assigned to the shield of interconnecting cable.

The two circuits reserved for data set testing (RS-232-C contacts 9 and 10) have not been included in order to minimize the size of the interface connector.

4. Some changes have been made to the circuit function definitions. For example, operation of the data-set-ready circuit has been changed and a new name, data mode, has been established due to the inclusion of a separate interchange circuit (test mode) to indicate a DCE test condition.

5. A new set of standard interfaces for selected configurations has been established. In order to achieve a greater degree of standardization, the option in RS-232-C that permitted the omission of the request-to-send interchange circuit for certain transmit-only or duplex-primary-channel applications has been eliminated.

6. A new set of circuit names and mnemonics has been established. To avoid confusion with RS-232-C, all mnemonics in this standard are different from those used in RS-232-C. The new mnemonics were chosen to be easily related to circuit functions and circuit names.

7. A different interface connector size and interface connector latching arrangement has been specified. A larger size connector (37-pin) is specified to accommodate the additional interface leads required for the ten newly defined circuit functions, and to accommodate balanced operation for ten interchange circuits.

In addition, a separate nine-pin connector is specified to accommodate the secondary channel interchange circuits. The 37-pin and nine-pin connectors are from the same connector family as the 25-pin connector in general use by equipment conforming to RS-232-C. A connector latching block is specified to permit latching and unlatching of the connectors without the use of a tool. This latching block also permits the use of screws to fasten the connectors together. The different connectors also serve as precautions with regard to interface voltage levels, signal rise times, failsafe circuitry, grounding, etc. before equipment conforming to RS-232-C can be connected to equipment conforming to the new RS-449. The pin assignments have been chosen to facilitate connection of equipment conforming to this standard to equipment conforming to RS-232-C.

Close attention was given during the development of RS-449 and RS-423 to facilitate an orderly transition from the existing RS-232-C equipment to the next generation without forcing obsolescence or costly retrofits. It will therefore be possible to connect new equipment designed to RS-449 on one side of an interface to equipment designed to RS-232-C on the other side of the interface.

This standard is compatible with the specifications of the International Consultative Committee for Telegraphy and Telephony (CCITT) and the International Organization for Standardization (ISO). However, it should be noted that this standard is under further study in CCITT and ISO.

The U.S. is actively participating in CCITT and ISO to gain international agreement on all items.

Work is proceeding, in cooperation with CCITT, toward the development of a more efficient all-balanced "mini" interface that minimizes the number of interchange circuits. It is expected that RS-449 will provide the basis for this work.

RS-449, like RS-232-C, applies to both synchronous and asynchronous data communications networks. The standard also applies to all classes of data communications service, including nonswitched-, dedicated-, leased- or private-line service of either 2- or 4-wire circuits, and switched-network service.

With the key mechanical difference between RS-449 and RS-232-C being the interface connectors, users wishing to interconnect RS-449 equipment as it becomes available to equipment with RS-232-C connectors will require interface adapters. Such adapters will crossconnect the appropriate circuits from, say, a 37-pin plug of RS-449, assuming no secondary channel is used, to the appropriate circuits on the 25-pin RS-232-C plug. Figure 9.3.1 illustrates the DTE connector face and 37-pin plug of RS-449. An adapter is shown that connects terminal equipment built to that standard with communications equipment (such as a modem) built with a 25-pin plug under the RS-232-C standard.

FIGURE 9.3.1   Connector and adapter

RS-449 INTERFACE REQUIRES 37-PIN PLUG

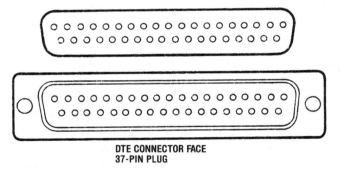

DTE CONNECTOR FACE 37-PIN PLUG

USING AN ADAPTER TO CONNECT RS-232-C EQUIPMENT

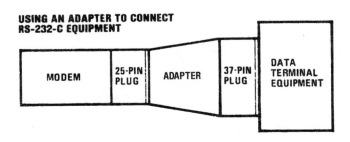

Interchange Circuits

The interchange circuits of the RS-449 standard fall into four general classifications: ground or common return circuits; data circuits; control circuits; and timing circuits. A list of the interchange circuits showing the circuit mnemonic, circuit name, circuit direction, and the circuit type is contained in Table 9.3.1.

Equivalency

A list of the RS-449 interchange circuits showing the nearest equivalent RS-232-C and CCITT identification in accordance with recommendation V.24 is listed in

TABLE 9.3.1   RS-449 INTERCHANGE CIRCUITS

Circuit Mnemonic	Circuit Name	Circuit Direction	Circuit Type	
SG	Signal Ground	—	Common	
SC	Send common	To DCE		
RC	Receive common	From DCE		
IS	Terminal in service	To DCE		
IC	Incoming call	From DCE	Control	
TR	Terminal ready	To DCE		
DM	Data mode	From DCE		
SD	Send data	To DCE	Data	Primary Channel
RD	Receive data	From DCE		
TT	Terminal timing	To DCE		
ST	Send timing	From DCE	Timing	
RT	Receive timing	From DCE		
RS	Request to send	To DCE		
CS	Clear to send	From DCE		
RR	Receiver ready	From DCE		
SQ	Signal quality	From DCE	Control	
NS	New signal	To DCE		
SF	Select frequency	To DCE		
SR	Signaling rate selector	To DCE		
SI	Signaling rate indicator	From DCE		
SSD	Secondary send data	To DCE	Data	Secondary Channel
SRD	Secondary receive data	From DCE		
SRS	Secondary request to send	To DCE		
SCS	Secondary clear to send	From DCE	Control	
SRR	Secondary receiver ready	From DCE		
LL	Local loopback	To DCE		
RL	Remote loopback	To DCE	Control	
TM	Test mode	From DCE		
SS	Select standby	To DCE	Control	
SB	Standby indicator	From DCE		

Table 9.3.2. It should be noted that the RS-449 circuit definitions may vary to a degree with the equivalent RS-232-C or CCITT recommendations. The reader should consult the RS-449 standard for additional information.

9.4 RESOLVING INTERFACE PROBLEMS

Ideally, an interface standard such as the Electronic Industries Association's RS-232-C should guarantee the interconnection compatibility of all data communications hardware designed to its specifications, regardless of the manufacturer. In practice, though, complete electrical compatibility does not always exist, even if connectors physically mate. The modems and terminals covered by RS-232-C can run into interface problems, most often because of improper signal timing or the lack of an expected command or response. Sometimes, too, difficulties can arise with products built to international standards because the international standards do not entirely match U.S. counterparts.

Once the reasons for the problems are understood, however, the solutions often turn out to be very simple—perhaps just cutting a line or adding a jumper. (Interface problems involving software or operating modes are another matter, since no standards exist in these areas.)

The RS-232-C standard defines signal functions and characteristics, cable length (limited to 50 feet), and pin assignments on standard 25-pin connectors. Compatibility of electrical characteristics such as voltage, current, or impedance usually is not a problem, because most manufacturers use standard drivers and receivers designed to meet interface standards. But there are many differences among signals in different types of modems because of speed and transmission differences.

A leading cause of incompatibilities is mistiming of signals or misinterpretation of commands and responses between two units, which can occur because the RS-232-C standard is open to different interpretations by designers with different perspectives on equipment design.

One problem arises from attempts to interconnect simple devices that fail either to produce or respond to some of these signals. A second problem occurs when unassigned lines in the interface cables are used for special functions and connected to equipment that lacks corresponding special-function pin assignments. A third group of incompatibilities is due to lack of understanding of international specifications set forth by the CCITT.

According to the RS-232-C specification, the circuits for transmitted and received data (pins 2 and 3) should be complementary, since the standard was originally intended for the interface between modems and terminals. Thus, the driver circuit that transmits data on pin 2 of a terminal should be connected to a receiver circuit feeding off pin 2 or a modem. But some of today's devices cannot clearly be categorized as either terminals or modems, giving rise to the possibility that connecting these pins may not link two circuits in a complementary manner. In such a case, the driver output of one may be connected to the driver output of the other and receiver input may be connected to receiver input, as shown in part A

TABLE 9.3.2 RS-449 EQUIVALENCY

RS-449		RS-232C		C.C.I.T.T. RECOMMENDATION V.24	
SG	SIGNAL GROUND	AB	SIGNAL GROUND	102	SIGNAL GROUND
SC	SEND COMMON			102a	DTE COMMON
RC	RECEIVE COMMON			102b	DCE COMMON
IS	TERMINAL IN SERVICE				
IC	INCOMING CALL	CE	RING INDICATOR	125	CALLING INDICATOR
TR	TERMINAL READY	CD	DATA TERMINAL READY	108/2	DATA TERMINAL READY
DM	DATA MODE	CC	DATA SET READY	107	DATA SET READY
SD	SEND DATA	BA	TRANSMITTED DATA	103	TRANSMITTED DATA
RD	RECEIVE DATA	BB	RECEIVED DATA	104	RECEIVED DATA
TT	TERMINAL TIMING	DA	TRANSMITTER SIGNAL ELEMENT TIMING (DTE SOURCE)	113	TRANSMITTER SIGNAL ELEMENT TIMING (DTE SOURCE)
ST	SEND TIMING	DB	TRANSMITTER SIGNAL ELEMENT TIMING (DCE SOURCE)	114	TRANSMITTER SIGNAL ELEMENT TIMING (DCE SOURCE)
RT	RECEIVE TIMING	DD	RECEIVER SIGNAL ELEMENT TIMING	115	RECEIVER SIGNAL ELEMENT TIMING (DCE SOURCE)
RS	REQUEST TO SEND	CA	REQUEST TO SEND	105	REQUEST TO SEND
CS	CLEAR TO SEND	CB	CLEAR TO SEND	108	READY FOR SENDING
RR	RECEIVER READY	CF	RECEIVED LINE SIGNAL DETECTOR	109	DATA CHANNEL RECEIVED LINE SIGNAL DETECTOR
SQ	SIGNAL QUALITY	CG	SIGNAL QUALITY DETECTOR	110	DATA SIGNAL QUALITY DETECTOR
NS	NEW SIGNAL				
SF	SELECT FREQUENCY			128	SELECT TRANSMIT FREQUENCY
SR	SIGNALING RATE SELECTOR	CH	DATA SIGNAL RATE SELECTOR (DTE SOURCE)	111	DATA SIGNALING RATE SELECTOR (DTE SOURCE)
SI	SIGNALING RATE INDICATOR	CI	DATA SIGNAL RATE SELECTOR (DCE SOURCE)	112	DATA SIGNALING RATE SELECTOR (DCE SOURCE)
SSD	SECONDARY SEND DATA	SBA	SECONDARY TRANSMITTED DATA	118	TRANSMITTED BACKWARD CHANNEL DATA
SRD	SECONDARY RECEIVE DATA	SBB	SECONDARY RECEIVED DATA	119	RECEIVED BACKWARD CHANNEL DATA
SRS	SECONDARY REQUEST TO SEND	SGA	SECONDARY REQUEST TO SEND	120	TRANSMIT BACKWARD CHANNEL LINE SIGNAL
SCS	SECONDARY CLEAR TO SEND	SCB	SECONDARY CLEAR TO SEND	121	BACKWARD CHANNEL READY
SRR	SECONDARY RECEIVER READY	SCF	SECONDARY RECEIVED LINE SIGNAL DETECTOR	122	BACKWARD CHANNEL RECEIVED LINE SIGNAL DETECTOR
LL	LOCAL LOOPBACK			141	LOCAL LOOPBACK
RL	REMOTE LOOPBACK			140	REMOTE LOOPBACK
TM	TEST MODE			142	TEST INDICATOR
SS	SELECT STANDBY			118	SELECT STANDBY
SB	STANDBY INDICATOR			117	STANDBY INDICATOR

of Figure 9.4.1. This problem can be overcome simply by cross-connecting the wiring between pins 2 and 3 as shown in part B.

For asynchronous operation, few if any of the control signals defined by RS-232-C are required. If there are no control signals, an asynchronous device operating full-duplex may use only three of the 25 pins: pin 2 (transmitted data), 3 (received data), and 7 (signal ground). This presents a problem if the asynchronous device is connected to a synchronous unit.

One handshaking mode specified by RS-232-C requires that data be transferred when the receiving device produces a clear-to-send signal on pin 5. (The side of the interface without the clear-to-send capability has a modem.) The problem occurs when the modem-interfaced device is not ready to receive, a state it signals by not producing a clear-to-send signal. If the terminal device cannot sense the absence of this signal and respond accordingly, then it may transmit data that will be lost at the modem. Obviously, the only way two such devices can be successfully interfaced is to add clear-to-send circuits to the terminal device.

FIGURE 9.4.1   Cross connecting

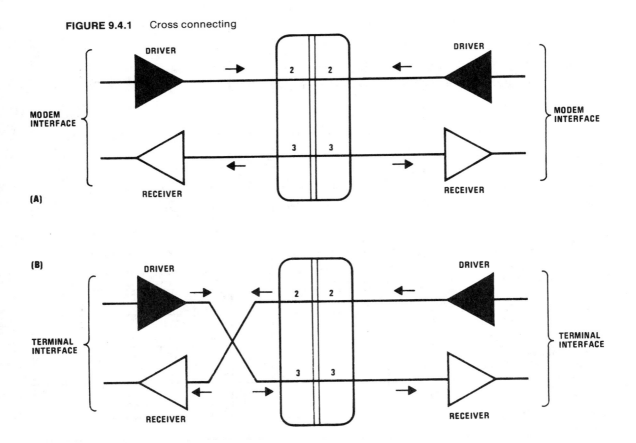

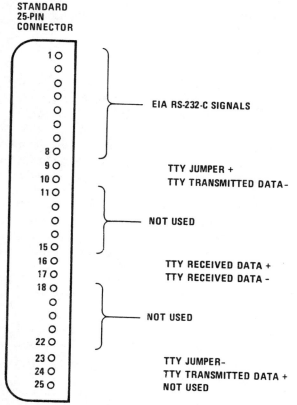

STANDARD
25-PIN
CONNECTOR

1 O

O

O

O

O ——⌐ EIA RS-232-C SIGNALS

O

O

8 O

9 O TTY JUMPER +
10 O TTY TRANSMITTED DATA-

11 O

O

O —— NOT USED

O

15 O

16 O TTY RECEIVED DATA +
17 O TTY RECEIVED DATA -

18 O

O

O —— NOT USED

O

22 O

23 O TTY JUMPER-
24 O TTY TRANSMITTED DATA +
25 O NOT USED

FIGURE 9.4.2   Current-loop modification

Unassigned Pins

A clever designer's trick that sometimes plagues users is to utilize unassigned pins—11, 18, 25, and any others not required for specific applications—for testing and special operating modes. For instance, if a modem does not provide a reverse channel capability, then all of the secondary lines (12, 13, 14, 16, and 19) may be available for other assignments. If, however, a device connected to such a modem has different lead assignments, then some aspects of its operation will be disrupted.

Such a disruption may occur when an RS-232-C connector is fitted to a low-speed, asynchronous terminal with a current-loop interface, like a teletypewriter, which requires signals only on pins 1 through 8 and on 20.

Figure 9.4.2 shows how a popular acoustic coupler is wired to such a connector. Here, the substitutions made for the RS-232-C signals on pins 9, 10, 16, 17, 23, and 24 convert the connector into an asynchronous current-loop interface. But if the terminal at the other end happens to be a synchronous/asynchronous device operating in the asynchronous mode, then it may be transmitting unneeded clock signals on line 24, making the acoustic coupler appear faulty. The solution is simply to cut the wire on the terminal's pin 24.

Not Quite The Same

A common belief is that the foreign counterpart of RS-232-C, the CCITT's V.24, is identical to the U.S. standard. This may be true in theory, but is seldom true in practice, since many countries require modems that conform to national standards that are slightly different.

One difference between the two standards is the definition of the data-terminal-ready signal (pin 20). In RS-232-C, this signal indicates to the modem that the terminal is connected and ready to interact with the telephone line, so that when the telephone rings, the modem will answer if it has an automatic answer feature. When the signal disappears, the modem will "hang up the telephone." The problem is that many nonprogrammable terminals obtain the data-terminal-ready signal by simply wiring pin 20 to a positive voltage level, so that the terminal is always ready if it is connected to the modem and the power is ON. This approach is practical for RS-232-C.

However, CCITT V.24 has two modes of operation for pin 20, specified in paragraphs 108.1 and 108.2. The 108.2 approach is virtually the same as RS-232-C, but 108.1 is intended only for private lines. If a terminal in which pin 20 is always positive is used on a private line, then the terminal will always be connected to the line. This may be undesirable because the terminal cannot be taken off line. It is possible, however, to use the 108.1 mode on dial-up lines, provided the terminal can control the signal on pin 20.

To minimize compatibility problems and to facilitate connector modifications, the user should take the following precautions:

- When connecting two RS-232-C devices, insure that the RS-232-C connection from one device is a DCE interface and the connection from the other device is a DTE interface. RS-232-C was defined to connect DCE to terminal equipment and cannot be used, as an example, to connect two terminals directly to each other.
- Check whether an RS-232-C compatible device has pin functions that truly meet those of the specifications.
- Look for a method to disable unused signals either by switches, jumper options, or software.
- For RS-232-C terminals that will be used outside the U.S. and Canada with CCITT modems, look for a way to cross-wire signals within the RS-232-C connector housing.

9.5 EQUIPMENT OPTIONS

No discussion of interfacing data communications devices would be complete without talking about equipment options. Like the interface between devices where signals from one component will affect another, options available on both DTE and DCE must be considered in tandem when interfacing such equipment.

TABLE 9.5.1 COMMON MODEM OPTIONS

Operating mode	Originate, Answer
Automatic answering	Permanently wired, No
Loss of carrier disconnect	Yes, No
Receive space disconnect	Yes, No
Send space disconnect	Yes, No
Data-set-ready (CC) Indication	Early, Delayed
Data-set-ready (CC) Indication for analog loopback	On, Off
Common grounds	Yes, No
Received data squelch	156, 9 millisecond, or none
Clear-to-send delay	180, 60, 30, 8 millisecond
Soft carrier turn off	In, Out
Transmitter timing	Internal, External, Slave

Modem Options

Most modems shipped to customers are configured with standard factory settings designed for normal optimum operation. Since different applications require different functions, users may have to change factory settings to obtain peak performance. In some situations, where a modem may have a dual mode of operation, such as originate or answer on Bell System series 100 data sets, the mode option enables the customer to specify the operating frequencies. Hence, for a point-to-point application one modem will be in the originate mode while the other modem will have its operating frequencies assigned for the answer mode. Table 9.5.1 lists some of the common options available for user consideration on many sets.

Automatic answering—For the automatic answering option, if NO is selected at installation, incoming calls must be answered manually. This can be accomplished by depressing the associated locking line key on a telephone set connected to the modem and then lifting the telephone handset. The data set can then be connected to the line by momentarily depressing the data key. Some manufacturers denote this option as key-controlled answering.

Loss of carrier disconnect—YES option will cause the modem to terminate a data call when a prolonged loss of received carrier energy is detected. For Bell System 100 Series data sets, the data set ready (CC) circuit will turn OFF 200 to 350 milliseconds after the carrier falls below the carrier detector threshold, disconnecting the telephone line. If the carrier interruption is less than 100 milliseconds, a disconnect will not occur. A carrier interrupt in excess of 250 milliseconds will always cause a disconnect.

Receive space disconnect—With YES option installed, the modem will disconnect a call after receiving approximately two seconds of continuous spacing.

Send space disconnect—With the data terminal ready (CD) circuit being turned OFF, the YES option will cause the modem to transmit approximately three seconds of spacing signals to the modem at the opposite end of the connection before disconnecting itself. This spacing signal causes the far-end modem to go "on hook" if the receive space disconnect feature is installed at that location.

Data set ready (CC) indication for analog loop—If the data terminal equipment connected to a modem requires an ON condition of the CC circuit to transmit and receive test data during an analog loopback test, the CC indication for analog loop ON option must be set.

Data set ready (CC) indication—For some Bell System 100 series modems, circuit CC is turned ON when the data set enters the data mode if "CC-indication early" is installed. If the "CC-indication delayed" is installed, CC is turned ON when carrier from the called data set is detected.

Common grounds—Through the use of the ground wire of a modem's power cord, a protective (frame) ground circuit is established. This cord also provides grounding of the modem housing and chassis. The signal ground circuit on the 25-pin connector is the common reference potential for all circuits on the interface. On most modems, signal ground and protective ground circuits are tied together by an option in the modem housing, installed as the common grounds—YES option. Tying these two circuits together is intended to provide additional protection against power line noise.

Received data squelch—This option is available on a few Bell System Series 200 modems, such as the 202S and 202T. When a modem that is transmitting in the half-duplex mode on a two-wire circuit turns its request-to-send circuit OFF, the telephone line may echo or reflect signals back to the transmitting device for a period up to the round-trip delay of the circuit. This round-trip delay or signal propagation time within the continental United States is less than 100 milliseconds. The received data squelch option prevents the receiver of the modem that has been transmitting data from delivering the reflections as data to the received-data circuit.

These reflections, or echoes, of the transmitted signal are created when a change of impedance occurs on the line. The circuit impedance acts as a mirror and reflects the signal back to the transmitting station at a reduced amplitude. Echo conditions normally occur on the public switched telephone network. However, echo suppressors are employed to stop the signal reflection by attenuating the echo and inserting loss into the echo's return path to the transmitter. While echo suppressors work well with voice transmission, data transmitted in the half-duplex mode could encounter significant problems if the echo suppressors are not disabled. Thus, when a call is placed on the switched network and a connection established, echo suppressors on the circuit must be disabled before data transmission can start. Modems can disable the suppressors by transmitting a frequency tone at 2,000 to 2,250 Hz for approximately 400 msec, which appears to the operator as a high-pitched whistle and informs him that the line is ready for data transmission.

During half-duplex operations, each change in direction will require between 50 to 250 msec for the echo suppressors to reverse direction, and this delay contributes to the total transmission turnaround time. Since no turnarounds are required in full-duplex transmission, the echo suppressors do not have to reverse direction and the transmission time is reduced.

For AT&T 202S and 202T modems, the 156-msec option is recommended for public switched telephone network, two-wire private-line, and four-wire private-line facilities. When transmission distances on two-wire facilities are less than 50 miles, the 9-msec option may be used. For distances over 50 miles, the 9-msec option is used only if the associated data terminal can ignore echoes. If the data terminal is able to ignore echoes, the no-squelch option can be used on four-wire facilities and in certain subscriber-engineered applications on two-wire facilities.

For transmission over the switched telephone network, it is impractical to attempt to optimize turnaround time if the data terminal cannot ignore echoes by using the 9-msec or no-squelch option in conjunction with 60-, 30-, or 8-millisecond clear-to-send options that will be covered later in this section. This is because the propagation time and echo delay vary widely on the switched network due to the alternate routing capability that makes the transmission distance for two calls between the same points differ. In addition, even if the data terminal can ignore echoes, it is difficult to optimize the turnaround time on the switched network because echo suppressors may be employed in the connection and their turnaround time may be as long as 100 milliseconds. If a terminal can ignore echoes and keep echo suppressors disabled by using the reverse channel of the modem, then the turnaround time can be optimized by using the 9-millisecond or no-squelch option in conjunction with the 60-, 30-, or 8-millisecond clear-to-send delay.

Clear-to-send delay—The availability of this option is similar to that of the received-data-squelch option previously discussed. This option concerns the time delay between the ON condition of a request-to-send circuit and the ON condition of the clear-to-send circuit. Bell System 202S and 202T modems permit delay settings of 180, 60, 30, or 8 msec. The delay option selected must be chosen to be compatible with the remote modem's squelch and receive-line signal-detector acquisition timing and for soft carrier turn-off operations on two-wire media.

The 180-millisecond option is recommended for use on the switched telephone network, four-wire leased line facilities with talkback, and two-wire leased-line facilities. This option is required when a 202S or 202T modem has the 156-msec squelch option installed. When used on the switched network, the 180-msec delay insures that the echo suppressors on the circuit are turned around prior to data being transmitted.

For four-wire point-to-point and multipoint facilities requiring fast startup, the 30- and 60-msec options should be used. The 8-msec option can be used in certain modems for full-duplex multipoint applications that require a fast modem startup.

Soft carrier turn-off—At the conclusion of a data transfer, when a terminal turns request-to-send OFF, transients can cause spurious spacing signals to be received at the other end of the circuit. When the soft-carrier turn-off-IN option is used, the data set will transmit a soft-carrier frequency at 900 Hz for either 8 or 24 msec for 202 type modems after the request-to-send circuit is turned OFF. The 8-msec option is used when the distant modem has a fast mode carrier detection option that permits a fast response time to the soft-carrier turn-off. When the OUT option is selected, the carrier is turned OFF in less than 1 msec after the request-to-send circuit is turned OFF.

Transmitter timing—This option is available on synchronous modems and provides a method of bit timing to the modem's transmitter. When the internal timing option is selected, the transmitter timing will be provided by the modem. An external timing option will use the DTE as the clocking source. If the modem has a slave timing option, the transmitter will be driven by the receive clock from circuit DD.

Terminal options—Terminal options vary considerably, depending upon the manufacturer and type of terminal employed. For a simple teleprinter, options may include an answerback station identification that is automatically transmitted in response to receiving a special control character to the type of stop bit (one, one and a half, or two elements) that it can accept. New terminals have up to 30 user-selected options, including interpreting received control characters and performing predefined functions for maintaining high, low, or no voltage on certain interface circuits that can be used to modify the RS-232-C transmission sequence.

9.6 IMPORTANCE OF TURNAROUND TIME

For applications where a large volume of data is to be transmitted between a terminal and a computer, or where many terminals share a common circuit, turnaround time becomes extremely important and can seriously reduce transmission efficiency. Turnaround time is the time it takes a modem to switch from receiving data to transmitting data and vice versa, and consists of a number of components. These components include the modem's internal delay time, which is the time it takes between a digital signal entering a device until the first modulated tone is put on the line; the propagation time for the signal to travel to its source; and the request-to-send/clear-to-send delay, which is the time between a terminal raising its request-to-send signal and the modem informing the terminal that data can be transmitted by returning a clear-to-send signal.

For transmissions over the public switched telephone network, request-to-send/clear-to-send delays between 100 and 200 milliseconds are typically available. These timings are greater than for modems designed to operate on private lines, because that time on the switched network must be allowed for echoes and transient signals to decay.

Modems designed for operation on private lines have short request-to-send/clear-to-send times, ranging from about 5 to 60 milliseconds. When designed specifically for multipoint private line operation, modems with short request-to-send/clear-to-send times are also commonly referred to as fast-poll modems.

Effect on Data Transfer

In order to determine the turnaround time effect on data transfer, let us assume our data transfer rate is 2,400 bit/s. Suppose we are transmitting data synchronously and our data blocks consist of 50 8-bit characters, or a total of 400 bits per transmitted block. When this block is transmitted, it takes

$$\frac{400 \text{ bits}}{2,400 \text{ bit/s}} = 166.6 \text{ milliseconds}$$

for the last bit in the block to leave the transmitter. If we assume that the modem's request-to-send/clear-to-send delay time is 100 milliseconds, then the transmission overhead is

$$\left(\frac{100}{100 + 166.6}\right) \times 100 = 37.5\% \text{ overhead}$$

Based upon the above, it is interesting to note that the 37.5% overhead is actually a minimum overhead time, since the transmission control-character overhead has not been considered. This overhead time can be reduced by enlarging the size of the data blocks to be transmitted. Thus, if the data block size is doubled to 800 bits, the time to transmit the block will double to 333.2 milliseconds if the transmission rate remains at 2,400 bit/s. Since only one turnaround time is required, overhead decreases to

$$\left(\frac{100}{100 + 333.2}\right) \times 100 = 23.1\% \text{ overhead}$$

While this blocking approach can be used to increase data transmission efficiency, the reader should be aware that the larger the data block, the longer it takes to retransmit that block when it is received in error. Thus, the user must consider additional factors, including the expected error rate of the medium, in order to determine an optimum block length for transmission.

QUESTIONS

9.1 Into what four basic groupings can the RS-232-C interface circuits be arranged?

9.2 What is the difference between protective ground and signal ground circuits?

9.3 What effect does the request-to-send signal have on transmission in the half-duplex mode and full-duplex mode?

9.4 Define the transmission directions of the following circuits:

    A. Request to send
    B. Clear to send
    C. Data set ready
    D. Received line signal detector
    E. Transmit data
    F. Receive data
    G. Data terminal ready
    H. Ring indicator

9.5 How does a reverse channel differ from a secondary channel?

9.6 Why is transmission speed on a secondary channel at a much lower speed than that possible on a primary channel?

9.7 What is the key mechanical difference between the RS-232-C and RS-449 standards?

9.8 What is the purpose of a mode option on some AT&T Series 100 modems?

9.9 If an automatic answering—NO option is selected for modems at a computer site, what effect does this selection have on terminal-to-computer transmissions?

9.10 If data is to be transmitted at 4,800 bit/s with blocks of 200 8-bit characters and the modem's request-to-send/clear-to-send delay time is 80 milliseconds, what is the transmission overhead in percent?

9.11 If a fast-poll modem with a request-to-send/clear-to-send delay time of 10 milliseconds is used, what happens to the overhead of question 9.10?

9.12 What effect on transmission overhead (question 9.10) does an increase in the size of the data block to 300 8-bit characters have?

9.13 If the transmission speed in question 9.10 is raised to 9,600 bit/s, what happens to transmission overhead?

CHAPTER 10

FUNCTIONAL NETWORK SUBSYSTEM RELATIONSHIPS

Regardless of the application, a data communications network's fundamental task is to economically and reliably connect remote terminals to a host computer, which may perform data processing activities, or to a message switch that routes messages between terminals. Once management has defined a network's operational requirements, the network analyst will find that he has available numerous options in equipment, software, and operating procedures. The major choices generally involve decisions about

- Terminals
- Transmission devices employed (couplers, modems, service units)
- Transmission medium
- Multiplexers and remote data concentrators
- Software and error-control procedures
- Front-end processors
- Fault isolation and backup features

Before any design decisions are made, some type of analysis must clearly establish the economic and performance benefits of the planned network. This analysis is known as a feasibility study. It is conducted to determine if the economic and performance benefits outweigh the cost and effort involved, or if alternative approaches to the problem are preferred.

Next, upon a positive result from the feasibility study, a communications plan is formulated. Involved in the plan are the kinds of transactions to be processed and their urgency, volume, geographic disposition of company sites, expected growth rates, and the accuracy needed.

In order to develop a practical communications plan, the network analyst must know the functional network subsystem relationships of terminals, transmission devices, transmission media, and central-computer-site hardware. In addition, hardware devices and techniques to optimize networks must be known to permit the design to be fine tuned. The focus of this chapter is on functional network subsystem relations, and following chapters are designed to expand the reader's knowledge of communications devices and optimization techniques.

10.1 TERMINALS

Because the remote data terminal is the only device in a data communications network that interfaces directly with business activity, it must be subject to several levels of critical evaluation. Management must be certain that terminals satisfy functional requirements within a prescribed cost. Operators must find them acceptable in the work environment. And planners must be sure the terminals are technically compatible with the rest of the network.

Fortunately, today the user can select from many different kinds of terminals. They range from simple, low-cost keyboard/printers—basically Teletype machines and their emulators—to rather sophisticated, high-speed terminals, which can also serve as stand-alone data processors. Typical of the latter are the proliferation of "personal" business microcomputers. This variety is due to rapid advances in terminal design, the most significant of which is the addition of programmable microprocessors.

Programmability makes a general-purpose terminal suitable for tailoring to many different business applications. It enables the terminal to take over certain data manipulations, and so reduces the amount of data sent over the communications lines and relieves the central computer of some jobs unrelated to its basic work of data processing. That is, when needed in a given situation, programmability enhances terminal performance in the business environment and can reduce communications and computer expenses.

Business requirements dictate the nature and form of the information to be sent to the computer, the urgency with which this information must be processed, and the nature and form of the processed information delivered back to the sending site. Therefore, the first thing to consider when selecting a remote data terminal is the input/output data requirements of the application. This takes any of four forms:

- Enter transaction-oriented data.
- Enter batch data.
- Output batch data.
- Retrieve—or ask for—information from a database.

Input/Output Classifications

In transaction-oriented data entry, data is keyed in at the place where the transaction occurs, and goes at once to the host computer to update the database. For example, an operator at a remote branch warehouse might key in data describing a shipment and so update the central inventory-control database immediately. (Sometimes, though, data from several transactions may be briefly stored in the computer mass memory and then processed in small batches.) Terminals suited for transaction-oriented inputs resemble those used in "interactive" or "conversational" applications, in which the operator engages in a dialog with the computer or with an operator at another terminal.

Being dependent on the operator's peak keying rate, idle time, and other performance factors, data enters the transaction terminal relatively slowly. Consequently, transaction-oriented functions employ terminals that can be classified as having slow input and slow-to-medium output.

In batch-data entry, a large quantity of data is gradually accumulated on magnetic disks or some other machine-readable medium, and later sent to the host computer as one long message. The accumulated data, usually in fixed record lengths, could represent eight hours of local business operations, but the total batch may take perhaps just 10 minutes to transmit. This type of terminal may therefore be classified as slow input/fast output.

In batch-data output the host computer quickly transmits a quantity of data to the local site, where it is recorded as fast as possible on punched cards, magnetic tape, disk packs, or—most commonly—paper. A high-speed line-printer terminal, for example, could print out invoices generated by the computer based on batch data that had been entered earlier. For this application, the terminal would be classified as fast input/fast output.

Database inquiry is the retrieval of a fairly small amount of information from a centrally situated database, for display at the local site. The classic example is an airlines reservations system. Here, the terminal has a keyboard for requesting specific flight data, and a CRT screen for displaying the answers. Often database inquiry requires a hard copy—for example, a completely filled-in airline ticket, which is produced by a teleprinter. The inquiry function has much in common with the transaction function.

To satisfy one or more of these basic data input/output requirements, manufacturers have developed several classes of terminals. Besides the keyboard/printers (or teletypewriters), alphanumeric CRT displays, and remote batch terminals already mentioned, they include such special units as point-of-sale and bank-teller terminals, as well as optical scanning units and other once-considered-exotic devices.

More Distinctions

Terminals with a slow, manual input generally fall into the asynchronous class. They have a keyboard, much like that of a conventional typewriter, and generate a coded character each time the operator strikes a key. Therefore their output is normally asynchronous, in that it depends not on a fixed time base, but on the irregular performance of the operator.

Machine-input terminals, and manual-input batch terminals that accumulate slow input data, generally deliver output data at a fast rate to the line, and use synchronous transmission. In synchronous transmission, long data blocks made up of a string of coded characters are transmitted, with each block—rather than each character—framed by a special synchronizing character.

Finally, remote data terminals can also be categorized as senders, receivers, and sender/receivers. Each has a controller and a buffer memory. The sender has a data-input mechanism, most commonly a keyboard, while the receiver has a data-output mechanism, most commonly either a character or line printer, or a CRT display. The sender/receiver consolidates the send/receive functions into one physical device as, for example, in a keyboard/printer terminal.

The buffer in an electronic terminal is a memory that stores enough bits to represent at least one character. Larger buffers store a word, a line, or even a whole message. With the development of "floppy" disks (diskettes) and integrated-circuit memories with their high-volume production, buffering cost has come down, so terminal makers can afford to install more internal buffering in their terminals. External buffers, too, like a disk pack, may be used to enhance a terminal's versatility.

Basic Tasks

The controller is a logic device—it directs all the tasks that the terminal must perform to convert, say, a keystroke into a sequence of bits for transmission on the communications link. Depending on the particular terminal, the controller may be hard wired and thus have been fixed in its functions when the terminal was designed, or it may be programmable so that its functions and tasks can be suited to one or several applications.

Whether hard wired or programmable, the terminal's controller must perform several basic operations. One of its simpler tasks is to handle the few signals that govern the input or output device. Here, the controller sends or receives signals to start up or shut down such devices as keyboards, card readers, CRT screens, character and line printers, magnetic tape drives, magnetic cassettes, and punched-paper-tape drives. A control signal also initiates translation of data from human-readable form to machine-readable form, and vice versa.

As for buffers, the controller in a sender fills this memory with bits from the input device and then empties it bit by bit in proper sequence onto a communications line. The reverse occurs, of course, when the terminal is a receiver.

Buffer control may be quite complex, when the controller simultaneously manages separate buffers for send and receive functions in the same terminal, or when the terminal employs double buffering to improve terminal speed. (In double buffering, one buffer is being filled while the other is being emptied; then the buffers reverse roles, and so on.) Control of simultaneous and double buffers, while complex, is a relatively fixed function and well within the capability of hard-wired logic.

A third task is code translation. The controller converts a character from the code form in which it was sensed by the input device, into another code form, one suited to transmission and computation, or vice versa. In a sender, for instance, it might translate Hollerith (punched card) code into ASCII code. Most modern teleprinters and CRT displays contain internal logic that directly accepts ASCII-coded information sent by the computer and translates (or generates) the coded information into characters.

In the generation of error-detection codes, the controller adds a 0 or 1 parity bit, if necessary, to a coded character before it is sent to the receiving terminal. The controller there scans the received character, including the parity bit, and its logic tells whether an error has occurred during transmission.

The character (or block, or message, depending on the particular requirement) must be stored in the sender's buffer until it is told by the receiving terminal the character has been received correctly. Otherwise, the transmission is repeated until it has been correctly received. Because the buffer cannot be filled with a new bit sequence until it is emptied, and time elapses while the receiving terminal evaluates the correctness of the received character, terminals often increase their data rate by using the double buffering mentioned earlier.

Automatic answering and transmission enable a sending terminal to be used with no operator present. Data can be "telephoned" in by an unattended remote batch terminal in response to a request made during the evening, when lower-cost night-rate telephone tariffs apply. The automatic answering equipment is not a part of every terminal's controller but can usually be obtained as an option.

The Host Computer's Overhead

However much is done by the terminal's controller, the host computer is still left with the job of handling terminal signals. This is overhead as far as the computer is concerned, since any time the computer spends other than in processing data reduces its efficiency. Remote-data-concentration and front-end-processing equipment intervening between the terminal and the host computer alleviates the host computer's data communications overhead. However, regardless of whether the terminal interfaces with a remote data concentrator, a programmable front-end processor, or a host computer, one of these devices will have to provide the data manipulation services required to interpret the hard-wired terminal's output. In the following discussion, it will be assumed the terminal feeds directly into the host computer.

For character-by-character (asynchronous) transmission, the computer must continually observe the lines coming in from the terminals. It can do this by frequent polling—that is, by asking each terminal if it has any messages to send—or by watching for an interrupt signal, which forces the computer to read the interrupting terminal's message.

After connection has been established, the computer must assemble each sequence of incoming bits into a full character, strip off the start and stop bits, translate the data from transmission code into computer-processable code, test the parity bit to see if an error has occurred, and place the character in the correct location in its memory for assembly into words and messages. Furthermore, the computer must determine whether the received character is a message character or a control character. A control character sets up a different level of activity within the computer. For example, it could indicate the end of a message, which allows the computer to disconnect the terminal and go on to other communications or data processing tasks.

In character-by-character transmission, the computer must perform each of the above activities from six to 10 times each second for each terminal in the network in turn. Comparable activity occurs for outgoing characters, which have to be handled at up to 30 times each second for each terminal. All this is a considerable burden on the computer.

Batch terminals with hard-wired controllers also place a data manipulation load on the computer. Because such terminals produce blocks of bits and operate in a synchronous mode, they do relieve the computer of some of the burden of individual character detection, validation, and removal of sync bits. Even so, the computer still has much to do to support their operation and communications requirements.

Such batch terminals as punched-card readers and magnetic-tape readers transmit information on a record-by-record basis. For example, one punched card may constitute a record. The computer must read the record, test it for accuracy, and either accept it or ask for a retransmission. For a good record, the computer must then perform necessary code translation, interpret card data for special commands, and position the data correctly in its memory.

Note that the entire record of a punched card, usually 80 characters, must be transmitted by the terminal and processed by the computer, even though the card itself may only contain perhaps 20 or 30 meaningful characters. The balance of the 80 fields on the card may be blank, contain card "deck" identification, long sequences of zeros, and other extraneous characters. Most hard-wired batch-terminal controllers cannot distinguish meaningful from extraneous information, and thus when the computer sends a record to a card-punch terminal, it must transmit all 80 fields—even though some are meaningless.

Most large host computers are designed for data processing, and not for such data communications tasks as terminal control, character and block analysis, and message assembly. Programmability has been added to terminals for one main reason: to take much of the specialized work away from the general-purpose computer and do it instead at the terminal site. As a side benefit, the programmable terminal—sometimes called a "smart" or "intelligent" terminal—also reduces the data load on the communications links.

Benefits of Programmability

What has made programmability economical and therefore feasible are the advances in semiconductor memory technology. It is now easy to build special memories, called read-only memories (ROMs), program them for a fixed application, and insert them into the terminal. The ROM is basically an expanded equivalent of hard-wired logic, which adds significantly to the functions the controller can perform.

Some terminals even contain a stored-program computer—a minicomputer or microprocessor with its functions programmed by software, just as in the large host computer. Such a programmable terminal, with its own mass memory or other peripherals, then becomes very flexible and powerful. It can serve as a standalone data processor in a local environment, besides communicating with the host computer. It also permits the development of distributed data processing networks.

The stored-program terminal, therefore, depending on the amount of electronic equipment it contains or on the creativity of its programmer, can perform a selection of the following functions:

Formatting input and output. Many normal business applications require information to be displayed or entered in a highly structured form. Cases in point are invoices or insurance applications that could best be prepared on preprinted forms, and customer records that could do with a standardized form for display on a CRT screen.

From a careful description of the form, a receiver-terminal controller can be programmed to generate the necessary spaces, tab stops, carriage returns, line feeds, and other device-control characters to properly position the carriage on a character printer or a cursor on a CRT display.

Similarly, with suitably described field formats for a sender-terminal, an operator simply enters the necessary information in each field. If the information does not fill a fixed-format field, the operator then keys in a delimiter symbol, and the controller fills in the field automatically with characters that are meaningless in the context—dollar signs, zeros, or spaces. The computer is programmed to ignore field-filling characters, but as a check will count all characters to make sure the field is filled to its prescribed length—no more and no less.

Data compression. Instead of transmitting entire field-filling and other extraneous character sequences, the controller in a programmable terminal may simply send a two- or three-character number to indicate how many filler characters were removed from the data stream. The receiver then skips that many characters. Or the terminal can send a short code giving the position (or address) in the record at which the next meaningful character or sequence starts. Removing sequences of extraneous zeros or spaces is a simple application of data compression.

More significant compression can take place if the terminal stores several fully expanded (English-language) text messages to be displayed or printed on receipt of a short code corresponding to each piece of text. Such texts might be the specific payment terms to be printed on an invoice, an account credit status to be displayed on a CRT terminal, or a full product description to be printed on an inventory status report. Since some of these texts may be quite long—perhaps 50 characters—the ability to store them at the terminal, rather than at the host computer, and call them up with a short address code, reduces line traffic significantly.

Content-oriented error detection. Though all receiver-terminal controllers check parity bits to determine whether an error has occurred during transmission, parity checking cannot tell whether the correct data was sent. However, programmable logic at the terminal, particularly if it is based on a minicomputer, can undertake a more thorough check for errors. It relies on the content and context of the data being transmitted. The programmable terminal can make sure that received data conforms to prescribed format rules. It will, for example, prevent a field that should contain alphabetic characters from accepting numeric characters. It will count characters to make sure a field is filled and, if the field is not filled, will ask for a retransmission. It will perform quantitative checks, making sure a received number does not fall outside a prescribed minimum-maximum range.

Buffering multiple batches. An effective use of the terminal's buffer storage is the accumulation of character-by-character input data, as from a manually operated keyboard. This accumulation may last for as little as a line or as much as a page of information. The terminal assembles characters into messages, inserts redundancy-check characters where appropriate, interprets control characters, and responds as necessary to the display or printer to let the operator know his input has been correctly received at the computer. Here, each time a line or a page is completed, it is immediately sent out as one long continuous message at high speed to the computer. In short, the programmable terminal performs those functions that a central computer might otherwise do for character-by-character transmission, but much less time is taken on the communications link and the computer's overhead is substantially reduced.

At a more complex level, one programmable terminal can handle batches accumulated from several input devices (keyboards). In this situation, it operates as a gathering place for what amounts to multiple keypunch operations being performed away from the central computer site. The input from each keyboard may be assigned its own area on a disk pack, with each keyboard operator perhaps performing a different processing task. When all work is finished at the remote site, or on demand from the computer, information stored on the disk is transmitted at high speed to the computer.

Local editing of data. When the programmable terminal contains a large local buffer, a complete line or page can be reviewed by the operator, who then edits the message to correct keying and other errors. When he spots an error in a displayed message, he simply backspaces the cursor to the error position and keys in the correct data. Once satisfied with the message's accuracy, he causes the buffered data to be transmitted. Local editing thus reduces the communications link and computer overhead that would otherwise have been used to handle wrong data.

Handling simple computations. With programmability in the controller, the terminal can perform computations on accumulated data locally, rather than having to send all raw data to the host computer. Typical examples of such computations are price extensions from unit prices and quantitites, quantity discounts, and tax amounts. With such local computations, the terminal can then prepare an invoice locally.

Appending local constant data. During a business day, constant data is added to each document or business transaction serviced by the terminal. The controller can be programmed to include terminal location and identification, operator identification, date and time, and security code to allow only authorized access to the terminal.

Such data is automatically added to the variable data being inputted by the operator. In a sense, appending local data is a form of data compression.

Control sequence numbering. To avoid confusion within a business operation, it often is important to consecutively number messages, invoices, and other documents. If the terminal is programmed to assign and print numbers in sequence and to use a number only when it produces a valid document, no skips will occur in numbering sequences.

Automatic restart and recovery. From the standpoint of operating integrity, one attractive use of a programmable terminal is to accumulate a local log, with checkpoints along the way, of all transactions passing through it. Then, should the data communications/data processing network malfunction, operation can be backed up to the last checkpoint and restarted, and the logged data automatically transmitted up to the point at which the malfunction occurred. This eliminates the need for the operator to find source documents and rekey information, because the terminal's "audit tape" simulates the operator's actions. When recovery transmission has been completed, the operator continues the transmission with new manual inputs.

Local operator guidance. Some programmable terminals are designed to handle a single type of operation, but others, particularly ones based on a minicomputer, can be changed by the operator to handle several different assignments during the day. In either case, the input has to be entered in a structured form. Often, the operator will make mistakes either in keying in good data or in entering the wrong kind of data for a particular field in the prescribed format. To prevent these situations and thus to improve overall efficiency, terminals can be cleverly programmed to display a specific message on a CRT screen that will tell the operator what to do next. And if the operator does it wrong, the program can even lock the keyboard, preventing any further input, and flash a message telling the operator what he did wrong and what to do instead.

10.2 REMOTE DATA CONCENTRATORS

A data communications network may grow so complex that it needs a remote data concentrator to interface clusters of terminals with the long line to the host computer. This concentrator is designed to combine many low-speed lines into one or more high-speed lines for transmission to the host computer. The functions performed by remote data concentrators vary considerably, from simple data concentration to code conversion, code compression, speed conversion, traffic smoothing, and error control. Today, a number of communications components on the market perform one or more of the previously mentioned functions. These devices are known as multiplexers (frequency division and time division), statistical or intelligent multiplexers, wideband multiplexers, and concentrators.

In hardware form, the differences between multiplexers and concentrators have narrowed considerably. Today, the functions performed and capabilities of such devices may be the same due to advances in hardware technology and the incorporation of microprocessors into multiplexers.

Initial Developments

In the late 1960s and early 1970s, concentrators not only combined many low-speed lines into a high-speed line or lines, as conventional time-division multiplexers did, but also handled more terminals than a TDM could. With its computer architecture, the concentrator could perform such functions as line servicing, code and speed conversion, traffic smoothing, and error control—in short, all the data communications overhead functions necesssary for improving line and host-computer utilization.

Concentrators

In hardware form, concentrators are implemented with a general-purpose stored-program minicomputer or with a communications-control computer designed specifically for the purpose. The difference between them, essentially, is that a minicomputer (or microcomputer) includes certain hardware, like an arithmetic multiplier or floating-point hardware, not needed in data communications, and it usually uses software to service communications lines. Conversely, the communications-control computer contains no superfluous equipment, and employs hardware for multiplexing, logical programming, and data manipulation at the line interface. Either, however, can be programmed to implement specific functions required in a particular network and can be readily modified to suit changes and growth. And each contains extensive memory in which input data can be temporarily stored.

Code and Speed Conversion

Any fairly large data communications network contains a variety of terminals operating at different speeds and in different code formats. Transmitting this intermix over a high-speed line to different ports in the host computer again places a severe overhead burden on both line and computer. Instead, the programmable concentrator can convert both speeds and codes at a relatively local level. Concentrators contain a hardware interface that accommodates such standard terminal speeds as 110, 134.5, 150, 300, and 1,200 bit/s.

This hardware, in combination with suitable software, detects the incoming speeds prior to reading the data, and executes code and speed formatting. For example, it will strip out start-stop bits from asynchronous codes—a procedure that by itself improves line utilization by about 20%—and will arrange mixed codes into a synchronous bit stream, with a fixed format suited to the host computer. In this manner, one computer port can service a variety of terminal speeds, instead of a separate expensive port being needed for each speed.

The concentrator's code- and speed-conversion capability has several advantages. It allows users in remote cities to dial up the computer, through the concentrator, and insert data from various terminals operating at any common speed. It permits the concentrator to undertake message switching between terminals operating with different speeds and codes. Furthermore, it allows for network expansion without disturbing the host computer's software or hardware, and permits a new, more efficient type of terminal to be substituted for another without any modification at the host computer installation.

When implementing line servicing and code and speed conversion, the concentrator uses a special form of memory called a buffer. Each input channel to the concentrator has its own buffer. This memory accumulates one or more characters that are then read into the concentrator's fast internal-core memory, which performs immediate processing of the data streams.

The concentrator also has mass memory—usually disk packs or drums—in which it holds data for long time intervals, as may be needed for traffic smoothing and for saving data in case of temporary outages of the line. The concentrator also has output buffers to interface the accumulated high-speed data stream onto the line between the concentrator and the computer. Often, these output buffers serve instead of software to implement error-control procedures. Consequently, how much and what kind of memory is needed depends on two major functions of remote data concentration—traffic smoothing and error control—both of which have to be carefully matched to user requirements.

Traffic Smoothing

Conventionally, network planning includes an analysis of traffic to be carried from the terminals to the computer and to other terminals. Peak load occurs at certain times of the day, and will determine the number of high-speed lines needed to carry the peak traffic. But if this peak-load determination assumes all terminals will operate simultaneously at their full rated speeds, the network may be overspecified.

Many terminals, particularly the manually operated low-speed keyboard types, may be connected to the line, but there will be scattered intervals during which operators will not be hitting the keys. Thus, the network's actual data throughput will be less than rated capacity. Therefore, with the traffic-smoothing function made available by adding mass memory to the concentrator, the fully utilized average speed on the line to the computer can be less than the sum of the rated speeds of the terminals going into the concentrator.

For traffic smoothing, the mass memory acts as a temporary reservoir for bits entering the data concentrator when the total input rate is higher than the output rate to the line. When traffic slows, stored messages leave the memory for their destinations. That is, properly designed traffic smoothing takes care of the effect of random variation in terminal traffic, and assembles the message completely in the memory before transmission to assure full utilization of the high-speed line.

Even though the memory size may be economically selected for some assumed peak traffic load, this load may be exceeded from time to time. In this case, the concentrator, under software control, will have to be able to raise a busy signal to incoming terminals to prevent them from transmitting.

Besides providing maximum utilization of the line to the computer during peak load periods, the mass memory can aid integrity. It can store one or more consecutive outgoing data blocks as needed for a request-for-retransmission error-control procedure, and it can store incoming terminal messages during an outage on the line between the concentrator and the computer.

Outages occur for many reasons. For instance, the common carrier may have to switch the primary leased line to a backup line when trouble arises. A Bell System document defines two types of outages: a hit, lasting less than 300 milliseconds (as might happen from a lightning strike), and a dropout, lasting 300 milliseconds or more. A dropout of 300 milliseconds on 4,800-bit/s lines means a loss of 1,440 bits. The loss of so much data, which could have originated at many different terminals, could upset company operation—unless the bits are retained within the concentrator's memory for retransmission in case of an outage.

The mass memory can also be made large enough to implement a store-and-forward feature, particularly desirable in networks handling considerable traffic between terminals. With this feature, the sending terminal does not have to wait for a busy receiving terminal to finish a call and hang up. The store-and-forward memory acts as a temporary receiving terminal. Then, for example, the line protocol can allow each "free" terminal to request messages addressed to it, if any, that are stored in the concentrator's mass memory. The feature may also be desirable for data communications networks requiring especially high operational certainty. Here, the need may be not only to forward messages but also to store all traffic for up to 24 hours, to provide repeats of messages that may have gotten lost, or to retain data until an audit of the day's work has been completed.

Error Control

One of the main benefits of using a remote data concentrator is that it can check data coming in from all terminals for errors and add a checking code to traffic between the concentrator and the host computer. That is, if the concentrator detects an error, it can request retransmission of a message over a short link, without involving the host computer. Moreover, the corrected messages can be sent in long, economical blocks over the high-speed line to the computer.

Error detection and control can be implemented using several techniques, such as automatic request for repeat (ARQ) and forward error correction (FEC).

One thing all these procedures have in common is that extra coding bits are added to the data block. These redundant bits, which can range from a simple parity bit to perhaps one-third redundant bits in a forward error-correction method, require memory to store messages temporarily while they are being analyzed for proper coding and decoding. An extensive memory is available in remote data concentrators at a relatively low cost per bit.

Error control can be implemented by software or hardware. For the commonly used cyclic redundancy check, for instance, special dedicated hardware is assigned to each line. Although such hardware raises the concentrator's installed cost, its advantage is that checking is done in real time with no software overhead required at the data concentrator. Software implementation reduces the concentrator's cost, but adds a burden to the computer within the concentrator. For example, a single

4,800-bit/s link controlled by a concentrator with a 1.8 microsecond memory cycle can use up to 10% of available real time for performing the checking function by software. The decision whether to use hardware or software error control will fall out as part of the overall technical and cost analysis of the network requirements.

Multiplexers

As previously mentioned, there are four types of multiplexers: frequency division, time division, wideband, and statistical or intelligent. While there are significant differences between the first three types of multiplexers and concentrators, statistical multiplexers are based upon microprocessors and today perform the same functions of most concentrators at a fraction of the cost. Also, the use of multiplexers maintains network transparency—not requiring any programming changes. This is usually not true for concentrators. While the specific capabilities and differences between devices will be covered later, what is most important is to recognize the types of data sources that can be concentrated at remote locations for transmission to the host computer, as illustrated in Figure 10.2.1.

Concentration Sources

Figure 10.2.1 shows six examples of data sources that may be concentrated. In part A, a multiport line connecting four remote terminals may be serviced by the data concentrator. In part B, a terminal on a point-to-point line is directly interfaced to the data concentrator. Parts C and D illustrate the concept of "remultiplexing" or "recombining." In parts C and D, data is first concentrated by time- or frequency-division multiplexers for transmission to a hub area where the data concentrator is located. At the hub area, additional data sources are combined with the previously multiplexed data into one or more high-speed composite channels for transmission to the host computers. Local terminals may be directly connected to the concentrator, as illustrated in part E. Part F shows how many terminals can connect to the concentrator by using the public switched telephone network as the initial transmission medium.

10.3 FRONT-END PROCESSORS

When computer-based data communications networks began coming into use in the 1960s, the preferred interface between the host computer and the communications lines was the hard-wired transmission controller—notably IBM models 2701, 2702, and 2703 (or 270X). Occasionally even then, small computers, called data communications preprocessors, were installed at the front of the host computer by such computer makers as Burroughs and Digital Equipment Corp.

In 1969, several minicomputer makers began to advocate actually replacing the hard-wired units with programmable front-end processors. The idea took hold so well that IBM developed the model 3705—and more recently, the 3725—series of programmable communications controllers.

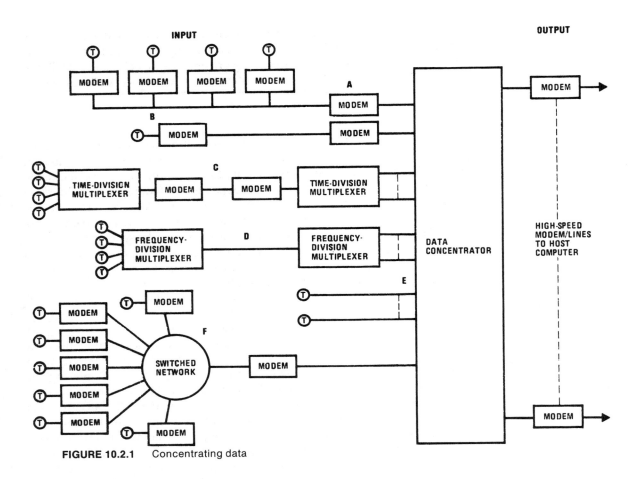

FIGURE 10.2.1 Concentrating data

A programmable front-end processor (PFEP) today may cost less than a hard-wired controller. Its real advantage, however, is its ability to free the host computer's internal memory, software, and execution time of much of the burden of data communications. First, compared with the hard-wired unit, the PFEP makes much less demand on the host computer for line control. Second, being far more versatile than the hard-wired unit, the PFEP takes over such data communications tasks as polling, code conversion, formatting, and error control.

In a well-designed data processing configuration, with the computer operating in a batch data processing mode, average computer utilization is about 75% to 80%. The balance of 20% to 25% has to be left available as a reserve for servicing peak loads. But adding a data communications mode increases the average load by perhaps another 20%, eliminating the reserve capacity.

In this situation, if the extra load is handled by upgrading the host computer to a larger mainframe or more memory or both, thousands of dollars will be added to the cost of the setup. But when retaining a peak-load reserve is accomplished by adding a PFEP, costs are kept relatively low.

Today, only the simplest data communications networks employ hard-wired controllers. But the line-control discipline implemented by the hard-wired controller is so thoroughly embedded in the technology of computer-based data communications that the front-end processor was initially programmed to emulate the hardwired controller.

Later, the evolutionary development of front-end processors resulted in the transfer from the host computer to the FEP of most, if not all, of the software related to specific data communications functions—as illustrated in Figure 10.3.1. The result of this transfer was to make the network managed by the processor appear to the host computer almost like a single input/output device that is ideally compatible with the design and operation of the host computer.

Serial Bits Into Parallel Bits

A typical data communications network includes several types of terminals as well as multiplexers and perhaps a remote data concentrator, operating asynchronously and synchronously and with several codes and speeds. Thus, when all bits in all characters in all messages converge at the central computer site, the host computer is confronted with a random, interleaved, and intermittent data stream from all on-line terminals and other devices.

The host computer is not designed to process these diverse inputs directly. The bits composing a character are entered one after the other at the terminal and continue as a series along the transmission link to the computer. But the host computer takes in all the character bits in parallel, at one time.

In computer terms, this bit-parallel character is called a byte. Moreover, the host computer can accept bytes at a rate at least 1,000 times faster than characters come off a high-speed voice-grade line. It would be wasteful for such a machine to spend its time, worth perhaps $5 to $20 a minute, on slowly accumulating bits and converting them into bytes.

Instead, this job is done by hardware registers in the interface. There, each serial-bit character coming from a given terminal is directed into that terminal's interface channel and converted into a parallel byte for the computer. The computer, in turn, temporarily stores that byte in a dedicated address space in its internal memory, from which the byte, or character, moves either to another area in internal memory or to a secondary memory that accumulates words and messages. One address space is needed for each line.

All this the hard-wired controller does under control of communications programs stored in the host computer, as illustrated in Figure 10.3.1, part A. When the processor is used only as an emulator (Figure 10.3.1, part B), it operates under control of the same communications software and has as many channel addresses between the host computer and the processor as there are lines into the processor.

For the true front-end processor, note that just one channel (Figure 10.3.1, part C) is used by the processor to communicate with the host computer. This means

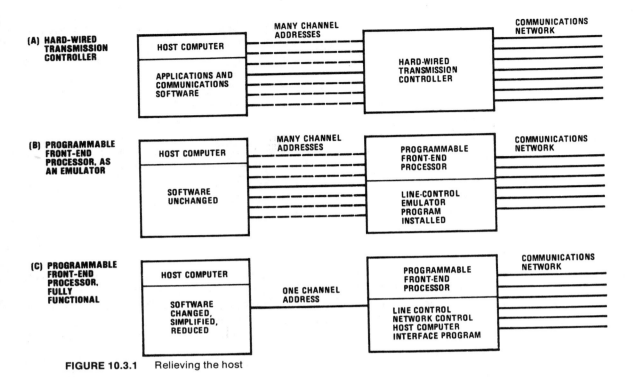

FIGURE 10.3.1   Relieving the host

that only one address space is needed in the host computer, leaving more space for use by other peripherals. Also, the access-method program, which "connects" input lines to the application program, is simplified, since the host computer interfaces with only one line to the processor.

Acting solely as an emulator, the processor offers no real economic advantage since the data communications overhead still burdens the host computer. This overhead consists of extensive data manipulation, or preprocesssing, that must be accomplished by the host computer before it can actually operate on the messages. These preprocessing programs require host-computer execution time and internal memory, both of which may be in short supply in a given application.

When most of the overhead is transferred out of the host computer and into the processor, the front-end processor will, among other things:

• Poll the input and output devices to determine whether an information transfer should take place.

• Restructure incoming data to more compact forms to increase host-computer input efficiency.

• Convert data to the code most suited to the host computer.

• Check incoming data for errors. Reject data blocks if errors are present.

• Route messages from one terminal to another. That is, perform message switching without the data having to enter the host computer at all.

No Channel Limitation

Conserving the host computer's internal memory and execution time is not the only reason for preferring a front-end processor to a hard-wired transmission controller. Another is that the processor's programmability makes it easier to change the network—when, for example, substituting one type of remote terminal for another—without having to make actual wiring changes at the host computer. A third reason is that a minicomputer, the kernel of the front-end processor, is designed to handle more, and more-varied, types of input and output devices than is the large computer, which is primarily designed to process large batches of data rapidly.

Thus, in its data communications mode using a hard-wired controller, the host computer may be restricted in the number of lines it can handle either by the limit of the computer's channel addresses (address space) or by the fixed number of channels available on a particular hard-wired controller. In either case, the installation is channel limited, not throughput limited.

The minicomputer, on the other hand, is not channel limited but throughput limited. By way of example, if the minicomputer has an instruction execution time of 1 microsecond, it can perform 1 million instructions each second. Suppose that sampling a line to tell if a pulse is a 1 or a 0 takes 25 instruction times and that to define the start and stop edges of a bit's pulse, each bit is sampled eight times. Thus, each bit uses 200 instruction times. Therefore, the minicomputer can service this throughput as eight (input or output) lines at 600 bit/s, 30 lines at 150 bit/s, 45 lines at 110 bit/s, or some combination of speeds that does not exceed 5,000 (1 million ÷ 200) bit/s. More than likely, assuming a random traffic pattern, the processor could handle even more lines. Moreover, if network analysis indicates that the instantaneous data rate may exceed 5,000 bit/s, then the peak data can be stored at the processor, in a mini disk pack, for inputting (or outputting) when traffic slows down. This small mass memory can also augment the host computer's larger memory.

However, most minicomputers have inexpensive hardware interfaces to perform serial-to-parallel conversion of bits to bytes. Depending on the particular minicomputer, throughput can thus be increased by 5,000 to 20,000 bytes, or characters, per second.

The whole business of a programmable front-end processor unburdening a host computer is easy to grasp. The practical problems lie in performing a technical and economic analysis to assure that a processor of adequate size, including all necessary peripherals, is specified. Then one must manage software modifications to keep abreast of changing network requirements, such as new terminals needing different protocol support. The hardware and software relationship between a front-end processor and a host computer is illustrated in Figure 10.3.2.

10.4 NETWORK INTEGRATION

For the network analyst to plan efficiently for the addition of terminals to an existing network, or to design a new network, the provisions for integration of the

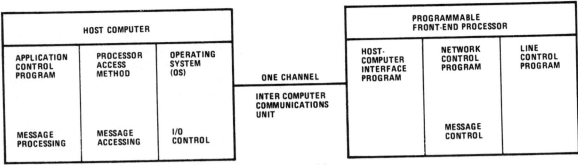

FIGURE 10.3.2   Processor-host computer interrelationship

components and their limiting factors must be examined. To do so, one can first begin by exploring the methods used to connect remote terminals to a host computer.

Individual Service

As the first example, let us assume that every terminal is given individual access to the host computer, as illustrated in Figure 10.4.1. If each terminal transmits and receives large volumes of data and must be connected on line to the computer most of the working day, then this configuration could be an optimum one. However, very few, if any, terminals are connected on line during the entire working day, and alternate approaches can be considered to service such terminals, as illustrated in Figure 10.4.2.

FIGURE 10.4.1 Individual access

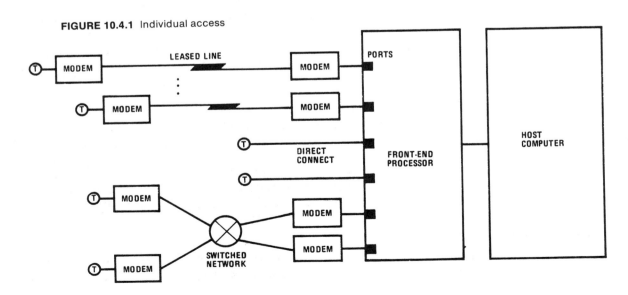

Access Contention

In comparison to the first configuration, access contention in Figure 10.4.2 employs a multipoint circuit and a rotary switch to reduce the number of ports required on the front-end processor to service a larger number of terminals than in the first example. These ports or channels are the physical interfaces through which communications devices are connected to the front-end processor. Not only are such ports expensive, but there is a physical limit to the number of such ports per front-end processor. Once that number is reached, the network planner must either plan for an additional processor or implement ways to reduce port requirements. All this time, the planner must continue a high level of service to each terminal that requires access to the network.

By the use of appropriate poll and select software, the two leased lines of Figure 10.4.1 can be converted into a multipoint circuit as shown in Figure 10.4.2. If the locations of the terminals are right, not only will port requirements be reduced from two to one, but the total length of the leased line required may be reduced. Since a poll and select protocol is now employed, each terminal on the multipoint line contends for access to the computer, which is the price one must pay for this type of connection. If the terminals used are CRTs operating at 2,400 or 4,800 bit/s, then the terminal operator will experience "direct access" to the computer because of the high data transfer rate and fast-polling power of the front end. Only when perhaps five to 10 or more terminals share a multipoint circuit will an operator notice degraded performance, such as increased response time.

The lower portion of Figure 10.4.2 shows a two-position telephone company rotary switch installed at the front-end processor local business lines to connect those lines to two dial-in modems. This rotary facilitates a number of terminal

FIGURE 10.4.2 Contending for access

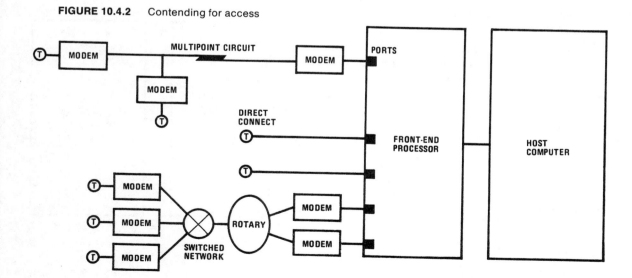

operators dialing the local numbers for a connection to the computer via the public switched telephone network. Basically, the rotary acts as a stepping device. If the number that is dialed is busy, the rotary will step the calling party to the next number on the rotary, alleviating the calling party from hanging up and dialing the next telephone number. (Refer to Section 5.4, Operations.) While only two telephone numbers would be associated with the two dial-in modems shown, imagine the operator inconvenience if there were 10 or 20 dial-in lines to try for each connection attempt.

Assuming each terminal that uses the switched network only transmits data for a portion of the business day, then some number over two (say four or five) terminals can use the two dial-in lines on a contention basis before waiting times become excessive. The methodology to determine delay times and how to reduce such delays by adding more "servers" or dial-in connections is called queuing theory.

Data Concentration

Another method that can be used to connect terminals to a computer through a network is by first concentrating the data from a number of terminals for retransmission over one or more common high-speed lines to the computer, as illustrated in Figure 10.4.3. While only two concentration devices, a concentrator and a multiplexer, are illustrated, a number of devices are now available for the user. These devices include frequency- and time-division multiplexers, wideband multiplexers, multiport modems, line- and modem-sharing units, as well as concentrators and intelligent multiplexers—and are covered in more detail in Chapter 11, Methods of Data Concentration.

FIGURE 10.4.3   Data concentration

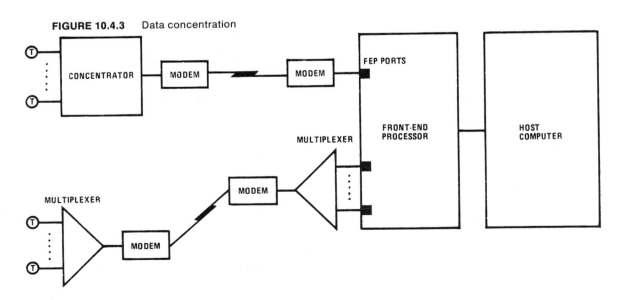

In Figure 10.4.3, the key differences between a multiplexer and a concentrator are recognizable. Here, the concentrator can group data into a format that the front-end processor is capable of processing, and may require only one front-end-processor port. Since the front-end processor is normally capable of processing the concentrated data, no complementary device is required at the central computer site.

When a multiplexer is used, normally the routine for data concentration is not compatible with the software in the front-end processor, so another multiplexer, functioning as a demultiplexer, must be employed at the computer site. This demultiplexer reverses the data concentration process and regenerates the individual terminal data streams from the composite high-speed line, feeding each data stream into a separate port on the front-end processor.

Although the use of a concentrator can reduce the physical number of ports required by the front-end processor, the reduction will be accompanied by additional software processing requirements for the processor. These and additional trade-offs between the use of different data concentration devices will be discussed in Chapter 11.

QUESTIONS

10.1 What is the difference between a feasibility study and a communications plan?

10.2 List some of the functions an "intelligent" terminal might perform that normally a "dumb" terminal cannot.

10.3 How might an "intelligent" terminal be used to reduce the host computer's overhead?

10.4 What general functions does a concentrator perform? What additional functions might a concentrator be programmed to do?

10.5 When we talk about front-end processors, we normally speak about the functions they perform in reference to off-loading the software burden of the host computer. Discuss some of these functions that can be off-loaded.

10.6 Discuss the key differences between a multiplexer and a data concentrator.

10.7 What are some of the common functions of multiplexers and concentrators?

CHAPTER 11

METHODS OF DATA CONCENTRATION

11.1 INTRODUCTION

Today, the network analyst can select from over 10 types of devices to concentrate many low-to-medium-speed data streams into one or more high-speed aggregate data streams for retransmission to a host computer. By combining a number of data streams from a geographical area into one high-speed link, one may be able to reduce either the number of long leased circuits or the expense of long-distance calls on the public switched network. If the cost of the special equipment required for data concentration is less than the savings that can be realized through a reduction in circuit transmission costs, then, from a cost standpoint, the use of such equipment is justified.

In addition to economics, performance parameters must be examined. In many uses, data concentration equipment may reduce the number of line errors. This is because the concentration equipment may employ error-checking features. Here, data from a number of terminals is grouped into blocks of data for transmission, and a block check character is computed and appended to the block. At the receiving site, another device checks received data blocks by recomputing its block check character and comparing it with the transmitted block check character. If the check characters do not match, the receiving concentration equipment will request a retransmission (NAK) of the data block. This sequence is invisible to the terminal operator, who will not be aware that the long-distance circuit was experiencing line hits, and the same blocks of data were being transmitted more than once. If, instead, the terminal operator had a direct (i.e., no error control) long-distance transmission patch to the computer, these error conditions would become visible. This is especially true when using asynchronous terminals whose printed data would appear garbled, since such devices have no provision for error checking and automatic retransmission before printing.

11.2 MULTIPLEXERS

One of the most common types of concentration devices is the multiplexer. Data communications users usually multiplex their high-capacity traffic on leased voice-grade lines between major data-accumulation centers so that they can transmit large amounts of data at reasonable cost. By multiplexing, one high-speed link can carry the same amount of traffic that several low-speed ones could handle without it.

By taking advantage of the rate structures for the various types of leased lines available from common carriers, the user can lease one high-speed link for much less than a number of low-speed lines would cost. More than likely, the savings realized from multiplexing traffic into one high-speed line would pay for the multiplexing equipment.

If a preliminary analysis indicates that multiplexing may save money, consideration must then be given to selection of either frequency-division multiplexing (FDM), time-division multiplexing (TDM), or a combination of the two. As the name implies, FDM achieves its concentration by dividing the telephone-line frequency band into smaller frequency segments. TDM, on the other hand, allocates time segments to the various traffic channels. Generally, FDM is used when one line must service many terminals in a local area through a multidrop arrangement. In contrast, TDM is usually used in long-distance point-to-point configurations, typically between major cities.

FDM

In FDM, a voice-grade line with a certain bandwidth, typically 3,000 Hertz, is split into narrower channel segments, often called derived channels or data bands. Each channel, tuned to a specific frequency, has a transmitter at one end and a receiver at the other end. The width of each frequency band determines the data-rate capacity of the subchannel. For example, the band can be made narrow enough to pass only 75-bit/s data streams or wide enough for 150 or 300 bit/s, if required by the terminal speeds. "Guard" bands separate the data bands to prevent data on one channel from interfering with data in an adjacent channel.

FDM normally provides full-duplex operation on a four-wire circuit. Each channel set (of equipment) has a transmit and a receive section. All transmit tones go out on one pair of wires, and all receive tones come back on a second pair. However, FDM can also operate full duplex on a two-wire circuit. For example, with 24 channels available on the line, one channel set is tuned for line channel 1 to transmit, and channel 13 to receive; another for channel 2 to transmit, and channel 14 to receive; and so on. Here, the number of data channels is halved, but this technique saves the difference in costs between four-wire and two-wire lines in a network servicing a small number of full-duplex terminals.

TDM

Time-division multiplexing's time segments utilize the full bandwidth of the line. A typical TDM network configuration is shown in Figure 11.2.1. Note the optional

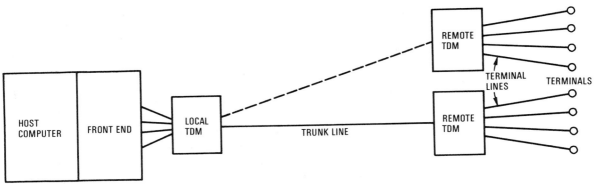

FIGURE 11.2.1 Typical multiplexer configuration

additional remote TDM. Several operator terminals are connected to the ports of the remote TDM, and the local TDM is connected to the host computer's ports. Alternatively, if the front-end processor is programmed to act as the local TDM, then just the remote TDM is required.

The high-speed-trunk line's (Figure 11.2.1) transmission rate equals the maximum aggregate of data rates available to all the terminal (or host) lines. For example, if the trunk capacity is 9.6 kbit/s, then no more than four 2.4 kbit/s terminal lines can be connected.

Each of the TDM's time segments is assigned a character (or bit) from each low-speed port. At the trunk's other end, the process is reversed. The bit stream is demultiplexed and the characters (or bits) are assembled into the messages as they appeared at the low-speed ports of the sending (remote or local) TDM.

The character-interleaved bit stream contains the bits in each character in a continuous data stream, the multiplexer having assembled a full character into one frame for transmission. In the bit-interleaved bit stream, the multiplexer takes one bit from each source device, in turn, and combines them into a frame for transmission. Since character interleaving requires the multiplexer to assemble bits into a character before multiplexing, the buffer area is larger than for bit interleaving.

The conventional TDM is a hard-wired (non-programmable) device that allocates a fixed portion of the high-speed trunk's bandwidth to each of its low-speed channels. Since terminal devices are rarely in operation full time, the fixed-allocation scheme uses the trunk's capacity inefficiently. When a terminal has nothing to send, its allocated time segments—carrying only null or fill characters—are still part of the data stream.

Configuring the Network

A more efficient device—the intelligent or statistical TDM (STDM)—has just about obsoleted the conventional TDM.

A local STDM communicates with a remote one by using a higher-level full-duplex protocol, such as high-level data link control (HDLC), synchronous data link control (SDLC), or Digital Equipment's digital data communications message protocol (DDCMP)—or variations on one or other of them. The line is typically a 9.6 or 19.2 kbit/s trunk. The possible interface arrangements include:

- Two or more hosts to one local STDM;
- One or more local STDMs to two or more remote STDMs (Figure 11.2.1);
- Use of the STDM as a network node, with connections to high-speed remote job entry (RJE) equipment, in addition to conventional user terminals and to other multiplexers.

If a conventional remote TDM is connected to a 9,600 bit/s trunk and services user terminals rated at 110 bit/s, the configuration can support 9,600 divided by 110, or nearly 90 terminals. But it can be determined statistically that, at any one time, a certain number of terminals, say 20, are going to be idle. As pointed out earlier, the conventional multiplexer continues to allot high-speed line segments to these idle terminals, sending nulls on the trunk to the local TDM, then on to the host for discard.

Statistical multiplexing eliminates the nulls by allocating trunk line segments only to terminals actually transmitting data. The TDM is driven by time; the STDM is driven by data. Since it was shown in the example that, statistically, 20 terminals are idle at any one time, at least 20 terminals may be added at the remote STDM without exceeding the capacity of the trunk. The local STDM will, of course, have to sort out and keep track of host port assignments, since the number of ports at the host remains the same (90 in the example). However, the determining statistics represent only normal conditions. There will obviously be situations when more terminals will seek access than there are host ports available.

Two factors determine if a terminal is to gain access to a host port: availability of the port, and availability of bandwidth on the trunk. Port contention will likely take place during times of peak traffic. And transmission delays will result when a terminal operator will hear a busy signal and will have to wait for an available port. Port contention may be considered the penalty paid for the conveniences of statistical multiplexing.

The delays can be minimized, however, by scheduling—where possible—peak periods for different terminals at different times. This may not be as difficult as it sounds, especially if the user's network touches more than one time zone. By considering what delays are acceptable, and establishing a realistic limit on the total number of terminals able to seek access, the user can best reap the economic benefits of statistical multiplexing in spite of port contention.

Another intelligent feature, which also causes contention, is dynamic allocation of the high-speed trunk's bandwidth or number of channels. This feature is realized when a terminal user seeks access at the remote STDM. With a conventional TDM, each time slot is for a fixed data rate and is not easily changed; the data from each terminal accessing the remote TDM goes into its assigned slot. On the other hand, the STDM has considerably more flexibility, since there are no assigned time slots and no fixed data rates. Depending at what data rate the terminal operates, as detected, and how much of the trunk's bandwidth is available, the STDM determines if the traffic can be accepted at that time. So with bandwidth contention, if the terminal seeking access demands more high-speed bandwidth than is then available, it cannot reach a port even if one is available. The remote STDM will return a busy signal, and the terminal operator will have to try again. The number of available trunk channels is not constant, and depends on trunk capacity (maximum bandwidth) and how much of the bandwidth is not in use at the time.

To make transmission between STDMs even more efficient, data compression techniques allow information to be sent using fewer bits than when the data is not compressed, or "normal."

The simplest form of data compression calls for the remote STDM to scan the high-speed data stream, at some time prior to transmission, and pick out repeated characters, such as a string of periods or space characters. The STDM counts the number of times a character is repeated, then sends the character once, followed by a short combination of bits that represents the number of times the character is to be sent. The receiving STDM could restore the original data stream, or leave the task to the host computer, whichever is necessary so as to maintain transparency.

A conventional multiplexer may accept and tag a received character as errored. But no provision is made to correct that error. The STDM, however, has the ability to correct errors by the automatic repeat request (ARQ) feature, using the cyclic redundancy check (CRC) code to detect errors.

In ARQ, a sending STDM stores each transmitted data frame while awaiting a positive or negative acknowledgment (ACK or NAK) from its correspondent STDM. On receipt of an ACK, the sending STDM discards the stored frame, and continues transmission. If the receiving STDM recognizes an error in the CRC code of a received frame, it sends back a NAK to the sending unit. The sending STDM then retransmits the errored frame and all following frames sent while awaiting the ACK/NAK. This process is repeated until the errored frame is accepted as correct, or until a frame transmission counter reaches a preset limit, and causes an alarm to go off.

But ARQ can cause substantial inherent transmission delays. It may be more convenient for a user to tolerate an occasional error—which would be recognized and flagged by the receiving equipment, and could then be corrected by interpretation—rather than accept reduced throughput.

Traffic Buffering

As mentioned earlier, unacknowledged transmissions are stored until no longer needed for retransmission. The storage takes place in a buffer that allows dynamic (temporary) retention of a certain amount of transmitted traffic. The prospective user should check the buffer storage capacity of whichever STDM is being considered for his network. Typically, from 10 to 20 seconds of a user's data may be retained before buffer overflow is threatened. Overflow is likely to occur only during a trunk line outage, or during a noisy trunk line condition causing many repeated transmissions under ARQ, and warning of the overflow's imminence may or may not be provided to the terminals, depending on the sophistication of the circuitry.

One additional buffer consideration that the user should be aware of is the relative "weight" assigned to each terminal port. Even when terminals of identical bit rates are connected to a remote STDM, it may be possible to program their ports so that one terminal may be treated at a higher priority than the others. Priority is accomplished by emptying the preferred terminal's port buffer at a faster rate than the others. In fact, a series of priorities may be assigned to establish different buffer-emptying rates for each port. Besides treating certain terminals preferentially, the weighting parameter may also be used to compensate for differing traffic volumes—in addition to what the statistical multiplexing feature accomplishes in this area.

Automatic Rate Detection

To make most efficient use of its port contention and bandwidth allocation characteristics, the STDM has a deluxe attribute of the conventional TDM: automatic data rate detection—also known as autobaud or autospeed. Under this feature, a terminal user seeking access to a host computer through a time-division multiplexer must transmit a short group of preliminary characters (usually up to three). The remote TDM analyzes them and determines the terminal's transmission rate. The bandwidth and port contention phases are then exercised, as described previously. Also, when the port on the host (or on its front-end processor, if one is used) is of the autospeed type, the local mux will supply the preliminary characters to the host, which will do its own rate recognition and will accept regular traffic.

Autospeed does not really apply to synchronous transmission, since the applicable modems would require a range of data rates that would make the modem equipment economically impractical at present. And there does not appear to be demand for such an application. However, a minimal form of synchronous autospeed does exist. If a host port can accept, say, either 2,400 bit/s or 4,800 bit/s, then the remote STDM has that much more latitude in assigning terminals to ports. For example, if all fixed-rate host ports of 2,400 bit/s and 4,800 bit/s are in use, and one multi-rate port for both speeds is still available, then a terminal of either speed can gain access to the host.

A corollary of autospeed is the automatic detection of code or character format. This feature enables the remote STDM to decipher the preliminary character or characters transmitted to detect the use of either the ASCII or the binary-coded decimal (BCD) code, as well as for data rate as described earlier.

Echoplex

An operator at a remote terminal usually creates a copy of what is being sent, either on the terminal screen or on an associated printer. This procedure provides no assurance to the operator of the data being received in that form.

Echoplex is a technique that attempts to provide such assurance. With the terminal's line connected directly to a host computer (or front-end processor, as in Figure 11.2.2A), the data as received from the terminal is returned to its printer

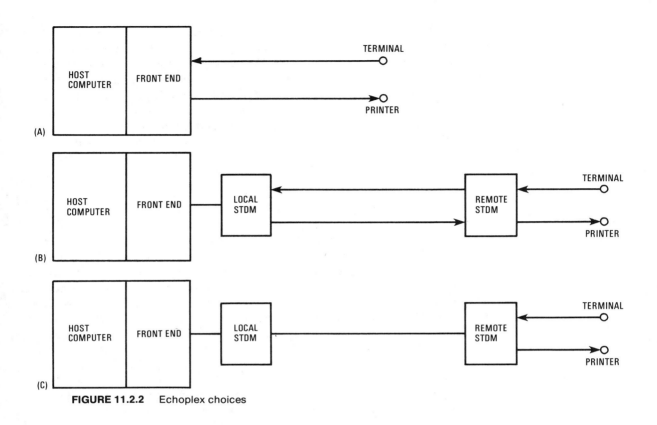

FIGURE 11.2.2 Echoplex choices

or screen. This method enables the operator to verify that the transmission was received correctly.

Some STDMs offer the option of relieving the host of the processing time required by the echoplex function. If the local (host-end) STDM returns the received data (Fig. 11.2.2B), then reception is verified for both the terminal and high-speed lines. If the remote STDM does the echoplexing (Fig. 11.2.2C), verification is obtained for just the terminal line.

For low-speed terminals, such as those operating up to 300 bit/s, the delay between transmission and the echoplexed reception may be excessive—causing operator disorientation. In such a situation, full verification may be sacrificed and echoplexing from the remote STDM is accepted ("pseudo-echoplex").

When a network problem occurs, the STDM can also become a diagnostic tool. It assists in localizing and diagnosing the trouble with both its own indicators and the associated printouts. The STDM can initiate remote and local loopback testing of trunk and terminal lines under off-line or dynamic conditions. At the local site, the entire network may be monitored and abnormal conditions logged, with a note of the time of day.

Diagnostic routines are usually initiated by an operator at the local STDM. Some vendors offer a "hot" backup unit ready to take over for the primary unit when a failure is detected. The backup unit may be given the task of running non-interfering diagnostics automatically, until it is needed as a replacement.

Some STDM vendors also provide the modems for the terminal and trunk lines. These modems may occupy circuit board slots in the mux equipment, or could be external depending on the vendor's design and practice. The buyer/user should include modem costs when comparing STDM prices.

11.3 COMMUNICATIONS PROCESSORS

The communications processor (CP) is often not a single device, nor are its functions limited to one network location. Basically, a CP is used as (1) a front-end processor, (2) remote concentrator, and (3) message switch. The packetizing processor represents another CP use, but is considered a special form of the message switch communications processor.

Each of the three basic categories is shown in Figure 11.3.1, represented in somewhat simple network arrangements, and explored later in more detail. As a front-end processor (FEP), the CP is located at its host computer. A prime function of the FEP is to relieve the host of network communications overhead.

When physically located at or near the distant terminal devices served, the CP is known as a remote concentrator. The connection back to the host may be direct (dashed line, asymmetrical) or through a similar CP acting as an FEP (solid line, symmetrical). (Many network applications such as that of the remote concentrator can be filled by statistical multiplexers.)

The prime purpose of locating the CP remotely is to reduce the cost of running multiple lines to distant terminals by running fewer to the remote CP. A combination of short runs between the terminals and the remote concentrator plus the CP connections back to the host are usually more cost effective than multiple long runs. In the symmetrical arrangement, when some terminals are located near the host, access to host applications may be made through the FEP rather than through the remote concentrator, as shown in Figure 11.3.1B.

Another CP function is store and forward when used as a message switch. Elements of this function exist in the FEP and remote concentrator. But when switching is the primary function, the network may be represented more accurately by Figure 11.3.1C.

As supplied to the user, a communications processor will resemble a minicomputer or look like an entirely different unit. In the latter case, the equipment is supplied by an independent vendor who designs and builds his own processor. Many minicomputer vendors are also represented by their products in the CP field. Another group of companies increasingly represented are the specialized common carriers with their offerings of CPs originally developed for use on their own public packet networks.

Compatible

Some vendors aim almost exclusively at the IBM user market. Their front-end processors are plug-compatible replacements for IBM's 3704 and 3705 (and later

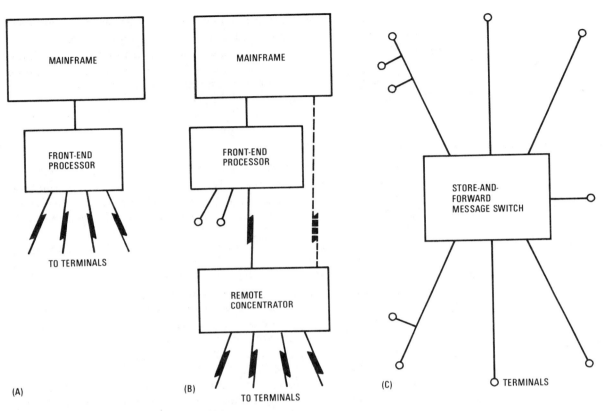

FIGURE 11.3.1 Processor variations

models) communications controllers, and are upgrades of IBM's hard-wired 270X transmission control units—as are the 370X units.

Where a user has a large network—one with several centralized host computers—employing just one multihost front-end processor can be very convenient. Hardware costs are lower, and programming is less complex.

Even with one host, a front-end processor is effective in relieving a mainframe of dealing with each terminal desiring access to particular application programs. As indicated in Figure 11.3.2, the FEP responds to a terminal's application request and gains access to the proper host region. Shown are three typical IBM applications: timesharing option (TSO); information management system (IMS); and customer information control system (CICS).

Application programs and multihost support come together when each host is dedicated to a particular application. Then, a terminal is directed to its application by the FEP switching the request to the proper host. If one host fails, then only that application is lost. Of course, to prevent loss of all applications if an FEP goes down, a back-up FEP should be included.

Networking

When a communications processor is used as a "pure" message switch (Figure 11.3.1C), no connection is needed to a host computer. Only when the network's terminals must also have access to a host's resources—such as particular applications—is switch-to-host connection required.

The CP's network functions—besides being a store-and-forward message switch—include buffering and queuing for load leveling. That is accomplished by pacing, otherwise known as throttling. The technique consists of the processor sensing an impending overflow situation at a receiving device, and either temporarily storing the data that would have caused an overflow, or stopping the sending device until the receiver is ready again.

A CP feature that exercises another form of traffic control is called fast/slow poll. Here, terminals are polled normally—fast—until a terminal does not respond or has no traffic to send. When such non-responses occur, the CP automatically

FIGURE 11.3.2   Accessing applications

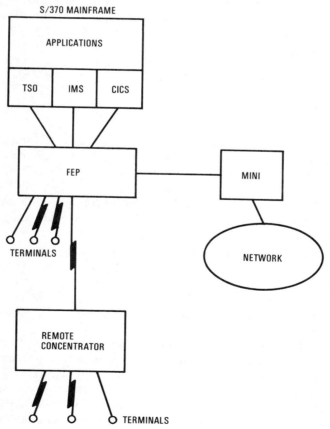

reduces the polling frequency of that terminal. When it again responds with traffic, the terminal is transferred back to a fast-poll mode. The algorithm for establishing polling frequencies and mode criteria are under user control. It is important to note that the operator of a remote terminal is not aware that he is dealing with an intermediate processor, and not directly with a host computer.

Another network function is logging and journaling. Such information is normally kept on magnetic tape or disk. Collecting and monitoring network statistics is yet another CP function. This data may include line and terminal usage, outages, numbers and types of messages, and repeat-request frequency. By keeping track of connect times, the CP can store—for access by the control console—accounting information such as charge-back data.

Network maintenance is aided measurably by the CP. Both software and hardware "bugs" may be detected, isolated, analyzed, and correction assisted by CP console action. Non-host-dependent diagnostic capabilities are featured in some communications processors.

One notable feature of the communications processor is the ability to deal with a variety of terminal types, speeds, and codes. Enabling each type to communicate with the others requires CP conversions, which are made possible by a combination of line interface devices and software. Standard speeds and codes are readily handled; non-standard ones may be accepted, but usually require some reprogramming. Similarly, standard protocols—such as asynchronous and binary synchronous (BSC) communications—are accepted by the CP, as are, increasingly, the bit-oriented ones and X.25.

Gateway Processor

As public networks proliferate, there is a growing need for a device on one network to communicate with devices on others. The need is becoming apparent with the various networks in different countries. But political considerations may slow implementation of internation data flow.

However, within the U.S., internetwork transmission may not be as difficult to implement. And with the proper software developed, and the guidance of standards, the CP can act as a gateway processor.

There are other situations when the CP, functioning as other than a switch, may operate without a host. For example, if the host computer shown in Figure 11.3.2 becomes disabled, the terminals—in the case of many processors—may still communicate with each other. Of course, there will be degraded service. But if the CP is so designed, it may queue application requests until the host is again operational and on line.

To relieve the host of as much of the network operational responsibilities as possible, the efficient CP manages such functions as message routing and network reconfiguration. Routing tables are maintained at the CP. When a table change or update is needed, some CPs require just a console entry for a simple change—such as a terminal identifier to correspond to a new location. But when the update is more complex, the new data is entered as part of an initial program load (IPL) or system generation.

Network reconfiguration data is entered similarly. This routing and configuration information is totally resident in the CP, with the host not involved.

One other network feature a communications processor may have that could be useful is called "pass through." As shown in Figure 11.3.2, if access is desired from a terminal to another network (mini-controlled in the figure), the FEP will recognize the request and pass the connection through to the other controlling hardware. This feature effectively widens the numbers of applications and terminals to which a CP-controlled device may have access.

As a network node, the CP combines intelligence with switching capabilities of hundreds of lines. Line speeds range typically up to 230.4 kbit/s.

Interfacing with Controllers

The typical hardware components included in a CP used in a concentration role are illustrated in Figure 11.3.3. The single-line controllers (SLCs) provide the necessary control and sensing signals that interface the concentrator to individual circuits. While single-line controllers can be asynchronous or synchronous, the majority are the synchronous type. The preponderance of synchronous transmission is due to the SLC's normally providing only one—or at most a few—high-speed transmission links from the concentrator to another concentrator or to a host computer (front-end processor).

Since the support of numerous lines would be expensive and would take up a lot of space if implemented with single-line controllers, most communications support for the concentrator-to-terminal links are implemented through the use of multiline controllers. Multiline controllers (MLCs) can be categorized by capacity (number and speed of lines supported) as well as by operation: hardware- or software-controlled.

Hardware-controlled multiline controllers place no additional burden on the concentrator's CPU, the hardware MLC requiring much less operating software than the programmed controller. However, programmed controllers have the lowest per line cost by reducing the hardware in the interfaces and the controller to a minimum, although a larger burden is placed on the processor. For a programmed controller, all sampling control, bit detection, and buffering is performed by the processor through software control. The amount of processing time required by the operational program is the main factor limiting the number of lines that can be connected to the concentrator via software-controlled MLCs.

To reduce the complexity of circuits in hardware multiline controllers, as well as

FIGURE 11.3.3   Concentrator hardware

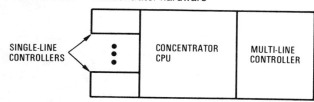

SINGLE-LINE CONTROLLERS   CONCENTRATOR CPU   MULTI-LINE CONTROLLER

to reduce software overhead of programmed controllers, incoming lines are often arranged in groups. These groupings are by bit rate, code level, and the number of stop bits for asynchronous terminal support. Figure 11.3.4 illustrates a typical grouping by channel for a multiline controller. This controller requires a minimum of four channels per group—all four channels of the same terminal class (same bit rate and code). Groups 1 and 3 are of the same class. The MLC may have any mixture of classes, until the number of groups multiplied by four equals the total number of channels supported by the controller (64 in the example).

Pure Contention

In essence, a pure-contention concentrator is a port selector. In performing this function, any of M input lines are connected to any of N output lines as one of the N output lines becomes available. The M input lines are commonly called the line side of the concentrator, whereas the N output lines are referred to as the port side—to interface the ports of a front-end processor. The basic hardware components of a contention concentrator are illustrated in Figure 11.3.5.

Incoming data on each line of the line side of the device is routed through the concentrator's processor, which searches for a non-busy line on the port side to transmit the data to. The determination of priorities can be programmed so that groups of incoming lines can be made to contend for one or a group of lines on the

FIGURE 11.3.4　Groupings by channel

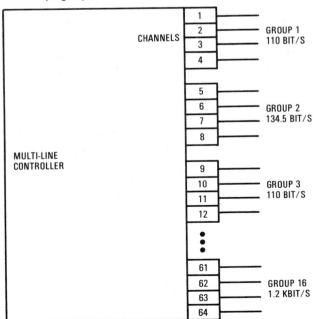

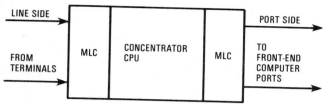

FIGURE 11.3.5   Contention concentrator

port side. When all ports are in use, messages can be generated to notify terminals attempting to access the host of the "busy" situation. Through the addition of peripheral storage devices, incoming jobs can be batched to await the disconnection of a user from the host. Then connection to the newly available port side line is made to gain entry to the computational facility, and the stored job is transmitted.

If one needs store-and-forward message concentration, emphasis should be placed upon peripheral equipment, data transfer rates, and software appropriate for this particular application. In addition, if the application is critically time dependent, examining hardware reliability by itself may not suffice, and the user will most likely want to consider a redundancy configuration.

As shown in the redundant store-and-forward arrangement of Figure 11.3.6, both configurations are directly connected to each other by an intercomputer communications unit and share access to incoming and outgoing lines and peripherals via electronic switches. During operation, one configuration is considered the operational processor or master, while the other is the slave or standby, monitoring the master. Upon a hardware failure or power interrupt, the master signals the slave to take over processing via the intercomputer communications unit, generates an alarm message, and conducts an orderly shutdown.

Since the slave has been in parallel processing, it resets all controls and becomes the master, holding the potential of losing data to a minimum. This procedure can usually be completed within 500 microseconds for processors with a cycle time of 750 nanoseconds or less. In this case, 666 cycles or more (500 microsec ÷ 750 nanosec) are available with that time slot to execute the required instructions to transfer control and effect the orderly shutdown. Actually, just two to four computer cycles are needed for the execution of such instructions.

Switching the Message

To effect message switching, incoming data is routed to a central point where messages are concentrated for processing. Then, based upon some criteria, messages are routed over one or more lines connected to the processor. In message switching, all terminals can communicate with every other terminal connected to the configuration—once the message has been processed and the destination data contained in the message is acted upon.

The hardware required for a message switch is quite similar to that required by

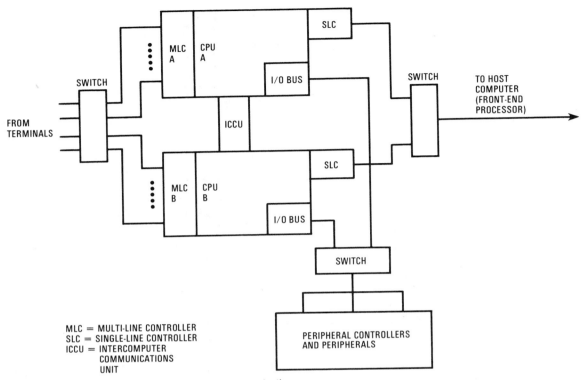

FIGURE 11.3.6 Redundant message concentration

a store-and-forward message concentrator. The primary differences are the application software, and that incoming messages are not stored, but are processed and then routed over one or more of the incoming lines. And accesses to peripherals such as disks are handled via direct memory access (DMA) channels instead of the lower speed available from data transfers conducted via a processor's I/O bus.

The interface used to transfer data to communications controllers and peripherals is usually determined by the necessary I/O transfer rate. Interfacing may occur at the computer's I/O bus or via such devices as direct memory control (DMC) and DMA. Data transferred on the I/O bus is bit-serial and under control of the program. In the DMC mode, data transfers are effected independent of program control, and data blocks are transferred on a word basis (bit-parallel) to and from any portion of main memory. The DMC mode is used for medium-speed data transfer, and requires a starting and ending address, as well as the number of characters to be transferred. Although similarly word-oriented and a direct-to-memory medium, the DMA mode requires only the starting and ending address. For high-speed data transfers, the DMA mode is used, but at a cost higher than with DMC. The speed at which DMA permits transfer of data is such that a computer using DMA on a high-speed channel can exchange data with several devices (peripherals) and controllers concurrently on a timeshared basis.

Figure 11.3.7 illustrates a typical data communications network consisting of several different types of concentrators and a front-end processor. This network combines examples of much of what was discussed previously.

At location 1, a standard concentrator is used to concentrate the traffic from 32 terminals onto a high-speed line for transmission to the front-end processor. Since location 2 has a requirement for remote batch processing as well as connecting 12 terminals to the host computer, a remote network processor has been installed to perform these two functions. And since location 3 has a significant number of terminals doing an important application, a redundant store-and-forward message concentrator was installed.

Terminals remaining in the network (location 4) total 128. However, it was felt that at most only 56 would ever become active at any given time. Therefore, to economize on front-end processor ports, a contention concentrator was "front-ended" to the front-end processor, making the 128 channels connected to terminals contend for the 56 front-end processor ports.

FIGURE 11.3.7   Integrating into a network

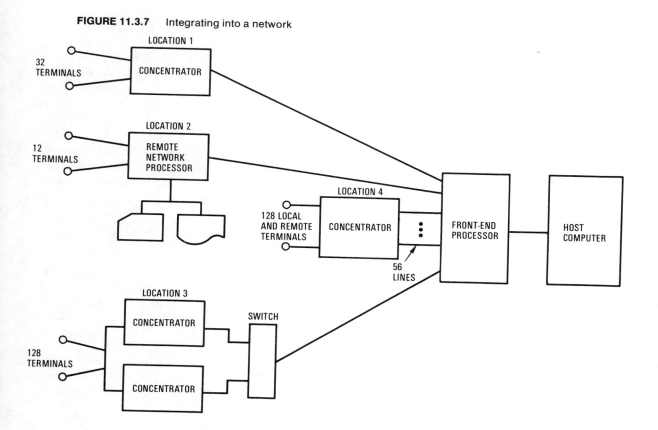

11.4 MODEM- AND LINE-SHARING UNITS

It may be evident that a single communications link is less costly than two or more. What is sometimes less obvious is the most economical and effective way to make use of even a single link.

Multiplexing is usually the first technique that comes to mind. But there are many situations where far less expensive, although somewhat slower, equipment is quite adequate. Here terminals are polled one by one through a "sharing device" that acts under the instructions of the host computer.

Typically, the applications where this method would be most useful and practical would be those where messages are short and where most traffic between host computer and terminal moves in one direction during any one period of time.

The technique, which can be called "line sharing" (as distinct from multiplexing), may work in some interactive situations, but only if the over-all response time can be kept within tolerable limits. The technique is not as a rule useful for remote batching or remote job entry, unless messages can be carefully scheduled so as not to get in each other's way because of the long run time for any one job.

Line sharing, then, is comparatively inexpensive—but has some limits to its usefulness in situations where a multiplexer, most likely a TDM, can bring in more economic leverage.

A line-sharing network is connected to the host computer by a local link, through which the host polls the terminals one by one. The central site transmits the address of the terminal to be polled throughout the network by way of the sharing unit (Fig. 11.4.1). The terminal assigned this address (01 in the diagram) responds by transmitting a request-to-send (RTS) signal to the computer, which returns a clear-to-send (CTS), to prompt the terminal to begin transmitting its message (ABCD in diagram). When the message is completed, the computer polls the next terminal.

Throughout this sequence, the sharing device merely routes the signals to and from the polled terminal and handles supporting tasks, such as making sure the carrying signal is on the line when the terminal is polled, and inhibiting transmission from all terminals not connected to the computer.

FIGURE 11.4.1 Line sharing

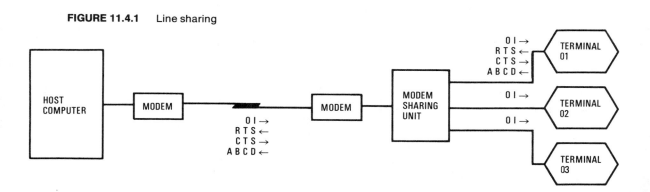

There are two subspecies of device used in this technique—modem-sharing units and line-sharing units. They function in much the same way to perform much the same task—the only significant difference being that a line-sharing unit has an internal timing source, while a modem-sharing unit gets its timing signals from the modem it is servicing.

Remote Operation

A line-sharing unit is mainly used at the central site to connect a cluster of terminals to a single computer port (Fig. 11.4.2). It does, however, play a part in remote operation—when a data stream from a remote terminal cluster forms one of the inputs to a line-sharing unit at the central site, so as to make it possible to run with a cheaper single-port computer.

In a modem-sharing unit, one set of inputs is connected to multiple terminals or processors (Fig. 11.4.2). These lines are routed through the modem-sharing unit to a single modem. Besides needing only one remote modem, a modem-sharing network needs only a single two-wire (for half-duplex) or four-wire (usually, for full-duplex) communications link. A single link between terminals and host computer allows all of them to connect with a single port on the host, a situation that results in still greater savings.

If multiplexing were used in this type of application, the outlay would likely be greater, because of the cost of the hardware and the need for a dedicated host computer port for each remote device. A single modem-sharing unit, at the remote site, is all that is needed for a sharing configuration; but multiplexers usually come in pairs, one for each end of the link.

The polling process makes sharing units less efficient than multiplexers. Throughput is cut back because of the time needed to poll each terminal and the

FIGURE 11.4.2   Line sharing and modem sharing

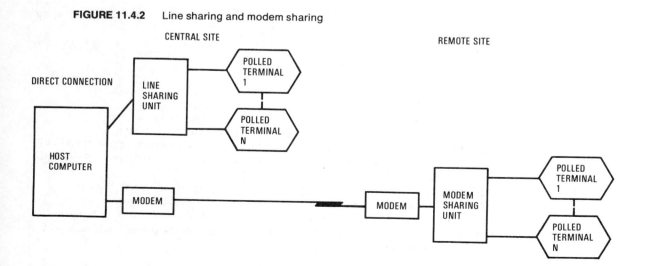

line turnaround time on half-duplex links. Another problem is that terminals must wait their turn. If one terminal sends a long message, others may have to wait an excessive amount, which may tie up operators if unbuffered terminals are used.

Sharer Constraints

Sharing units are generally transparent within a communications network. There are, however four factors that should be taken into account when making use of these devices: the distance separating the data terminals and the sharing unit (generally set at no more than 50 feet under RS-232-C interface specifications); the number of terminals that can be connected to the unit; the various types of modems with which the unit can be interfaced; and whether the terminals can or cannot accept external timing from a modem through a sharing unit. Then, too, the normal constraints of the polling process, such as delays arising from line turn-around and response, and the size of the transmitted blocks, must be considered in designing the network.

It is advisable to check carefully into what types of modems can be supported by modem-sharing units, since some modems permit a great deal more flexibility of network design than others. For instance, if the sharing unit can work with a multiport modem, the extra modem ports can service remote-batch terminals or dedicated terminals that frequently handle long messages. Some terminals that cannot accept external timing can be fitted with special circuitry through which the timing originates at the terminal itself, instead of at the modem.

QUESTIONS

11.1 Name five data sources that could be candidates for data stream multiplexing.

11.2 What are the two basic techniques commonly used for multiplexing, and how do they differ?

11.3 Discuss the equipment differences between multiplexers that employ bit interleaving and those that employ character interleaving.

11.4 If a multiplexer frame contains two SYNC characters, what is the overhead when the frame's data characters are

A. 2   C. 6
B. 4   D. 8

11.5 Why is the employment of a multiplexer as a front end not common?

11.6 Employing an intelligent multiplexer with a 4:1 asynchronous compression ratio will permit how many 1,200-bit/s asynchronous circuits to be multiplexed if the composite high-speed line is to operate at 4,800 bit/s?

11.7 Discuss the limitations of multiport modems in comparison with multiplexers.

11.8 What is the difference between a concentrator and a remote network processor?

11.9 Discuss the difference between a modem- or line-sharing unit and a multiplexer.

11.10 Where would a line-sharing unit normally be physically placed? Where would a modem-sharing unit be located?

CHAPTER 12

NETWORK TOPOLOGY AND OPTIMIZATION

Before we can apply the devices covered in Chapter 11 to the optimization of a network, we must first examine the different types of network structures that can be developed. Once the different structures, known as network topologies, are covered, we can explore how different network layouts can be developed, and some of the tools available for the network analyst to use in optimizing his design.

After the preceding has been accomplished, this chapter will explore how one can develop a minimum-cost network. Such a network will not only consider the cost of the communications medium, but also such factors as the types and costs of terminals, transmission equipment, and central-site hardware, including front-end-processor equipment.

This chapter devotes an entire section to a case study that applies the information previously discussed to a requirement representing a typical user request for service. Through an analysis of the requirement, and the application of knowledge previously discussed, several network possibilities will be developed. A minimum-cost network design is proposed as a solution to the requirement.

Note again, as in Chapter 8, that all costs and means of establishing them in this and the next chapter, such as those detailed in the rate tables included herein, should be considered as typical, not necessarily current, and to be used primarily for the examples and exercise questions. If readers have actual current applications, they are urged to refer to the latest figures, obtainable from the appropriate vendors or government organizations.

12.1 NETWORK STRUCTURE

The arrangement of data links and nodal points (where data is concentrated) is called topology. There are many varieties of network structures. As will be seen, the topology employed has a direct bearing on the operation, reliability, and operating cost of a network.

To develop a specific topology, we may use different types of data links, such as point-to-point and multipoint, combining them in some manner, with or without specialized data communications equipment.

Centralized (Star)

A centralized, or star, network configuration is illustrated in Figure 12.1.1. When this topology is employed, each communications link is directly connected to the host computer. Data movement is directly from each terminal to the computer. There are no delays due to concentrator buffering times or the internal delay of a multiplexer, since no such devices are employed. Moreover, if any link should fail, only the terminal on that specific link will be affected by the line outage.

The star topology is suitable where each terminal has a large volume of data traffic and must operate at 9,600 bit/s or another high data rate on a leased line, or each terminal has a low traffic volume and a correspondingly low connect time via the public switched telephone network. Otherwise, this configuration results in economic inefficiencies that can be corrected by the use of a hierarchical, or tree, structure.

Hierarchical (Tree) Structure

In a hierarchical, or tree, structure, data is transferred through intermediate points where one or more operations may be conducted prior to the data continuing on to the host computer. Figure 12.1.2 is an example of a hierarchical, or tree, topology. Here the concentration equipment could be a multiport modem, multiplexer, modem-sharing unit, or concentrator. When this configuration is employed, the traffic from a number of low-to-medium-speed terminals is combined for retrans-

FIGURE 12.1.1   Centralized or star

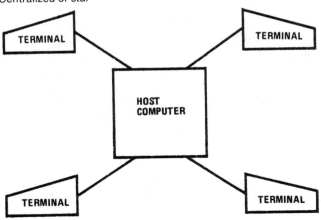

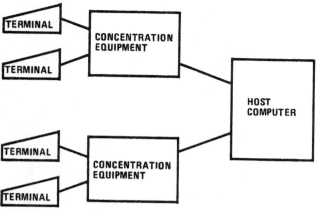

FIGURE 12.1.2   Hierarchical, or tree, structure

mission to the host computer via a high-speed link. Such an arrangement may result in a substantial reduction in circuit costs, since one or a few lines from the concentration device replace numerous terminal lines to the computer that would be required without concentration.

One of the primary disadvantages of such an arrangement is that if either the concentration equipment or high-speed line should fail, all terminals connected via that arrangement may become inoperative, unless alternative data links are available to reestablish a connection to the computer.

Loop, or Ring, Structure

One topology normally used to link computers rather than terminals is the loop, or ring, structure illustrated in Figure 12.1.3. Here, terminals may first be connected via a star (or tree) structure to a computer or other type of intelligent (programmable) device, which, in turn, is connected via a loop or ring structure to the host computer. In this arrangement, most of the terminals connected to the ring do not communicate directly with the intended host computer but have their data looped around the ring until it reaches the proper host computer.

This structure is economical when many remote terminals and computers are located close to one another. If remote terminals are geographically dispersed over long distances, line costs could become very expensive for such a structure.

Distributed or Multistar

As data processing requirements have evolved, many firms recognized a need to decentralize a portion of their computational power and locate such power at branch or regional locations. This movement of processing power to the field offers considerable advantages with respect to communications costs by reducing the

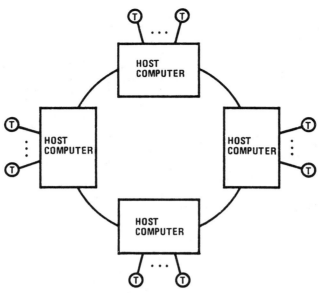

FIGURE 12.1.3   Loop or ring structure

distance and charges for terminal-to-computer communications, as illustrated in Figure 12.1.4. Although all three computers are shown connected to each other, this is not a requirement of distributed processing nor of a distributed network.

When the computers are interconnected, there are more paths through which data can flow. Hence the failure or outage of any one circuit between computers may be temporarily alleviated by the rerouting of data onto an alternate path. Although the extra circuits to interconnect computers result in extra communications costs, the additional transmission paths improve the overall network performance.

In order to determine the number and capacity of the high-speed intercomputer data links, a network traffic analysis must be conducted. Depending on the number of computers and terminals in the network, this study can become very complex. Other factors must also be considered, including computer software modifications to resolve the problems of linking distributed data bases. Very few truly distributed networks have been implemented, due to the cost of modifying application software. This cost can be quite high in comparison to that of the communications mediums required. A number of computer manufacturers have introduced distributed computer networks that include the required software to interconnect computer databases, relieving the user of this development expense.

Mixed Structure

The topology of a network can vary considerably, as illustrated in Figure 12.1.5, where a mixed structure configuration is shown. In this example, a hierarchical or tree structure, using multiplexers or other types of data concentration equipment, may be employed to concentrate many data sources within a geographical area for retransmission to a host computer. Due to particular operating characteristics or traffic volumes, a number of terminals may be directly connected to the computer in a centralized or star arrangement, as shown in the upper-right-hand portion of Figure 12.1.5.

And another star structure connects terminals directly to the computer located in the lower portion of Figure 12.1.5. The latter computer, when connected to the other computer, forms a distributed or multistar structure.

12.2 NETWORK LAYOUT

Prior to initiating the design of a network, several items must be considered by the network planner. One of the first is the type and anticipated usage of terminals to be connected via a data communications network to the computer.

Numerous approaches can be used to obtain the required information, with these approaches being covered in considerable detail in Chapter 15. For our initial investigation into the concepts of network design, we will limit our problem by considering only a few alternative transmission media and assuming that our terminal operating statistics are given.

VH Coordinate System

In the United States, the distance of the telephone connection is one of the cost variables that has to be considered for all land-based transmission methods, with the exception of packet switching. Although the communications carrier routes

FIGURE 12.1.4   Distributed, or multistar, network

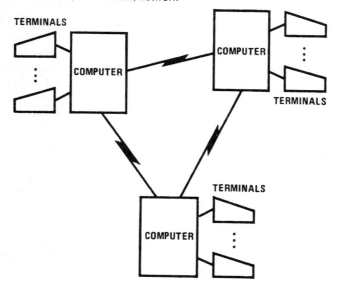

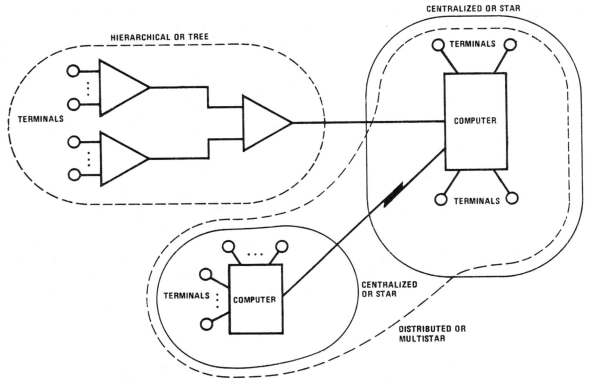

FIGURE 12.1.5 Mixed structure

both leased lines and connections over the public switched telephone network over any desired path, charges are normally independent of actual routings and are based upon the straight-line airline distance between locations connected.

First filed as a tariff by AT&T, the VH coordinate system of distance measuring is now used by almost every communications carrier in the United States. This system divides the continental United States by vertical and horizontal grid lines so that every location is capable of being expressed as a pair of vertical (V) and horizontal (H) coordinates that can then be used to calculate distances between locations.

Once the VH coordinates for two locations are known, the distance between those locations can be computed by the Pythagorean theorem:

$$\text{Distance} = \sqrt{\frac{(V_1 - V_2)^2 + (H_1 - H_2)^2}{10}}$$

In using the VH system and the theorem for distance computation, since fractional miles are considered as full miles, the result of taking the square root will be rounded to the next higher number.

As an example of the use of the theorem, consider determining the mileage between Reading, Pennsylvania (V = 5,258, H = 1,612) and Atlanta, Georgia (V = 7,260, H = 2,083). Substituting in the previous equation, the distance between the two cities becomes

$$D = \sqrt{\frac{(5{,}258 - 7{,}260)^2 + (1{,}612 - 2{,}083)^2}{10}}$$

$$= 650.37 \text{ miles}$$

which becomes 651 miles when rounded to the next higher whole number.

While a table of airline mileages may appear to be easier to use than obtaining the VH coordinate of every terminal location, then computing the distances from each terminal to possible data concentration equipment locations, VH coordinates lend themselves to computerization. Today, several consulting firms offer subscribers the use of their optimization programs. Here, the user enters the terminal type and location as a city and a state, and the program then assigns from its database the corresponding VH coordinates. The program computes an optimum path for transmission based on the terminal's activity factors and the location and activity factors of other terminals in the network.

IXC Mileage

IXC, or intercity exchange channel mileage, is the airline distance between locations. Although tables of VH coordinates are available from a number of sources, unless the subscriber wishes to computerize his network design, VH coordinates can be cumbersome to work with. Instead, subscribers can contact their AT&T Long Lines account representative and provide that person with a list of cities for which he desires the IXC mileage. The AT&T representative may then access a special timesharing program, which will produce a tabulation of the distances between each location. If the cities of concern are as listed in Table 12.2.1, the IXC program would produce a series of tables showing the mileage from each location to all other locations. Portions of the first and last two such tables are shown in Tables 12.2.2 through 12.2.4.

12.3 MINIMAL-COST NETWORK DESIGN

Let us consider the situation in which our computer center is located in Denver, Colorado, and we desire to connect a number of terminals in the western region of the United States to it. For this example, let us limit our choice of transmission media to the public switched telephone network and to leased lines, and eliminate any expansion requirements from consideration. (In actual situations, planned expansion must be considered.)

To develop a minimal-cost network, the first priority is to compute the most economical method of data transmission from each terminal location into Denver. To do this, direct-dial long-distance costs are computed and compared with the

TABLE 12.2.1 TERMINAL CITY LOCATIONS

City No.	City	City No.	City
1	Denver, Col.	34	Montrose, Col.
2	Boise, Idaho	35	Durango, Col.
3	St. Anthony, Idaho	36	Grand Junction, Col.
4	Burley, Idaho	37	Pueblo Dam, Col.
5	Salem, Oregon	38	Salida, Col.
6	Forest Grove, Oregon	39	Loveland, Col.
7	Spokane, Wash.	40	Albuquerque, N.M.
8	Ephrata, Wash.	41	Farmington, N.M.
9	Yakima, Wash.	42	Cuba, N.M.
10	Grand Coulee, Wash.	43	Oklahoma City, Okla.
11	Sacramento, Cal.	44	Austin, Texas
12	Willows, Cal.	45	El Paso, Texas
13	Fresno, Cal.	46	Amarillo, Texas
14	Auburn, Cal.	47	San Angelo, Texas
15	San Bernardino, Cal.	48	Harvey, N.D.
16	Shasta Dam, Cal.	49	Garrison, N.D.
17	Folsom Dam, Cal.	50	Bismarck, N.D.
18	Tracey, Cal.	51	Watford City, N.D.
19	Goleta, Cal.	52	McCook, Nebr.
20	Altadena, Cal.	53	Grand Island, Nebr.
21	Boulder City, Nev.	54	Billings, Mont.
22	Carson City, Nev.	55	Great Falls, Mont.
23	Reno, Nev.	56	Fort Peck, Mont.
24	Phoenix, Ariz.	57	Kalispell, Mont.
25	Parker, Ariz.	58	Huron, S.D.
26	Tucson, Ariz.	59	Watertown, S.D.
27	Salome, Ariz.	60	Rapid City, S.D.
28	Yuma, Ariz.	61	Courtland, Kan.
29	Page, Ariz.	62	Riverton, Wyo.
30	Salt Lake City, Utah	63	Casper, Wyo.
31	Provo, Utah	64	Laramie, Wyo.
32	Dutch John, Utah	65	Washington, D.C.
33	Logan, Utah		

TABLE 12.2.2 IXC MILEAGE FROM POINT 1 TO ALL OTHER POINTS

From	To	Mileage
1	2	636
1	3	450
1	4	496
1	5	985
.	.	
.	.	
.	.	
1	63	224
1	64	112
1	65	1,489

TABLE 12.2.3 IXC MILEAGE FROM POINT 63 TO ALL OTHER POINTS

From	To	Mileage
63	64	112
63	65	1,547

TABLE 12.2.4 IXC MILEAGE FROM POINT 64 TO ALL OTHER POINTS

From	To	Mileage
64	65	1,511

cost of a leased line on a monthly basis. Assume 22 working days in a month, and that the number, operating speed, and location of terminals requiring a connection to the computer center in Denver are as listed in Table 12.3.1.

To develop a cost table of public-switched-telephone network vs. leased-line cost, we must determine the average daily connect time per terminal and the distance between each terminal location and the computer center. This information is listed in Table 12.3.2.

It should be noted that the daily terminal connect time could be determined from a communications survey. Or, the data could be extrapolated from terminal

TABLE 12.3.1 REMOTE-TERMINAL DATA

Location	Operating Speed	Quantity
Billings, MT	300 bit/s	1
Salt Lake City, UT	1,200 bit/s	4
Boise, ID	300 bit/s	1
Boulder City, NV	1,200 bit/s	4
Phoenix, AZ	1,200 bit/s	4
Casper, WY	300 bit/s	1

TABLE 12.3.2 TERMINAL CONNECT TIME AND DISTANCE TO COMPUTER CENTER TERMINAL

Location	Daily Connect Time (Hrs.)	Mileage To Denver
Billings, MT	0.25	451
Salt Lake City	2.0	370
Boise, ID	4.0	536
Boulder City, NV	4.0	595
Phoenix, AZ	3.5	583
Casper, WY	0.5	224

usage of other locations that are using the computer to solve similar problems for which the six new locations in Table 12.3.2 may be installed. The mileage to Denver could come from numerous sources, such as the telephone company's IXC program, or a table of airline mileages between points.

With the information in Tables 12.3.1 and 12.3.2, a comparison of leased vs. public-switched-telephone-network usage is made for each terminal location. This comparison is contained in Table 12.3.3. In columns 3 and 4, the monthly connect time is divided into the number of initial one-minute connections and the number of additional minute connections, since the toll charge per long-distance call is based upon this division. Since 22 working days per month are assumed, a further assumption of only one call per day enables the monthly connect time costs in columns 3 and 4 to be readily computed.

As an example, for Billings, MT, where the daily connect time (column 2) is 15 minutes, assuming one call per day results in 22 (column 3) initial minute costs per month. The total monthly connect time is 15 minutes/day × 22 working days/month, or 330 minutes/month. Subtracting the 22 initial minutes produces a total of 308 additional minutes per month of connect time, as shown in column 4.

The mileage to Denver comes from Table 12.3.2. The cost-per-call data contained in columns 6 and 7 were taken from Table 8.2.1 in Chapter 8, Section 2, and represents the Intra-U.S. Rate Table for telephone calls over the public switched telephone network based upon mileage, type of call, and call duration. For the data in columns 6 and 7, it is assumed that calls are made during the day on a station-to-station basis. Next, the monthly switched network cost per terminal was computed (column 8) by multiplying column 3 by column 6 and adding the result to that obtained by multiplying column 4 by column 7.

To determine the cost of a leased line, the rate center category of cities to be connected by the circuit must be known. This information is contained in column 9. Column 10 shows the monthly cost of the line. This cost was computed by using the mileage from column 5, the rate center category from column 9, and Table 8.2.4 from Chapter 8, Section 2. Since each leased line is assumed to be a point-to-point structure, two station terminals will be required per line at a monthly cost of $36.05 per station terminal, for a total of $72.10 per month, as shown in column 11. The total monthly leased line cost is then obtained by adding the line cost (column 10) and the station terminal cost (column 11). The total is shown in column 12. Lastly, the more economical method was determined by comparing the monthly switched-network cost (column 8) with the monthly leased-line cost (column 12). The results were placed in columns 13 and 14.

Network Layout

Once a tabulation of the switched- and leased-line costs per terminal have been completed, a network layout can be constructed. Use an appropriate map of the locations to be connected to the computer center. Then, via a progression of steps in conjunction with other information (detailed here), obtain a minimum-cost network design. In the design of the minimum-cost network, the data communications devices listed in Table 12.3.4 and their associated monthly costs are used.

TABLE 12.3.3

① LOCATION	② DAILY CONNECT TIME (MINUTES)	③ MONTHLY CONNECT TIME — NO. OF FIRST MINUTE (1)	④ NO. OF ADDITIONAL MINUTES	⑤ MILEAGE TO DENVER	⑥ COST/CALL DAY RATE — INITIAL MINUTE	⑦ EACH ADDITIONAL MINUTE	⑧ MONTHLY SWITCHED NETWORK COST/ TERMINAL	⑨ RATE CENTER CATEGORY	⑩ MONTHLY LEASED LINE COST	⑪ MONTHLY STATION TERMINAL COST	⑫ TOTAL MONTHLY LEASED LINE COST	⑬ MOST ECONOMICAL TYPE	⑭ MONTHLY COST
BILLINGS, MT	15	22	308	451	.62	.43	146.08	B A	676.77	72.10	748.87	SWITCHED	146.08
SALT LAKE CITY, UT	120	22	2,618	370	.59	.42	1,112.54	A A	506.72	72.10	578.82	LEASED	578.82
BOISE, ID	240	22	5,258	536	.62	.43	2,274.58	B A	756.67	72.10	828.77	LEASED	828.77
BOULDER CITY, NV	240	22	5,258	595	.62	.43	2,274.58	B A	812.13	72.10	884.23	LEASED	884.23
PHOENIX, AZ	210	22	4,585	583	.62	.43	1,990.78	A A	706.94	72.10	779.04	LEASED	779.04
CASPER, WY	30	22	638	224	.58	.39	261.58	B A	463.39	72.10	535.49	SWITCHED	261.58

NOTE (1) ASSUMES ONE CALL/DAY

With the data in Table 12.3.1, we can first place the terminal quantity and operating data rate at each location, using as an example the symbol 1 X 300 to denote 1 terminal operating at 300 bit/s at a given location. This is illustrated in Figure 12.3.1. Next, the more economical method of transmission per terminal as computed in Table 12.3.3 can be indicated on the network layout, by placing an S for switched and an L for a leased line, and denoting the monthly cost of the connection. This additional information is illustrated in Figure 12.3.2.

Once the cost per terminal is placed on the network layout, we examine the utilization of data concentration equipment, such as multiplexers. One of the best places to initialize a multiplexer location is at a site with a large number of terminals, with each terminal having a large monthly communications cost from the location to the computer site. Let us assume that the cost of a 4-channel asynchronous multiplexer is $100 per month, and a 4,800-bit/s modem rents for $135 per month. Using two multiplexers (one at a remote site and one in Denver to demultiplex data), the cost of the two pieces of equipment and the two high-speed

TABLE 12.3.4 DATA COMMUNICATIONS EQUIPMENT FOR NETWORK

Device	Monthly Cost
2,400-bit/s modem	65
4,800-bit/s modem	135
7,200-bit/s modem	210
9,600-bit/s modem	235
4-channel multiplexer	100
4-channel expansion	50
8-channel statistical multiplexer	175

modems necessary to service four terminals becomes ($100 + $135) × 2 = $470 per month. Using this equipment cost we can modify Figure 12.3.2 as illustrated in Figure 12.3.3. In this illustration the cost of installing four-channel multiplexers at Phoenix, Boulder City, and Salt Lake City are compared with the cost of the previously computed most economical method. As an example, in Phoenix the cost of the multiplexing equipment and modems plus the cost of one leased line, becomes $1,249 per month. This cost is now compared with the $779/month cost of a leased line from Phoenix to Denver. If we assume that the terminals in Phoenix cannot be polled, then four such lines would be required, for a total monthly cost of $3,116. Since the multiplexing cost of $1,249 per month is less, we can intially position a 4-channel multiplexer in Phoenix.

We conduct a similar analysis for Boulder City and Salt Lake City, with the results indicating the 4-channel multiplexers can be initially positioned at those sites as well. We modify our network layout to indicate the initial multiplexer placements, as illustrated in Figure 12.3.3.

Homing Points

Using the initial multiplexer locations, we next examine the cost trade-offs of using each location as a hub, connecting other remote terminals in the geographical area through the multiplexer to the computer center in Denver. From the layout in Figure 12.3.3, it is apparent that Boise is closer to Salt Lake City than to the other two multiplexer locations, while Billings and Casper are closer to Denver than to any multiplexer site. Thus, it would be impractical to connect either Billings or Casper terminals through a multiplexer. This would increase costs, since switched service was originally computed to be more economical than a leased line, and a leased line from Billings or Casper to a multiplexer is longer and costlier than a leased line to Denver. Thus, we now concentrate on Boise, whose formerly computed most economical cost was $829 per month using a leased line to Denver. From an IXC mileage table, we obtain a distance of 297 miles between Boise and Salt Lake City. Since this line involves category B and A rate centers, we use Table 8.2.4 in Chapter 8, Section 2, to compute the cost of a leased line between Boise and Salt Lake City. The cost of this circuit is $532.01 plus $72.10 for two station terminals for a monthly cost of $604.11— which is less than the $829-per-month

FIGURE 12.3.1

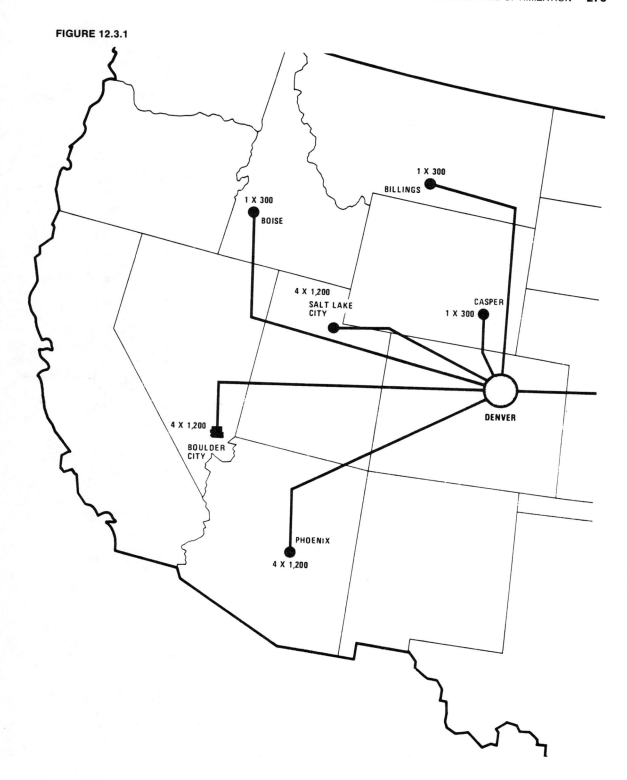

FIGURE 12.3.2

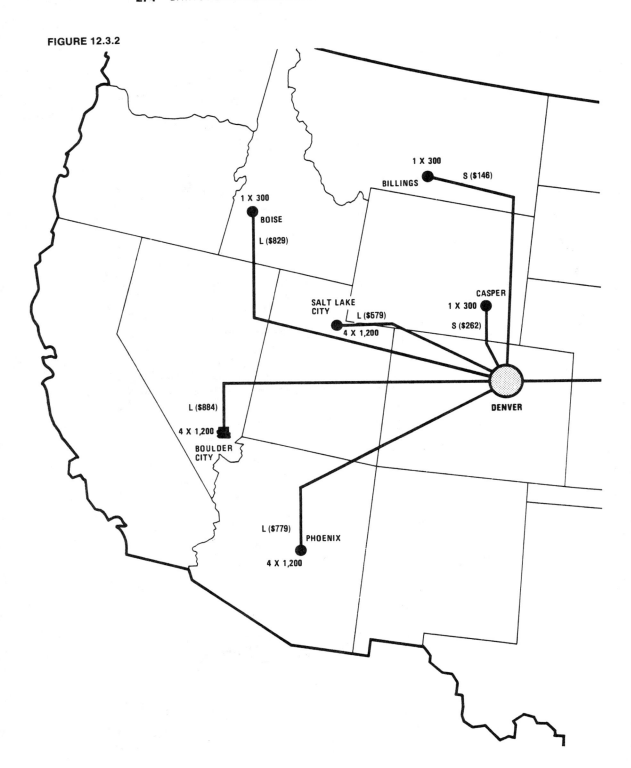

FIGURE 12.3.3

cost of the leased line from Boise directly to Denver, representing a potential savings of $225 per month.

Since the Salt Lake City 4-channel multiplexer is operating at 4,800 bit/s, higher-speed modems connecting Salt Lake City with Denver and a larger-capacity multiplexer will be required. Note that the cost of modems for the line connecting Boise with Salt Lake City is not considered, since a modem is required at Boise in any event, as well as one at the computer site in Denver.

Let us suppose that a larger-capacity multiplexer rents for an extra $50 per month per device. Since two are required, this reduces our potential savings to $125 per month. Now comes the bad part. Upgrading our modem to the next higher synchronous data rate, say, 7,200 bit/s, costs an extra $75 per month per modem as well as $21.15 per month for line conditioning, converting our potential savings to an extra expenditure of $46.15 per month.

Instead of using an expanded conventional multiplexer and obtaining a higher-speed modem, suppose we install a statistical multiplexer at Salt Lake City and Denver to support the four 1,200-bit/s channels at Salt Lake City and the one 300-bit/s channel from Boise. Suppose the statistical multiplexer rents for $175 per month and has an asynchronous compression ratio of 4:1. This means that the total input data rate of (4 × 1,200) + 300 or 5,100 bit/s requires a modem capable of transmission at 1,275 bit/s or above. Thus, although the statistical multiplexer costs $25 per month per device greater than the conventional multiplexer and its expansion unit in this example, its use may result in considerable modem cost reductions.

The statistical multiplexer permits use of 2,400-bit/s modems on the Salt Lake City-to-Denver circuit, which can be obtained for approximately $65 per device per month. Using the configuration in Figure 12.3.4, the monthly cost to support Boise and Salt Lake City terminals is listed in Table 12.3.5.

In comparing the cost shown in Table 12.3.5 with the costs listed on Figure

FIGURE 12.3.4   Supporting Boise through Salt Lake City

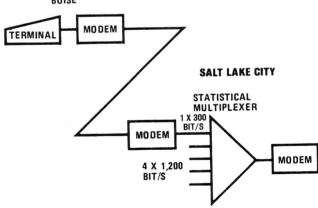

TABLE 12.3.5

Salt Lake City — Denver	
Statistical multiplexers 2 @ $175	$350.00
Leased line cost	579.00
Modem cost 2 @ $65	130.00
Subtotal Salt Lake City to Denver	$1,059.00
Boise to Salt Lake City	
Leased line and terminations	604.11
Total	$1,663.11

12.3.3, the Salt Lake City-to-Denver transmission cost has increased $10 per month, to $1,059. This is because the extra cost of the statistical multiplexers ($175 vs. $100 per month) is not completely offset by the lower cost of the modems required ($65 vs. $135). However, the total cost for supporting both Boise and Salt Lake City terminals has been reduced from $1,878 ($829 + $1,049) to $1,633.11 per month. Thus, the new network configuration would be as illustrated in Figure 12.3.5.

Prior to finalizing the network layout, we can examine each of the three multiplexer locations to determine if additional cost reductions may be realized. We consider transmitting data from one multiplexer location to another in order to eliminate or reduce the leased-line mileage charges for long-distance circuits. The distances between the three multiplexer locations and the computer site in Denver are illustrated in Figure 12.3.6.

In examining the distances between locations, connecting Boulder City to Denver via Phoenix would appear to offer the best possibility for potential savings. This is because the distance from Boulder City to Phoenix (236 miles) is less than any of the other interconnection distances. The cost of a pair of multiplexers and high-speed modems, as well as the leased line between Boulder City and Denver, was $1,087 per month as computed in Figure 12.3.3. If the line cost between Boulder City and Phoenix plus multiplexing equipment cost and any additional modem charges are less than that amount, multiplexing the data from the terminals in Boulder City through Phoenix will be more economical than directly to Denver.

Since Boulder City is a category B rate center and Phoenix is a category A center, the cost of a 236-mile circuit is $474.67 per month. $72.10 per month for two station terminals makes a total monthly cost of $546.77.

One method that can be used to service Boulder City through Phoenix is illustrated in Figure 12.3.7. Here a pair of conventional multiplexers are employed with 4,800-bit/s modems to multiplex the data from four 1,200-bit/s terminals in Boulder City to Phoenix. They are then demultiplexed, passed into a statistical multiplexer with an 8-channel capacity, and remultiplexed with local Phoenix terminal traffic for transmission to Denver.

It should be noted that statistical multiplexers are not used on the Boulder City-to-Phoenix circuit. If we assume monthly costs for such multiplexers and 2,400- and

FIGURE 12.3.5

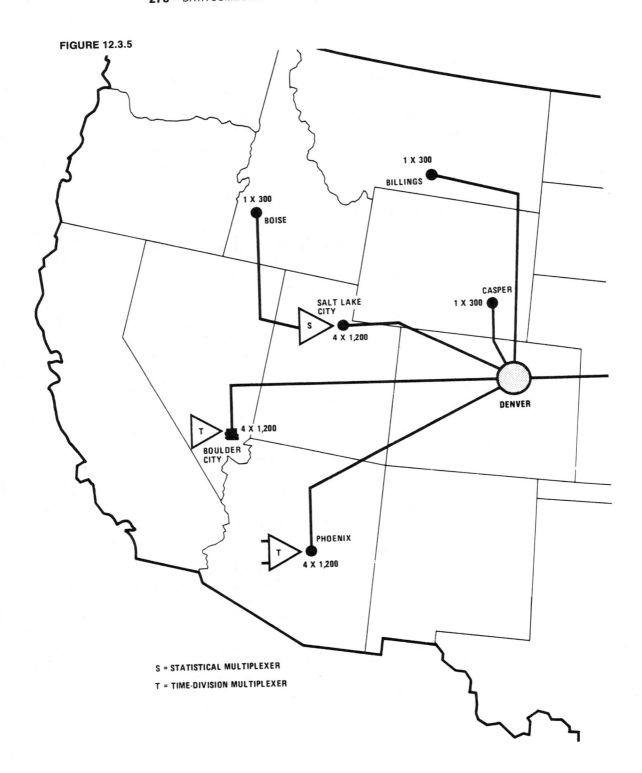

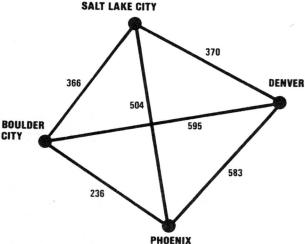

FIGURE 12.3.6   Multiplexer interconnection distances

4,800-bit/s modems as previously discussed, the cost of statistical multiplexers and 2,400-bit/s modems would be higher than the cost of conventional multiplexers and 4,800-bit/s modems on that segment of the network.

For the Phoenix-to-Denver segment, statistical multiplexers are employed since their absence would require a data rate of 9,600 bit/s on that line and 9,600 bit/s modems. Since a 9,600 bit/s modem costs $235 per month, using 2,400-bit/s modems will result in a monthly modem savings of $170 per end, or $340. Since a statistical multiplexer costs only $25 per month over an expanded conventional 4-channel multiplexer, employing that type of multiplexer will cost $290 per month less ($340-$50) than employing conventional TDM's with 9,600-bit/s modems.

Based upon the preceding, the cost of servicing Boulder City through Phoenix, is listed in Table 12.3.6.

In comparison to the $2,275.77 cost of servicing Boulder City and Phoenix, the previous cost can be found in Figure 12.3.3. Boulder City to Denver costs $1,354 per month while Phoenix to Denver costs $1,249, for a total of $2,603 per month on an individual basis. Based upon the preceding analysis, it is more economical to transmit the multiplexed data from Boulder City through Phoenix on to Denver.

With this, the initial network can be finalized as shown in Figure 12.3.8. In this illustration, the total monthly service cost per segment is shown in parentheses. Note that the monthly network cost is now $4,347 per month. In comparison, the network illustrated in Figure 12.3.8 with the initial multiplexer placements would cost $4,884 per month. The most economical method from Table 12.3.3, column 14, results in an expenditure of more than $10,000 per month, since data concentration equipment had not yet been considered. While the obvious use of multiplexers reduced the network cost from over $10,000 to $4,889 per month, through an optimization process, the cost was reduced more than $500 per month.

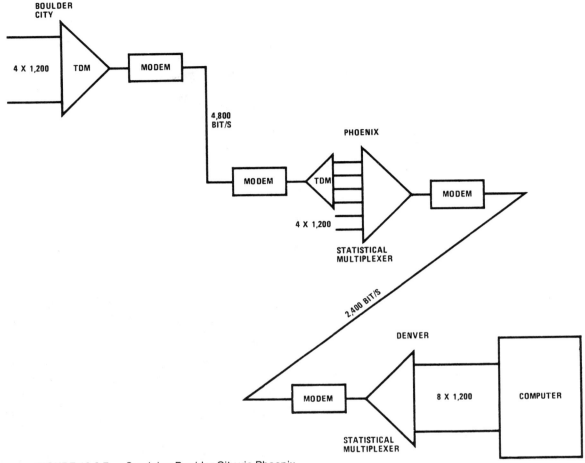

FIGURE 12.3.7   Servicing Boulder City via Phoenix

12.4 OPTIMIZATION PROGRAMS

The task of topology optimization can be long and tedious, even when not considering performance constraints—which may have a large effect on the design of complex networks. The interconnection of network locations as economically as possible while also meeting performance constraints is one of the most complex tasks facing the network analyst.

In addition to initially selecting the types and locations of data concentration equipment, each terminal in the network must be examined to determine if it is economical to transmit data through a concentration device or directly to the host computer. Next, concentration points must be examined. The routing and data rates of the circuits from each of the concentration devices are routed to other such devices to determine if transmission costs can be reduced while maintaining a desired level of performance.

TABLE 12.3.6   BOULDER CITY — PHOENIX — DENVER COST

Boulder City to Phoenix	
Multiplexers 2 @ $100	$200.00
4,800-bit/s modems 2 @ $135	270.00
Leased line cost and terminations	546.77
Subtotal Boulder City to Phoenix	$1,016.77
Phoenix to Denver	
Statistical multiplexers 2 @ $175	$350.00
2,400-bit/s modems 2 @ $65	130.00
Leased line cost	779.00
Subtotal Phoenix to Denver	$1,259.00
Total cost	$2,275.77

While these tasks are being pursued, the network analyst must evaluate the tariff structures not only of telephone companies but of specialized carriers, satellite carriers, and value-added carriers. For large networks containing several hundred terminals scattered over a large geographical area, the calculations required could result in a considerable effort, and a change in one or more tariffs could result in errors in the initial computations, making obsolete the initially designed minimum-cost network.

Fortunately for the network analyst, a number of data communications software network planning tools have been developed by several consulting organizations.

These tools can be purchased, leased, or used on a timesharing-agreement basis. They assist the network analyst in automatically creating least-cost network layouts, once specified parameters are entered. They help analyze network performance under varying conditions, and create and maintain computerized network databases. These databases then form the foundation for network analysis under numerous changing environments. One of the leading network planning tools is MIND.

The MIND System

The MIND (modular interactive network designer) system was developed by Network Analysis Corp. (now Contel) of Great Neck, New York, for users with little or no computer experience who desire to implement the most modern and cost-effective network solutions.

Using any type of asynchronous terminal, one can access the MIND system through dialing a timeshared computer service organization at which the software and tariff databases reside. With the aid of a users' manual, reinforced by the on-line prompting of MIND, users describe their network requirements to MIND's network editor module, which is used as the database for later design and analysis. Through the editor, one can move, add, or delete terminals, concentrators, multiplexers, and lines, and change traffic patterns or hardware characteristics. MIND analyzes each set of requirements, tells the user how best to satisfy

FIGURE 12.3.8   Final minimal-cost network

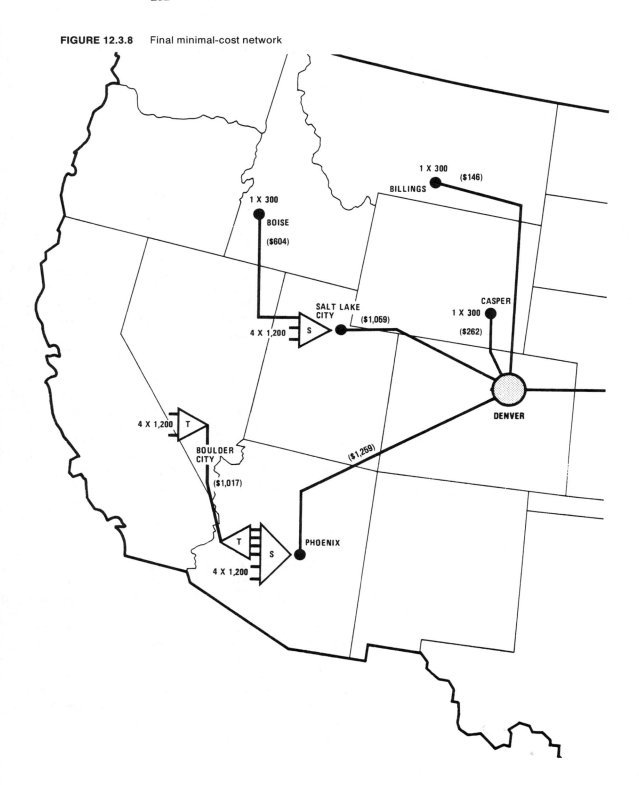

them with a least-cost line layout, and provides accurate data on operating cost, response time, reliability, and a host of other factors.

Optimization with MIND

In order to use the MIND program, let us assume that we wish to connect one terminal located in each of seven cities to our computer center in Macon, Georgia. Let us also assume that the terminals operate synchronously and can be connected via one or more multipoint lines due to the availability of appropriate poll and select software in the front-end processor.

From an analysis of anticipated operations, we estimate the transmit and receive traffic in kbit/s as illustrated in Table 12.4.1. This data is used to build the database required by the computer program for analysis and design of the network.

In Figure 12.4.1, a portion of the process required for building and verifying the database is shown.

FIGURE 12.4.1

```
    *** MIND II *** Version 8.1.1 *** MAR. 2, 1982
%
% 4/2/82 MIND CONTAINS REVISED ATT TARIFF RATES
%          REPRESENTING AN APPROX. 1.6% RATE INCREASE
%
% Type HELP for more info. End all input with a carriage return.

NDS198I: PAGE LENGTH IS          66

READY AT HOME !EDIT
.ENTER EDITING COMMAND OR ?.   !ET
READY AT EDIT/ET    !AN
.ENTER NODE ID OR ? . !MACGA,ATLGA,HOUTX,DALTX,CINOH,CLEOH,COLOH,DENCO, ①
EDT304I: NODE MACGA HAS BEEN ADDED.
EDT304I: NODE ATLGA HAS BEEN ADDED.
EDT304I: NODE HOUTX HAS BEEN ADDED.
EDT304I: NODE DALTX HAS BEEN ADDED.
EDT304I: NODE CINOH HAS BEEN ADDED.
EDT304I: NODE CLEOH HAS BEEN ADDED.
EDT304I: NODE COLOH HAS BEEN ADDED.
EDT304I: NODE DENCO HAS BEEN ADDED.
READY AT EDIT/ET    !
.ENTER EDITING COMMAND OR ?.   !EP
READY AT EDIT/EP    !SN
.ENTER NODE ID OR ? .      !MACGA
ENTER KEYWORD OR ?   !ACEX
ENTER Terminal Area Code and Exchange (AAAXXX)    !912744   ②
ENTER KEYWORD OR ?   !ROLE
ENTER Role of Terminal in Network   !CONC
ENTER KEYWORD OR ?   !
READY AT EDIT/EP    !SN ③
```

TABLE 12.4.1

Location	Area Code/ Exchange	Traffic in Kbit/s	
		Transmit	Receive
Atlanta, GA	404363	.05	.125
Houston, TX	713220	.06	.250
Dallas, TX	214321	.06	.125
Cincinnati, OH	513242	.10	.250
Cleveland, OH	216921	.06	.125
Columbus, OH	614221	.05	.125
Denver, CO	303292	.05	.125

As illustrated by the numeric 1 circled, all cities in the network are entered with identification by city and state abbreviation, including the computer center which is entered as MACGA. Next, area codes and exchanges are entered for Macon and the other network locations. The numeric 2 circled indicates the data entry for area code and exchange to identify Macon.

Next, by the entry of the characters SN, denoted by the numeric 3 circled, the program is instructed to accept traffic data for the six remote cities. A portion of the data entry interaction between the terminal operator and the computer is illustrated in Figure 12.4.2 for Houston and Dallas.

Once traffic data as well as the terminal area codes and exchange locations have been entered for all cities, the terminal operator lists the previously entered data

FIGURE 12.4.2

```
READY AT EDIT/EP     !SN
.ENTER NODE ID OR ? .      !HOUTX
ENTER KEYWORD OR ?   !ACEX
ENTER Terminal Area Code and Exchange (AAAXXX)       !713220
ENTER KEYWORD OR ?   !HOME
ENTER Homing Point of Terminal!MACGA
ENTER KEYWORD OR ?   !RC
ENTER Receive Traffic Value    !.250
ENTER KEYWORD OR ?   !TX
ENTER Transmit Traffic Value   !.06
ENTER KEYWORD OR ?   !
READY AT EDIT/EP     !SN
.ENTER NODE ID OR ? .      !DALTX
ENTER KEYWORD OR ?   !ACEX
ENTER Terminal Area Code and Exchange (AAAXXX)       !214321
ENTER KEYWORD OR ?   !HOME
ENTER Homing Point of Terminal!MACGA
ENTER KEYWORD OR ?   !RC
ENTER Receive Traffic Value    !.125
ENTER KEYWORD OR ?   !TX
ENTER Transmit Traffic Value   !.06
ENTER KEYWORD OR ?   !
```

```
READY AT EDIT/T       !TN
.ENTER NODE ID OR ? .     !*
NODE    ACEX      CITY    ST NDEV    RC     TX    AVAIL    ROLE HOME     TER
MACGA 912744  MACON     ,GA   1   0.000  0.000  .0000  CONC              0.00
ATLGA 404363  ATLANTA   ,GA   1   0.125  0.050  .0000  TERM MACGA       0.00
HOUTX 713220  HOUSTON   ,TX   1   0.250  0.060  .0000  TERM MACGA       0.00
DALTX 214321  DALLAS    ,TX   1   0.125  0.060  .0000  TERM MACGA       0.00
CINOH 513242  CINCINNATI,OH   1   0.250  0.100  .0000  TERM MACGA       0.00
CLEOH 216921  CLEVELAND ,OH   1   0.125  0.060  .0000  TERM MACGA       0.00
COLOH 614221  COLUMBUS  ,OH   1   0.125  0.050  .0000  TERM MACGA       0.00
DENCO 303292  DENVER    ,CO   1   0.125  0.050  .0000  TERM MACGA       0.00
```

FIGURE 12.4.3

for verification, entering the symbols TN to the program. Next, by the use of the symbol *, which denotes "all," all node data is printed in tabular form as illustrated in Figure 12.4.3. Here the column TER denotes the monthly station terminal charge, which is zero for all locations, since up to now data has been entered in the build mode of the program and the optimization portion has yet to be executed.

Once the database is completed, the network optimization program is executed. This program will not only provide routing and pricing information, but is also used to graphically display a network map of the resulting multipoint circuits.

Figure 12.4.4 shows a portion of the output available from the execution of MIND: the Trunk Line Summary. From the Trunk Line Summary, the total monthly cost of the multipoint circuits is $3,219.32. The drop-cost of $288.40 per month is actually the sum of the station terminal costs. The V and H coordinates listed and used for computing airline mileage between points was based upon the

FIGURE 12.4.4

```
 TRUNK LINE SUMMARY:
NO TRUNK LINES IN NETWORK

*** NAC'S MIND: A DESIGN TOOL OF NETWORK ANALYSIS CORPORATION ***
   TOPO: CIRCUIT REPORT               Tue 18-May-1982 12:27PM
 AT CONCENTRATOR MACGA:
     CIRCUIT MACGA1    :

          STATION DETAILS
  TERID ---LOCATION--- ---CITY--- ST  TRANSMIT    RECEIVE  NDV --COST--
  MACGA                 MACON      GA    0.000      0.000    0    0.00
  DENCO                 DENVER     CO    0.050      0.125    1   36.05
  DALTX                 DALLAS     TX    0.060      0.125    1   36.05
  HOUTX                 HOUSTON    TX    0.060      0.250    1   36.05
  CINOH                 CINCINNATI OH    0.100      0.250    1   36.05
  COLOH                 COLUMBUS   OH    0.050      0.125    1   36.05
  CLEOH                 CLEVELAND  OH    0.060      0.125    1   36.05
  ATLGA                 ATLANTA    GA    0.050      0.125    1   72.10
```

```
INTEREXCHANGE CHANNEL DETAILS
                        CITY        ST -ACEX- VVVV HHHH AB ALMI      COST
         FROM  DENCO  DENVER        CO 303292 7501 5899 A
         TO    DALTX  DALLAS        TX 214321 8436 4034 A   660.    779.32
         FROM  DALTX  DALLAS        TX 214321 8436 4034 A
         TO    HOUTX  HOUSTON       TX 713220 8938 3536 A   224.    369.48
         FROM  HOUTX  HOUSTON       TX 713220 8938 3536 A
         TO    ATLGA  ATLANTA       GA 404363 7260 2083 A   702.    818.80
         FROM  ATLGA  ATLANTA       GA 404363 7260 2083 A
         TO    CINOH  CINCINNATI    OH 513242 6263 2679 A   368.    504.84
         FROM  CINOH  CINCINNATI    OH 513242 6263 2679 A
         TO    COLOH  COLUMBUS      OH 614221 5972 2555 A   101.    253.86
         FROM  CLEOH  CLEVELAND     OH 216921 5574 2543 A
         TO    COLOH  COLUMBUS      OH 614221 5972 2555 A   126.    277.36
         FROM  MACGA  MACON         GA 912744 7364 1865 A
         TO    ATLGA  ATLANTA       GA 404363 7260 2083 A    77.    215.66

     TOTALS FOR CIRCUIT MACGA1      :
 LOCATIONS =  7   TRANSMIT=      0.430   DROP COST=$     288.40
 DEVICES   =  7   RECEIVE =      1.125   LINE COST=$    3219.32
 MILEAGE= 2258.   TOTAL   =      1.555   TOTAL     =$    3507.72
```

FIGURE 12.4.4   (CONT.)

area code and exchange location of each terminal that was previous entered. Thus, the program alleviates the necessity of obtaining VH coordinates by permitting users to enter the more commonly known area and exchange data elements. Again, referring to the interexchange channel details (Figure 12.4.4), the AB column heading denotes the rate category of the circuit.

Lastly, Figure 12.4.5 shows the line layout for the optimized network. As shown, one circuit links Cleveland, Columbus, Cincinnati, and Atlanta to Macon, while the second multipoint circuit connects Denver, Dallas, and Houston via Atlanta to Macon. One line connects Macon to Atlanta, which, through the use of split-stream modems, connects the two multipoint circuits on one line to Macon.

FIGURE 12.4.5

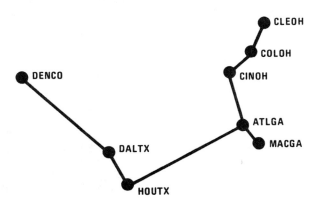

QUESTIONS

12.1 Design a minimum-cost network based upon the following information:

A.

	Terminal Data		Terminal Call Data	
Location	Data Rate	# of terminals	# of calls/day	connect time/call (min)
1	300	1	2	05
2	1,200	4	1	20
3	1,200	1	2	20
4	300	4	1	50

B.

Terminal Location	Distance To Computer	Rate Category
1	750	A-A
2	400	B-A
3	375	A-A
4	1,040	B-A

C. **Interchange mileage between locations**

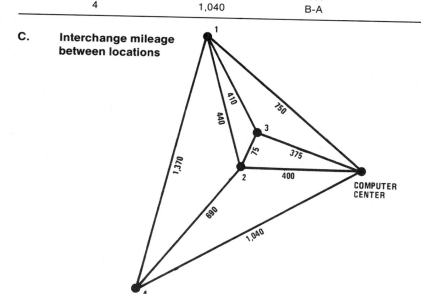

D. **Equipment rental charges/month**

4-channel multiplexer	$100
8-channel statistical multiplexer	$175
2,400-bit/s modem	$ 65
4,800-bit/s modem	$135
9,600-bit/s modem	$235

Note: Statistical multiplexer has a 4:1 compression ratio for asynchronous data.

CHAPTER 13

EMPLOYING SPECIALIZED DATA COMMUNICATIONS COMPONENTS

13.1 INTRODUCTION

This chapter introduces the reader to the operating characteristics and employment of several specialized data communications components.

Once the descriptive material has been completed, the reader can turn to the four network integration problems, starting with Section 13.10. These problems can be solved by the use of the information contained in this chapter and material previously covered.

13.2 LIMITED DISTANCE MODEMS AND LINE DRIVERS

Savings can be realized by using hardwired, twisted-pair lines driven by limited distance modems (LDMs). However, choosing the most economical way to drive data pulses down these lines involves tradeoffs in cost, performance, and quality of transmission. Although LDMs lack capabilities found in conventional modems, they are often chosen because of their lower cost for localized configurations such as office complexes, universities, and factories.

Typical point-to-point, multipoint, and repeater configurations are shown in Figure 13.2.1. Since such applications often have large numbers of terminals, the savings that can accrue by selection of the most economical transmission devices can amount to a substantial portion of the total network cost. However, in evaluating the possible savings, the cost of wire and its installation should not be overlooked, since these expenses can be considerable. If wiring costs are prohibitive, the alternative is to use limited distance modems in conjunction with leased telephone lines, but there may be problems in selecting units that meet telephone company standards, which will be covered later.

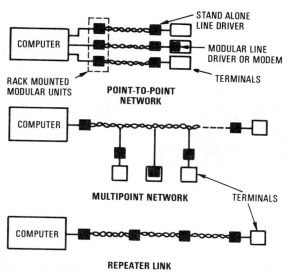

FIGURE 13.2.1   Link configurations

The four methods of transmitting data, each more expensive than the preceding one, should be carefully evaluated:

- Direct connection by ordinary copper-wire pairs.
- Line drivers, which reshape distorted pulses.
- LDMs, which are simpler versions of conventional modems.
- Conventional telephone-line modems.

The range of distances that can be achieved by the various interconnection methods are shown in Figure 13.2.2. As might be expected, the greater the distance, the greater the cost.

The RS-232-C and CCITT V.24 standards limit direct connections to 50 feet for data rates to 20 k bit/s. For distances greater than 50 feet, first consideration should be given to line drivers.

A single line driver generally provides adequate performance for hundreds of feet (depending on the unit) at data rates up to 9.6 kbit/s. Beyond the distance normally specified for the line driver, signal attenuation and line distortion become significant, and tradeoffs between line drivers and LDMs must be considered. However, line drivers can be strung out as repeaters (Fig. 13.2.1).

The distortion that results from long line lengths is caused by electrical characteristics of twisted-pair cables, which round off the leading edges of pulses and displace them in time. Pulse rounding, in turn, causes pulse sensing to be delayed, adding to existing delays. The effect of increasing attenuation as distance increases sometimes makes signal levels fall below the thresholds of pulse sensing circuits, thereby causing bits to be dropped.

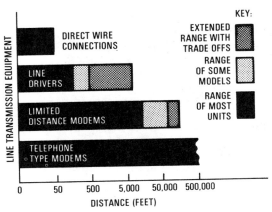

FIGURE 13.2.2   Four ways to link terminals

The factors affecting the usable distances of line drivers and LDMs for long wire runs are transmission rates, distances between points, and wire types. By using line drivers, low data rates may be transmitted over several miles of wire. For instance, at speeds up to 300 bit/s, data can be transmitted over 5,000 feet of #22 twisted-pair wire without excessive distortion. But to minimize errors, high data rates require squarer pulses than low data rates. Therefore, data rates much higher than 300 bit/s suffer from reduced range. For example, 2.4 kbit/s is limited to several hundred feet between line drivers.

When to Use LDMs

If line drivers cannot do the job, the next consideration should be LDMs. The basic elements of an LDM are shown in Figure 13.2.3. These devices are simpler and less expensive versions of conventional telephone-line modems. The cost advantage of an LDM increases with the data rate because three major functions performed by conventional modems can be eliminated or relaxed. At low data rates, the cost differences are not great. At high speeds, the differential may be thousands of dollars.

Among the unnecessary modem functions are multilevel modulation schemes, which compress high data rates into the narrow voice grade channels supplied by telephone companies. Another function that can be eliminated in LDMs is immunity to frequency offset. This effect often occurs in the modulation and demodulation processes in long distance telephone circuits. If the modulation and demodulation carriers are not precisely at the same frequency and phase, then the received signal is offset, causing demodulation errors.

A requirement that can be relaxed in LDMs is noise rejection. This factor often plays an important role in dictating the modulation technique of a conventional modem and tends to make it costly.

Settling for Less

In return for low price, LDMs lack some capabilities, which could limit their usefulness. Therefore, in considering tradeoffs between LDMs and conventional modems, the buyer must decide whether his network will tolerate the deficiencies.

First, LDMs are used mostly for private line, hardwired links. Some also can operate over local-loop voice grade telephone lines, provided that: there are no loading coils between the two points; the total distance the signal must travel can be guaranteed to be within the range of the modem; the bandwidth is within the range of the telephone lines; and the power level meets standards for metallic circuits (Bell System Technical Reference 43401).

Some LDMs require a degree of technical expertise and certain test equipment to change speeds and make line matching adjustments. Others must be returned to the factory for these jobs. However, a number of LDMs do facilitate these adjustments by means of front panel controls or wire jumpers. As might be expected, the ease with which adjustments can be made often depends on the price of the unit.

What Else to Look For

At short distances, the error rates specified for most units are about 1 error in 10^8 bits, but these rates increase rapidly with respect to distance. Diagnostic capabilities vary from one LDM model to another. Self-testing methods permit the user to find out if his unit is defective or if trouble exists elsewhere, with one or more lights to indicate equipment status and alarm conditions.

The self-testing features usually involve some form of loopback testing. The simplest diagnostic is a local loopback test, which returns the transmitter output to the receiver of the same LDM so that the transmitter signal can be checked for

FIGURE 13.2.3   Limited distance modem

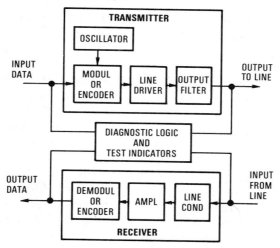

errors. Another test, dc busback, transmits the received data and clock back to the LDM at the other end of the line to provide an end-to-end test. Still another test, remote loopback, triggers dc busback at a remote site to test the elements bypassed in the preceding test. In all of these tests, an internally generated message may be used instead of existing data.

In a polled network, only one driving unit is needed at the primary site. For networks in which the wire runs exceed the limits of the line driving units, repeater stations may be needed.

Data rates of most LDMs range between 2.4 and 9.6 kbit/s. However, some units offer speeds down to 300 bit/s or less and others reach data rates up to 1 Mbit/s.

Hooking Up the Network

An important consideration in designing a network containing LDMs is selection of the most economical form of wiring. If the equipment is wholly situated on private property, cables can be strung, or telco lines can be leased.

Wire sizes and types deserve special attention. Twisted-pair wire serves for relatively short distances, and coaxial cable may be needed for longer runs. For example, one vendor specifies that a data rate of 4.8 kbit/s may be transmitted over 15 miles of #19 twisted-pair wire, but only five miles for #24 wire. At speeds near 1 Mbit/s, these distances drop to 10 percent of the 4.8 kbit/s distances. If, instead, the units are interconnected by video quality coaxial cables, the signals can be reliably transmitted as far as 17 miles at 4.8 kbit/s and 2.4 miles at 1 Mbit/s. Each manufacturer can provide a set of curves showing suggested bit rates for wire lengths of various sizes. An example is shown in Figure 13.2.4.

13.3 PORT SHARING UNITS

Port sharing units are devices that sit between host computer and modem and control access to and from the host for up to about six terminals. In this way port sharing units are able to cut down on the number of computer ports needed for these terminals.

The port sharing unit is versatile, comparatively inexpensive (about $500), and available from many modem and terminal manufacturers. It can save the cost of a relatively expensive multiplexer that does essentially the same job but may have more capabilities than are needed. Port sharing units can also be used on local peripherals, and so expand the job that can be done by a single port on the host computer.

To put the concept of port sharing into perspective, the reader should be aware of related devices designed to cut networking costs. Modem sharing units and line sharing units are available to minimize modem and line costs at remote locations, but they do not deal with the problem of overloading the host computer's ports. Modem and line sharing units are a partial solution to the high cost of data

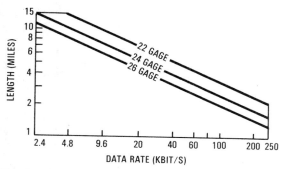

FIGURE 13.2.4   Heavier wire means more distance

communications networking, but they are limited as to the types of problems they can handle. They can, by themselves, complicate the life of the network designer.

One problem that surfaces when either modem or line sharing units are used by themselves is the distribution of polled terminals within the network. For either kind of sharing unit to be effective, the terminals should be placed so that several are grouped close together. Modem sharing units with an RS-232-C interface option can be used to serve remote terminals. Although this interface allows the data communications network a slightly more flexible configuration, with a number of terminals remote from the sharing unit, the number of remote terminals that can be served by any one unit is usually limited to one or two.

Another disadvantage of this arrangement is that if either modem on the high-speed link between the computer and the modem sharing unit should fail, or if the circuit itself goes down, all the remote terminals become inoperative. Multiplexed terminals can use the dial-up network to restore data communications if the dedicated line fails. Polled terminals, however, do not have this advantage, since the host computer software is set up to seek and recognize the addresses of specific terminals in a certain order on the line. Thus, polled terminals must stay in their respective places, relative to each other, along the communications route. Any change in route necessitates changes in hardware at the terminals as well as software at the host computer.

Port Sharing Alone

Port sharing, then, is presented either as an alternative or as a supplement to modem and line sharing, in networks without multiplexers. A port sharing unit is connected to a computer port and can transmit and receive data to and from two to about six either synchronous or asynchronous modems (Fig. 13.3.1). Data from the computer port is broadcast by the port sharing unit, which passes the broadcast data from the port to the first modem that raises a receiver-carrier-detect (RCD) signal. Data for any other destination will be blocked by the unit until the first modem stops receiving. The port sharing unit thus provides transmission by

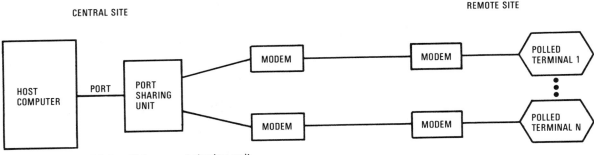

FIGURE 13.3.1   Using a port sharing unit

broadcast and reception by contention for the port connected to it. Like a modem sharing unit, a port sharing unit is transparent with respect to data transmission. Data rates are limited only by the capabilities of the terminal, modem, and computer port.

To gain the same results without a port sharing unit would require a multidrop configuration. Both the port sharing unit and a multidrop network allow a large number of terminals to be served by one computer port, but in a multipdrop network the failure of any part of the circuit will put all terminals beyond the failure out of action. In the configuration in Figure 13.3.1, however, failure of a modem or an outage on the line will only cut out a terminal on that segment. Failure of a computer port or of the port sharing unit would of course bring down the entire network, but these devices are stable and such failures are fairly unusual.

Port Sharing as a Supplement

Port sharing units may also be used alongside modem sharing units. If modem sharing units alone are used, a situation can arise where there are not enough ports to serve the network, as in Figure 13.3.2A. If each modem sharing unit serves its full complement of terminals, and all the computer ports are in use, expansion of the network, even by just one port, may require a second mainframe computer.

This problem can be dealt with by the use of a port sharing unit at the central site, which, by cutting down the number of ports needed, allows a network to expand without using additional computer ports. Figure 11.3.2B shows how one port sharing unit with a two-modem interface can free a computer port from the configuration shown in Figure 11.3.2A.

One versatile feature of port sharing units is an option that allows the unit to accept a local interface instead of the normal RS-232-C interface, so that up to two local terminals may be operated without modems at the central site.

While both modem sharing units and port sharing units are similar in the way they are used, there is an important difference in the normal placing of their interfaces. Table 13.3.1 compares the characteristics of a port sharing unit with those of modem and line sharing units. Table 13.3.2 compares the typical monthly cost of a four-terminal network in multiplexed and port sharing configurations.

FIGURE 13.3.2   Two sharing techniques combined

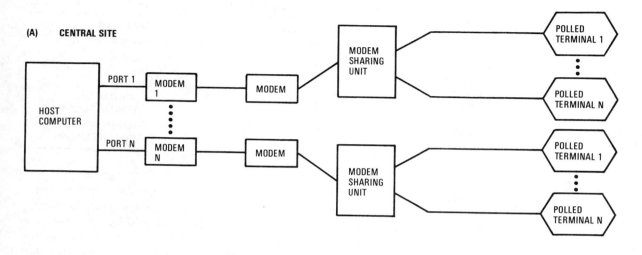

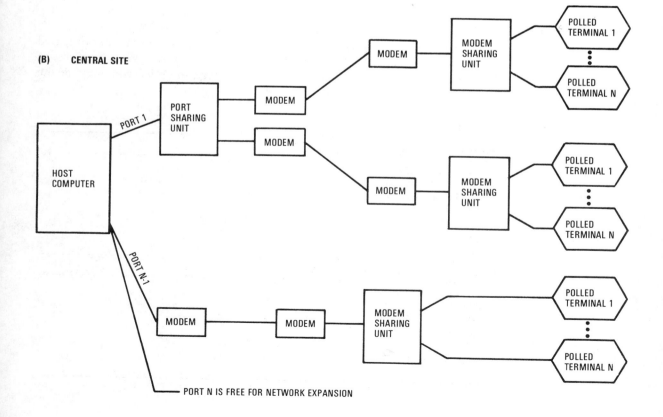

TABLE 13.3.1 FEATURES OF SHARING-UNITS

Feature	Modem Sharing/ Line Sharing Unit	Port Sharing Unit
Transmit Mode	Broadcast	Broadcast
Receive Mode	Contention	Contention
Number of Modems Interfaced	2 to 32	2 to 6
Terminals Supported	Polled	Polled
Options	RS-232-C Interface (MSU to Modem)	Local Interface (PSU to Terminal)
Normal Interface Placement	Between Modem and Terminal	Between Computer Port and Modem

The break-even point comes when the cost of each leased line (X) reaches $180 a month. This figure can be arrived at by taking the total known costs (for multiplexers, computer ports, modems, and terminals), and adding an unknown cost—for the leased line—which remains constant. Balanced against this is the somewhat smaller total rental amount for a single port sharing unit, one computer port, four lower-speed modems, and four terminals.

More Leased Lines

The lower part of the table, however, shows an increase in the number of leased lines from one to four. The upper prat of the table, therefore, gives a fixed cost of $1,420 with a variable amount on a one-time basis for a single leased line, while the

TABLE 13.3.2 COMPARISON OF MONTHLY COSTS

Multiplexed Configuration Costs

Two 4-channel TDM's @ $120	$ 240
4 Computer Ports @ $35	140
2 9,600 Bit/S Modems @ $220	440
4 Terminals @ $150	600
1 Leased Line	X
Where X = Monthly Cost of A Leased Line	$ 1,420 + X

Port Sharing unit Configuration Costs

1 Port Sharing Unit @ $25	$ 25
1 Computer Port @ $35	35
4 2,400 Bit/S Modems @ $55	220
4 Terminals @ $150	600
Leased Lines	4X
Where X = Monthly Cost of A Leased Line	$ 880 + 4X

lower part shows a significantly lower equipment cost but gives a variable cost for leased lines four times that for a single-line multiplexed configuration.

In this example, $1,420 less $880 equals $540 or 3x (with x still representing the variable cost of the leased line). Dividing $540 by three gives a break-even point of $180. Thus, until monthly leased-line charges total $180 for each line, the use of a port sharing unit is more economical.

In addition, users can (without increasing network costs) add up to two more local terminals to a configuration based on a port sharing unit, since the table is based on the costs related to four terminals, and the average port sharing unit can support up to six. The only additional cost would be for the rental of the terminal units.

In order to carry two additional terminals in a multiplexed configuration, however, the user would have to pay substantially more. On the basis of the table, $150 would be required for each terminal, and an additional $35 each for two more computer ports. As explained earlier, the cost of adding two computer ports can be further aggravated if all ports are already in use on the host computer, so that any extra load requires another entire processing unit.

The port sharing unit, therefore, is most evidently a cost-saving tool when the user is already straining the CPU to its limits. While saving money is a full-time preoccupation for all cost-conscious data communications managers, and port sharing should be considered in any polled-terminal situation where instantaneous response is not the most important network condition, there are times, such as when the CPU runs out of capacity, that the cost of any further network expansion takes a leap from a few hundred dollars to perhaps tens of thousands for another CPU.

13.4 PORT SELECTORS

Even in a network in which terminals must contend for access to ports on the host computer, it is unlikely that all ports will be busy at the same time. So most networks can operate with more terminals than computer ports. But because each terminal is not connected to its own dedicated port, a switching device, called a port selector or intelligent patch panel (IPP), is needed to connect incoming messages to available ports.

Port selectors allow terminals to be added to a network without increasing the number of computer ports. When a network is being designed, the selectors can reduce the cost of its host computer by cutting back on the number of ports needed.

These IPPs operate in a manner similar to telephone rotaries (stepping switches that sequentially search for available outgoing lines), except that the selectors provide appropriate interfaces between computers and terminals. Some selectors have extra features specifically applicable to data networks.

The difference between port selection units and port sharing devices is that port sharing units are used in polled networks (where the host controls the traffic flow), while port selection units are in contention networks, in which terminals transmit to the host on a random basis. With a port selection device, access to any port is on a first-come, first-served basis.

The port selector looks for incoming data from terminals connected to its line side, and at the same time keeps track of any computer ports that are idle. Some port selectors can be arranged to form subgroups of contending terminals and ports, so that certain terminals can only be connected to an assigned group of ports. When one of these terminals requests access, the selector searches for an available port in its group and connects the terminal to that port. If all the designated ports are taken, the selector continues to scan until one becomes available, or until the request for access ceases. Another option is a "busy out" feature whereby the port selector signals to new callers that all available ports are in use.

Port selectors can be used at remote locations to make input terminals contend for a smaller number of communications lines or multiplexer ports. Consider a remote location with 32 terminals each communicating with the central computer at 300 bit/s. One economical method to move the data is to multiplex transmission from the 32 terminals over a single leased line, at an aggregate transmission speed of 9,600 bit/s. This requires two 32-port multiplexers and 32 computer ports. Assume that 16 additional 300 bit/s terminals must be added to the remote site. Since the leased line is already operating at its 9,600 bit/s limit, one alternative is to upgrade the multiplexers by adding 16 ports to each one, and to replace the modems and voice-grade communications link with wideband facilities. This method requires 16 additional computer ports to service the additional terminal traffic. But the added line capacity would be very expensive, because wideband facilities are far more costly than voice-grade lines.

Another option would be to install a pair of 16-port multiplexers, one additional leased line between them, and two 4,800-bit/s modems to transmit on the new line. But 16 additional computer ports would still be required to service the additional terminals.

Evaluating Port Selection

Increasing the number of terminals tht can be handled by the central site by means of a port selection arrangement may indeed be less expensive than doing it by expanding the capacity of the multiplexing equipment. To find out if port selection is the practical answer to a particular situation, the user should first assess the demands the present terminals are making on the network, then estimate the additional demands that will arise because of the proposed new terminals. If, for example, it is found that even though 48 terminals are needed, the total number demanding access to the central computer at any one time is unlikely to be more than 32; and that this limit of 32 is going to be exceeded during a total of perhaps two hours a week; and that even in those two hours, the total demand will hardly ever mount to more than 35 terminals at any one time: Then, if the user is willing to risk the chance that three terminals may not immediately be able to reach the computer during about two hours in the week, a standard 32-port selector can be installed (Fig. 13.4.1). It services 48 lines at 32 ports on a contention basis.

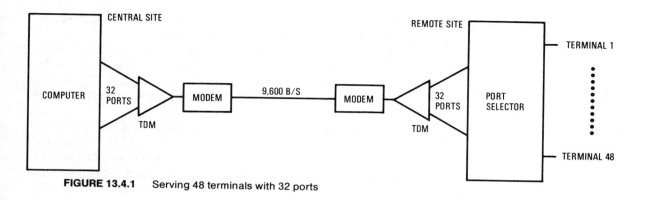

FIGURE 13.4.1   Serving 48 terminals with 32 ports

The port selector then offers a contention ratio of 48 to 32, or 3 to 2 (48 terminals connected to the line side of the selector and 32 outputs to the multiplexer ports). It eliminates the need to add 16 computer ports, to upgrade or add multiplexers, or to upgrade or add communications links. Although a telephone company rotary could be used for the port selection process, 80 modems would then be needed (48 for the terminals and 32 for the carrier lines). A port selector can thus cut back on the number of modems needed for port selection by rotaries, as well as the expense of 48 communications links. By directly connecting the terminals to the line side of the port selector it becomes possible to do away with the low-speed modems. A port selector than can make 48 lines contend for 32 ports might cost about $15,000. But the rotary cost would equal that of a port selector in a little less than a year.

A typical computer network, as in Figure 13.4.2A indicates what must be taken into account in coming to a decision about port selectors. In this example 48 computer ports handle messages from two multiplexers and a local rotary. Each multiplexer provides 16 terminal-to-computer connections, as well as 16 dial-in ports at the computer site. If the network is distributed over several time zones, peaks in utilization of the terminals will occur at different times in different places (Fig. 13.4.2B).

Load Patterns

A typical profile of the number of users logged onto the network from each geographical area can be computed with statistical software packages provided by computer manufacturers. While other networks may not reveal the same patterns, they may be similar, because normal working habits are a significant factor in the fluctuations of network utilization.

At the start of working hours, use gradually builds as people arrive at the office and settle down to work. During the morning coffee break period, the number of users decreases temporarily, with the length of time and the degree of the dropoff varying from place to place. Morning peak use is followed by a drop in activity during the lunch period. Use then builds up until the afternoon break, and peaks again as people rush to complete the day's work. As close of business approaches, activity tapers off until only a few terminals remain on line.

By combining profiles, an overall network profile can be developed, which presents the total number of terminals on line. Typically, 95 percent of the time, there will be up to 37 terminals on-line or seeking access between 4:15 p.m. and 4:45 p.m. and 99 percent of the time there will be as many as 40 users (between 4 p.m. and 5:30 p.m.).

Returning to the network in Figure 13.4.2A, it is now apparent that 99 percent of the time eight or more of the 48 computer ports are not in use, and that 95 percent of the time, 11 or more ports will be idle. Thus, the use of a port selector becomes a question of economics against inconvenience. Is the cost of a number of mostly idle computer ports worth the seldom used advantage of being able to connect all terminals, simultaneously and without delay? A related question that the network designer must answer is whether the computer can process all messages rapidly enough when all terminals are on-line.

Let us assume (Fig. 13.4.2A) that the 90th percentile of port usage is decided on. This would mean that a 32-port selector would be needed (Fig. 13.4.2B). After calculating the cost saving possible with such a port selector, we can determine if the sacrifice of 16 continuously available ports is justifiable. Investigations might also be made into the savings possible with a 48-line by 37-port selector (95th percentile), or a 48-line by 40-port selector (99th percentile).

Although the saving may be considerable for a single computer installation, additional saving is possible for installations that have redundant computers, because every excess computer port that can be eliminated on one front end can also be eliminated on the other. In addition, reductions may also be possible in the capital outlay for devices that switch between central processing units.

'Blue-sky' Outlook

The intelligent patch panel evokes much wishful thinking because of its inherent flexibility. The three most frequently mentioned "wish-list" items are:

1. Speed, code, and protocol conversion to make the IPP a truly universal interface and allow its use with large mainframes

2. Preprocessing capability so that certain CPU functions could be off-loaded to the IPP

3. Demultiplexing of remote multiplexers to further enhance network cost savings (such as a remote eight-channel multiplexer connected to a single local IPP interface, with the IPP acting as the local multiplexer).

However, these desirable features also increase the price and complexity of such equipment and push its function into the realm of the large, expensive front-end, or communications, processor.

The intelligent patch panel benefits both the user and the site manager. For the user, the IPP is a simple interface that affords keyboard selection of authorized computer resources and the feedback and control to minimize intervention by computer-site personnel. To the computer-site manager, the IPP gives the infor-

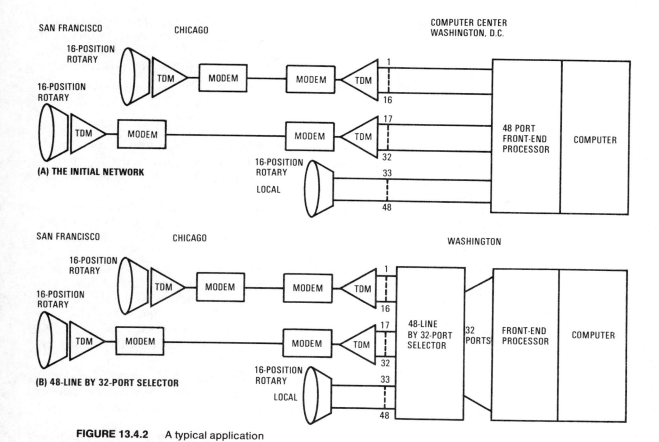

FIGURE 13.4.2   A typical application

mation and control necessary to dynamically change the entire network. This results in a cost-effective configuration, savings in computer ports and operator time, and increased user efficiency.

Finally, because of the nature of any microprocessor-based device, the IPP is inherently programmable, thus allowing for future enhancements and avoiding rapid obsolescence.

13.5 DATA COMMUNICATIONS SWITCHES

At one time, data communications switches were found mainly in technical control rooms, where they help in on-line monitoring, fault diagnosis, and digital and analog testing. But now they are also being used to reroute data quickly and efficiently and to replace several dedicated backup units with just one, enabling a single terminal (say) to act as standby for several on-line terminals.

The four basic categories of switches are fallback, bypass, crossover, and matrix.

Two or more of these, from the same or different categories, may be chained to serve still other data communications requirements. Furthermore, within each category there are two types of switches: the so-called telco switches, which transfer four-wire leased or two-wire dialup telephone lines, and the EIA switches, which transfer all 24 leads of an EIA RS-232-C interface.

Fallback Switches

The fallback switch is a rapid and reliable means of switching network components from on-line to standby equipment. The EIA version selects either of a pair of 24-pin-connected components, which, as shown in Figure 13.5.1, may be terminals, modems, or channels on a front-end processor.

In the first example, two terminals share a single modem. This configuration might be required—for example—when terminals have the same transmission speed but use different protocols, so that each communicates with a different group of remote terminals or computers.

In the second example (Fig. 13.5.1B), one terminal is provided with access to two modems, one of which is redundant but needed for uptime reliability. Alternatively, the first modem might enable the terminal to transmit to another terminal at 2,000 bit/s during one portion of the day, while the second lets it "talk" to a central computer at 9,600 bit/s during other periods of the day. Then, depending on operational requirements, one terminal with a fallback switch for modem selection could be more practical than installing two terminals.

In a third application, an EIA fallback switch (Fig. 13.5.1C) permits a modem to be transferred between front-end procesors. Although called a line-transfer device by some manufacturers, in effect what one obtains is a device that selects which front-end processor will service the modem.

A telco fallback switch similarly allows the user to select one of two sets of telephone lines. As shown in Figure 13.5.1D, it can select one line from among various combinations of dedicated and dial-up lines that may have been installed to fit the needs of a particular application. For a critically large data-transfer application, for instance, it might be connected to a pair of leased lines, one a primary circuit and the other an alternate circuit.

Bypass Switches

The EIA bypass switch connects several EIA interfaces of one type (say, modems) to the same number plus a spare of another EIA interface type (say, terminals) and can switch any member of the first group to the spare member of the second group. One application is at a computer installation (Fig. 13.5.2A). Here, one front-end channel is reserved as a spare in case any of the existing channels, which normally service predetermined modems, should need to be connected quickly to a spare channel.

In another application (Fig. 13.5.2B), the EIA bypass switch can substitute a standby spare terminal for a failed on-line terminal and do away with the need for

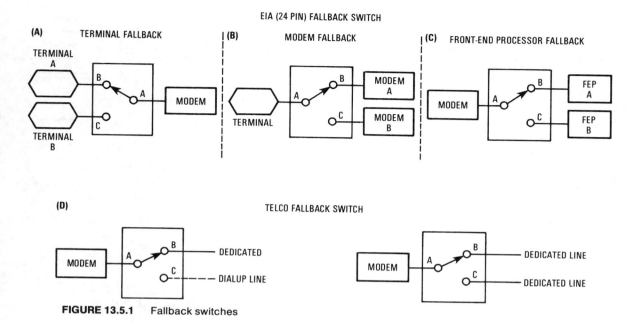

FIGURE 13.5.1   Fallback switches

a spare modem. Although seldom used for multiple-terminal access, a bypass switch can also enable many terminals to share a single modem and line.

A telco bypass switch transfers any one of a group of two- or four-wire telco lines to a spare communications component. For example, as shown in Figure 13.5.2C, if modem 1 should fail, line 1 can be switched to the spare modem. Conversely, a telco switch may transfer a spare line to an operational communications component like a modem (Fig. 13.5.2D). Telco bypass switches can be used to switch leased or dial-up lines to modems, automatic dialers, or acoustic couplers.

Crossover and Matrix Switches

Crossover switches supply their user with an easy method of interchanging the data flow between two pairs of communications components. Each switching module has four connectors, one for each of the two pairs of communications components connected to it. As shown in Figure 13.5.3A, an EIA crossover switch permits the data flow to be reversed between two pairs of EIA-interfaced components. Here, modem A (which is normally connected to the front-end channel A) and modem B (normally connected to front-end channel B) swap channels when the switch is moved by the network operator from the normal to the crossover mode of operation.

Similarly, a telco crossover switch permits the user to interchange the data flow between two telco lines and two modems (Fig. 13.5.3B). Although two dedicated

EIA BYPASS SWITCH

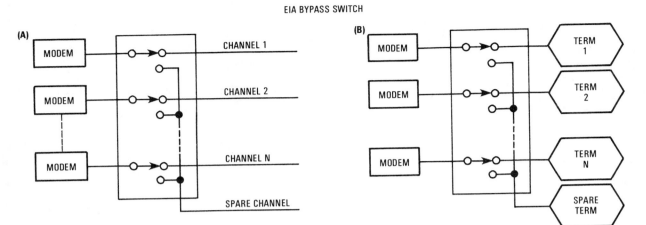

TELCO BYPASS SWITCH

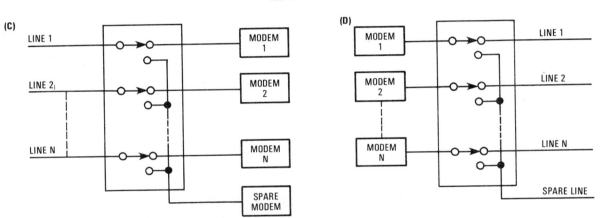

Figure 13.5.2 Bypass switches

lines are shown connected to the crossover switch, the switch can also be used to cross over two dialup lines or one dedicated and one dialup line. In any of these cases, crossover line A (which is normally connected to modem A) becomes connected to modem B, and vice versa.

With a matrix switch the user can interconnect any combination of a group of incoming interfaces to any combination of a group of outgoing interfaces. Matrix switches are manufactured as N-by-N, with 4-by-4, 8-by-8, and 16-by-16 combinations typically available.

As shown in Figure 13.5.4A, an EIA 4-by-4 matrix switch is a quick and efficient way of connecting any combination of four modems to any combination of four front-end-processor channels. The circles represent the activated switch combinations, so that, in this case, modem 1 serves front-end processor (FEP) channel 1, modem 2 serves FEP channel 3, modem 3 serves FEP channel 2, and modem 4 serves FEP channel 4. Further, with this configuration the user is free to designate one or more modem or front-end-processor channels as spares, or a combination of modems and channels as spares.

The telco 4-by-4 matrix shown in Figure 13.5.4B similarly permits the transfer of any combination of four incoming lines to any combination of four outgoing lines. One type of application warranting use of telco matrix switches arises when remote terminals require access to two or more adjacent computers. If the terminals are used heavily enough to justify installing leased lines from the remote sites to the central computers, the telco matrix switch enables the user to switch the incoming leased lines to outgoing cables, which, via modems, are connected to different computers.

Derived Functions

From the four categories of switches discussed, a number of additional switching functions have been developed. For instance, a spare-component backup switch is basically a pair of fallback switches contained in one housing. As shown in Figure 13.5.5A, this switch permits a normal and a backup mode of operation. The normal mode permits data to be transferred through the primary component, whereas the backup mode switches the data flow through the spare components.

Figure 13.5.3   Crossover switches

(A)

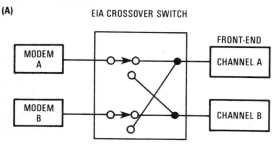

(B)

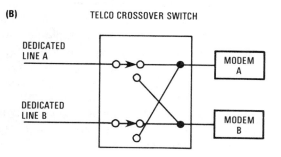

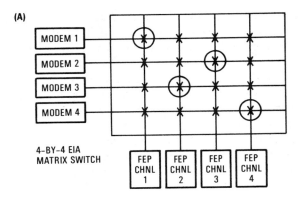

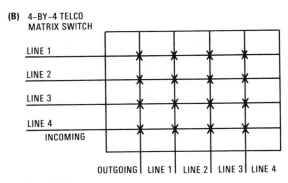

Figure 13.5.4 Matrix switches

In another configuration (Fig. 13.5.5B), a pair of modems are the primary and spare components connected to one terminal, and the switch selects the modem to be used in transferring data between the terminal and the telco line. Because three EIA interfaces are involved, this configuration is called a 3-of-4 EIA interface bypass switch.

In a 4-of-4 EIA interface (Fig. 13.5.5C), four interface devices are connected to the switch. In this configuration the switch selects one of the two encoders to encode terminal data for transmission through the attached modem.

A second common switch derivation is a multiple fallback switch. Besides the EIA and telco versions, this switch is manufactured in a 1-of-N version, with N being the number of possible selections. Figure 13.5.6A shows two possible configurations for a 1-of-4 EIA fallback switch. At the left, the switch allows the terminal to be connected to any one of four modems, while at the right, any one of four terminals may be connected to a single modem. Similarly, Figure 13.5.6B shows how the 1-of-4 telco fallback switch allows either four modems to share a single line or four lines to share a single modem.

Figure 13.5.5   Backup-switch variations

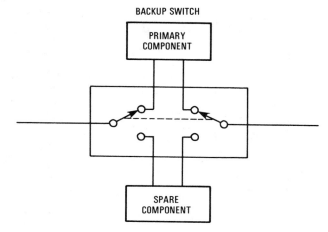

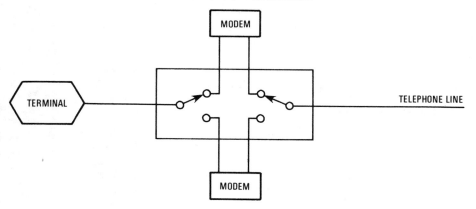

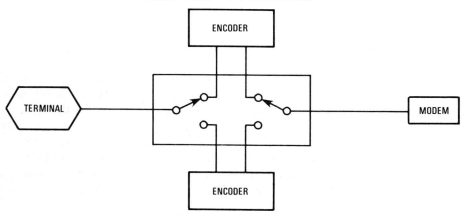

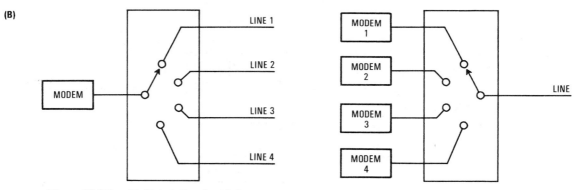

Figure 13.5.6   Multiple fallback switches

Chaining Switches

Switches can be chained to develop additional switching functions or to increase the capacity of existing network devices. Even more usefully, different categories of switches and different types of switches within the same category can be chained. Figure 13.5.7 shows a 4-by-4 telco matrix switch chained to a 4-by-4 EIA matrix switch so that the user may interconnect any combination of lines, modems, and front-end-processor channels to arrange the information path he desires. For this example, the number of possible configurations is increased to N^3 from the normal N^2 combinations available with a single N-by-N matrix switch.

Switch Control

The commonest methods of activating a switch are local and remote manual, ASCII unattended remote, and via a business machine or central host computer.

For a remote manual switch a manufacturer produces a remote control panel equipped with a push button and a cable connecting it to the remote switch. This setup also has the advantage that shorter cable lengths can be run from communications components to the switch.

The ASCII unattended remote control permits a switch to be controlled or monitored at any remote site at which a telephone line can be installed. An adapter interfaces the switch (or switches) to the telephone line and turns it on or off upon receiving a coded message consisting of the switch number and the state to transfer to. The adapter then reports back the switch's new status. Also available is a query mode that allows the operator to check a remote switch's position.

When a business machine (computer) is involved, switching is controlled directly by the machine—normally through a 5-volt TTL logic circuit.

Figure 13.5.7   Chaining telco and EIA matrix switches

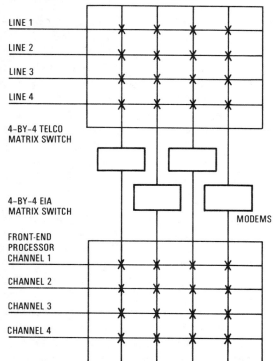

13.6 SWITCHING APPLICATIONS

The cost of providing communications switches can range from less than a few hundred dollars to well over $50,000. What makes the price vary so much rests on the answers to such questions as:

- Which devices are most likely to fail?
- What tangible and intangible effects will a failed network device, such as a concentrator, have on the organization's operation?
- Would the operational loss be so great that it warrants the cost of including backup equipment and transmission lines?
- When a network component goes down, how much down time—if any—is allowable to activate backup devices and get the network back into full-scale operation?
- To obtain speedy network recovery, what are the best types of switches for the application, and where should they be placed in the network?

In this section, the discussion will center around the ramifications of switching between dual colocated concentrators. Here, one concentrator may be assigned completely to back up the other unit, or each concentrator may be servicing its own terminals during normal operation. In either case, on failure of one concentrator, the other takes over all duties if it has enough capacity to do so. In the latter case, if the reserve capacity isn't available, then a secondary job, such as driving a line printer, may be suspended as long as concentrator down time continues.

In the basic setup of the following applications, each concentrator location services a number of relatively local low- and medium-speed terminals, so that each has a number of terminal-to-concentrator links. Each concentrator merges all traffic from its terminals and sends it on a high-speed line to a remote host computer.

As will be seen, the applications tend to become more complex and more expensive. The actual choice depends to some extent on network application and on the severity of the consequences of a device failure.

Hot-Start Configuration

The two main methods of integrating colocated concentrators to service remote terminals are commonly called "hot start" and "cold start." The hot-start approach (Fig. 13.6.1) means that a backup computer is energized, fully programmed with a duplicate of the software in the primary concentrator, and may be continuously tracking the traffic in and out of the primary concentrator. When the primary computer fails, a computer-controlled switch can put the backup concentrator in control substantially instantaneously.

Full effectiveness of such a hot-start arrangement requires the installation of an intercomputer (that is, interconcentrator) communications unit. When a failure such as memory-parity errors or power loss occurs, the concentrator experiencing difficulty sends appropriate software commands through the communications unit. Additionally, an automatic command to a bank of computer-controlled telco

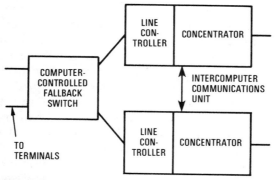

FIGURE 13.6.1   Hot-start

fallback switches provides instantaneous transfer of the line from each terminal to the line-controller of the operating concentrator.

The near-instantaneous switching and the minimization of the loss of data are the important advantages of the hot-start configuration. However, there are significant hardware costs associated with the computer-controlled switches and the intercomputer communications unit. In addition, the necessary software modifications to permit the desired switching are complex, involving experienced personnel, much patience, and large amounts of machine time for testing the developed software. Overall, the cost for hot start may well reach over $100,000—not counting the cost of the concentrator itself. But it may be well worth the money to assure that the network remains continuously operational and available.

Cold-Start Configuration

Telco fallback switches represent one method of providing an alternate path between the remote terminals and the two concentrators (Fig. 13.6.2). Here, the

FIGURE 13.6.2   Cold-start

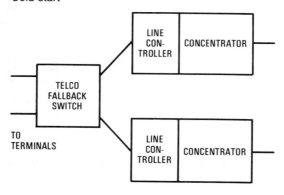

occurrence of a concentrator failure or a concentrator-to-host link failure will require manual intervention. When one or both failures occur, it becomes necessary to switch the telco units to insure that the remote terminals are connected to the operating concentrator. Furthermore, the standby concentrator must have its programs loaded from a high-speed storage unit such as a disk. Thus, if the concentrators are initially sharing the terminal workload, the failure of one concentrator may require the other concentrator's software to be reconfigured to service the entire workload. This configuration can be completed in a few minutes by manually activating the switches and reading the backup programs from the disk into the operational concentrator's memory.

Some data being transmitted through the concentrator may be lost during the reconfiguration time. But the low cost of the cold-start configuration may justify the extra time associated with satisfying retransmission requests for lost messages.

Sharing a Backup Concentrator

The availability requirements of the network may be such that neither operating concentrator has the reserve to serve as backup for the other. But it may be possible to service both devices with a single backup concentrator (Fig. 13.6.3). Here, telco fallback switches allow the terminals in Building 1 or Building 3 to be connected to the backup concentrator in Building 2. The number of modems interfaced to the telco switching units in Building 2 only need equal the maximum of the number of such devices in either Building 1 or Building 3. Thus, if the possibility of two concentrators failing at the same time is disregarded, the cost of the fallback switches is more than offset by the savings due to the lesser number of modems necessary at the backup concentrator.

Backup with EIA Switches

An alternative approach to servicing the terminals in Buildings 1 and 3 by the backup concentrator in Building 2 can be obtained through the use of EIA fallback switches (Fig. 13.6.4). Instead of installation between the modems as with the telco switches in the preceding application, the EIA switches are between the modem and the line controller of the concentrator. Depending on the distance between either primary concentrator and the backup concentrator, line drivers or modems become necessary to permit an undistorted output signal to reach the backup. Assuming relatively short distances that permit the use of lower-cost line drivers, rather than modems, a telco fallback switch will suffice in Building 2 for each pair of terminal-to-concentrator links in the other buildings.

In the normal mode of operation the terminals in Building 1 or 3 communicate with their respective concentrator via a pair of modems and an EIA fallback switch. Should either concentrator fail, the operator must position the fallback switch into its backup mode and position the telco switch in Building 2. Doing this provides a new set of circuits from the affected terminals to the concentrator in Building 2.

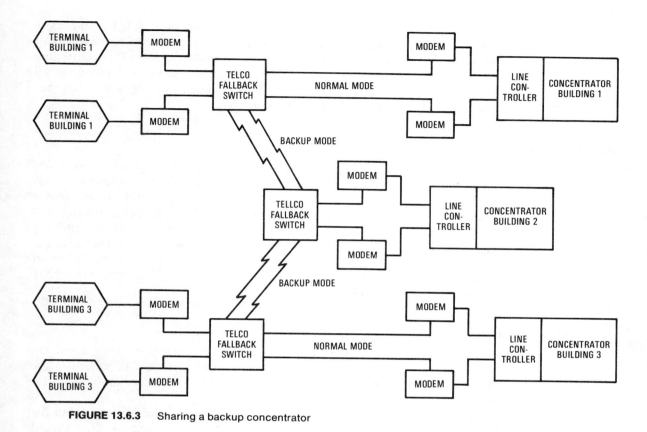

FIGURE 13.6.3   Sharing a backup concentrator

FIGURE 13.6.4   Backup with EIA switches

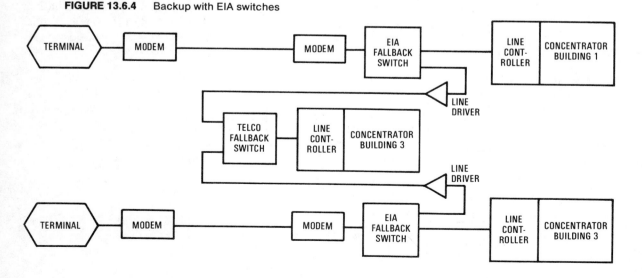

This and the previous application have a concentrator added to the basic configuration of two such devices. In either case, the user may set up a network of three primary concentrators that share the backup duties. As well as connecting terminals directly to the concentrator in Building 2, the user would have to install EIA or telco fallback switches to transfer the new data paths to either of the other two concentrators when backup service is needed.

Concentrator to Central Computer

If data transfer from each concentrator to the central computer is via a few high-speed lines, EIA fallback switches permit the transfer of modems and lines between the concentrators. In Figure 13.6.5, two switches permit each concentrator to communicate over its own dedicated link to the central-computer complex.

This type of configuration compensates for a concentrator failure by permitting the remaining concentrator to communicate with the host computer over its line and the line of the other device. However, the failure of either one of the dedicated lines or of a modem would require selection of one of the concentrators to use the remaining data communications link.

Adding a Third EIA Fallback Switch

If the user wants to overcome the shortcomings of the preceding configuration, the inclusion of a third EIA fallback switch and another modem interfaced to the dual-concentrator configuration can either prevent or minimize the failure of a modem or of a dedicated line (Fig. 13.6.6).

In the normal mode of operation, each concentrator communicates with the central computer via its own dedicated line. If a modem or dedicated line should fail, the proper positioning of two of the switches allows the concentrator to communicate with the central computer via the middle modem over an alternative path—either a dial-up line or another dedicated line. A disadvantage of this

FIGURE 13.6.5 Concentrator to computer

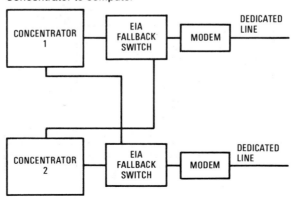

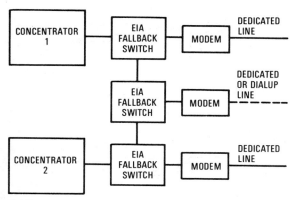

FIGURE 13.6.6   Adding a third EIA fallback switch

configuration is that each concentrator has access to only one line at a time, unlike the configuration in the previous application.

Adding More Switchable Lines

Access to more than one dedicated line at a time may be obtained by adding lines for each concentrator and reconfiguring the EIA fallback switches as shown in Figure 13.6.7. If one concentrator should fail, the other can communicate over both dedicated lines, and it still has access to the backup line. In this manner, throughput degradation should be minimized.

Chaining Adds Options

Chaining two EIA fallback switches results in another way of providing an alternative central-computer link for a dual-concentrator installation (Fig. 13.6.8). Only one channel is required for each concentrator. In normal operation, each switch

FIGURE 13.6.7   Adding more switchable lines

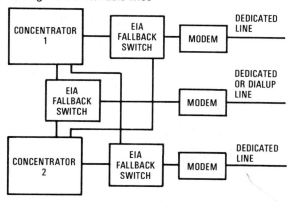

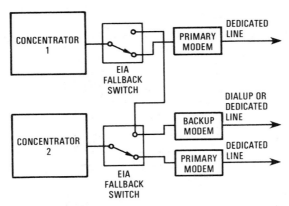

FIGURE 13.6.8   Chaining adds options

interfaced to each concentrator channel remains in the primary-modem position. If the dedicated line or the primary modem of either concentrator should fail, the associated switch is positioned so that a path is provided to the backup modem. As previously, this backup modem can use a dial-up or a dedicated line to communicate with the central computer.

This configuration requires only one concentrator channel to provide a link in the event of modem or dedicated-line failure. However, should a concentrator fail, the other one is not provided with access to the failing device's line. Thus, if terminals from the failing concentrator are switched to the operational concentrator, the operational link to the computer may not be sufficient to satisfy the increased terminal traffic. Redundancy for this link through the use of EIA fallback switches can become rather complicated when more than a few lines require multiple access.

FIGURE 13.6.9   Access to other lines

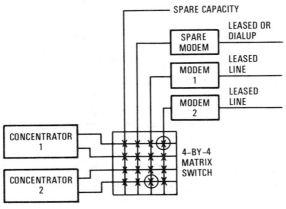

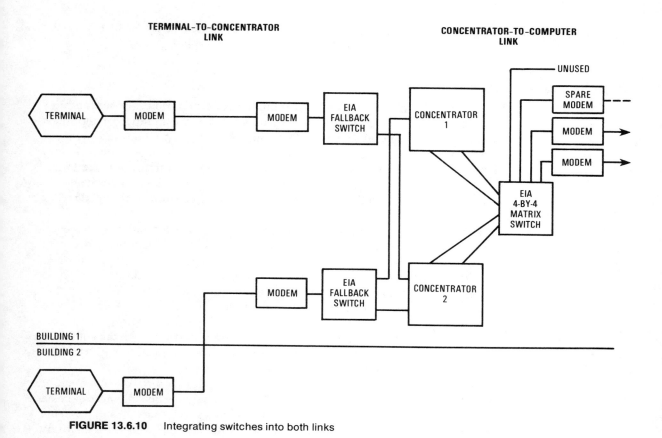

FIGURE 13.6.10   Integrating switches into both links

Access to Other Lines

Use of one or more EIA matrix switches (Fig. 13.6.9), can alleviate switching complexity as well as provide each concentrator access to the other dedicated line. For example, with a single 4-by-4 switch, each concentrator can have ready access to the spare modem and to any modem and line connected to the other concentrator. Although only one spare modem is shown here, a second modem and its associated line facilities could be added, since the output side of the 4-by-4 switch can interface one additional device.

As shown by the circles, concentrator 1 normally transmits data through modem 2 to the central computer, and concentrator 2 via modem 1. Either concentrator can be connected to the spare modem and associated line, should its primary modem or line fail.

If a concentrator fails, the other one can be connected to the failing device's primary modem and line, thus ensuring the continuation of full throughput to the central computer. If each concentrator communicates with the central computer through more than one link, the use of an 8-by-8 or a 16-by-16 switch, or the chaining of more than one matrix switch, should be explored.

Integrating Switches into Both Links

The number of concentrators and of communications lines from each concentrator to the host computer depends upon such factors as the number of terminals serviced by each concentrator in both primary and backup modes of operation, terminal-traffic patterns, and line-protocol overhead. The configuration in Figure 13.6.10 represents one possible way of integrating switches into both the terminal-to-concentrator and the concentrator-to-host-computer links. It provides an alternative path for both links when dual concentrators are within about 50 feet of each other.

Here, it is assumed that the remote terminals are in two buildings. However, because the distances between each terminal and the concentrators preclude direct attachment or the use of line drivers, modems are necessary. An equipment study establishes each terminal's need for access to a second concentrator in order to maintain the desired level of backup. At the same time, to maintain throughput at the full transmission speed after the failure of one concentrator, it is necessary to have the capability to switch the links of the failing device to the other one. Furthermore, should any modem or line of the concentrator link to the computer become inoperative, switching to a spare modem communicating with the host computer via the dial-up network is desirable.

If the equipment study shows that each concentrator requires one channel for communicating with the host computer, then two channels become necessary on each device in order for each to use the other's link as well as its own at the same time. Thus, as shown here, the failure of concentrator 1 can be compensated for by positioning the EIA fallback switches on the terminal-to-concentrator link so that the terminals in Building 1 connect to the second concentrator. In addition, each concentrator link to the computer is connected via a 4-by-4 EIA matrix switch to the other concentrator. The same procedure applies to the failure of the second concentrator.

Should a modem or line from either concentrator link to the computer become inoperative, the 4-by-4 matrix switch permits a ready configuration to the spare modem and the dial-up network.

The procedures discussed here apply to a network with any number of terminal and host links.

13.7 AUTOMATIC ANSWERING AND CALLING UNITS

Automatic answering units (AAUs) and automatic calling units (ACUs) reduce the necessity of network intervention by an operator. An AAU is normally integrated into a modem that interfaces a computer. When the AAU detects a remote user's dial-up ring, it automatically connects the user to a computer port (if available).

An ACU, on the other hand, permit a computer or other intelligent device to automatically dial other devices. Dial-up numbers, calling times, and redial quantity and sequence (if necessary) may be programmed in the computer.

AAUs are normally in use in computer-timesharing applications, where many subscribers randomly call several computer dial-up lines. ACUs are cost-effective where transmissions are of short duration. The ACU, normally at a central location, enables automatic dial-up polling of remote devices during preprogrammed time intervals.

13.8 SPEED AND CODE CONVERTERS

Lower speed, low-level-code terminals can communicate with faster, higher-level devices on the same network, thanks to comparatively low-cost converters for speed and code. The converters may be temporary or permanent network additions.

They make otherwise incompatible terminals compatible with the network. Compatibility brings the chance to reduce the number of expensive multipoint lines and computer ports, and to standardize on one modem speed.

Just how and where speed and code converters can be applied in the network is covered in the accompanying illustrations. First, though, it's important to point out that speed and code converters are by no means standardized interchangeable products. All convert speed, but not all convert codes. They also differ in speeds and codes handled.

The network of Figure 13.8.1 has a mixture of 110- and 150-bit/s terminals connected to the computer. This requires at least one computer port and one multidrop circuit to service each type of remote terminal. Furthermore two different modems are required at the computer site (one 110-bit/s and one 150-bit/s) and at any remote site with both types of terminals.

If the user wishes to install 300 bit/s terminals at a few of his remote locations due to workload growth, he normally would have to add one more multidrop circuit similar to the setup in Figure 13.8.2. He would need a computer port and enough 300 bit/s modems to service the addition of the 300-bit/s terminals. However, through the installation of speed converters for each of the 110-and 150 bit/s terminals (Fig. 13.8.2), all terminals could be serviced via the single 300-bit/s multidrop line shown. This reduces the number of lines needed and requires only one modem and one computer port at the central site. Also, because all modems in the network can now operate at the same speed, the number of spare modems is reduced.

Like speed converters, code converters permit different types of terminals to be mixed within a multidrop line of the same network. They can be very useful during network upgrading, when a user gradually replaces a large number of older Baudot terminals with more modern ASCII or EBCDIC ones. Depending upon the mix of new and old terminals and the conversion schedule, the user can go one of two ways. The existing network (Fig. 13.8.3A) operates by the computer transmitting five-level Baudot code on a multidrop line to the five-level Baudot terminals interfaced to that line.

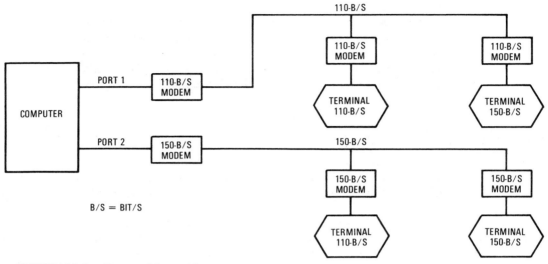

FIGURE 13.8.1   Nature of the problem

In Figure 13.8.3B, the user has converted transmission to eight-level ASCII code by installing Baudot-to-ASCII code converters between each five-level Baudot code terminal and the transmisssion line. Eventually these terminals may be replaced with ASCII terminals, or the network may be left as shown with the converters for permanent operation.

In Figure 13.8.3C, the user continues to transmit in five-level Baudot code, and so has installed an ASCII-to-Baudot converter between the new ASCII terminal and the transmission line. If he then decides to convert to eight-level ASCII

FIGURE 13.8.2   Adding higher-speed terminals

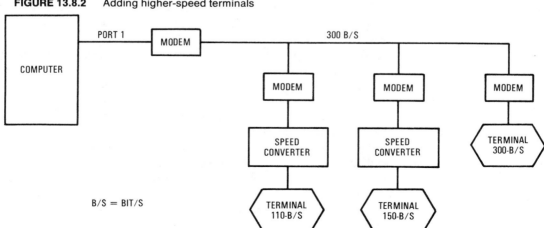

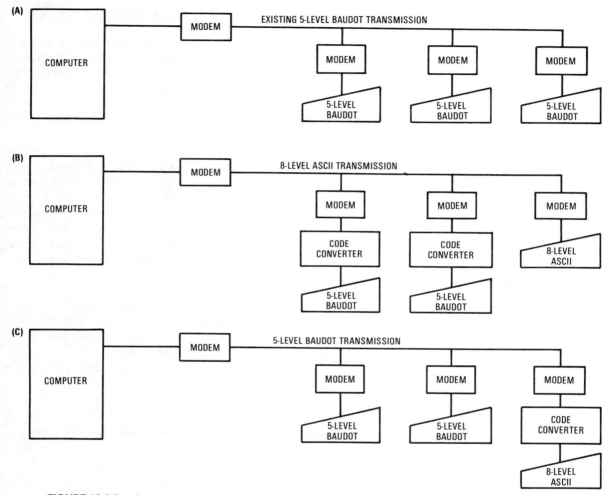

FIGURE 13.8.3   Implementing code conversion

transmission, he must decide whether to convert the older five-level terminals or replace them with eight-level terminals.

A combination of speed-and-code converters permits the user to satisfy two or more dissimilar communications requirements with a single terminal, thereby reducing both the number of terminals necessary and capital investment. Consider an organization with many ASCII-code eight-level Teletype models 33 and 35 used on the TWX network and in timesharing, and with some older, five-level Baudot Teletype models 28 and 32 used on Telex and international-record-carrier networks.

It is desirable to standardize on the models 33 and 35 because they are more widely used and more readily available. A combination of speed and code converters will make them usable on Telex- and TWX-like networks as well as in timesharing (Fig. 13.8.4).

The ASCII even-parity serial code of 11 bits (100 words per minute) is converted to a Baudot serial code of 7.5 bits (66 words per minute) and vice versa. Since most ASCII terminals can be interfaced by a converter, CRT terminals can also be used to send messages through the Telex- or TWX-like networks.

13.9 DIGITIZING VOICE

In the past, few users required, or even seriously entertained, exclusive reliance on end-to-end digitized voice transmission because of the high cost associated with analog-to-digital (A/D) and digital-to-analog (D/A) conversion devices. However, the cost of both digital transmission service and A/D and D/A conversion hardware is declining. As a result, digitized voice is emerging as a serious alternative to analog service. Moreover, given the continuing proliferation of digital transmission media, and many users' desire to integrate both voice and data in one network, digitized speech has become an increasingly important traffic component in the planning of future networks.

Digital voice communications (DVC) offers:

Compatibility Because of high conversion costs, compatibility with digital network facilities is not always beneficial in the short term, but eventually compatibility will be a necessity. This will come about because of the long-range phased elimination of analog-based media by common carriers.

Less Degradation Information transmitted digitally suffers less degradation

FIGURE 13.8.4   Combining speed and code conversion

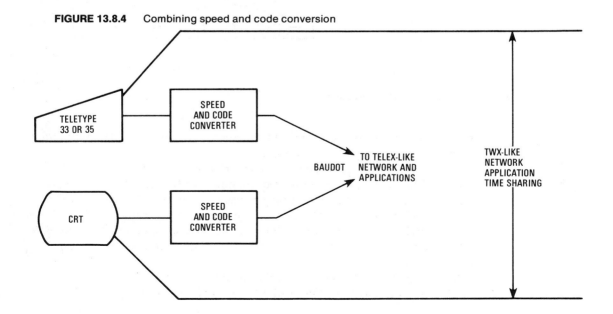

for a number of reasons. First, digital signals are easily regenerated via repeaters. Second, sophisticated error control is more simply applied to digital signals. As a result, analog transmission impairments normally associated with telephone networks—crosstalk, intermodulation interference, echo, and filter nonlinearities—can be eliminated. A related attribute of DVC is that any distortion, introduced into speech at the input, can be confined to a source digitizer. Thus, received speech quality can be made essentially distance-independent, a major difference compared to speech quality associated with analog voice transmission.

Secure Communications   For many years, the military and several large corporations have desired the ability to transmit conversational speech in a secure (encrypted) fashion. A modicum of protection from eavesdroppers is offered by analog scramblers. Although adequate for many applications, even the most sophisticated analog scramblers do not provide the degree of protection afforded by digital encryption techniques.

Reduced Bandwidth   By the appropriate choice of speech digitization technique, voice signals can be compressed in digital form to a point where they require less equivalent channel capacity than the original analog signals. For example, if speech is digitized at 2.4 kbit/s, four simultaneous full-duplex conversations can be multiplexed over a single voice-grade line driven by 9.6-kbit/s modems or 9.6-kbit/s digital trunks. This effectively quadruples communications capacity. With the inevitable decline of A/D and D/A hardware conversion costs, these configurations become increasingly attractive.

Voice/Data Integration   Once voice has been digitized, it can be freely intermixed with (digital) data traffic. Such flexibility relieves network planners of the burden of separate facilities management for individual dedicated networks. This also enables users to take advantage of inherent economies of scale resulting from integration.

Compatibility with Computers   Speech in digital form can be readily processed, transformed, and stored by computers. Obviously, with the appropriate processing capabilities, communications networks provide voice-related services, including automatic speaker authentication, speaker identification, speech recognition, and computer-generated voice answerback in response to keyed inquiries.

Trade-offs Will Favor DVC

Many of these advantages are long-term in nature and are highly technology dependent and cost sensitive. The trade-offs will ultimately favor DVC.

The first trade-off to consider is cost versus voice digitization rate (VDR). The techniques are well understood and the complexity of the conversion hardware is minimal. For useful DVC, however, high VDR has limited practical appeal due to the high transmission cost associated with even a single conversation. From the standpoint of bandwidth efficiency, the lowest possible VDR is always desirable. However, the cost of low VDR conversion devices is still quite high. Therefore, trade-offs between conversion device costs and transmission bandwidth must be made in order to arrive at the most cost-effective strategy.

To analyze this trade-off, an optimum voice digitization rate must be determined. Combining transmission costs and hardware conversion costs, as shown in Figure 13.9.1, a total-cost curve can be computed. From this graphic view, the "optimum" VDR is found at the point of least cost. This is only a representative analysis of a DVC cost picture, and any actual cost trade-off must take into account such real factors as current specific tariff charges, conversion device costs, and network topology.

Voice "quality" must also be considered. Voice quality is both difficult to define and difficult to quantify. Yet no single characteristic of DVC is more crucial to the user. Perceptual voice quality encompasses several different characteristics. The barest requirement is intelligibility or, stated simply, the listener's ability to understand what the speaker is saying. Several devices that operate at low VDR can distort specific phrases and impair intelligibility. Other digitization techniques provide adequate intelligibility, but sound synthetic or machine-like. In many instances, therefore, voice naturalness is also required.

At higher VDRs, additional speaker-related attributes are easily preserved, such as a listener's ability to recognize the speaker, and even discern his emotional state. In order to reduce VDR, some speech characteristics are compromised. This degradation depends, however, not only on the VDR, but also on the digitization technique used.

Converting Speech to Digital

All human languages consist of certain basic sounds called phonemes. English, for example, has approximately 40 phonemes. In normal conversational speech, at most 10 phonemes per second are uttered. Therefore, if six bits are used to encode each phoneme, a bandwidth of 60 bit/s is required to transmit human speech. Table 13.9.1 lists several major voice digitization techniques, and illustrates the

FIGURE 13.9.1   Trade-off speed and cost

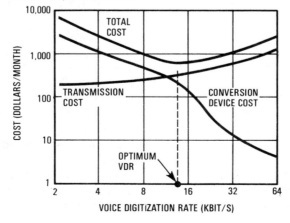

TABLE 13.9.1   DVC TECHNIQUES

Digitization Technique	VDR (Kbit/s)	Cost Characterization	Digitization Methods
Linear Pulse Code Modulation (PCM)	90–110		
Log PCM	48–64	Relatively Inexpensive Devices	Waveform— Reconstruction
Differential Pulse Code Modulation (DPCM)	32–48		
Continously Variable Slope Delta Modualtion (CVSD)	16–32		
Sub-band Coder (SBC)	7.2–24		
Linear Predictive Vocoder	2.4–9.6	Currently Expensive	Analysis Synthesis
Channel Vocoder	2.4–4.8		
Cepstrum Vocoder	2.4–4.8		
Formant Vocoder	0.6–2.4		

typical range of associated voice digitization rates at which "acceptable" quality speech may be obtained.

Caution must be exercised in order to reconcile the apparently large differences between the VDR which is theoretically required and that which is realized in practice, since a great deal more information than only speech is normally conveyed. For example, phrasing, stress, articulation, and emotional content are all important parameters of conversational speech. Indeed, purely computer-driven synthesis techniques yield a singularly monotone output, yet have achieved rates as low as 75 bit/s. But, these devices are not applicable for conversion of user-generated speech in real-time applications.

The indicated VDR associated with each technique in Table 13.9.1 represents the typical bit rate required for acceptable voice quality. Each technique's VDR may be increased or decreased, but either change will have an effect on quality. For instance, in many of the strategies, the voice quality associated with different techniques is not comparable. Table 13.9.1 contains both commonly used digitizing techniques, as well as many techniques still considered experimental.

The most widely used method of digitizing voice is pulse-code modulation (PCM). It is employed by carriers worldwide, and, in fact, implementations of PCM have been standardized by CCITT for voice digitization. With PCM, analog inputs are low-pass filtered and sampled at a fixed rate. The sampled waveform is quantized to a discrete level and then encoded. The VDR in PCM depends on the sampling rate.

A technique known as companding is often used to reduce the analog signals' dynamic range. Companding takes advantage of the human ear's operation, which is logarithmic—with higher sensitivity at lower amplitudes. Two standard companding techniques—μ-255 and A-law—are used most often. Both techniques employ fixed digitization rates.

Differential pulse-code modulation (DPCM) differs from PCM in that it uses the difference between sample amplitudes and not the actual value as in PCM. Delta modulation (DM) is a special case of DPCM, which approximates a speech waveform with a "staircase" function. By employing automatic gain techniques, the staircase can be made to adaptively track the analog waveform. A special form of adaptive DM is called continuously variable slope delta modulation (CVSD). CVSD varies the staircase step size as a function of its average signal power. LSI-based CVSD devices have become cost competitive with PCM at equivalent performance levels.

Another voice digitization technique, sub-band coding, is still largely experimental. Sub-band coding techniques divide speech into continuous sub-bands, and each sub-band is quantized independently. Experiments indicate that sub-band coding provides greater control of quantization errors and can improve signal quality.

What's Available

The preceding are all waveform reconstruction techniques. The other digitizing scheme, analysis-synthesis, uses vocoders, which exploit certain intrinsic properties of human voice. By digitizing only these parameters, a significant reduction in VDR can be achieved. As Table 13.9.1 points out, a number of different vocoder types are employed in reconstructing waveforms. The choice of a speech digitization technique is a non-trivial affair; there exists a variety of competing strategies, each differing in device cost, complexity, VDR, quality of synthesized speech, and performance in the presence of errors.

Once speech has been encoded in digital form, it can be handled in a fashion similar to data traffic. Speech packets could be formed and transmitted in a store-and-forward manner through a packet network. Although new protocols would be required for accommodating speech packets (due to their different error and delay performance requirements compared to data), there exists a potential for saving of transmission bandwidth by a combination of packet switching and speech-actuated vocoding. By not transmitting information or utilizing communications facilities during periods of silence, approximately a 50 percent reduction in bandwidth requirements can be realized.

The future reliance on DVC will also spur the growth of man-machine communications applications on a network-wide basis. Speech is man's most natural form of communications, and thus, ample motivation exists for "communicating" with computers in this manner. The widespread existence of digitized voice using quantizers and vocoders will facilitate such applications and, with additional research, will transfer them from the laboratory environment to on-line services.

Synthesize Answerback

Computer-generated answerback already exists in the analog world, and is used extensively in banking and order-entry applications. A synthesized voice could be used in response to user-entered queries via standard keyboards or dual-tone multifrequency keyboards (such as AT&T's Touch-Tone pad). Both speaker identification ("Who is this individual?") and speaker authentication ("Is this person who he says he is?") could be supported under DVC. Vocoders intrinsically generate certain unique parameters of voice, such as pitch. These parameters can then be used to verify or determine the caller's identity. The potential for erroneous identification is much higher when analog signals are used for this, due to noise. In DVC using vocoders, however, the vocoder supplies the raw speech parameters required for identification.

Finally, the support of speech recognition and speech understanding devices under which users can verbally input commands and/or data to a computer (although still a major research topic at many universities and laboratores around the world), is facilitated in a digitized environment.

13.10 NETWORK INTEGRATION

Current Facilities

The V.S. Cracker Co. operates a large computer installation at its corporate headquarters in Greensboro, N.C. Until recently all corporate accounts were in New England. As a result of this, the company's network consisted of a number of leased lines from Greensboro to several branch offices in the northeast United States.

Due to a high demand for crackers on the West Coast, a branch office is scheduled to open in San Francisco. Based upon a recently conducted feasibility study, the San Francisco office will require the installation of one remote batch teminal (RBT) operating at 4,800 bit/s and ten 1,200-bit/s interactive Teletype-compatible Terminals.

The prime-time activity factor of the RBT is expected to be unity, meaning that the device will be connected to the network continuously during the prime shift, although it may not necessarily be transmitting or receiving data during that time. For the interactive terminals, during prime time an average of four terminals are expected to be connected to the network. For 90 percent of the time, six or less terminals will be connected.

At San Francisco, all interactive terminals will be located on the same floor of one building, geographically distributed in several work areas. A room is reserved for the RBT and any required communications equipment. The average distance from any interactive terminal to the inside of the RBT room is approximately 275 feet. In discussing terminal operations with San Francisco personnel, it was ascertained that all terminals will be in fixed locations.

Since terminal operators also serve as order entry clerks, separate telephones must be installed for each terminal to insure that no customer encounters a period of busy signals when a terminal is in use.

At the central computer site, 30 slots are available on the front-end processor for network expansion. Each slot can service a dual-capacity asynchronous/synchronous channel module, which is available from the computer manufacturer.

Requirement

Design an equipment configuration to service the terminals to be installed in San Francisco so that the remote- and central-site costs are minimized. For the interactive terminals, analysis shows that six terminals would not result in any measurable loss of productivity, and the servicing of ten terminals might actually result in a gain to the company of $100 per month. Assume that the servicing of four such terminals would result in a loss of productivity worth $400 per month. The following equipment should be considered at the denoted monthly lease rates:

Equipment	Monthly Cost
Acoustic coupler	$ 30
Auto-answer modem, 1,200 bit/s	40
Telco Rotary	30
Telephone	15
Dial-in-line	15
Line driver	10
TDM (4-channel)	90
TDM (8-channel)	120
Statistical TDM (12-channel)	275
9,600-bit/s modem	200
9,600-bit/s multiport modem	220
Front-end processor channel	35
Cable, per foot	0.10
Leased line, San Francisco to Greensboro	1,873

13.11 NETWORK INTEGRATION

Current Facilities

Jiffy Jewelers presently has a corporate data processing center in Dallas, Texas, that is connected on line to a number of regional offices located throughout the United States. At the Chicago regional office, a remote batch terminal (RBT) is connected via a leased line to the computer in Dallas. This RBT internally performs code compression and operates throughout the prime shift, transmitting to Dallas at 9,600 bit/s.

Expansion Requirements

Due to the employment of new marketing techniques, sales at the Chicago office have been increasing faster than the national average. The manager of the Chicago office believes sales can increase even more if his marketing staff had access to small portable terminals operating at 300 bit/s that could be carried to customer sites. Such terminals would enable the sales force to verify current prices and delivery schedules as well as directly enter orders for goods whose prices fluctuate according to the price of silver and gold.

During a meeting with the regional manager, he mentioned that although at any time up to 20 salesmen could be visiting customers, the maximum number of simultaneous terminals in operation should not exceed eight. With sales increasing, the RBT would either require a partial second shift operation or an increase in the transmission rate to 14,400 bit/s. Responding to your question, you ascertained that the cost of a second shift operation would be approximately $1,080/month.

Right before the meeting adjourned, the regional manager mentioned that he would like a CRT with an attached printer installed in the Chicago office. This terminal would enable his staff to enter orders called in from customers, check delivery schedules, and access the new MIS that provides information on sales trends and profit forecasting by region. For this application, a transmission rate of 2,400 bit/s would be acceptable.

Equipment and Operating Cost

In examining alternative communications equipment configurations, you compiled a list of available equipment and their monthly costs, as well as the monthly second shift operating cost and leased line costs. The costs of such equipment and facilities are tabulated:

Equipment	Monthly Cost
Voice-grade leased line	$ 910
Wideband circuit	4,075
TDM (8-channel sync/async input)	120
TDM (12-channel sync/async)	200
Wideband multiplexer (4-chnl sync input)	250
Inverse multiplexer	300
9,600-bit/s modem	200
9,600-bit/s multiport modem	220
4,800-bit/s modem	135
2,400-bit/s modem	50
300-bit/s auto-answer modem	20
Dial-in line	15
Telco rotary	30
Second shift RBT	1,080

Requirement

Design a minimum-cost network configuration to service the remote data processing requirements of the Chicago office. Assume that the CRT will be co-located with the RBT and any required additional communications components.

13.12 NETWORK INTEGRATION

Current Facilities

Your organization operates a large multidimensional (batch, remote-batch, and timesharing) computer in Chicago. Currently, two dual-function (asynchronous/ synchronous) ports are unused and available for network expansion on your existing front-end processor. An additional front-end processor can be obtained with a minimum of 16 dual-function ports and leased for $1,500 per month.

Expansion Requirements

Management has decided to open a branch office in St. Louis and a customer-inquiry office in Little Rock. At the branch office, five CRTs and one remote batch terminal are required. At the Little Rock office, one additional CRT is required. If each terminal is connected to an individual port, asynchronous 1,200-bit/s CRTs can be used. If CRTs are clustered, 4,800-bit/s synchronous devices must be obtained. The remote batch terminal must operate at 4,800 bit/s.

Communications Cost

Voice-grade leased-line costs per month are:

From	To	Monthly Cost
St. Louis	Chicago	$404
Little Rock	Chicago	675
Little Rock	St. Louis	432

Equipment Cost

The following equipment should be considered at the indicated monthly cost:

Equipment	Monthly Cost
4,800-bit/s modem	$ 120
9,600-bit/s modem	200
9,600-bit/s multiport modem	220
8-channel TDM	160
Modem-sharing unit	35
1,200-bit/s terminal	100
4,800-bit/s terminal	125
Computer port	35
Front-end processor	1,500
Remote batch terminal	500

Requirement

Assuming that existing facilities cannot be modified, what network configurations should be considered and what are the implications of those configurations?

13.13 NETWORK INTEGRATION

Current Facilities

Presently, your organization has five warehouses in major cities throughout the southeastern United States, with a distribution center in Atlanta. Each regional office has data communications equipment and facilities as illustrated here.

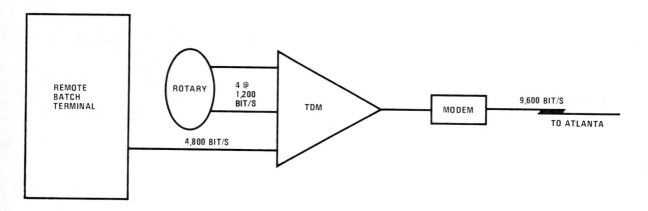

Expansion Requirements

Currently, each warehouse terminal communicates with only the distribution center, since goods are shipped from the distribution center to each warehouse directly. The low-speed terminals at each warehouse interrogate the company master database in Atlanta to determine the status of items. The remote batch terminal transmits "ticket" information of goods leaving the warehouse en route to various distribution centers.

Management would like to transship goods between warehouses. To do so, the lowspeed interactive terminals would continue to access the database in Atlanta. However, the remote batch terminal at each warehouse would now require direct communications with the RBTs located at other warehouses. Based upon a feasibility study, it was estimated that each RBT would average 12 warehouse-to-warehouse calls per month for transmission of data at an average cost of $5.50 per call.

Upgrading the Present Network

At the central computer site, a message-switching software package could be added to the front-end processor. This package costs $900 per month and would require an additional memory module, at a cost of $750 per month.

Examining Other Options

The hardware cost, which should be investigated for alternative communications, is

	Monthly cost
4,800-bit/s modem	$ 120
Fallback switch	10
Matrix switch	200

If the switching is not automatic, as can be obtained from using appropriate software, an additional 50 cents per call will be required for coordination.

PROBLEM

In addition to message switching, what other options are available, and what is the economic impact of such operations?

CHAPTER 14

NETWORK DIAGNOSTIC AND MONITORING CONSIDERATIONS

Once a data communications network becomes operational, a number of transmission problems are likely to occur, mostly on a random basis. Due to the evolution of networks with computers, modems, circuits, and terminals supplied by many different vendors, a method to pinpoint transmission problems to specific devices must be available to the user. Ideally, only the responsible vendor is notified of the fault in the equipment or on the circuit.

To assist in fault isolation, a number of devices have built-in test-character generators and circuitry to compare data transmitted with data received during a loop-back test. While such test features may resolve certain fault-isolation problems, they will not normally denote such factors as the sources of transmission distortion. To obtain additional information, line monitors and other test equipment must be employed.

In this chapter we will first review some of the sources of transmission errors and how line monitors can be used to trap and display data to provide a precise picture of line activity. Since many computer installations justify spare equipment to maintain operations continuity if a device or circuit should fail at the central site, the design and construction factors involved in a technical control center will be covered. Personnel at a well-designed center not only can monitor and determine the causes of transmission problems, but may also be able to patch users around those problem devices and circuits while remedial action is taken.

14.1 SOURCES OF TRANSMISSION-LINE DISTORTION

Transmission-line testing is a well-developed subset of electronic knowledge. An understanding of how lines are tested, the parameters utilized as variables, and the interpretation of the results will aid any network designer or user in the understanding of a network. Consideration of these testing procedures will entail giving attention to the following points:

- Key parameters relevant to transmission-line testing
- Common-practice measurement techniques
- References to specifications and procedures

Knowledge of these factors gives an understanding of the parameters that affect the data transmission capabilities of transmission lines. Transmission lines as discussed here are the voice-bandwidth private-line data circuits provided by a communications carrier.

Basic Measurements

As detailed in Section 5.2, the decibel (dB) is a unit that is defined as the ratio of output signal power to input signal power.

$$dB = 10 \log_{10} \frac{\text{output power}}{\text{input power}}$$

Logarithms are used because a signal level in dB can be easily added and subtracted, and because the ear responds to signal levels in an approximately logarithmic manner. Note that if the output power is less than the input power, the result is negative and the channel is said to have a dB loss. Decibels are simply the measure of a power ratio. Measurements made in this way are expressed in decibels relative to one milliwatt (dBm), where

$$dBm = 10 \log_{10} \frac{\text{signal power in milliwatts}}{\text{1 milliwatt}}$$

Therefore, 0 dBm means 1 milliwatt, and absolute power levels may be expressed as so many dBm.

For reference, common carriers establish a zero transmission level point (TLP) as some measurable point in a channel at which a specific test tone level (0 dBm) is expected. A +7 TLP, for example, is a point at which the test-tone level should be +7 dBm. For voice circuits, the test tone used is a 1,004 Hz, 0 dBm tone at the zero TLP. This is normally referred to as a 1-kHz test tone, or simply a test tone.

Other tones can be used for testing. These tones are all 1 kHz, but are at different levels. To reference them back to test-tone level, another unit of measurements is used. Decibels referred to one milliwatt with respect to test-tone level (dBm0) are defined as:

$$dBm0 = \text{signal level in dBm} - \text{test tone level in dBm}$$

Data is normally transmitted at a level 13 dB below test-tone level. Therefore, data level is –13 dBm0. At a zero TLP, data level would be –13 dBm; at a +7 TLP, data level would be –6 dBm. It is important to note that data transmission-line measurements are made with a l-kHz tone—called a holding tone—at data level, not at test-tone level.

The Noise Factor

In theory, noise is the limiting factor in data transmission. In actuality, noise alone rarely is the cause of errors in low- and medium-speed transmission. For high-speed transmission, the effects of other transmission impairments reduce the noise margin—the signal above noise level—that makes noise the figure of merit in comparing different modulation schemes (as will be discussed under modems).

The audible hiss on a telephone line is noise. This uniformly distributed, random background noise is measured in several ways. Noise measurement units are decibels above reference noise, where

$$0dBrn = -90dBm$$

is the reference noise level. This arbitrary level represents the lowest noise level an "average" listener can hear on a telephone. A C-message filter is used as a "front end" to a level meter to give a representative noise measurement. Although this is a voice telephone measurement, it has carried over into data transmission. When a C-message filter is used in measurement, the units are called decibels above reference noise C-message weighted (dBrnc).

Noise on a channel is a function of the telephone channel and telephone equipment, so an increase in signal level will bring about an increase in noise distortion. To measure noise under "actual" conditions, a 1-kHz holding tone (data level) is transmitted. At the receiving end, a second filter is used to remove, or "notch out," the tone. This is strictly defined as a C-notched noise measurement.

Figure 14.1.1 shows the response of a C-message filter. Notice how it severely attenuates power line harmonics (60, 120, 180 Hz, etc.). A second filter, 3-kHz flat, is used as a check for power-line harmonics. Both C-message and 3-kHz-flat noise measurements are made, if power line harmonics are suspected.

As with the dBm, an absolute reference level for noise is often specified, based on a transmission-level point. Decibels above reference noise, C-message weighted, with respect to test-tone level (dBrnc0), are dBrnc0 = noise level in dBrnc – test-tone level in dBm. Figure 14.1.2 illustrates the relationships between the above measurements.

In practice, a telephone channel will transmit frequencies from 300 to 3.3K Hz. The amplitude loss at each frequency may be different. Curves of level vs. frequency, referenced to the loss at 1 kHz, define the amplitude response—or attenuation distortion—of a transmission channel.

Another source of distortion is from different frequencies propagating through a channel with different velocities. This means that if a number of different frequency tones are transmitted simultaneously into a channel, they will be received at different times. This is significant because a data signal is composed of many different frequencies. Figure 14.1.3 shows that there will be a difference in arrival times (or in phase) between two tones of different frequencies.

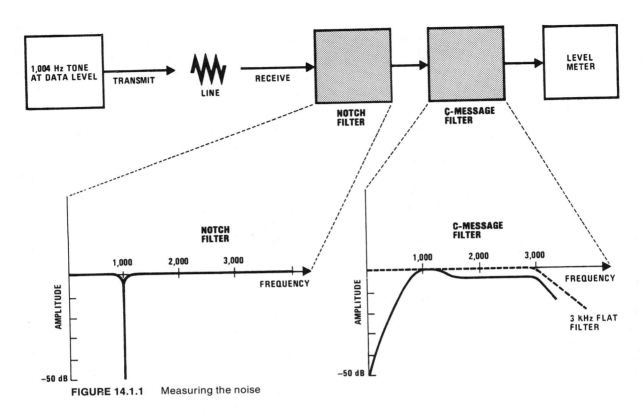

FIGURE 14.1.1 Measuring the noise

This difference may be expressed in terms of microseconds of delay. Absolute delay is not really measurable, since a frame of reference (When did the signal start?) cannot be established. The relative difference between two tones can be measured, however. Envelope delay distortion at a given frequency is, then, measured as the difference in microseconds when compared with the delay experienced by a reference tone at 1.8 kHz. Note that a 1-kHz tone is not used for reference. Sophisticated methods are used to actually measure envelope delay distortion.

Distortion caused by power-line harmonics, in multiplex configurations for example, creates "jittering" of zero crossings, or of the instantaneous phase of a signal, as shown in Figure 14.1.4. This phase jitter is measured by looking at zero crossings of a holding tone. Noise, which can affect zero crossings as shown, can strongly influence phase jitter measurements. To make accurate measurements, a data-level holding tone should be used, since the ratio of signal level to noise level is a factor. Notched-noise measurements should be made in conjunction with phase-jitter measurements. This should help to determine what is actually being experienced: true phase jitter or just the effects of a high noise level.

At low to medium speeds, phase jitter is rarely noticeable compared with the effects of amplitude-response distortion, envelope-delay distortion, and line hits (discussed later). For high-speed transmission, phase jitter is more critical, as will be discussed under modems.

Nonlinear Distortion

A channel has many nonlinear components. These components distort a data signal by generating unwanted harmonics that add to the signal in a detrimental manner. As illustrated in Figure 14.1.5, for a single tone, the effects can be pronounced. The example is a simplification, but the "clipping" effect on the wave

FIGURE 14.1.2   Relationships between measurements

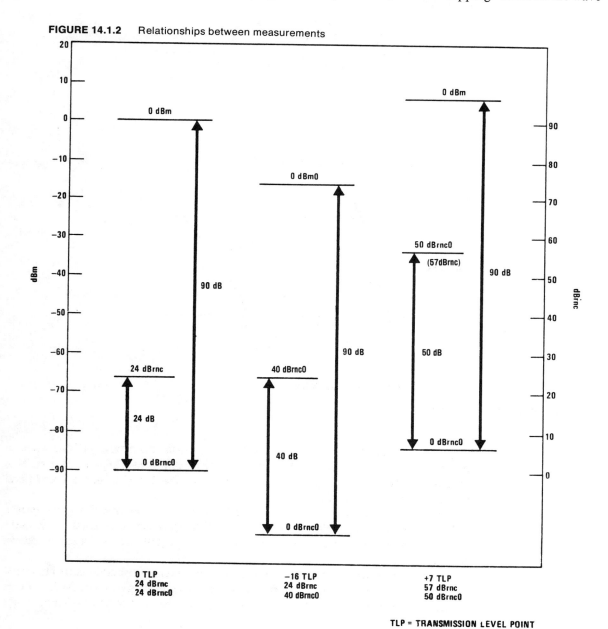

TLP = TRANSMISSION LEVEL POINT

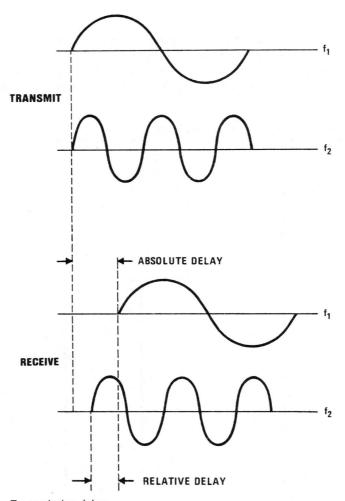

FIGURE 14.1.3   Transmission delay

(Fig. 14.1.5, Part C) is a characteristic of harmonic distortion. At one time, a parameter called harmonic distortion was measured in just this way. A tone was transmitted down the channel, and the level of the fundamental, second, and third harmonics was measured.

To more accurately simulate a working data circuit, a newer technique is in use today in which two sets of closely paired frequencies are used, and their harmonics and cross harmonics are measured. This is called a nonlinear-disortion measurement.

Nonlinear distortion causes intersymbol interference (discussed later) of a low magnitude. However, equalization (also discussed later) largely corrects the effects of amplitude response and delay distortion. So nonlinear distortion—which is not corrected by equalization—can be the limiting factor in high-speed transmission. The presence of nonlinear distortion is the reason for "D" type conditioning provided by the telephone company for high-speed lines.

Another source of transmission errors is called a "line hit." It is the primary source of error in low- and medium-speed transmission. Any hit of this type can render unrecognizable any data transmitted for the duration of the hit, and to the end of the block in progress. A line hit can be separated into specific types, such as:

• Dropouts—sudden, large reductions in signal level that last more than several milliseconds.

• Phase hits—sudden, uncontrolled changes in phase of the received signal.

• Gain hits—sudden, uncontrolled increases in the received signal level.

• Impulse noise—sudden "spikes" of noise of very short duration. In telephone reception it is those clicks that can be heard on occasion.

Four-wire, full-duplex private lines have independent transmit and receive "sides" or channels. Transmission test instruments normally have independent

FIGURE 14.1.4   Phase jitter

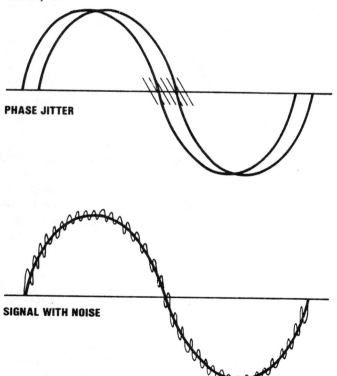

PHASE JITTER

SIGNAL WITH NOISE

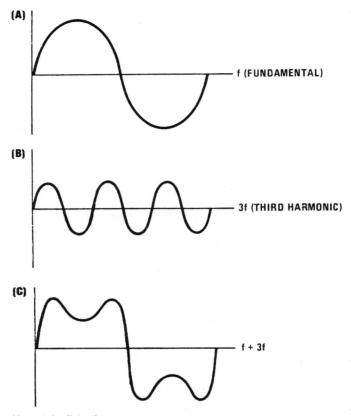

(A) f (FUNDAMENTAL)

(B) 3f (THIRD HARMONIC)

(C) f + 3f

FIGURE 14.1.5 Harmonic distortion

transmit and receive sections. The transmit section is usually capable of generating a 1-kHz tone and variable-frequency tones at adjustable levels. The receive section may simply be a level meter. In addition, the test instrument could contain a frequency counter, noise measurement filters, as well as phase-jitter, envelope-delay, impulse-noise, and hit-measurement equipment. The cost of a transmission test set is proportional to the extent of measurement equipment in the receive section.

Measurement Methods

There are several basic techniques associated with test sets. These involve some items to be careful of.

• Bridge vs. terminate—A transmission line is assumed to have an impedance of 600 ohms. This means that on the transmit side it presents a resistance or load of 600 ohms to the transmitter, and that correspondingly it expects to "see" a load of

600 ohms on the receive side. If this is not the case, level—and level-dependent—measurements will be erroneous.

The test-set transmitter physically replaces the modem at its connection to the line, so the test set must expect to see a 600-ohm load. On the receive side, two possibilities exist. The test set may again physically replace the modem at its connection to the line. In this case, the test set must "terminate" the line into a 600-ohm load. Or, the test set may be attached to the line without replacing the modem. In this case, the test set "bridges" across the line and must present a high impedance to the line, so that the line does not see both its load and that of the modem. Level, and all level-dependent, measurements will be wrong if a line is bridged when it should be terminated, or vice versa. Most test receivers can switch between these modes.

• Setting levels—The correct transmit and receive levels must be established. Common practice is to have a + 13 TLP on transmit, and a –3 TLP on receive. This means that the transmit level should be 0 dBm and that the receive level should be –16 dBm, since data level is –13 dBm0 (Fig. 14.1.2). All measurements with tone should use a data-level tone at 1,004 Hz, except for envelope-delay distortion, which uses a 1.8-kHz tone.

• Circuit loss—With the proper level tone being transmitted, the user should verify that the proper tone level is received. Care should be taken about whether a bridged or terminated measurement is being made. The received level should be within 1 dB of the expected level. If it is not within this tolerance, circuit-level adjustments should be made to correct the error. It is not good practice to attempt to compensate for the difference with the test set, since all level-dependent measurements will then be incorrect.

• Noise measurement—C-notched noise—using both a notch filter and a C-message filter (Fig. 14.1.1)—is normally what is measured. Care should be taken to use a data-level holding tone, and to know what the test set is actually measuring (dBrn, dBrnc, or dBrnc0). A 3-kHz flat measurement should be made to check for powerline interference.

If the test set has an audio monitor, it may be worthwhile to measure idle channel noise and listen to the circuit. This is done by leaving the test set receiver in a C-message noise measurement mode and putting a "quiet" termination—the characteristic impedance—on the transmit end. Most test sets have this termination, which may simply be a 600-ohm resistor placed across the transmit line with the transmitter disconnected. Listening on the receiver, one may well hear muffled conversations from other lines (crosstalk), or tone interference (a tone). There is not a specified measurement technique for single-tone interference, so the ear may be the only practical detection device.

• Envelope delay—The test set manual should be checked for arrangements to measure forward (transmit)- or reverse (receive)-channel delay. A 1.8-kHz tone is used as the zero millisecond reference for the delay measured at other frequencies.

• Phase jitter—A data-level tone—the 1-kHz holding tone—should be used. Phase jitter measurements should be distinguished from the measurement of high noise levels.

● Distortion—Distinction should be made between the measurement of harmonic or of nonlinear distortion. Noise affects distortion measurements, so that a part of the measurement process is to check the noise contribution. The measurement may then be corrected by a table-look-up procedure.

● Hit measurements—Again a data-level tone should be used. Test readings are normally made for a duration of 15 minutes. Correlation should not be made with the results for tests of other time durations because of random phenomena.

It is often possible to mistake dropouts, gain and phase hits, and impulse noise for one another. To avoid this misidentification, hits are normally measured simultaneously in a prescribed order. The hit-count order is: First, a dropout locks out all other hit counters. Second, a gain or phase hit preempts any impulse-noise count.

Improving the Line

Consider a line with ideal phase and amplitude response. Assume that a pulse with a baseband frequency response as shown in Figure 14.1.6A is modulated, passed through the line, and demodulated. The resultant time response of the pulse at the receiver would be as shown in Figure 14.1.6B. Suppose that at time T, a second pulse is transmitted. At the receiver, the result would be the addition of the two pulses shown in Figure 14.1.6C. Note that if the received signal is being sampled at a rate of T times a second, the received pulses can be accurately interpreted since there is no interference between the received pulses at time T. (One pulse is at its maximum amplitude, while the other is at zero.) This conclusion means that under ideal circumstances, it is possible to signal at an unmodulated rate of double the f1 pulse rate through a line that is band limited to f1 Hz. This rule is a simplification of a Nyquist criterion of communications.

For an actual line with a given amplitude and phase response, the situation changes. First, since the amplitude and delay response are so bad at the edges of the voice band, only the center portion of the band is used to transmit data. Normally, only 2.4 kHz (1.6 kHz in severe cases) of the band centered around 1.7 or 1.8 kHz is used, as shown in Figure 14.1.6D. Next, a method is used to compensate for the amplitude and phase response to approximate an ideal line more closely.

In order to understand the need for this compensation, consider an example of the effects of delay distortion. Suppose that a pulse like one of those discussed previously is transmitted on an actual line. The received pulse is distorted as shown in Figure 14.1.6E. Note that now at intervals of time T, there is some contribution of amplitude of other pulses which could be transmitted at multiples of time T. This effect is known as intersymbol interference. Compensation is, then, used to minimize this type of interference.

The compensation process is called equalization. Equalization can be fixed, manual, automatic, or adaptive. Equalization is discussed in detail in Section 5.4.

For speeds up to 1.8 kbit/s, the standard modulation method is frequency-shift keying (FSK). This type of modulation is very simple to implement, costs little, and is quite rugged for this low-speed transmission. For 2.4-kbit/s transmission,

FIGURE 14.1.6 Why line equalization is needed

(A)

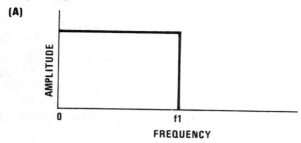

(B)

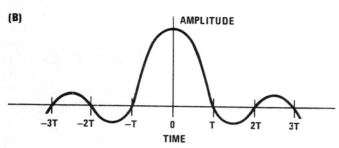

(C)

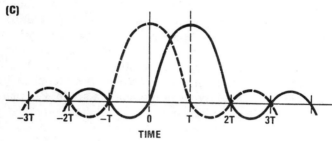

(D)

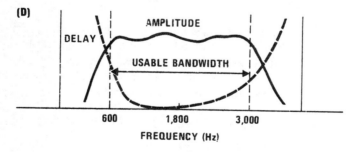

(E)

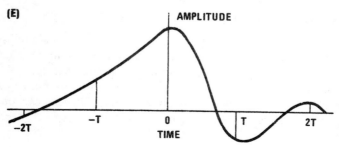

343

differential phase-shift keying (DPSK) has become the standard. In DPSK, the reference phase required for signal detection "rides" with phase jitter and other impairments of the line. That is, to correctly sample and interpret a symbol, all that is required is the previous symbol; whatever distorted the current symbol probably affected the previous symbol the same way, so that a type of immunity to signal impairments is inherent. DPSK gives reasonable efficiency at a moderate cost.

The Higher-Speed Modem

The choices of modulation are not as simple for higher speeds. Recall that about 2.4 kHz of the voice band is used for data transmission. As a rule, one signaling interval (or bit per second) can be transmitted per cycle of bandwidth. This means that 2.4 kbit/s is the maximum normal transmission capability of a line. At speeds above 2.4 kbit/s, therefore, another method, called multilevel coding, must be used.

The number of bits transmitted per modulated signaling intervals is limited by noise. All transmission impairments contribute to errors, and may be related back to noise. Therefore, the primary design criterion in modems becomes one of maximizing the margin against noise (signal-to-noise ratio).

Different types of modulation methods on lines with identical bit-error rates may be compared for various coding levels and signal-to-noise ratios. Modem-vendor data may be useful for conditions encountered by users with certain line conditions not listed in the available reference literature. For speeds between 4.8 and 9.6 kbit/s, several types of modulation are in use: phase-shift keying (PSK), vestigial sideband (VSB), quadrature amplitude modulation (QAM), and combined PSK and amplitude modulation (AM).

Some general observations are appropriate:

- VSB schemes are efficient, but very sensitive to phase jitter and noise.
- PSK schemes are extremely sensitive to noise and phase-jitter.
- Amplitude-phase-modulation schemes—including QAM—appear superior in the presence of noise and phase jitter. Note that different implementations will vary in their noise and phase jitter immunity.

Section 5.3 has additional detail on modulation techniques.

14.2 LINE MONITORS AND TEST EQUIPMENT

When trouble hits a data communications network, finding the fault fast is paramount. That's why an investment in a line monitor and other test equipment is a wise decision. Such devices permit a capable operator to isolate faults to a component such as a modem, terminal, line, or a communications processor. In the hands of an experienced technician, these devices can pinpoint problem areas within a defective unit to expedite troubleshooting.

Line Monitors

Line monitors trap and display data and control characters to provide a precise picture of line activity, eliminating the difficulty in deciphering pulses viewed on an oscilloscope. In addition, the monitors permit control signals on RS-232-C connections to be checked when there are problems in establishing and maintaining message exchanges.

In a multivendor installation, a line monitor can pinpoint a problem so that the proper service organization can be called to make repairs. Downtime and servicing costs can be excessive if the user calls the wrong service organization.

Conventional troubleshooting requires the measuring of voltage and current levels, reading phase jitter, and viewing bit streams with oscilloscopes. The proper application of these techniques requires more expertise than is ordinarily available in many communications installations. An equally valuable role of line monitors is frequent on-line testing to check for degradation of service, which often signals incipient failures. Problems found during such routine tests can be corrected before they cause costly, unexpected breakdowns.

Line monitors provide readouts for data and control characters. Information is displayed in one of four ways:

- Light-emitting diodes (LEDs) that indicate the states of individual bits. This readout must be converted into the appropriate code.
- Labeled indicator lights.
- Alphanumeric displays.
- Alphanumeric on cathode-ray tubes.

Most units permit data or control characters to be trapped and displayed on a selective basis. Trapping may be initiated upon detection of errors, or by decoding specified characters, such as a synchronization character. The ability to read the states of the RS-232-C control leads allows the user to check the "handshaking" sequence if there are problems in establishing and maintaining message exchanges. Many line monitors also permit these leads to be "clamped" at desired voltage levels, or programmed to simulate any aspect of operation.

Some units also provide test messages for polling and answerback, which are used in end-to-end network tests. Parity indications and counts, also common features, are used both in checking out specific problems and in determining line quality. Advanced data link controls, such as IBM's SDLC and Digital Equipment Corp.'s DDCMP, can be accommodated, so long as the message lengths do not exceed the buffer size of the line monitor.

The compactness of integrated circuits permits line monitors to be built into small enclosures. The makers of units that have binary readouts squeeze them into suitcases small enough to fit under an airplane seat. Line monitors with cathode ray tubes are bulkier, but, nevertheless, they are still fairly small.

Most line monitors are built around serial buffer memories that store the data selected for trapping, as illustrated in Figure 14.2.1. Operation of the buffer is

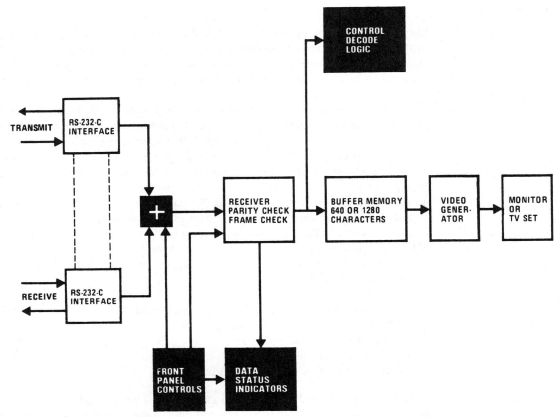

FIGURE 14.2.1   Inside a line monitor

dictated by logic circuits, which route the trapped characters to the memory and direct the readout into the selected mode. Monitors interface the line with connectors compatible with RS-232-C standards.

Line monitors are used in two ways: to check out control signals at the RS-232-C interface (establishing and maintaining a proper connection); and to check for the correctness and proper sequencing of control characters and data.

If the message exchange cannot be initiated or maintained, the RS-232-C lines should be checked with the line analyzer at both ends of the data link. If there is difficulty in transmitting, then, for most modems, the line monitor should check the data-terminal ready, data-set-ready, and request-to-send states. Each manufacturer provides for the display of different combinations of RS-232-C lines. The prospective buyer should ensure that the unit he is considering includes those tests deemed necessary for his troubleshooting requirements.

The next level of troubleshooting consists of testing data-link control characters and data. Some line monitors trap only control characters, while others also capture data. This should also be considered in selecting a unit.

Some line monitors provide a complete, self-contained testing capability, which includes polling, answerback, and generating test messages. Other types can participate in these tests only if additional equipment is used to generate signals and responses. Examples of tests using line monitors are shown in Figures 14.2.2 through 14.2.7.

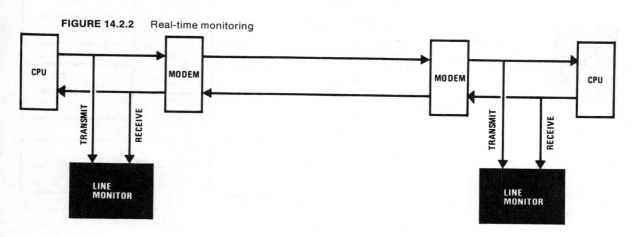

FIGURE 14.2.2   Real-time monitoring

FIGURE 14.2.3   Addressing a terminal

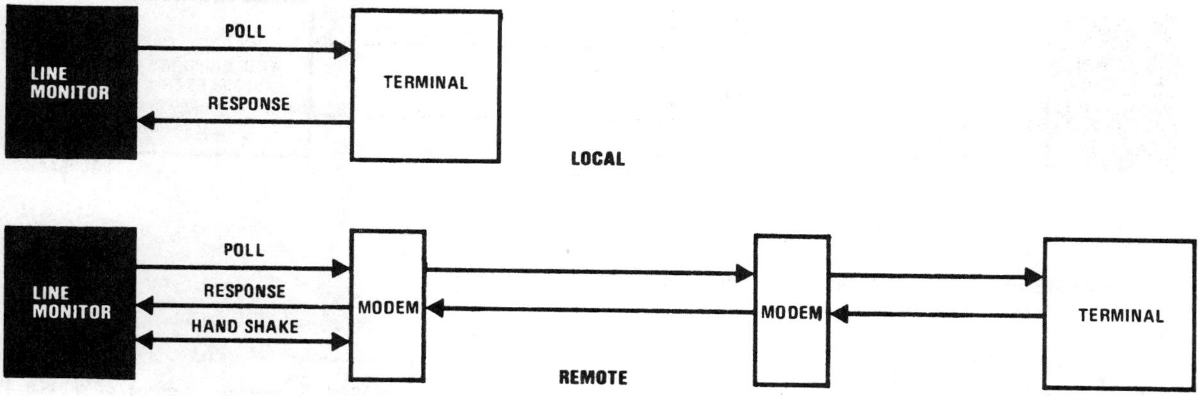

FIGURE 14.2.4   Testing modems

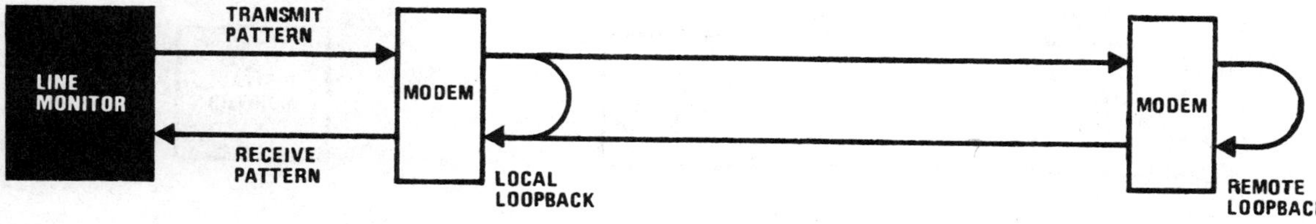

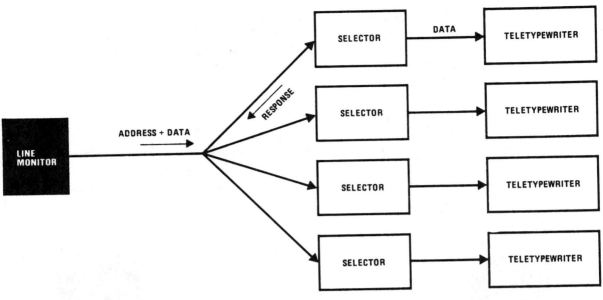

FIGURE 14.2.5 Polling selectors

FIGURE 14.2.6 Testing TDMs

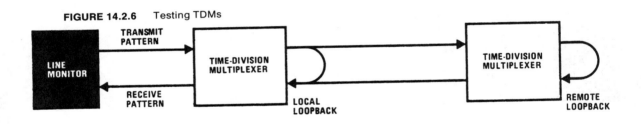

FIGURE 14.2.7 Digital and analog monitoring

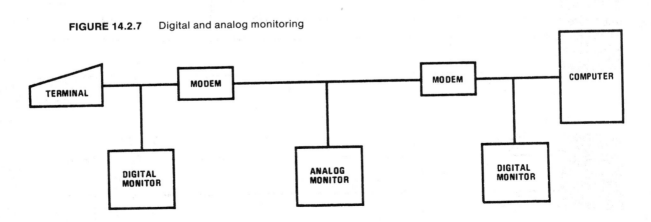

Line Monitor Features

To check the correctness and proper sequencing of control characters and data without having to obtain a terminal and operator to transmit sample data, many line monitors contain special features that can generate the desired test data. While some features listed in Table 14.2.1 are immediately understandable, they are discussed in their order of appearance.

- Code level—The level of a code is defined as the number of information bits used to encode the characters in an alphabet, generally 5, 6, 7 or 8 bits, Baudot, ASCII, or EBCDIC.
- Stop-element length—For asynchronous formats, the stop element consists of a pulse with 1-, 1.42-, 1.5-, or 2-bit intervals, depending on the code and equipment used.
- SDLC—Several sets offer automatic SDLC (IBM's synchronous data link control) capability as an option. With SDLC, block-check-character treatment is important. While it is not difficult to calculate and manually enter the BCC (block check character) for BSC (binary synchronous communications) protocols, it is cumbersome to do so for SDLC formats.

In such cases, block-check-character entry involves additional manipulations for zero-insertion and zero-complementing NRZI (nonreturn to zero, inverted). The inverse of these manipulations must be performed on the received message for it to be intelligible. Unlike the BSC protocol with its negative-acknowledgment response, an absent or wrong BCC and zero insertion means a polled station will not reply.

- Stored-message generator—Stored messages—generally in a programmable read-only memory—are available in such codes as Baudot (International Telegraph Alphabet No. 2), ASCII, and EBCDIC. The stored message may be a standard "fox" (the quick brown fox jumps over a lazy dog's back, 1234567890) or some other combination of characters.
- Send RY/U*—Alternating 1s and 0s may be sent instead of information bits in a string of characters by using the character pairs RY for 5-level code and U* for 8-level code.
- Character-error count—For error-rate determination, parity-error count is generally regarded as being equivalent to character-error count. The latter is

TABLE 14.2.1   LINE MONITOR FEATURES

Code-level selection	Modulation rate
Stop-element length selection	Random-word generator
SDLC	Dot-pattern generator
Stored-message generator	Error count
Send RY/U*	Nonvolatile program memory
Character-error count	Selectable character trap
Distortion Analysis	Programmable sync characters

obtained by bit comparison of received characters with the generated message. On the average, 80% of the character errors are found by parity checks.

• Peak- or bias-distortion analysis—Peak distortion refers to peak individual distortion when operating in the synchronous mode (EIA Standard RS-334 explains synchronous distortion), and to peak "gross stop-start distortion," or "telegraph distortion," during operation in the asynchronous mode. This type of distortion is explained in EIA Standard RS-404 and Bell System Technical Reference PUB 41003. Peak-distortion analysis refers to both synchronous and asynchronous kinds. Bias distortion refers to the elongation of either the mark intervals (marking bias) or the space intervals (spacing bias).

• Modulation rate—The distortion display on some test sets can indicate overspeed; that is, the difference between the modulation rate of the received signal and a standard speed provided by the internal clock. If the internal clock has a fine enough adjustment, it can be used to measure the actual modulation rate of the received signal.

• Random-word generator—Up to six pseudo-random bit sequences can be stored in the test set. An example is the 511-bit pattern in CCITT recommendation V.52.

• Dot-pattern generator—A dot pattern—that is, a square wave, also known as reversal, or 1:1—is obtained by generating alternate mark and space levels for analysis.

• Error count—Error count and error-rate capability may be used as interchangeable terms by some manufacturers. Some vendors use the acronym BERT (bit error rate test). Normally the line monitor will provide a direct readout of the error rate and a readout of the total count and time interval associated with an error count.

• Nonvolatile-program memory—Devices with this feature permit retention of programs fed into memory via the keyboard or bit switches, even though the power is disconnected. The retention time varies, depending on the equipment.

• Selectable character trap—With some devices, incoming data can be compared with one or more "trap" characters that the operator has programmed into a storage register. When a sequence of incoming characters matches the programmed characters, the operator can turn on a trap indicator that will initiate some function, such as transmitting an acknowledgment of a poll message to the station where the test set is located. For simplicity, the selected trap character(s) could be the station's address.

• Programmable sync characters—For transmitting text over synchronous data links, one or more synchronization characters are required to bring the receiver and transmitter into the correct character-phase relationship. If the device has this feature, its receiver circuit is programmed with the correct character(s).

Analog Measurements

Up to now, our discussion in this section has been limited to digital monitoring between the transmission device and the terminal equipment as illustrated in Figure 14.2.7. Although such monitoring is important to ascertain such information as why a specific terminal does not respond to a poll—using a line monitor may show that the line address generated by the computer is incorrect, or perhaps an end-of-transmission character inadvertently follows every poll due to a software error—digital monitors will not provide information on dropouts, phase hits, gain hits, impulse noise, envelope delay, and other circuit data in order for the technician to determine the cause of problems on the line. For such measurements, an analog line monitor, capable of measuring the previously discussed information as well as such additional data as signal strength, amplitude modulation, and harmonic distortion, must be employed. Since the control of a circuit normally rests with the communications carrier, only a few organizations employ analog test equipment. Most organizations merely report an outage to the communications carrier by informing the carrier that a loopback test generates lots of errors, whereas a local loopback test on both ends of the circuit in question shows both transmission devices to be working properly.

14.3 DIAGNOSTIC CENTER COMPONENTS

Any ad hoc approach to troubleshooting in a data network can run into problems and duplication almost as soon as it can be classified as a network; i.e., when there are two locations. With large networks, these and other considerations make a centralized and systematized troubleshooting operation practically essential. Commonly called a tech control center, such a diagnostic facility often pays off additionally by pinpointing and pruning unnecessarily complex line routings, thereby keeping the network neat and easy to maintain.

The first step in designing a tech control center is to define the network clearly. Up-to-date information might be readily available in a new network, but in an older network, it often is not updated frequently enough. The information on the central computer site should include the computer's line address for each channel, identity of the digital line that connects the front end to the modem, the modem type, the party responsible for the modem, the modem's telephone or leased-line number, the modem's data-transmission rate, type of data-access arrangement if applicable, routing of remote lines, and the party responsible for remote lines. Similar information is needed at terminal sites, including locations and terminal types.

Once this data is mapped out, the next step involves adjustments to include future network elements, so that they can be accommodated in the tech control center.

The mapping and documentation indicate the number and types of channels that must be monitored. The types are categorized first in terms of transmission medium (cable, satellite, line-of-sight), then whether the medium is dial-up or leased, digital or analog, synchronous or asynchronous, and two-wire or four-wire. This information indicates the number of channels that are needed in the patching and test equipment, and the types of lines that must be handled by this equipment.

Obviously, not all channels need to be monitored simultaneously; thus the actual number of parallel channels in the tech center might be substantially less than the total. But knowing the total of present and future channels provides the basis for an intelligent estimate of the channel capacity.

The basic equipment must include a patchfield for interconnection and a bit-error-rate test set (BERT). The patchfield permits network components to be connected or bypassed, provides for test equipment to be connected into signal lines without disturbing them, and provides for loopback tests. A BERT generates bit sequences. These can be applied to various portions of the network, and checks made to see if the bits are properly transmitted and received.

Other important devices are a set of lights to indicate the status of the interface cable's control leads, a voltmeter and oscilloscope to monitor signal levels and pulse shapes, and, if the carrier cannot be relied upon for adequate or prompt line testing, a variety of analog line-monitoring test instruments. Error detection and control-lead monitoring often are included in line-monitoring equipment, which also provides for readout and trapping of characters, and operation in specific line protocols.

In the following diagnostic center component discussions, examples are based upon synchronous transmission on a four-wire (full-duplex) circuit.

Patchfield

A patchfield provides a way for monitoring lines, injecting signals, and reconfiguring a network. If it is well designed, a patchfield also provides access to any local equipment interface.

As illustrated in Figure 14.3.1, the equipment and line jacks are normally connected together internally. If a plug is inserted in the equipment jack, the V-shaped metal prong is lifted and the internal contact is broken, disconnecting the line and connecting the equipment at the opposite end of the plug. (Note that the circuit shown is for a two-wire connection, with ground not shown. A four-wire connection requires two sets of jacks.)

In the diagram, the modem is connected to the front end. But if a BERT is used to simulate the front-end output to the modem, then the test set is plugged into the modem jack so the actual front end is automatically disconnected. The same is true for the computer jack, except that the test equipment is connected to the front end to substitute for the modem. The patchfield can be used in a similar manner to switch out a defective unit and replace it with a spare piece of equipment.

The monitor jack is used to provide access to a line without disturbing it. Plugging into the monitor jack does not break the circuit, but only provides a point of contact for connecting test equipment.

The diagram is simplified for the purpose of illustration in Figure 14.3.1. For an actual setup such as one that conforms to RS-232-C specifications, there are a total of 25 data, clock, and control lines in the interface cable between the front end and the modem. Their signals are combined in the modem into each two-wire channel. Therefore, the tech center should have provision to patch many leads simultaneously, but not necessarily all equipment in the network.

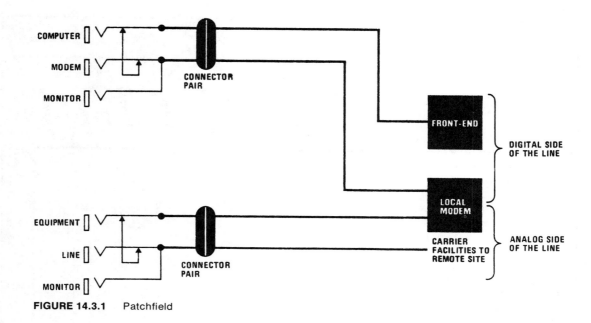

FIGURE 14.3.1   Patchfield

RS-232-C Lead Assignments

The RS-232-C lead assignments (Fig. 14.3.2) that must be patched (assuming the protective ground is common) are:

- Transmit data (TD)
- Receive data (RD)
- Transmit clock (TC)
- Receive clock (RC)
- Data terminal ready (DTR)
- Data set ready (DSR)
- Request to send (RTS)
- Clear to send (CTS)
- Carrier detect (CD)
- Signal ground (SG).

Normally, at least one or more of the following leads must also be patched:

- Ring indicator (RI)
- Signal quality detector (SQD)
- External transmit clock (XTC)
- Data-rate selector (DRS).

Note that provision for the variety and combinations of leads that can be patched must be based on operating conditions— both present and future.

LEAD	DESCRIPTION	COMMON GROUND	DATA		CLOCK		CONTROL	
			TO MODEM	FROM MODEM	TO MODEM	FROM MODEM	TO MODEM	FROM MODEM
1	PROTECTIVE GROUND (PG)	X						
2	TRANSMIT DATA (TD)		X					
3	RECEIVE DATA (RD)			X				
4	REQUEST TO SEND (RTS)						X	
5	CLEAR TO SEND (CTS)							X
6	DATA SET READY (DSR)							X
7	SIGNAL GROUND (SG)	X						
8	CARRIER DETECT (CD)							X
9	DATA SET TEST (DST)							
10	DATA SET TEST (DST)							
11	UNASSIGNED							
12	SECONDARY CARRIER DETECT (SCD)							X
13	SECONDARY CLEAR TO SEND (SCS)							X
14	SECONDARY TRANSMIT DATA (STD)		X					
15	TRANSMIT CLOCK (TC)					X		
16	SECONDARY RECEIVE DATA (SRD)			X				
17	RECEIVE CLOCK (RC)					X		
18	UNASSIGNED							
19	SECONDARY REQUEST TO SEND (SRS)						X	
20	DATA TERMINAL READY (DTR)						X	
21	SIGNAL QUALITY (SQD)							X
22	RING INDICATOR (RI)							X
23	DATA RATE SELECTOR (DRS)						X	X
24	EXT TRANSMIT CLOCK (XTC)				X			
25	UNASSIGNED							

FIGURE 14.3.2   RS-232-C lead assignments

Employing BERT

The most common application of the bit-error-rate test set is in connection with loopback tests. The bit pattern produced by the BERT is passed through one or more elements of the network. The output is returned to the test set and compared to the original test pattern. Each time a mismatch is sensed, an error counter on the BERT is incremented. This count is an indication of the channel's error rate (errors per unit of time).

Loopback testing is generally performed in successive stages, encompassing a greater proportion of the network at each stage. In the first stage, the test set is looped back on itself to determine that it is operating properly. Then the BERT is connected to the local modem, the output is looped back, and the error rate is checked. The signal is turned back at the modem output before it enters the transmission line. Connections are made through the patchfield, as shown in Figure 14.3.3.

Next, the test is repeated, this time including the front end and modem. The signal is turned back just before it enters the remote modem, so that the line is also checked out. Then the remote modem is included, with the signal being turned around at the digital side. The test sequence continues in this manner until all elements of the network have been added to the chain. At each stage, any added error rate indicates the degradation of signal quality contributed by the last unit connected.

In looping back the data from any point on the digital side of the remote modem, some changes in clock synchronization are needed. The transmit- and

FIGURE 14.3.3   Bit-error-rate-test setup

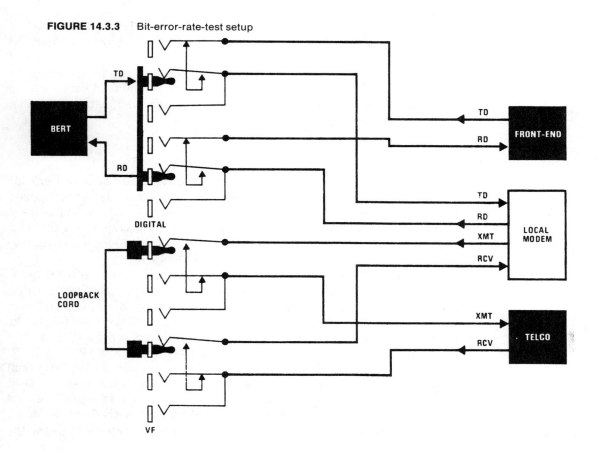

receive-clock signals in a modem are not normally synchronized with respect to each other. The transmit clock is produced by an internal oscillator, while the receive-clocking signal is derived by phase-locking on the received data stream. The receive clock is thus synchronized to the transmit clock at the remote modem. But when the data is looped back, the received data must be synchronized more accurately, so it can be properly sampled. To accomplish this, the transmit clock at the local site becomes the master clock, and both the transmit and receive clocks at the remote site must be slaved to it for synchronization.

This is achieved at the remote modem by strapping it for operation with an external transmit clock, connecting pins 15, 17, and 24 so that all three clocking signals are synchronized. In some modems, the receive clock is connected automatically to the external transmit clock in the loopback mode. To achieve loopback of the data itself, the transmit data and receive data pins (2 and 3, respectively) are connected. Some modems also require the presence of request-to-send (pin 4) and/or data-terminal-ready (pin 20) signals to operate in a loopback mode. The 12-volt dc supply needed to simulate these signals in most modems can be derived by connecting a lead from the data set test line (pin 9) to pins 4 and/or 20.

A return path is not available on two-wire channels. Therefore, a BERT is needed at both ends—one to transmit the test signal and another to receive and count the errors.

Line monitors used instead of BERTs may be arranged to transmit special bit patterns, such as protocol-control characters, to check the ability of the network to establish and maintain a link, in addition to sending character patterns treated as data. Some monitors also trap selected characters.

Digital Signal Monitoring

The activity on the control and clock leads of the RS-232-C cable can provide valuable insight into the setup's operating sequence. Knowledge of the signals' conditions and their sequence often points to the source of a failure. The simplest method of monitoring the signals on these leads is to connect them to light-emitting-diode indicators, as illustrated in Figure 14.3.4. The LEDs are individually illuminated when their respective inputs are in the ON state.

When connecting new equipment that is supposed to conform to RS-232-C standards, it is often assumed that the interface signals will match perfectly. This is not always true. Because of differences in manufacturers' standards, interpretation, and quality-control, some units will work well together and others will not. Hence waveshapes, timing, and signal levels must be carefully checked.

The most important leads are TD, RD, RTS, CTS, CD, DSR, and DTR. Understanding the function and timing of these leads is extremely helpful in fault isolation. For instance, if the terminal and modem are operational, DTR and DSR should be ON. If control signals are being exchanged, RTS, CTS, and CD should be active. And if data is being transmitted or received, TD and RD should be active.

Two other useful monitoring devices are a voltmeter and an oscilloscope. The

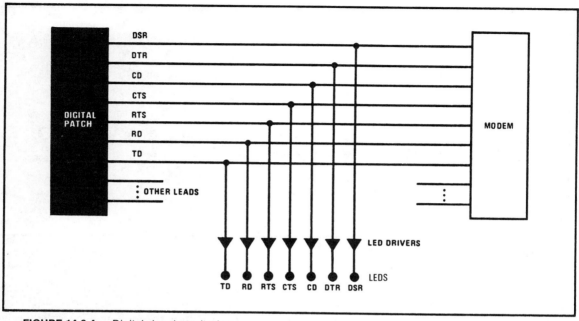

FIGURE 14.3.4   Digital signal monitoring

voltmeter measures the dc voltages on the interface leads, while the scope permits viewing of activity and waveshapes on data and clock lines. Still another useful feature of a tech center is a 12-volt dc source to simulate RS-232-C signals for controlling the operating modes of the equipment under test, as described for loopback testing. An example of a monitoring panel with jacks, control leads, LEDs, and power-supply leads appears in Figure 14.3.5.

Analog Signal Monitoring

In addition to the basic digital test equipment, a tech control center may contain equipment to measure carrier-line characteristics. Among the parameters measured are circuit loss, noise, attenuation distortion (frequency response), delay distortion, phase jitter, frequency shift, phase hits, gain hits, dropouts, and nonlinear (harmonic) distortion. Of these, the simplest ones to measure are circuit loss, noise, attenuation distortion, and frequency shift. These can be measured with a single instrument, called a level/noise/frequency test set.

Other integrated instruments measure both phase jitter and impulse noise. Delay-distortion test sets can be valuable for testing conditioned lines.

Several instruments that measure all the aforementioned parameters are now available. One even provides a visual display of frequency response and delay distortion simultaneously. In the absence of these instruments, however, an oscilloscope can be used to obtain a qualitative visual indication of the important

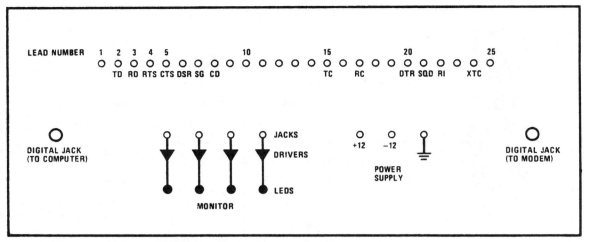

FIGURE 14.3.5   Monitoring panel

transmission characteristics. The resulting display is called an eye pattern because of its characteristic shape, as shown in Figure 14.3.6.

For an eye pattern, two signals are needed from the modem. One is the received baseband data signal (analog) and the other is the symbol timing wave, a binary signal. On low-speed modems, one bit is transmitted for each one-bit sampling interval. In high-speed modems, which use multilevel coding, each symbol bit represents more than one data bit. In most modems, this signal is not available at the outside of the modem, but instead must be tapped from an internal test point.

The eye pattern is produced by applying the demodulated data input to the vertical oscilloscope channel, and triggering the oscilloscope with the symbol timing wave. Positive-going signals form the upper half of the eye; negative-going signals, the lower half.

The waveform is illustrated in Figure 14.3.6. The pattern shown is for a modem with one-level coding. With multilevel coding, modems will show several "eyes," stacked one above another at each coding interval. Also of significance is the shape of the eyes. A pulse gated at the sampling instant is determined positive or negative by whether it is above or below the threshold level. In order for the pulses to be correctly recognized, the eye must be open, and the sampling instant and threshold level should be in the center.

The vertical amplitude is affected by noise, intersymbol interference, echoes, and gain variations. Excess amounts of any of these factors, as well as timing degradations, will tend to narrow the eye. A properly shaped eye, therefore, indicates the excellent "health" of a number of transmission characteristics. Even a nontechnical viewer can be relied upon to check it. If the shape is incorrect, further testing is required.

Line testing is a gray area of responsibility. Assuming that the lines are not privately owned, testing must be done with the consent of the carrier, and it should not interfere with the carrier's normal operations. Line-test equipment should therefore be fully compatible with the line. In the event of cooperative testing, it should be compatible with the equipment used by the carrier.

14.4 BUILDING A DIAGNOSTIC CENTER

Generally a diagnostic test center (commonly called a tech control center) must, in addition to providing sufficient space for the equipment, allow access to connecting and test points, use only as much cable as necessary, and provide adequate ventilation. Taken one at a time, these considerations may be fairly obvious, but to overlook any one of them is to invite problems later on.

Human factors also deserve attention. The effectiveness of a tech control center is determined to a great extent by the willingness of people to use it. And if its operation involves excessive bending, stretching, or other difficulty in taking readings or making connections, users might try to work around it.

In Section 3 of this chapter we dealt with selecting and applying the test equipment and patch panels for a tech center. In this section we will concentrate on the layout and installation of the previously discussed components.

The most important consideration in selecting a location is to minimize cable lengths, bearing in mind that to avoid signal degradation, RS-232-C cables should not exceed 50 feet. The optimum location from this point of view is between the

FIGURE 14.3.6   Eye pattern display

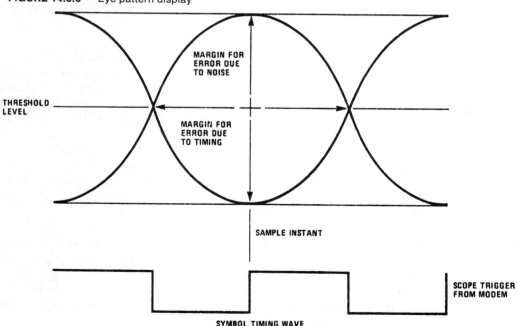

modems and the front end. Moreover, to facilitate access to modems for line and other network tests, the modems are often housed right in the tech center.

For distances exceeding 50 feet, cable drivers can extend the usable cabling distances, sometimes by hundreds of feet, depending on the data rate. But be careful. Many equipment manufacturers will not support setups using cable drivers. And when they are used, be sure to test the cables with the tech center's test equipment, and the data processing and communications equipment, before the cables are placed in normal operation. This is to be sure that any signal degradation caused by the drivers and long cables is acceptable.

In designing a tech center for a network not yet installed, the cable routings must be carefully planned and their lengths accurately computed. All obstructions that interfere with direct routing should be carefully taken into account, because 50 feet of cable can easily be consumed, even when the straight-line distance between interconnected units is only a fraction of the 50 feet.

Computer-type cabinets provide the best housing for tech center equipment. Rack-mountable units usually conform to their standard widths and can be ordered or fitted with appropriate mounting hardware. Typical cabinets are 6 feet high, 2 feet wide, and 2 to 3 feet in depth. The deeper cabinets are recommended because space is needed behind the equipment for cables and air flow. Rails are usually provided at the front and rear of the cabinets for mounting the equipment. The standard spacing between rails is 19 inches, the most common width of rack-mounted equipment.

Other desirable features are roller slides and rear doors to facilitate access to equipment, and open cabinet bottoms to permit installation of under-floor cabling. For additional cooling, the top of the cabinet should be open, as well. The cabinets should have hardware for distributing ac power and "loops" or "ladders" for routing cables.

A word about space for cables and connectors—design parameters that are easily underestimated. Providing access to each unit entails the ability to interconnect through a patch panel, also called a patchfield. A full-duplex channel—both channel types can be housed in a single cable—usually requires four lines: two RS-232-C cables for connecting the terminal or computer to the modem via the patch panel, and two telephone cables to tie the modem to the line, also through the patch panel. Therefore, as the number of channels increases, the number of cables and connectors needed at the patch panel and the amount of space needed to house them increase fourfold. Still more lines would be required if such items as multiplexers, switching equipment, and spares are also to be tied through the network's tech center.

To assure adequate room behind the cabinet for service workspace, a rule of thumb is that the rear of the cabinet should be at least 3 feet from the nearest obstruction. Therefore, the total floor space required for each cabinet is at least 5 to 6 feet deep and 2 feet wide.

An alternative to cabinets is inexpensive, open "radio-relay" racks. These are less attractive than computer cabinets, but they are easier to access, and their openness provides good ventilation.

An attractive, although more expensive, method of providing access to the patch panel, controls, and indicator lights is to build a wraparound console. But consoles also consume a great deal of floor space. So unless the tech center is visited constantly, a wraparound console may not be advisable.

Care must be taken in positioning test equipment, patch panels, and control and indicator panels in the cabinets so that they are at convenient heights. Test equipment, and control and indicator panels, should be as close as possible to eye level, which is 4 to 6 feet above the floor. Patch panels can be somewhat lower, from 3 to 5 feet. Modems and other equipment not frequently accessed can occupy the space in the lower 3 feet.

A list of recommended distances above the floor for various types of equipment is given in Table 14.4.1, Equipment Mounting Heights. Note that the table specifies equipment heights in RMS units, which here stand for rack-mounting space. A term frequently used by cabinet suppliers, one RMS unit is equal to a linear distance of 1¾ inches. So 2 RMS equals 3½ inches, and so on.

Patch panels can present some problems in finding enough room to locate all the jacks at convenient heights. Commercial patch panels are designed for 12 to 16 modems, and each modem requires two RS-232-C connectors. Experience indicates that the recommended height range provides room for a set of three panels, which can accommodate 36 to 48 modems.

Equipment layout can be simplified by using worksheets, as shown in Figure 14.4.1, for arranging the equipment, calibrated both in feet and RMS units. Note that the RMS measurements begin at the lowest possible mounting location, generally 6 to 8 inches above the floor, but the distance in feet is measured directly from the floor. The reason for the discrepancy is that RMS is used to measure

TABLE 14.4.1   EQUIPMENT MOUNTING HEIGHTS

Equipment Type	Equipment Height (RMS)	Mounting Range (Feet)
Cabinet	40	½ to 6
Patchfield (analog and digital for 12 to 16 modems)	4	3 to 5
Status monitoring panel (for 12 to 16 modems)	2	5 to 6
Test equipment	2 to 4	4 to 6
Miscellaneous patchfields (analog, digital, spare modems, etc.)	2	3 to 5
Asynchronous modems (typically eight per mount)	4	½ to 4
Synchronous modems, 2,400 bit/s or less (typically two per mount)	4	½ to 4
Synchronous modems, 4800 bit/s or more	4	½ to 4
Drawers (for patch cables, accessories)	2 to 4	3 to 4
Writing surfaces	1 to 2	3 to 4

Note: Distances are from the floor (feet) or lowest mounting point (RMS) to the bottom of the mounted equipment. (1 RMS = 1¾ inches)

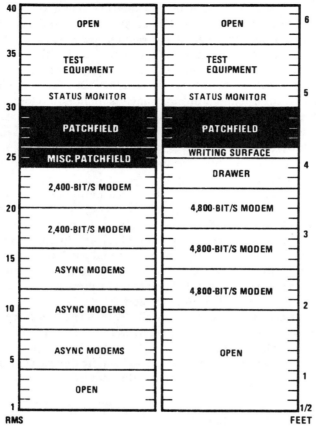

FIGURE 14.4.1   Arranging the equipment

usable mounting space, whereas the distance in feet—the actual distance from the floor—is used for measuring cable lengths.

The procedure for designing a tech control center is first to estimate the amount of front mounting space needed to house present and future equipment, and then to lay out the equipment in the cabinets. The final step is to arrange the cabinets on the floor to minimize digital cable lengths.

The balance of this section illustrates this procedure for a setup with 12 low-speed modems, two of medium speed, and two of high speed. Assume that space must also be provided for expansion by 50% to 18 low-speed modems and three each of the medium- and high-speed modems.

How Many Cabinets?

After choosing the test equipment, obtain the rack-mounting dimension in RMS units. For the setup described, assume that the test equipment consists of two patch panels, two status monitor panels, and a bit-error-rate tester. Also assume that the modems will be housed in the tech center, so that their mounting dimensions must also be determined. As indicated in Figure 14.4.2, Estimating total mounting space, the total height of the equipment is 52 RMS units. Computer-type cabinets that are 6 feet high provide about 40 RMS of mounting space. Taller cabinets are available, but the extra height makes it difficult to reach the equipment on top. As a result, the 52 RMS units of height should be built into a double-width cabinet or two cabinets bolted together. Another advantage of two cabinets is that the equipment can be spread out to assure sufficient cabling space and ventilation. Also, the loose arrangement provides adequate space to mount additional test equipment, should the need ever arise.

Arranging the Equipment

Once the total mounting space has been estimated, and the required number of mounting racks determined, the equipment can be laid out in the cabinets, with the locations selected according to the recommended equipment heights.

In Figure 14.4.1, a drawer and a writing surface have been added. The drawer holds cables, documentation, and other accessories. A "miscellaneous" patch panel also is provided for access to backup modems, special test points, or to expand the patching capability to other units in the network. The need for an extra patch panel often develops as troubleshooting and maintenance techniques evolve.

FIGURE 14.4.2   Estimating total mounting space

EQUIPMENT	HEIGHT (RMS)
PATCHFIELD (MOST FOR 12 OR 16 MODEMS; TWO FOR 24 MODEMS)	2 X 4 = 8
STATUS MONITOR (TWO REQUIRED)	2 X 2 = 4
MOUNT FOR ASYNCHRONOUS MODEMS (IF THERE ARE EIGHT PER MOUNT, THREE MOUNTS REQUIRED)	3 X 4 = 12
MOUNTS FOR 2,400-BIT/S MODEMS (IF THERE ARE TWO PER MOUNT, TWO MOUNTS REQUIRED)	2 X 4 = 8
MOUNTS FOR 4,800-BIT/S MODEMS	3 X 4 = 12
MOUNT FOR TWO PIECES OF TEST EQUIPMENT	2 X 4 = 8
	TOTAL EQUIPMENT HEIGHT = 52 RMS

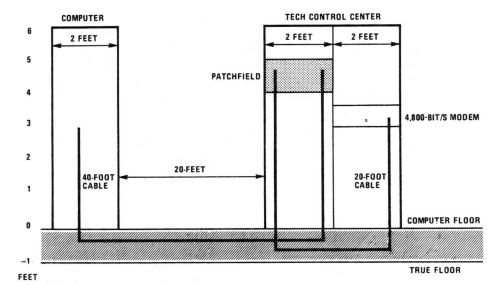

FIGURE 14.4.3 Cable runs

FIGURE 14.4.4 Estimating cable length

CABLE LENGTH FROM MODEM TO PATCHFIELD:	
MODEM TO FLOOR (ASSUMING 1 FOOT OF CABLE IN THE CABINET)	1 + 4 + 1 = 6 FEET
UNDER BOTH CABINETS	2 + 2 = 4 FEET
FLOOR TO PATCHFIELD (ASSUMING 1 FOOT OF CABLE IN THE CABINET)	1 + 5 + 1 = 7 FEET
CABLES USUALLY MADE IN MULTIPLES OF 5 FEET, SO A 20-FOOT CABLE WOULD PROBABLY BE USED	**TOTAL LENGTH = 17 FEET**
CABLE LENGTH FROM PATCHFIELD TO THE COMPUTER:	
PATCHFIELD TO FLOOR (ASSUMING 1 FOOT OF CABLE IN CABINET)	1 + 5 + 1 = 7 FEET
UNDER FLOOR (AND BOTH TECH CONTROL AND COMPUTER CABINET)	2 + 20 + 2 = 24 FEET
FLOOR TO COMPUTER (ASSUMING 1 FOOT OF CABLE IN CABINET)	1 + 3 + 1 = 5 FEET
THEREFORE, A 40-FOOT CABLE WOULD PROBABLY BE USED	**TOTAL LENGTH = 36 FEET**

Minimizing Cable Runs

Since the patch panel is connected between the modem and the digital equipment, the cable run should be determined by summing the lengths of the cable between the modem and the patch panel, and the cable between the patch panel and the digital device. From Figures 14.4.3 and 14.4.4, we can determine, for example, that a 24-foot straight-line distance between a modem and computer (indicated as underfloor distance) might require a 60-foot cable.

The problem now is how to reduce the cable length to 50 feet to meet RS-232-C standards. If the digital device and tech center cannot be moved closer to each other, then one way to save a few feet is to use a cabinet without a partition or to drill holes in an existing partition so that the cables connected across the cabinet can be routed directly, instead of around the partition. Another solution is to move the modems and patch panels closer to the floor.

QUESTIONS

14.1 What are the gain or loss in decibels of the following signal power measurements?

  A. Output power 10 mw, input power 100 mw
  B. Output power 100 mw, input power 1 mw

14.2 Discuss the differences between dropouts, phase hits, gain hits, and impulse noise.

14.3 Discuss two methods that can be used to improve line transmission.

14.4 What is the key difference between digital and analog monitoring?

14.5 Discuss the use of five line monitor/digital test set features one should consider.

14.6 What elements are the specific concern of analog monitoring, and why is analog monitoring less frequently employed than digital monitoring?

14.7 What is a patchfield and how can it be used?

CHAPTER 15

NETWORK PLANNING AND DESIGN ALTERNATIVES

Preceding every efficiently designed network is proper planning. The network plan can be considered a roadmap that will result in the network analyst achieving an effective network that meets the requirements of his organizational users.

In this chapter, we will examine some of the methods used to collect information, the typical data elements that should be collected and their use, and the types of operational requirements one should query network users about. Next, current and anticipated resources will be examined. Some of the typical types of hardware limitations, and methods that can be used to alleviate those limitations, will be covered. Finally, a discussion of carrier and equipment selection, installation, and operation will show the relationship of those elements to the network plan.

15.1 INFORMATION COLLECTION

In formulating a network plan, the most difficult element may be obtaining the requirements of current and anticipated network users. If these requirements are stated incorrectly or glossed over due to misunderstandings, then the most methodical network plan will not be successful.

Several methods can be used in the information collection process, ranging from personal interviews to surveys, forms, and checklists. While an interview can be costly and time consuming, especially if current or anticipated users are scattered over a wide geographical area, often this method of information collection results in the discovery of items or classification of certain factors that no amount of survey forms or checklists can accomplish. When sitting down with the network user, the analyst could discover, for instance, that lower seatbelt production for the next six months will result in the termination of second and third shifts at a plant during that period. The analyst might then recognize that the factory on-line data collection network will be inoperative during half the year for all but the first shift. Therefore, the circuit connecting the factory with the company's data processing center could be used to support a remote batch terminal that is now using the public switched telephone network for transmission.

While checklists have been employed on occasion, they are very difficult to use. They can result in user frustration, since they normally do not permit a deviation from listed elements. When using the checklist approach, the network planner prepares a menu of all possible responses to the information he requires, permitting the network user only to check the relevant block. Thus, if the analyst wants to know the planned operating speed of terminals to be acquired during the next year, he might have blocks denoting 300, 1,200, 2,400, 4,800 and 9,600 bit/s for the user to check. If the user required 110-bit/s terminals and another block were available, he could check that block and write in his requirement. In doing this, we have modified the checklist. By the use of these types of modifications, one may wind up with a survey.

The Survey

Although a survey may not be able to ferret out items of information that an interview may obtain, this method provides much more flexibility than a checklist. It is the most popular technique employed for obtaining information.

Figure 15.1.1 contains a terminal and data communications survey form, while one possible set of instructions for completing the survey is listed in Table 15.1.1. Since data traffic that must be supported by a communications network originates from remote terminals, the survey is called a Terminal and Data Communications Survey. For the particular requirements of the network analyst, only 12 items have been placed on the survey. However, we will discuss several additional items later in this section that might be included.

In this particular survey, the first item to be completed denotes the location of the terminal. This will be important when the analyst prepares a network layout in preparation for developing a minimal-cost network design. Although in Table 15.1.1 the survey respondent is not asked to indicate the street address and room number of terminals, this could be incorporated into the survey. The analyst may believe that remote terminals could be directly connected to communications equipment at one or more remote locations, or he may wish to explore the use of line drivers and limited-distance modems to connect terminals to data concentration equipment. For such cases, the analyst might request a diagram showing terminal locations by building floor and the layout of conduits on each floor.

The second item on the survey assumes that only three types of terminals will be considered. For the less knowledgeable individual, a definition of each type could be included in the survey instructions.

In the third item, the user is to indicate the number of terminals he will require over a three-year period. While the analyst could use the first year's information to develop a network if none already exists, he may wish to obtain one or two

1. Location: _____
2. Type of terminal: Type I — Teleprinter _____ Type II — A/N Display _____
   Type III — Batch _____
3. Quantity of terminals required (#): 1984 _____ 1985 _____ 1986 _____
4. Transmission speed required (bit/s): a. 110 _____ b. 300 _____ c. 1,200 _____
   d. 2,400 _____ e. 4,800 _____ f. 9,600 _____ g. other (explain) _____
   _____
5. Terminal options required: _____
   _____
   _____
6. Normal operating hours (EST) per day: _____ To _____
7. Peak hours (EST):
   To host: From _____ To _____ From host: From _____ To _____
8. Calls per day per terminal (#): To host _____
9. Connect time (hours and minutes) per call: Average _____ Peak _____
10. Messages per call per terminal (#):
    To host: Average _____ Peak _____ From host: Average _____ Peak _____
11. Average characters per message per terminal (#):
    a. To host _____ b. From host _____
12. Comments: _____
    _____
    _____
    _____
    _____
    _____

FIGURE 15.1.1 Terminal and Data Communications Survey

TABLE 15.1.1 INSTRUCTIONS FOR COMPLETING TERMINAL AND DATA COMMUNICATIONS SURVEY

The following explanation and examples are given to assist you in completing the survey. The survey form may be copied if more are needed.

For each or the twelve items on the survey, indicate the required information as follows:

Item #1 — *Location*

A separate survey form *must* be completed for each different location where a terminal will be installed. Indicate *city, state,* and denote if *Region* or *Area Office. Specific location must be indicated.*

Item #2 — *Type of terminal*

A separate survey form *must* be completed for each of the three categories of terminals. Indicate type of terminal by placing a *check mark* in the appropriate space.

Item #3 — *Quantity of terminals required*

A separate survey form may be required for each year if all other conditions are not the same. For example, if three teleprinters are required in 1984 and three more are required in 1985, but their usage is different, two separate forms should be completed. Indicate *number* of terminals required in the appropriate space.

Item #4 — *Transmission speed required*

Indicate transmission speed required by placing a *check mark* in the appropriate space.

Item #5 — *Terminal options required*

Indicate any *optional terminals features* you may require. Examples: (1) printers for CRT, (2) special printing features, (3) special keyboard requirements, (4) portability, (5) graphics, (6) protocol.

Item #6 — *Normal operating hours per day*

Indicate the hours (EST) during which the terminal(s) will normally be operating.

Item #7 — *Peak hours*

Indicate the *peak hours (EST)* during which you will be transmitting to and receiving from the host computer. More than one group of peak hours is possible.

Item #8 — *Calls per day per terminal*

Indicate the *number* of calls to the host computer per day per terminal.

Item #9 — *Connect time per call*

Indicate the connect *time (hours and minutes)* per call (average and peak).

Item #10 — *Messages per call per terminal*

Indicate the *number* of messages per call per terminal going to the host computer (average and peak).

Item #11 — *Average characters per message per terminal*

Indicate average *number* of characters per message per terminal going to and being received from the host computer. A carriage return constitutes the end of a one-line message to the host, and the end of a print line constitutes the end of a one-line message from the host.

Item #12 — *Comments*

Indicate any additional information which you feel may be pertinent to the survey.

---

additional years of projected information for planning purposes. In the instructions contained in Table 15.1.1, the survey respondent is instructed to complete different forms when terminal usage conditions change.

The fourth item, transmission speed required, permits the user to indicate the operating data rate he desires. In some organizations, the respondent may only be asked to furnish expected operational statistics. The network analyst will review them and then inform the requestor what his terminal operating speed should be, based upon the user's expected operational data transfers.

Item 5, terminal options required, could be expanded by the network analyst to obtain additional information. As an example, the analyst might inquire about the operating speed and usage of printers for CRTs. Such printers operate at one-half to one-fourth the data rate of CRTs. Extensive printer usage could permit more CRTs to be placed on a polled circuit than if the CRTs were extensively used for job output scanning that requires a fast look at extensive amounts of information by the terminal operator at the full data transfer rate of the CRT.

In items 6 through 11, operational communications data factors are requested to enable the network analyst to examine several methods of connecting each terminal to the host computer. If the computer is located in the Eastern Standard Time (EST) zone, then items 6 and 7 will request the normal and peak operating hours with respect to EST. This permits the analyst to examine the effect of terminal operations in many time zones on the host computer and the network. Thus, if peak usage occurs at the same relative time across the country, the difference in time zones may permit the analyst to reduce the number of front-end processor ports than if time zone differences were not considered.

The call-per-day and connect-time-per-call data requested in items 8 and 9 can be used to compare transmission cost over the switched network with, say, leased-line utilization. When items 10 and 11 are included, the analysts can cost out value-added carrier utilization and then compare that cost with that of telephone company and perhaps satellite carrier service. Lastly, item 12 permits any additional information to be added to the survey form. One of the problems with such a catch-all item is that personnel completing the form may not be knowledgeable enough to state other factors that are not asked for on the survey. A modified form of item 12 is illustrated in Figure 15.1.2.

As shown in Figure 15.1.2, supplemented by relevant instructions, users can now express special operational requirements as well as add comments. In part A of item 12, response-time requirements can be denoted. Applications of a critical nature that may require special communications backup and equipment redundancy can be listed in part B. If the application is of such a nature that data encryption may be warranted, this fact can be expressed in part C. For organizations that do not centrally fund communications but charge back costs to users, a billing or chargeback portion of item 12 should be considered. A variety of data, from a user's charge number to a dollar limit for the expenditure of funds on communications, could be filled in part D of item 12. Lastly, the catch-all "other" phrase can be used. However, the person completing this modified form now has four examples to think about before entering his comments.

FIGURE 15.1.2   Modified portion of survey form

12. Special Operating Requirements and Comments: _____
    A. Response Time _____
    B. Backup/Redundancy _____
    C. Security _____
    D. Billing/Chargeback _____
    E. Other _____

Survey Analysis

Let us assume that the Chicago customer service center of an organization completed one Terminal and Data Communications Survey form, as illustrated in Figure 15.1.3. From this completed form, the network analyst can plan the method of integrating the communications requirements of the Chicago customer service center with the other network requirements of the organization. From items 2, 3, and 4 of the survey, the service center will be using 300-bit/s teleprinter terminals and has a requirement for ten such devices in 1984, seven more for 1985, and an additional four in 1986. Thus, while the analyst must immediately concern himself with supporting ten terminals in Chicago, he should plan to support 11 additional devices over the next two years. In items 6 and 7 it appears that there are no peak hours of operation; thus calls will normally occur on a random basis throughout the normal business day.

Using the data furnished in items 8 and 9, the average and peak connect time per terminal can be computed by multiplying the calls per day by the average and peak connect times per call. Thus each terminal in Chicago will be on line an average of 180 minutes per day, and for high-volume days have a peak connect time of 270 minutes. This information can be used to determine the optimum size of data concentration equipment, or to determine the cost of switched-telephone-

FIGURE 15.1.3   Completed form sample — Terminal and Data Communications Survey

1. Location: _CHICAGO CUSTOMER SERVICE CENTER_
2. Type of terminal: Type I — Teleprinter _✓_ Type II — A/N Display _____
   Type III — Batch _____
3. Quantity of terminals required (#): 1984 _10_ 1985 _7_ 1986 _4_
4. Transmission speed required (bit/s): a. 110 _____ b. 300 _✓_ c. 1,200 _____
   d. 2,400 _____ e. 4,800 _____ f. 9,600 _____ g. other (explain) _____
5. Terminal options required: _Portable and Lightweight_
   will be moved throughout building due to frequent
   organizational changes.
6. Normal operating hours (EST) per day: _8 AM_ To _5 PM_
7. Peak hours (EST):
   To host: From _____ To _____ From host: From _____ To _____
8. Calls per day per terminal (#): To host _6_
9. Connect time (hours and minutes) per call: Average _30 min_ Peak _45 min_
10. Messages per call per terminal (#):
    To host: Average _40_ Peak _____ From host: Average _300_ Peak _____
11. Average characters per message per terminal (#):
    a. To host _25_ b. From host _60_
12. Special Operating Requirements and Comments: _____
    A. Response Time
    B. Backup/Redundancy
    C. Security
    D. Billing/Chargeback
    E. Other

network and private-line service, depending upon where the computer center is located.

Using the information in items 8 and 9 in conjunction with the data in items 10 and 11, the network analyst determines the cost of using a value-added carrier to support the Chicago service center's transmission requirements. From item 10, an average of 40 messages per call per terminal will be transmitted to the host computer. In item 11, the average characters per message per terminal to the host is 25. This results in a total of 1,000 characters on the average transmitted to the computer during one call. Similarly, an average of 18,000 characters will be transmitted from the host computer to the terminal during a call, for a total of 19,000 characters transmitted and received.

Multiplied by the six calls per day, this results in a daily average of 114,000 characters transmitted and received by each terminal, or a daily total of 1.14 million characters for the ten terminals. For the value-added carrier that has a charge element based upon packets and not characters, the information in items 10 and 11 can be used to determine the number of packets transmitted and received. As long as the number of average characters per message as indicated in item 11 is less than the maximum number of characters that can be contained in a packet, the messages per call per terminal in item 10 are equal to packets. If the average characters per message (item 11) exceeds the number of characters per packet, each of the messages in the messages per call (item 10) represents more than one packet. This normally occurs when terminals transmit synchronously and a large number of characters is grouped into a block for transmission. If the value-added carrier under consideration has a packet size of 128 characters and the average per message transmitted is 160, then each message per call (item 10) would represent two packets, one containing 128 characters, the second containing 32 characters.

15.2 RESOURCE EXAMINATION

In addition to collecting information on user requirements, the network planner must consider the resources he has and their expansion potential. These resources range from existing circuits and data concentration equipment to the central-site hardware. Especially included are existing front-end processors and the availability of additional ports to service additional terminal connections to the processor.

One method that can be employed by the network analyst to understand the capability and expansion potential of existing equipment and circuits is through the use of an "Expansion Table." Such a table might contain a list of present equipment, current monthly cost, expansion potential of equipment, and the anticipated cost of the expansion. In Table 15.2.1, a portion of the expansion table is illustrated for the Chicago segment of a network. Here an 8-channel time-division multiplexer and an 8-position rotary connecting eight dial-in lines are listed, and their expansion potential and cost of expansion indicated. As illustrated, one can indicate the channel data rates on the TDM, which can be used to determine how many of the expansion channels at various data rates can be used before the capacity of the high-speed modem or leased line is exceeded.

TABLE 15.2.1   POTENTIAL EQUIPMENT EXPANSION

Location: Chicago

Equipment	Monthly Rent	Expansion Capability	Projected Monthly Cost
TDM, 8 chnl (4 × 300, 4 × 1,200)	$150	8 channel	$100
Rotary (8 dial-in lines)	$35	10 contiguous Numbers XXX-444	Installation only
High-speed modem Bell 209	6,000 bit/s Effective Transmission on GD4726 circuit		

Although a telephone company rotary can step through a series of perhaps 1,000 numbers, when such devices are installed normally only a small group of contiguous telephone numbers will be left available upon user request to serve as expansion potential. In the expansion table, one might list the quantity of numbers reserved and their extensions. Information that can be added to the table for remote sites includes the type of transmission equipment used and transmission medium information, if applicable. In Table 15.2.1, a Bell 209 high-speed modem, which is capable of transmitting data at 9,600 bit/s, is listed with the notation, "6,000-bit/s effective transmission on GD4726 circuit." The GD4726 is the telephone company designation for a particular leased line that connects the customer's Chicago location with his computer facility. The notation about 6,000-bit/s effective transmission indicates that an additional 3,600 bit/s can be transmitted on that medium.

Central-Site Resources

Although the host computer site can have a very large number of communications components and circuits, a good starting place for resource investigation is the computer's front-end processor. This is because the available resources and expansion potential of that device are the governing factors behind the design, establishment, and growth of a communications network.

Software Limitations

If the front-end processor cannot support multipoint lines due to the unavailability of poll and select software, then the network designer may not be able to consider that method during the network configuration process. If multipoint lines can significantly reduce potential communications costs, then the analyst should explore the cost of modifying existing software, purchasing software from a vendor that will enable the front-end processor to poll and select terminals, or obtaining and using software from the computer manufacturer that may require some modifications.

Similarly, the network analyst should investigate the protocol software-support modules available from the computer manufacturer as well as from software houses. He will then know what other types of terminal support may be available and what the cost might be. In Table 15.2.2, some of the more common terminal software protocols are listed.

Even when a terminal protocol is available at no cost or for a nominal fee, care must be taken to examine the effect of adding another software module to the front-end processor. This is because each software module must be core resident at all times if terminals requiring that specific protocol support are to be permitted to connect to the network at any time during the day. Since the processor's memory size is fixed, the size of the protocol module must be examined to determine if that module will "fit" in the processor, or if an expansion memory module is required.

Obviously, if the processor is fully configured and not enough memory is available for the required module, then another front-end processor would be required. This would be very expensive, say, if the analyst were faced with the situation where only one remote user wanted to obtain a terminal whose protocol was not previously supported; if the organization's front-end processor were fully configured; and all memory were utilized by existing software modules.

Here, even if the analyst can obtain the required terminal protocol support module at no cost, the cost of an additional processor to support one terminal may not be justified. The analyst informs the user that the specific terminal he desires cannot be supported for a reasonable cost and that the user should select another terminal whose protocol is already supported by the front-end processor.

Hardware Constraints

In conjunction with software limitations, hardware constraints of front-end processors must be examined. Although no techniques exist for fitting software modules onto hardware once all memory is used, other than obtaining additional memory or another processor, a variety of techniques can be employed to alleviate

TABLE 15.2.2   COMMON TERMINAL SOFTWARE PROTOCOLS

Teletype   110 bit/s ASCII
Teletype   135.5 bit/s EBCDIC
Teletype   300 bit/s ASCII
Teletype 1,200 bit/s ASCII
CRT synchronous block mode
CRT poll and select cluster
IBM 2780/3780
IBM 3270
Honeywell RC 115

hardware constraints. These techniques range from front-end processor channel reconfiguration to obtaining devices to "front-end" the front-end processor.

To understand some of the options available to the network analyst for alleviating front-end processor hardware constraints, let us examine a typical hardware configuration, illustrated in Figure 15.2.1. In this configuration, sixteen 300-bit/s and sixteen 1,200-bit/s teleprinter channels are used to support the output of two 16-channel multiplexers. Four 9,600-bit/s batch terminals and four CRTs, each on an individual circuit, are supported by a total of eight processor channels. Eight channels are available for network expansion.

Let us assume that this 48-channel front-end processor cannot be expanded to accommodate additional channels in excess of 48. Also, due to the growth of the organization, there is a requirement for an additional 16-channel multiplexer at a third remote site to support 300-bit/s terminal operations and fourteen additional CRTs at various locations.

FIGURE 15.2.1   Typical front-end processor configuration

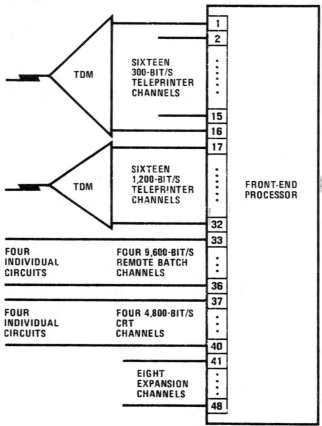

For the first expansion requirement, the utilization of a port selector may be an optimum solution, depending upon the cost of that device in comparison to the cost of an additional front-end processor. If we employ such a device and estimate that no more than 32 users will require simultaneous access 95% of the time, then the time-division multiplexers feeding the front-end processor via a port selector would appear as illustrated in Figure 15.2.2. In this illustration, a port selector capable of cross-connecting 48 input connections to 32 output lines is employed. During a typical day, 95% of the time users will not encounter a busy condition. When such a condition does occur, the user can reestablish the connection and obtain access to the network if another user has completed his processing activity in the interim. In this particular application, the port selector permits 16 additional teleprinter channel connections with no increase in the number of front-end processor channels.

The CRT expansion requirements depend upon the relationship of the location of the additional CRTs with respect to existing terminals of that type. Several approaches may be considered to alleviate processor hardware constraints.

If the CRTs are co-located at a few geographical areas, modem-sharing units could be employed to service those devices, as illustrated in Figure 15.2.3, part A. Modem-sharing units permit from four to 32 terminals to share a common modem. Thus one channel on the front-end processor services the CRTs connected via this configuration.

When the CRTs are geographically distributed, as illustrated in part B of Figure 15.2.3, one or more multipoint circuits connecting a number of terminals via a common circuit to the computer center may be employed. Again, for each multipoint circuit only one front-end processor channel is required, regardless of the number of terminals connected by that line, within the front-end's software limits.

FIGURE 15.2.2   Employing a port selector

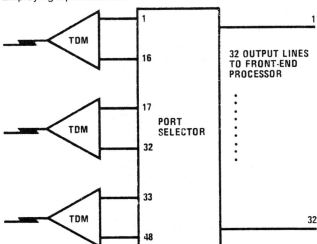

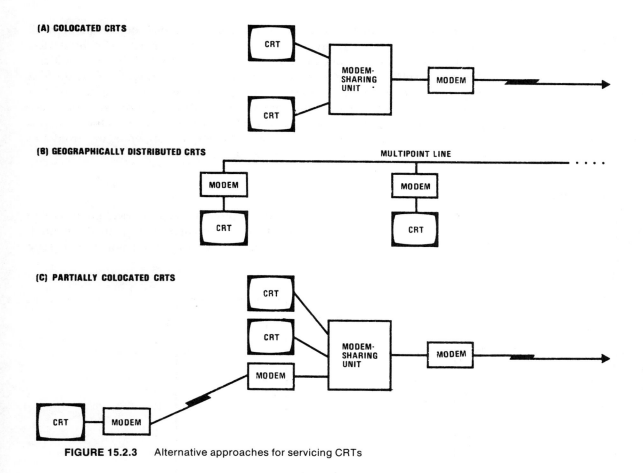

FIGURE 15.2.3 Alternative approaches for servicing CRTs

For partially colocated terminals, one or more modem-sharing units with DCE options may be employed. Illustrated in part C of Figure 15.2.3, colocated CRTs are directly serviced by the sharing unit at the terminal location. Each remote terminal is connected to the sharing unit via a pair of modems and an extra circuit. Since all CRTs connected via the sharing unit employ a common medium, only one channel at the front-end processor is required to support the colocated and remote CRTs connected in this manner.

Returning to our expansion requirement to service fourteen additional CRTs, let us assume that an optimum use of equipment and circuits results in the use of three multiport lines and two modem-sharing units to support the existing four CRTs and the 14 additional devices. Our final front-end processor configuration could now appear as in Figure 15.2.4. Here, after the use of three multipoint circuits and four modem-sharing units, four or five front-end processor channels are still available for network expansion.

Even if all channels are used, other hardware can be considered to free a channel on the front-end processor for other use. One such device the network analyst can investigate is a port-sharing unit. To realize the potential of this device, consider the partial network illustrated in Figure 15.2.5.A. Here four modem-sharing units, one at each of four remote locations, provide transmission to the host computer from numerous clustered terminals at each site. The use of this configuration requires four channels or ports on the front-end processor. In Figure 15.2.5.B, two port-sharing units have been installed, with each unit supporting two modem-sharing unit clusters. By the use of the port-sharing units, two front-end processor ports become available for network expansion.

Throughput Considerations

So far in our discussion of resource examination, we have restricted ourselves to alternative network configurations without being concerned about throughput. While it is obvious that one cannot continue to service more and more terminals by

FIGURE 15.2.4   Front-end processor after network expansion

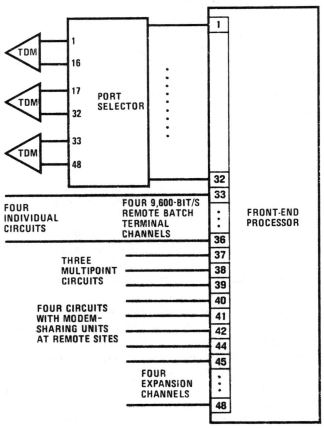

FIGURE 15.2.5   Employing port-sharing units

(A) FOUR CHANNELS OF THE FRONT-END PROCESSOR ARE REQUIRED TO SUPPORT FOUR MODEM-SHARING UNITS

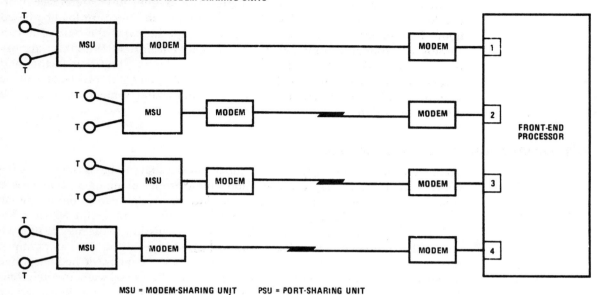

MSU = MODEM-SHARING UNIT   PSU = PORT-SHARING UNIT

(B) USING PORT-SHARING UNITS CAN FREE FRONT-END PROCESSOR CHANNELS FOR OTHER APPLICATIONS

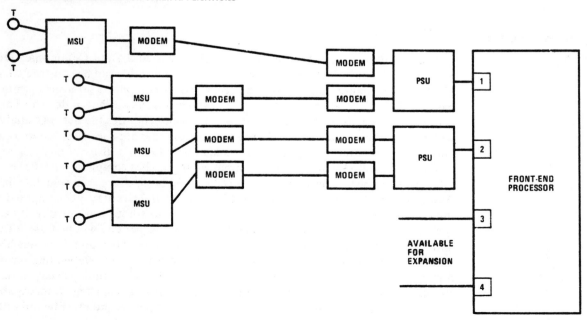

continuing to modify, add, and alter equipment and lines, computing throughput constraints can become very complex. One alternative to computing a large series of equations may result from using the processor manufacturer's reference manual. Many vendors have a series of curves that represent processor loading based upon the number of connected terminals of a specific type, the type of circuit employed, terminal data rate, protocol, and other parameters. With this information, the network analyst only has to read a series of utilization factors and accumulate a utilization sum. If the sum exceeds unity, the processor will be saturated under the projected loading conditions, and some service must be dropped or moved.

15.3 TRANSMISSION MEDIUM ALTERNATIVES

Today, the number and scope of transmission media that can be considered by the network analyst may result in confusion unless proper planning and analysis is conducted. Communications carriers' offerings are available from the telephone company, packet-switching vendors, specialized carriers, and satellite carriers.

Within each company, one or more types of transmission media may be offered, each with a number of transmission constraints and a specific tariff. As an example, services available from the telephone company are the public switched telephone network, leased lines, foreign exchange lines, and the use of wide area telecommunications service—all analog offerings, as well as the Dataphone digital service offerings.

In order to appropriately plan for the most economical transmission medium that is capable of servicing the anticipated traffic, the network analyst should construct a traffic-volume table.

Traffic-volume Table

Using the data from Figure 15.1.1, the Terminal and Data Communications Survey (or an equivalent mechanism), a traffic-volume table can be constructed, as illustrated in Figure 15.3.1. Note that each row is completed on a per-terminal basis, with the "Total" row reflecting the expected traffic at that node. The Total columns with checkmarks indicate the specific Total columns the network analyst will normally use to determine the type of medium that appears most economical, and at the same time be capable of servicing the required traffic volume.

Once the table (Figure 15.3.1) is completed, the analyst computes the number of bits/second to be transmitted from a specific nodal point over a common data link. As an example, assume that a peak of 15 million characters/day was computed as the total number of characters to be transmitted in an 8-hour working day. If each character is composed of 10 bits, then 150 million bits per day will be transmitted and received by the terminals at the specified nodal point. Over an 8-hour day, this represents 18,750,000 bits per hour, or 5,208 bits per second. Depending on the number of terminals, their operating data rate, and connect time per day, if data should be concentrated at the nodal point for transmission, then a medium capable of supporting a peak data rate in excess of 5,208 bits per second must be utilized.

NODAL POINT _____

	CALL/ DAY	CONNECT TIME/CALL		TOTAL TRANSMIT TIME		AVERAGE								
						MESSAGES/DAY TO HOST		MESSAGES/DAY FROM HOST		CHARACTERS/ MESSAGE		CHARACTERS/DAY	
		AVG	PEAK	AVG	PEAK	AVG	PEAK	AVG	PEAK	TO HOST	FROM HOST	AVG	PEAK
TOTAL				✓	✓							✓	✓

FIGURE 15.3.1   Traffic-volume table

Nodal Points

In the preceding discussion, we have intimated that a nodal point is a location where we may consider the concentration or multiplexing of data. However, we have not defined the geographical boundaries of the nodal point. Concerning its geographical boundary, a nodal point can be as small an area as an office building or as wide an area as perhaps the United States west of the Mississippi. The size of the nodal point will be governed by the number, type, and operational character- istics of terminals that will have their data transmitted and received from a central computer via a data concentrator. The selection of nodal points was previously discussed in Chapter 12.

15.4 INSTALLATION AND OPERATION

When planning the installation of a communications network, you must look beyond simply allocating sufficient floor space and appropriate power sources, and allow for the installation of air conditioning, new flooring, and electrical power receptacles, as well as fire-detection equipment, partitions, and environmental control systems. Also, unless you integrated such items as communications lines, modems, terminals, and data concentration equipment into the installation plan, there could be quite a time gap between the network's successful installation and the start of its useful operating life.

With turnkey systems, the vendor generally supplies not only all the hardware and software components, but also takes responsibility for combining them into an operational installation. Here, one key advantage for the user is that, for any maintenance or expansion problems, his point of contact is limited to a single source. While this is a valuable time-saver when maintenance problems arise, the user ultimately pays for the service. Most turnkey vendors employ a uniform profit markup. It's not uncommon for a user to pay 50 to 100 percent more for his terminals, modems, multiplexers, and communications lines, than if he assembled the network with components from different suppliers. This latter approach results in a more cost-effective network, since the middleman is eliminated. But if each vendor maintains only his own equipment, the user must know how to best select the required equipment, and also to plan ahead so that he can avoid "finger-pointing" when network problems arise.

Although the exact sequence of events to follow in communications-site preparation and planning varies from installation to installation, Table 15.4.1 serves as a useful guide for developing a pre-installation schedule. About three months prior to installation, the user should be at the stage where he has defined the necessary communications lines and ancillary equipment required for his network, and is ready to place his orders with the appropriate vendors. With the exception of local telephone companies, which can install a standard telephone circuit usually within a week after order, almost all other communications equipment is quoted on a 90-day after-receipt-of-order (ARO) basis. This means that, unless sufficient time is left for contingency purposes, a critical network component could just be leaving the vendor's factory on the date that the network is scheduled to become operational.

Consider Modem Options

In defining and ordering the required modems, check with vendors to investigate all the available options. Some of these may be of a convenience nature, but unless you consider all options carefully, it's possible that a modem of the properly rated

---

TABLE 15.4.1   PRE-INSTALLATION SCHEDULE

---

90 days before installation

- Define needs for and order long-distance telecommunications lines
- Define needs for and order local telecommunications lines
- Define needs for and order ancillary equipment—modems, multiplexers, rotary, data access arrangements, cable, and rack-mounting equipment

60 days before installation

- Define and install electrical power requirements according to specifications
- Complete environmental specifications
- Install convenience outlets
- Develop maintenance plan

30 days before installation

- Install all telecommunications lines and equipment
- Establish and check out the functioning of modems, remote terminals, local terminals, and communications lines
- Obtain test equipment

---

transmission speed may not be usable with other equipment in the network. The magnitude of customer options varies among modem manufacturers, as well as on the type of modem (bit rate) under consideration. One of the most common modems in use today, the Bell 103A, provides the user with 32 option possibilities, ranging from auto-call unit to mark or space hold, and from auto-answer permanently wired or key controlled to the terminal responding or not responding to disconnect and initiating or not initiating disconnect.

While some options may appear trivial, they can save the user a considerable amount of money. For example, consider a network where the central computer automatically dials numerous remote locations during each evening and requests transmission of the day's activities. If the modem options are selected so the terminal will respond to a disconnect signal, then, in effect, each remote terminal could be powered down after completion of the data interchange instead of drawing power throughout the night.

Link Schematic

One way to help define and order the required equipment is to prepare a link schematic. In the hypothetical situation represented in Figure 15.4.1, suppose that

FIGURE 15.4.1   Link schematic involving three locations

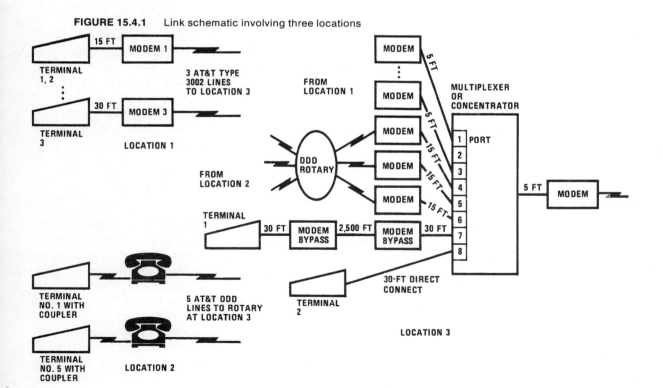

locations 2 and 3 are in the same state. (If the two sites are not within the same local telephone company area, the user will have to contact at least two local telephone companies to arrange for installation of the required modems, assuming such modems are obtained from the telephone company and not an independent manufacturer.) In this illustration, it is assumed that the terminals at location 1 will communicate with the multiplexer or data concentrator at location 3 via voice-grade leased lines, the installation of which may be arranged with AT&T Long Lines or the local telephone company. Assuming the terminals at location 2 are selected with built-in acoustic couplers, the user need only contact the local telephone company for installation of five telephones at this location.

At location 3, it's assumed the user desires to install two terminals close to the multiplexer. Here, one terminal is directly connected to port 8, while the other is connected to port 7 via a pair of modem bypass units—sometimes referred to as data transmit-receive extenders. In this arrangement, as long as the user limits his cable laying to his own property and does not use telephone lines, he does not require any connection to the telephone network.

Here, the three-number rotary is assumed to service the five terminals transmitting from location 2. If the user obtains non-Bell modems that are not registered under the Federal Communications Commission Equipment Registration program, he must contact the local telephone company or independent manufacturer for the installation of data access arrangements for transmission over the switched network.

Although the link schematic is a simplified one, it is interesting to note that the user could have conceivably chosen terminals from ten different vendors, the modems from ten suppliers, the rotary, DAAs, and telephones from three local operating companies, the modem backup units and cables from two additional vendors, and the leased lines from AT&T Long Lines Department.

To alleviate the problems that can arise from selecting modems from several vendors, one should ensure that either the modems are paired from the same vendor for each data link, or that the modem of one vendor can communicate with the modem of another.

Equipment Interface

One important point that is often neglected is to denote the type of interface for each item of equipment, as well as to define the differences between equipment when preparing a link schematic diagram. The two primary methods of interfacing equipment are based on voltage and current. For voltage interfacing, the EIA RS-232-C is an industry standard specification that dictates, for example, what the modem output must be for matching with telephone lines. With RS-232-C equipment, data is bipolar, voltage serial.

Current-loop interfacing replaces the mark and space levels by current rather than voltage. Some vendors offer three current-loop interfaces, with the difference being in the current level provided. Although current-loop interfacing can be more complex than voltage interfacing, its principal advantage is that it can eliminate the use of modems or acoustic couplers, since a current-loop circuit can drive a device at distances up to one mile, depending upon the amount of current and the gauge of wire used.

If the equipment employs a voltage interface, there's usually a 50-foot cable limit because of the high driver impedance associated with this technique. If equipment spacing exceeds the cable limit, a user can either rearrange his equipment, make provisions for obtaining a remote connection unit that allows an extension of line-driving capability up to 300 feet, obtain modem bypass units that allow communications at distances up to several miles, investigate the feasibility of using current-loop equipment, or use modems.

Most multiplexers, concentrators, and terminals can be selected with a current-interface option, which permits the user to eliminate modems or couplers when his terminals and multiplexers are located within his building or at a site where he can lay his own cable. When using current-loop interfaces, the user should consult the vendor's literature to determine the type of cable necessary. Usually, the vendor will specify the wire resistance and current-carrying capacity. Although 18 or 20 AWG (American Wire Gauge) copper conductor wire is commonly used, smaller-gauge (i.e. higher-number AWG) wire can be installed if distances are under 2,000 feet.

When transferring information from the link schematic, you should supplement the material with data from applicable vendor literature to complete a link worksheet. This worksheet not only serves as a guide in planning electrical outlet requirements, but can be furnished to selected vendors to help them meet your installation requirements. Also, the user can perform simple crosschecks to ensure that such taken-for-granted factors as cable-length limitations and modem compatibility are met to anticipate installation problems.

About two months before the installation date, all electrical power requirements should be defined at each site location, and arrangements made for installation according to the specifications developed for the network. Unless terminals are designed to operate from a fixed location, the cost of adding convenience outlets before installation will be less than trying to incorporate a degree of flexibility later.

Existing environmental (i.e. heating, cooling) tables should be updated to include all applicable communications equipment. Although it's doubtful if the addition of communications equipment will change air conditioner requirements, adding the dimensions, weight, temperature, and humidity characteristics to an environment table permits more complete analysis of the site.

For locations where you plan to install a large number of modems, multiplexers, or combination of ancillary equipment, consider the utilization of cabinets, enclosures, or rack mounts. Besides centralizing equipment and eliminating cluttered configurations, this will greatly facilitate test and maintenance procedures.

Maintenance Contact

For each site location, you should prepare a maintenance-contact sheet in addition to a master maintenance sheet, which should reside at the centralized location.

Each sheet should list the point of contact and negotiated responsibilities for the equipment of the appropriate vendors.

If the required equipment is ordered 90 days prior to installation, and the work plan is such that 30 days are allowed for installing and checking out the equipment, this latter period can be considered as contingency time. It can be utilized to establish and check out the functioning of communications lines and equipment. During this time, the user can familiarize himself with equipment maintenance requirements and diagnostic routines. Since most modems and multiplexers have on- and off-line diagnostics to help determine the operational status of each piece of equipment, the user should learn to pinpoint the source of problems to reduce fingerpointing once the network is functioning.

Besides relying on the built-in diagnostic capabilities of his equipment, the user should purchase test instrumentation with a high degree of flexibility. Portable test equipment is useful when installations have the operating equipment distributed over a wide area, so the test equipment can be taken to the work by the technical staff.

Cutover

Cutover is the point at which the new component replaces the old component, or the new setup replaces the old one. Several methods of cutover should be explored by the network analyst to determine the optimum method to employ based upon operating personnel, budget constraints, and other limitations.

The two primary methods of cutover are serial and parallel, with combinations of these two methods possible in an infinite variety of configurations. In the serial cutover method, as illustrated in Figure 15.4.2.A, the old method of communications ceases when the new method is installed. This is initally the least costly cutover method. However, if the new method does not work as designed, then operational problems could result that could force the reinstallation of the old method while "bugs" are eliminated from the new one.

In Figure 15.4.2.B, a parallel cutover method is illustrated. Here, the initial cost is higher due to operating two parallel networks for a period of time. But total costs may be reduced if—during the period bugs are being resolved—employees have the old network as fallback.

Monitoring and Reporting

A number of forms should be completed for both remote and central-computer sites, to facilitate network management and control.

At the central-computer site, a master station log can be completed by technical-control-center personnel and routed to network management the next business day. A sample completed log with four entries is illustrated in Figure 15.4.3. The purpose of this log is to record all outages and other significant occurrences pertaining to the organization's data communications network and its associated equipment. By examining the network log, managers obtain a better understand-

(A) SERIAL CUTOVER

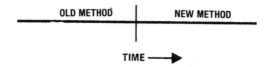

(B) PARALLEL CUTOVER

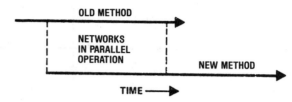

FIGURE 15.4.2   Cutover methods

FIGURE 15.4.3   Master station log

MASTER STATION LOG TECHNICAL CONTROL CENTER			DATE	TIME PERIOD	
				FROM	**TO**
			5-15-83	**0700**	**2400**
CHANNEL OR CIRCUIT	**TIME**	**OPERATOR INITIAL**	**ACTION/EVENT**		
GD 4720	0830	SN	OPERATOR S. BROWN AT WASH REPORTS CIRCUIT GD 4720 INOP, UNABLE TO GET INTO SYSTEM.		
GD 4720	0845	SN	CHECKED MODEMS BTB AND LINE WITH S. BELL; ALL APPEAR GOOD AND NO ERRORS.		
GD 4720	0855	SN	RAN-MODEM CHECKS AND LINE CHECKS WITH OPR BROWN FROM WASHINGTON TERMINAL; ALL NORMAL AND NO ERRORS.		
GD 4720	0905	SN	FOUND LOOSE CONNECTION ON FRONT-END, TURNED CKT BACK TO OPS AND NOTIFIED BROWN CKT RESTORED.		

FIGURE 15.4.4 Data transmission log

LOCATION _____		QUARTER ENDING _____		TERMINAL _____	
DATE	NO. OF CALLS	TOTAL TRANSMISSION TIME (MINUTES)	DATE	NO. OF CALLS	TOTAL TRANSMISSION TIME (MINUTES)

FORWARD NLT 15 DAYS AFTER END OF QUARTER TO:

CHIEF, DATA COMMUNICATIONS

ing of equipment and circuit operations, and problems experienced and reported by field personnel.

Another form that should be considered is a data transmission log, as illustrated in Figure 15.4.4. If communications funding is not centralized, then the network manager may not be able to obtain local and long-distance telephone bills and reevaluate portions of the network based upon new usage conditions. By submitting the data transmission log to terminal operators (who at the present time dial long distance to a computer), the network manager can periodically reanalyze the usage of the particular terminals in question. Then he may determine if a new transmission medium should be employed, based upon a change in transmission activity for a sustained period of time.

While there are no firm rules to follow in planning a network installation, these guidelines should help alleviate the more common problems that arise. If you devote careful consideration to the plan at an early enough date, it will go far in starting network operation at the scheduled time.

QUESTIONS

15.1 Name and discuss three methods used in the information-collection process.

15.2 What problems can occur when a checklist is distributed to users?

15.3 What are some of the advantages and disadvantages of interviews to obtain information?

15.4 Discuss the function performed by an expansion table.

15.5 Why is it important to know all protocols supported by a front-end processor when the processor is required to support one terminal type?

15.6 Discuss the possible effects of adding software modules to a front-end processor.

15.7 Name and discuss two techniques to alleviate front-end-processor port constraints.

15.8 What are the two primary methods of cutover? Discuss the advantages and disadvantages of each method.

CHAPTER **16**

NETWORK MANAGEMENT
AND ADMINISTRATION

With the evolution of data communications as a professional field of specialization, numerous techniques have been tested for their applicability to network management and administration. While some of these techniques were originally developed for use in other fields, certain techniques have been specially developed to assist the network analyst in the management and administration of a network.

In this chapter, two of the more important techniques the network manager can use for controlling cost, obtaining required equipment, and distributing the cost of operating the network will be discussed.

The first method, a procurement action, can be used with a high degree of success when a firm has a requirement for many devices, or one or more expensive pieces of equipment. By having many vendors compete for business, the competitive nature of organizations may result in a lower cost for the required product.

One problem now facing many organizations is how to distribute the cost of data communications usage in a fair and equitable manner. Until a few years ago, communications costs were an insignificant portion of an organization's total information processing budget. They were centrally funded and assessed to all company departments as an overhead expense. Due to the growth of remote processing, communications expenditures have increased dramatically to the point where they may not be suitable as an overhead expense. This is because the department that is located at the computer center feels, and rightfully so, that it should not pay for the data communications costs of other departments located in other cities that want to use the company computer for new applications. Recently a trend toward charging back of communications costs has evolved. This will be discussed further in this chapter.

16.1 PROCUREMENT ACTIONS

A procurement action can be considered a formal approach for obtaining required goods and services. Such an action can range from contacting a vendor directly and placing an order, to writing a series of specifications for the items required, issuing the specifications and a list of conditions to several vendors, and evaluating their responses from both a technical and cost viewpoint. For the latter case, this type of action is considered a competitive procurement, since more than one vendor is given the opportunity to compete for the business of the organization. For the former case, this type of procurement action is known as sole-source procurement, since only one vendor is considered.

In general, sole-source procurements can be used to obtain required equipment in a much shorter time frame than a competitive procurement. While a competitive procurement takes longer because a number of vendors must be contacted and their equipment and prices evaluated and compared, such procurement actions usually result in a reduction of cost to the organization.

Requirement Specifications

Prior to contacting vendors, the network analyst should prepare a list of requirement specifications. The formality, use, and transmission of such specifications to vendors will usually be a function of the rules of the organization's purchasing office.

For some organizations, the procurement of any items with an expected dollar amount over a certain limit must have the requirement specifications issued in a formal procurement document. The network analyst is responsible for preparing the requirement specifications that refer to the technical characteristics or operating parameters of required components. The purchasing office becomes responsible for including company-standard clauses concerning alternative proposals, contract forms, shipping costs, and other factors of a general nature common to most company procurements.

When writing the specifications of the devices required, the network analyst should divide the features of every component into two categories: mandatory and desirable. To be responsive, a vendor must meet all the mandatory requirements. Thus, mandatory features can be considered as items or performance specifications that, if not met, would degrade the overall performance of the required device to an unacceptable level.

A desirable feature can be considered an item or performance specification that would be nice to have, but without which the component would still be able to perform as required. Consider, for example, a multiport modem capable of operating at 9,600 bit/s. If the network analyst desires to multiplex two 4,800-bit/s data streams, then a two-port multiplexer, combining two 4,800-bit/s data streams, is a mandatory feature of the multiport modem. The analyst may believe that at some later date it is conceivable that, instead of two 4,800-bit/s data streams, he may lower one data stream to 2,400 bit/s and increase the support of the number of such devices operating at 2,400 bit/s to two. Then a multiport modem that can be reconfigured would be a desirable feature.

Feature Evaluation

In general, mandatory features are evaluated on a pass-fail basis. If the device has the item or items listed as mandatory, or meets the mandatory performance specifications, it is said to be in compliance with all mandatory features. If the device fails one or more mandatory features, then the device is excluded from further consideration.

A monetary value is normally assigned to each desirable feature. This dollar worth represents the typical cost to the user if he would have to procure the feature, or the value of the feature if his organization could use it. The price the vendor bids for a component is then adjusted by the value assigned to all the desirable features that the vendor's product includes. This cost value becomes the evaluated cost of the product for comparison with other vendor bids. This proposal evaluation method is known as the cost/value technique, since the value of desirable features is subtracted from the cost of the equipment.

Returning to the multiport modem example, consider the two devices in Table 16.1.1. Here, the modems of both vendors have been judged as meeting all mandatory requirements. However, vendor A's modem also has a desirable feature that, it is felt, could be used at a later date. A value of $500 is assigned to that feature. After subtracting the value of the desirable feature from the cost of the modem, vendor A's product has the lower evaluated price.

Award Consideration

Although price is an important factor, many additional items must be considered prior to awarding a contract. These considerations range from the equipment availability to maintenance and training support and equipment space and power requirements, as well as the methods available to obtain the desired equipment. Methods include lease, purchase, and lease with option to purchase.

For an organization that believes its requirements could change in the near future but requires certain items of equipment for current operations, leasing may be considered. Although the user can send back the equipment after giving ap-

TABLE 16.1.1   COST/VALUE TECHNIQUE

	Vendor A	Vendor B
Modem cost	$5,750	$5,580
Desirable feature	$ 500	---
Cost value	$5,250	$5,580

propriate notice, certain financial benefits that one obtains with equipment ownership cannot be used by the leaser. These financial considerations include the use of the investment tax credit and depreciation of equipment. Normally users request vendors to price their products with respect to both purchase and lease. This way, the user can evaluate both options and select the one most advantageous based upon his organization's requirements and financial circumstances.

16.2 NETWORK COST DISTRIBUTION

Providing adequate service at the lowest cost per user is one goal frequently sought in the design or modification of a data communications network. A problem occurs when the data communications staff receives and analyzes communications requests from other departments. Usually, these requests are formulated as a data communications service requirement for a particular activity or series of activities.

While a low price tag is often emphasized as an important part of these requests, the answer to the question of "How much is enough?" in the way of equipment and service is normally not left up to the data communications staff. The reason for this is that most organizations erroneously believe that the department that requests the service is the most knowledgeable about its data communications requirements. The primary goal of the data communications staff is believed to be to design and modify the network, leaving the requesting department responsible for determining its requirements.

One method that can be effectively employed to control costs despite this attitude is the implementation of communications chargeback. Through the utilization of communications chargeback, the cost of communications must be shared by all the users. Realizing that they will have to pay for the resources associated with the support of their requirements, departments requesting data communications support tend to become more concerned with cost. They tend to work more closely with the data communications staff, and usually start to eliminate frills. Thus, chargeback can be viewed as an effective method for bringing users down to earth by letting them know the dollar value of the services they want versus the services they really need.

A series of chargebacks projected over a period of time can be used by individual departments to generate the data communications portion of their operating budget. When properly formulated and defined, chargeback information gives all levels of management a realistic understanding of the nature and cost of data communications.

In developing a chargeback method, a distinction should be made between the recovery of direct costs and indirect costs. Direct costs relate to modems, multiplexers, and communications lines, and are clearly visible as expenses incurred in providing data communications support. Indirect costs for test equipment, patch panels, and equipment used in a technical control center (as well as the communications staff's salaries) should normally be omitted from chargeback, due to the problems one can encounter in trying to distribute these expenses equitably.

While the cost of test equipment could be assigned to all departments equally, such equipment may not be used on an equal basis. Even when test equipment is used by everybody, some departmental managers find it hard to justify their share of the payment when the equipment is often used to pinpoint a telephone line problem (for example), thus placing the onus of repair cost on the vendor. Due to these circumstances, most organizations centrally fund their communications staffs and their technical control facilities.

Chargeback Development

Two charges are associated with such communications components as lines, modems, multiplexers, and ancillary devices: non-recurring and recurring. Non-recurring charges include site preparation and equipment installation. If equipment is purchased outright, the cost of such equipment could be considered a one-time charge. However, a number of organizations centrally fund equipment purchases, and amortize the cost of the equipment to the user departments as a recurring depreciation charge.

Recurring charges are usually associated with the monthly rental cost of equipment. One recurring charge associated with purchased equipment, aside from depreciation, is maintenance. Although included in the monthly rental charge of leased equipment, this cost is usually separate for purchased equipment.

In computing depreciation for purchased equipment, several alternative methods are available for consideration. The most common method is called straight-line depreciation. This method assumes an equal write-off of the asset by dividing its cost by the length of its estimated life. The formula for straight-line depreciation is

$$D = \frac{C - S}{P}$$

where D = dollars/month depreciation
   C = the cost of the asset
   S = the estimated salvage value of the asset at end of its life
   P = the months of use

For a 9.6-kbit/s modem purchased for $7,600, with an estimated life of three years, and an estimated salvage value of $1,000, straight-line depreciation is

$$D = \frac{\$7,600 - \$1,000}{36}$$
$$= \$183.33/\text{month, or } \$2,200/\text{year}$$

Other depreciation plans include the "sum-of-the-year's-digits" and the "declining-balance" methods.

A point-to-point, single-use line is the easiest type of communications asset to charge to the user. This circuit is dedicated to a single department, and all communications costs are billed to it.

Sample Chargeback Methods

With M as the monthly cost per modem and L as the monthly cost of the leased line, the monthly charge to the user for a point-to-point circuit is

$$CB = 2M + L$$

For point-to-point, multiple-use lines, chargeback becomes more complicated. Consider the user of multiport modems with integral synchronous multiplexers that permit several streams of data to be transmitted over one line.

If TB is used to denote the total bandwidth of a line in bit/s, and BU denotes the portion of the bandwidth used by one cost center, then

$$CB = (2M + L)\frac{BU}{TB}$$

Each cost center is charged for its share of the line's bandwidth and for the use of the modems. If terminal 1 associated with cost center 1 operates at 2.4 kbit/s, and terminal N assigned to cost center N operates at 7.2 kbit/s, then the chargeback to each cost center would be as follows:

$$CB \text{ (cost center 1)} = (2M + L)\frac{2,400}{9,600}$$

$$CB \text{ (cost center N)} = (2M + L)\frac{7,200}{9,600}$$

What is specified is that since the first center utilizes 25 percent of the bandwidth, it should pay for one-quarter of the data communications cost, while the second cost center should pay the remainder.

The chargeback of communications facilities on multidrop lines can sometimes present a problem since some configurations may not appear fair and equitable to users receiving such chargebacks. Figure 16.2.1 shows a simple multidrop configuration and allows the examination of techniques that reduce communications costs, and chargeback problems.

For this multidrop line, all of the cities are on a horizontal plane and one cost center is associated with each city serviced by the multidrop line.

If N is the number of remote modems, L_i denotes the line cost for segment i, MC represents the modem cost at the central site, and M_i is the modem cost at each remote site, the chargeback debited to each cost center becomes

$$CB_i = L_i + M_i + \frac{MC}{N}$$

Simply stated, this formula charges to each cost center the expense of the line segment from the preceding city, its own modem cost, and the prorated share of the

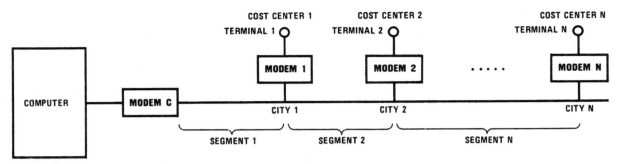

FIGURE 16.2.1   Multidrop line

cost of the central-site modem—which is distributed to each cost center based on the number of users on the line.

However, since most multidrop lines are not configured on a horizontal plane, certain network optimization routings can cause knowledgeable users to complain that their share of the cost is not equitable. One such network is illustrated in Figure 16.2.2.

Here, because of geographical locations, a "V" routing is employed from cities 1 to 2 and 2 to 3. While this routing reduces the total line cost of all locations, it increases the length and cost of the segment between cities 2 and 3, since connecting city 3 to city 1 is shorter than connecting city 3 to city 2. If one cost center is allocated to each city, cost center 3 could argue that it should not be forced to absorb higher individual costs to reduce the total cost to the whole organization.

While this argument has merit, it should be pointed out that without a corporate network, cost center 3 would have to pay for the entire line segment from the computer to its location, as well as the full cost of the modem located at the computer. The optimization of a network can produce certain inequities. However, very seldom do these inequities justify an independent approach in which cost centers establish their own arrangements.

FIGURE 16.2.2   Optimized multidrop line

COMPUTER
WITH
MODEM

Prorated Payment

Developing a chargeback methodology for contention equipment can also present problems. This is because the means of obtaining the most equitable determination of charges is the hardest to implement. Variable charges to different departmental cost centers are produced, and such charges are available only after the end of any given billing period.

One simple contention device is illustrated in Figure 16.2.3. Here, the contention equipment is a time-division multiplexer with two four-position telephone company rotaries connected to it at a remote location. One rotary connects four 300-bit/s auto-answer modems to the multiplexer, while the other rotary connects four 1.2-kbit/s auto-answer modems. With an aggregate throughput of 6 kbit/s, the multiplexer is connected to a 7.2-kbit/s high-speed modem, transferring data to the computer on the distant end at that speed. Assume that only two cost centers use the contention facility, with cost center 1 having six 300-bit/s terminals and four 1.2-kbit/s terminals, while cost center 2 has four 300-bit/s terminals and six 1.2-kbit/s terminals.

Several methods can be used to develop an equitable chargeback to both cost centers. One way to keep track of usage would be through terminal logs, with the total connect time of each terminal accumulated at the end of each billing period. The results of these logs might be as shown in Table 16.2.1 for one such period.

For simplicity's sake, assume that the monthly cost of the remote-site low-speed modems, the telephone rotaries, both TDMs, the high-speed modems, and the

FIGURE 16.2.3   Contention device

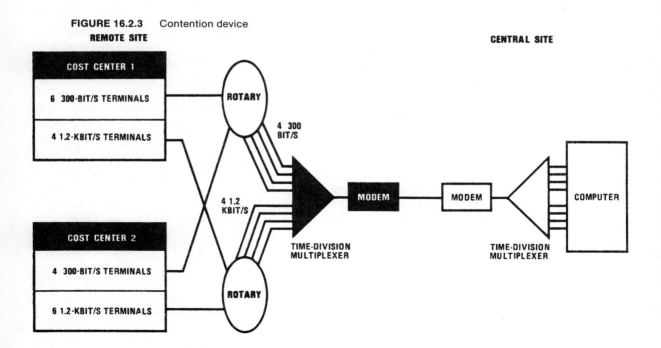

TABLE 16.2.1 CONNECT TIME (HOURS)

Modem Speeds	300 Bit/s	1.2 kbit/s
Cost center 1	35	87
Cost center 2	120	210
Total	155	297

leased line connecting the remote site to the central site is $2,000 per month. On a prorated usage basis, the cost debited to cost center 1 (chargeback) can be computed as follows:

$$CB1 = \frac{35}{155} \times \frac{1,200}{6,000} \times \$2,000$$
$$+ \frac{87}{297} \times \frac{4,800}{6,000} \times \$2,000 = \$559$$

For the above, 35/155 represents the prorated cost center 1 usage of the 300-bit/s port, and 1,200/6,000 represents the proportions of the four 300-bit/s ports to the total bandwidth of the network. Similarly, 87/297 is cost center 1's prorated usage of 1.2-kbit/s modems, with 4,800/6,000 representing the proportion of 1.2-kbit/s modems to the total bandwidth of the network.

Variations in connect times each month will cause the chargeback amount to change for each center sharing the contention equipment. One major problem in attempting to charge users on this basis is that logs are time consuming—both to complete and to analyze. In addition, users may neglect to record their usage, making such logs inaccurate.

Another method that can be used to generate chargeback costs for contention networks is by programming the corporate computer to do the required usage computations. A problem with this approach is that terminals are not necessarily fixed at a given location, and allowing a user to access the computer through different contention facilities would require a complex set of programs to produce the communications chargeback bill for each cost center.

Since contention facilities are normally accessed by timesharing or message-switching equipment, an easier way to use chargeback is to add a surcharge to the billing algorithm of each user. This surcharge is designed to recover the cost of providing communications for all contention facility users and is reviewed and modified as required to keep the total dollar surcharge as close to the communications cost as possible.

Returning to Figure 16.2.3, there is another, less sophisticated method to prorating the cost of a contention network. This method is based on the number of terminals used by each cost center. Using this approach, the chargeback for cost center 1 becomes

$$CB1 = \frac{6}{10} \times \frac{1,200}{6,000} \times \$2,000$$
$$+ \frac{4}{6} \times \frac{4,800}{6,000} \times \$2,000 = \$1,307$$

As shown, chargeback based on the number of terminals can produce results different from computation based on usage. One argument advanced for charge-back using terminal quantities is that the most important part of the initial design of many networks is the number of user terminals and the anticipated hours of their operation. While actual operation undoubtedly deviates from initial projec-tions, the information initially furnished to develop the communications network forms the basis for equipment procurement. Cost centers should be charged on the basis of the information furnished.

While this section has presented a sample of chargeback techniques, users should recognize that the wide variety of network configurations precludes the development of textbook solutions. Even under the Federal Communications Commission's ruling that permits nonaffiliated users to share a leased-line network (joint-use provision), the only guideline is that communications costs must be shared equitably. Thus, the present state of communications chargeback is best defined by the words fair and equitable.

QUESTIONS

16.1 What are the differences between sole-source and competitive procurements with respect to price and time?

16.2 Discuss the difference between a mandatory and a desirable feature.

16.3 What is the difference between mandatory and desirable features with respect to their evaluation?

16.4 If vendors A, B, and C respond to a procurement action with bids of $8,750, $8,827, and $8,905, and the value of their desirable features are $350, $500, and $150, respectively, who should we select and why?

16.5 Two departments share the use of common communications. Total costs are $4,500 per month. Each department's terminal usage for the month is:

| | Terminal Hours | |
	300 bit/s	1,200 bit/s
Department 1	450	750
Department 2	850	375

How much should each department be charged on a prorated usage basis?

CHAPTER 17

TRENDS IN DATA COMMUNICATIONS

17.1 INTRODUCTION

Data communications combines the technologies of digital communications and digital computers. As they are members of the so-called "high-technology" industries, improvements and new applications are almost daily occurrences. This chapter is intended to whet the reader's intellectual appetite. It describes some of the practicable trends that promise to make up just a small portion of what may be expected to emerge in the technology of data communications.

17.2 LOCAL NETWORKS

One readily defined parameter of a local network is its high speed. Its transmission rate is usually faster than that of networks covering a broad geographic area—such as a "long-haul" network. But what is a local network? Since there are several answers to that, it would be helpful to define some additional parameters.

One common ingredient is the transmission medium, usually shared by all user devices. Next is wide bandwidth, which translates to the aforementioned high-speed intercommunications. A local network must have rapid multi-addressing or broadcast capability, and it must have distributed control for flexibility. It must be able to offer distributed processing, host-to-host and host-to-peripheral transparent communications. A local network must also provide remote job entry (RJE) and file transfer, database management, and access (via gateways) to long-haul networks. Its range varies. It is not the area in itself that defines the local network, but its high-speed connection capabilities. If properly amplified, the local network has no range limitation. However, its common medium usually limits it to within a building or within an area in and around several buildings located near each other, such as a campus.

It is necessary to clear up a misconception about local networks—that a PBX or CBX is a local network. CBXs are often touted as alternatives, in some cases justifiably, to local networks. But their centrally controlled architecture and dedicated-line concept make them unsuitable for resource sharing. It is the cost-effectiveness of its resource sharing above all else that distinguishes local networks from other operational implementations.

Baseband, Broadband

The most common medium used by local networks is coaxial cable. And two prominent technologies using that medium are baseband and broadband. In baseband, all transmissions over the medium are at the same frequency. Xerox's Ethernet typifies this technique, and operates at up to 10 Mbit/s. Access by computers and workstations is facilitated by a statistical method known as carrier-sense multiple-access with collision detection (CSMA/CD). Carrier-sense means that each station "listens" to the cable before transmitting. If some other station is already transmitting, the first station senses the presence of the carrier signal and defers transmitting until the cable is quiescent. Multiple-access means that all stations tap into and share the same medium. Every transmission is "heard" by all connected stations. The intended recipients detect incoming message packets by recognizing their addresses embedded in the packets; other packets are discarded.

If two or more stations transmit at the same time, their signals will be intermixed on the medium—a collision. By listening while transmitting, each station can detect collisions and back off by waiting a random time interval before attempting to retransmit.

Another baseband-access scheme is token passing. Here, a control token—really a frame—is passed in turn to each station's interface unit, including those that have nothing to send. The method eliminates collisions, but has the overhead of passing the token, and somewhat complicated recovery mechanisms.

With broadband local networks, the medium is frequency-division multiplexed into many simultaneous, independent communications paths. The equipment used is that of the cable-TV industry, prominently the RF modem. Broadband vendors, such as Wang, claim that the CATV technology is mature and highly reliable, with active components having an MTBF in excess of 20 years. Theoretically, transmission rates could be greater than baseband's by at least a factor of 10. In practice, the medium is subdivided mainly to enable as much simultaneous traffic as possible, with at least one band reserved for video transmission.

There are several other local network topologies—such as ring—and access schemes—such as reservation access. If the reader wishes to pursue this topic in greater detail, the trade and technical literature abounds with detailed information.

17.3 ELECTRONIC MAIL

Electronic mail is often thought of as facsimile transmission. But the greatest potential for electronic mail lies not in paper transmission but in the integrated use of computers for performing each aspect of the communications tasks: word processing for preparation, store-and-forward networking for distribution, and database management for long-term organization (storage) and retrieval of the mail. Some commercial groups offer computer-based services for the store-and-forward function. Others provide a central computer facility through which users exchange messages, which are then stored on disks nearby.

As electronic mail grows in capability and availabilty, it becomes useful to split its different services into categories similar to those used for paper-based mail—posting, transport, and delivery. End-to-end services are public transporters of mail between users. The transport mechanism may be viewed as a simple packet-switched network, differing from the standard packet network mainly in the level at which the service operates. An electronic message is more structured and has more protocol layers than standard bit-segments of data.

User programs act as agents for individual users. They acquire a message, automatically construct it on the user's behalf, and then pass it on to the transport mechanism. On the receiving side, the user programs accept the message from the transport mechanism, make it available for viewing, and automatically act on special messages. Finally, they dispose of the message, either by discarding it or by filling it for long-term storage.

The typical computer-based mail service operates on a single computer. Message transfer is usually on disk, since the message stays on the same service machine, a minicomputer or mainframe that distributes the messages. Actual communications costs, therefore, are incurred during message entry and viewing, and it can be costly for a user to view a message repeatedly because of line charges.

Commercial versions of electronic mail implementations are proliferating. Tymnet and Telenet offer their users value-added electronic mail schemes called Ontyme and Telemail, respectively. Both services are available only to these companies' subscribers. ECOM is the US Postal Services's version of electronic mail, where the electronic portion of the service replaces the physical transport of paper between some major mail centers.

With Infomail, a Bolt Beranek and Newman scheme, no hardware investment is required. Operation is intended for popular computers, such as those of the Digital Equipment Corporation (DEC) and of IBM. Infomail permits not only the commonly available informal person-to-person messages but also those between people and computers (both directions) and between computers.

Typical of a hardware/software approach to electronic mail are Datapoint's ARC (Attached Resource Computer)-based EMS (Electronic Mail System) and Wang's Mailway. In this approach, the network is designed for data processing, word processing, and office communications, as well as for electronic mail. The software packages can be used only on the supplying vendor's network.

17.4 LIGHTWAVE COMMUNICATIONS

Communicating over a medium other than copper or via radio frequencies is a growing phenomenon. The alternative furthest along is optical glass fibers, with infrared of some limited availability. Showing tremendous promise is the use of unconstrained lasers—constrained being the laser source used in many fiber optic implementations.

Fiber optic offerings include the RS-232-C interface from many vendors. Cable runs of a kilometer without repeaters are commonly achieved. A frequently encountered light source is the light-emitting diode (LED), although greater distances are achieved with lasers. Field trial reports indicate that operation at several hundred megabits per second are in a transition phase from the laboratory to the field. And the medium is unaffected by electromagnetic interference, is considered extremely secure, takes up much less space than copper equivalents, and its price is comparable to—if not less than—copper's. Optical taps and multiplexers are still in the experimental stages, with much research work under way.

Of more limited use, but also commercially available, is the infrared link or relay. As embodied in one product, Datapoint's Lightlink, a pair of devices have a range of up to 2 miles, a data rate of 2.5 Mbit/s, and have a received beam width of 5 feet (making a bird's passing not likely to interrupt transmission). The major requirement is a clear field of sight.

Commerical use of data transmission via laser beams is slowly growing. Local connections to long-haul networks—replacing microwave—are proving cost-effective. Longer-distance use is still on the drawing board. One scheme envisions transmitting data from satellites via laser beams, establishing direct communications simultaneously with several earth stations. This "invention" comes from an IBM-Switzerland source and is strictly on paper at this writing.

ANSWERS TO QUESTIONS AND PROBLEMS

ANSWERS TO QUESTIONS AND PROBLEMS IN CHAPTER 1

1.1 In order to communicate one must have a transmitter, a receiver, and a transmission medium. For a telegraph system the wire conductor is the medium, and the telegraph key serves as both the transmitter and receiver. When we listen to a radio broadcast, the station we are tuned to serves as the transmitter, the atmosphere is the transmission medium, and our radio set becomes the receiver.

1.2 In Morse code, different characters have a different number of elements to denote the series of dots and dashes that define the character. The lack of uniform character length made it difficult to develop a machine to interpret characters that varied in length. In addition, the lack of a prescribed time interval between characters and of a method to denote the beginning and ending of characters resulted in the absence of a method to synchronize automatic sending and receiving units.

1.3 The Baudot code provided a constant length for each character in that code's character set. The addition of start and stop elements to each character by Howard Krum permitted transmitting and receiving devices to be synchronized.

ANSWERS TO QUESTIONS AND PROBLEMS IN CHAPTER 2

2.1 Both Babbage's analytical engine and modern-day digital computers are designed to include a storage or memory area, components to perform calculations (arithmetic unit), and a means of controlling the operation (control unit).

2.2 Not only were vacuum tubes bulky, but they consumed large amounts of power, produced large amounts of heat, and—due to their relatively low mean time between failure in comparison to solid state devices—at any given time a large computer consisting of vacuum tubes would have several such devices inoperative.

2.3 A. 182   **C.** 183
    B. 107   **D.** 255

2.4 A. 11011   **C.** 110011010
    B. 10111010   **D.** 11001110

2.5 A. 377   **C.** 305
    B. 253   **D.** 214

2.6 A. FF   **C.** C5
    B. AB   **D.** 8C

2.7

Decimal	Binary	Octal	Hexadecimal
17	10001	21	11
18	10010	22	12
19	10011	23	13
20	10100	24	14
21	10101	25	15
22	10110	26	16
23	10111	27	17
24	11000	30	18
25	11001	31	19
26	11010	32	1A

2.8 A. 100111 ones complement is 011000
Twos complement is 011001
Thus subtraction becomes addition with twos complements or:

$$\begin{array}{r} 101110 \\ -100111 \\ \hline \end{array} = \begin{array}{r} 101110 \\ +011001 \\ \hline 1\overline{\smash{)}000111} \end{array}$$

B.
$$\begin{array}{r} 1101110 \\ -1111001 \\ \hline \end{array} = \begin{array}{r} 1101110 \\ +0000111 \\ \hline 1110101 \end{array} \ (-10000000; \text{ or, in decimal: } -128 + 117 = -11)$$

C.
$$\begin{array}{r} 100011 \\ -011010 \\ \hline \end{array} = \begin{array}{r} 100011 \\ +100110 \\ \hline 1\overline{\smash{)}001001} \end{array}$$

D.
$$\begin{array}{r} 011111 \\ -100000 \\ \hline \end{array} \quad \begin{array}{r} 011111 \\ +100000 \\ \hline 111111 \end{array} \ (-1000000; \text{ or, in decimal: } -64 + 63 = -1)$$

2.9 Data should be represented octally in an 18-bit computer as follows:

X	X	X	X	X	X	X	X	X	X	X	X	X	X	X	X	X	X
17	16	15	14	13	12	11	10	9	8	7	6	5	4	3	2	1	0

For a 24-bit computer

X	X	X	X	X	X	X	X	X	X	X	X	X	X	X	X	X	X	X	X	X	X	X	X
23	22	21	20	19	18	17	16	15	14	13	12	11	10	9	8	7	6	5	4	3	2	1	0

For a 32-bit computer

X	X	X	X	X	X	X	X	X	X	X	X	X	X	X	X	X	X	X	X	X	X	X	X	X	X	X	X	X	X	X	X
31	30	29	28	27	26	25	24	23	22	21	20	19	18	17	16	15	14	13	12	11	10	9	8	7	6	5	4	3	2	1	0

2.10

	Procedure-Oriented Language	Assembly Language	Machine Language
Program machine dependency	Yes	Yes	Yes
Relative storage size for program	Larger	Smaller	Smaller
Execution time	Larger	Smaller	Smaller
Documentation	Easier	Harder	Harder
Debug time	Shorter	Larger	Larger
Programming complexity	Easier	Harder	Hardest
Program maintenance	Easier	Harder	Hardest

2.11 Several reasons exist that make assembly language the primary method of communications programming. First, no higher-level language has been developed exclusively for data communications. Such a language would require access to bit and byte manipulation, which is normally available only by the use of assembly language. Secondly, procedure-oriented languages are inefficient in object code and run time when compared to programs written in assembly language. Since communications programs are normally time dependent (i.e., gathering bits into a character before the first bit of the next character is received), time constraints may preclude the use of procedure-oriented languages for some types of communications applications.

2.12 A byte is the lowest addressable unit and can be used to group a series of bits to represent a character. Therefore, by manipulating bytes we can manipulate characters; whereas by manipulating bits we can manipulate only portions of a character.

2.13 Single and multiline controllers contain clocking and buffering circuitry and serve as an interface mechanism between a computer and communications lines. In the transmit mode they convert a character, comprised of a number of bits, from a parallel data stream of the computer into a serial data stream for transmission. In the receive mode they build characters by converting the received serial bit stream into a parallel group of bits that represents a character.

2.14 Using a front-end processor can reduce or eliminate the burden of communications processing from the host computer. Such functions as character generation or building by sampling incoming bit streams, code conversion, speed detection, and other communications functions can be moved to the front end, thereby permitting the host computer to concentrate on information processing.

ANSWERS TO QUESTIONS AND PROBLEMS IN CHAPTER 3

3.1 In the context of the data communications field, a terminal is a device that permits information to be transmitted on or received from a data communications network.

3.2 Basic communications links include:

Terminal-to-computer
Terminal-to-terminal
Computer-to-computer

These links can be modified by the inclusion of specialized data communications components to obtain such additional links as:

Terminal-to-concentrator
Concentrator-to-concentrator
Concentrator-to-host

3.3 Automatic send and receive (ASR) terminals have local storage capability, usually paper tape or cassette, permitting data to be generated off line and transmitted automatically, or received and recorded automatically. When a keyboard send and receive (KSR) terminal is used, as data is entered manually, a hard copy is produced on the terminal's printer; however, no local storage capability is available to permit automatic operations. A receive only (RO) terminal does not have a keyboard since it can only receive information transmitted to it and cannot be used to respond to the transmitted information. Thus an RO terminal operates as a simplex device. (See Section 4.3.)

3.4 The cursor on the CRT terminal is used to indicate the position on the display where the operator can enter, modify, or delete data. Via appropriate cursor movements, the operator can display characters at any point on the CRT screen.

3.5 The key advantage of a multipoint circuit is that it permits a number of terminals to share a single transmission path. When one company conducted business with a large number of other companies, it became physically impossible to connect large numbers of teleprinters to a single party line, resulting in the development of message-switching and circuit-switching networks.

3.6 Examples of terminals used for order-entry applications:

A. Optical scanner connected to point-of-sale terminal consisting of an electronic cash register
B. Credit card reader that reads magnetic encoding on card.

For both applications special equipment required includes the optical scanner, electronic cash register, and the credit card reader. To transmit the data to a computer off line, an off-line storage mechanism is required. If transmission is to be on line, specialized transmission devices, to be discussed in later chapters, are required.

3.7 Both teleprinters and remote batch terminals normally transmit and receive data. Received data is usually printed at the terminal or on a storage mechanism attached to the device. Normally, a remote batch terminal contains a small processer that permits limited local processing in addition to transmission and reception of data to and from the host computer. Usually a remote batch terminal has a much higher transmission volume than a teleprinter and thus operates at a much higher data rate.

3.8 Typical inquiry and response systems include:

A. Hotel reservations—requires terminal that can produce hard copy confirmation slips to be mailed upon customer request.

B. Police vehicle identification—requires terminal that can produce hard copy upon request and whose transmission can be scrambled so that unauthorized persons cannot intercept data.

3.9 By connecting an optical scanner to a terminal, information can be entered into a terminal more rapidly than if data is entered manually via a keyboard.

3.10 Terminal characteristics that should be evaluated prior to selecting a specific device include:

A. Input/output media
B. Operating rate
C. Off-line capability
D. Data codes and character set
E. Operator convenience
F. Cost
G. Security
H. Control of user errors
I. Error detection and correction

3.11 Code conversion can occur in the terminal, the front-end processor, the host computer, or in a specialized device employed between the computer and the terminal.

3.12 Parity is the addition of a redundant bit to make the number of bits that compose a character either odd or even. Through the use of parity checking, an error in transmission can be detected. As an example, consider the seven-bit character: 1011001

For the preceding character, four bits were set (to 1). If we employ odd parity, the parity bit would be set; whereas if we employ even parity, the parity bit would be reset on zero since the four bits set are an even number. Thus the character to include the parity bit would appear as:

Odd parity   10110011
Even parity   10110010

3.13 In asynchronous transmission, each character contains a start bit and one or more stop bits that provide synchronization between the transmitter and receiver. In synchronous transmission, groups of characters are blocked together for transmission, and special synchronization characters are employed to synchronize the transmitter and the receiver. Since data is blocked, and start and stop bits are omitted, synchronous transmission enables data to be transmitted at higher data rates than asynchronous transmission.

3.14 A. 10111010
B. 11101001
C. 11101111
D. 01110011

3.15 Synchronous terminals normally cost more than asynchronous terminals because they must buffer entered characters into data blocks for transmission. In addition to a buffer or memory area, synchronous terminals have more complex circuitry to include error-checking circuitry as well as circuitry to perform special functions such as inserting synchronization characters into messages to be transmitted and stripping such characters from received data blocks.

3.16 One parity check problem that can occur is a double bit error, which cannot be detected by that error-checking technique. Consider the seven bit character:

Bit position   1 2 3 4 5 6 7
Bit setting   1 0 1 1 0 1 0

With even parity, the parity bit would be zero, and the 8-bit character would be

1 0 1 1 0 1 0 0

If during transmission bits 1 and 3 are received in error, the result would be

0 0 0 1 0 1 0 0

which, from a parity-check view, would not indicate that an error had occurred.

3.17 Factors that should be considered during the terminal justification process include:

A. Time until information is required or it becomes obsolete.
B. Operational efficiency that can be gained through the use of terminals.
C. Management control through the use of terminals to enter data that becomes part of a database for a Management Information System.
D. Increased productivity and/or cost savings.

ANSWERS TO QUESTIONS AND PROBLEMS IN CHAPTER 4

4.1 A bit is the lowest level of information representation and signifies the presence or absence of a state or condition. A baud represents a unit of signaling speed equal to the number of discrete conditions or signal events per second.

When one bit is used as a signal unit, baud rate and bit/s are equivalent.

4.2 A computer word is fixed in size and can contain different size characters as long as the character size is less than the word size.

4.3 The three modes of transmission are simplex, half-duplex, and full-duplex. In the simplex mode, transmission occurs only in one direction. Half-duplex transmission can be in either direction but only in one direction at a time. Transmission can occur in both directions at the same time in the full-duplex tranmission mode.

4.4

	Asynchronous	Synchronous
Synchronization	Start/stop bits	Sync characters
Data rate	Under 2,000 bit/s	$\geq$ 2,000 bit/s
Idle time between characters	Yes	No
Data formed into blocks	No	Yes

4.5 In serial transmission, the bits that compose the character to be transmitted are sent in serial sequence over one line. In parallel transmission, the characters are transmitted serially, but the bits that represent each character are transmitted in parallel—over several parallel lines. Parallel transmission takes one bit time whereas serial transmission requires N bits, which comprise the character.

4.6 The three basic types of circuits are dedicated, switched, and leased. A dedicated line connects a device to a computer directly over a circuit owned by the user. A leased line is obtained from a common communications carrier. Dedicated lines normally connect local terminals to computers. Switched facilities normally connect terminals, requiring low usage, to a computer. Leased lines normally connect high-volume terminals to a computer.

4.7 The two basic types of line structure are point to point and multipoint. A comparison is shown below:

	Point to point	Multipoint
Many terminals can share line	Yes, if collocated	Yes
Special poll and select software required	Yes	No
Data throughput	Number of terminals is key constraint	Terminal operating speeds is main constraint

4.8 Control characters control data transfer by the use of such controlling functions as

Acknowledgement	ACK
Negative acknowledgment	NAK
End of transmission	EOT
Enquiry	ENQ
Start of heading	SOH

4.9 A transmission code creates a correspondence between the bit encoding of data for transmission or for internal device representation and printed symbols.

4.10 Since the number of dots and dashes that form a Morse character vary, depending upon character, this code is not practical for utilization in a computer communications environment that normally requires fixed-length characters for operation. In addition, Morse code uses the operator's ear to denote pauses between characters, while automatic data transmission requires a method of exact synchronization to indicate the start and ending of characters.

4.11 2^{10} or 1,024 characters

4.12 0.69 millisecond for one bit, or 0.69×12 or 8.28 milliseconds for a 12-bit character.

4.13 A protocol is a method employed to manage a data link. Protocol control tasks include

Connection establishment
Connection verification
Connection disengagement
Transmission sequence
Data sequence
Error control procedures

4.14	**BSC**	**HDLC**
	Half-duplex	Full-duplex
	Character oriented	Bit oriented
	Pseudo-transparent	Naturally transparent
	Fixed-length data blocks	Variable-length data message frames

4.15 In data transfer operations, a transparency mode of operation permits control characters to be transmitted without the expected operation (based upon the control character) taking place. In BSC a two-control-character group, of which one is a data link escape (DLE) character, is used to obtain data transparency. Since HDLC is naturally transparent, no control characters are required to obtain a transparency mode of operation. But a 0 is inserted after five consecutive 1s to prevent a flag character from appearing in the information field. The receiver deletes it.

4.16 Analog service was developed for voice transmission, while digital service was developed for digital transmission. To transmit digital signals over an analog medium, data must be modulated into an analog or continuous signal, whereas data is transferred digitally end to end over a digital medium.

4.17 A leased line connects two or more points, or nodes, on the line to each other via a permanent routing. A WATS line permits users to employ the switched network, at special tariffed costs, to call a number or receive calls from many telephones within a geographical area. An FX line is a hybrid combination of a leased line and the public switched telephone network.

4.18 An analog extension is a leased line that connects a location that does not have Dataphone digital service to a location that does. Analog extensions can be employed to extend transmission to the digital network from non-digital network locations.

ANSWERS TO QUESTIONS AND PROBLEMS IN CHAPTER 5

5.1 Factors affecting shape of digital signals include the transmission distance, the transmission medium (type of wire gauge, low-capacitance shielded cable, etc.), and the pulse rise and fall time, which is proportional to the transmission speed.

5.2 The signal-to-noise ratio is the signal power divided by the noise power and can be used to characterize the quality of a circuit.

5.3 Power ratio $P = 10 \log_{10} \dfrac{\text{Power transmitted}}{\text{Power received}}$ dB

A. $P = 10 \log_{10} \dfrac{1}{.1} = 10 \log_{10} 10 = 10$ dB

B. $P = 10 \log_{10} \dfrac{.2}{.005} = 10 \log_{10} 40 = 16$ dB

C. $P = 10 \log_{10} \dfrac{.05}{.00025} = 10 \log_{10} 200 = 23$ dB

5.4 A line driver is employed on a direct-connect circuit. It samples, amplifies, and regenerates data pulses and then retransmits such pulses, which now have their structure reformatted back into their original shape.

5.5 The key difference between amplitude, frequency, and phase modulation is how the carrier signal is varied by the data signal. In amplitude modulation, the amplitude can be varied so that the carrier signal is either present at a certain amplitude or absent due to zero amplitude. In frequency modulation, the frequency can be shifted according to the bit pattern. For phase modulation, the phase can be changed to represent a particular bit pattern.

5.6 Basically the larger the channel's bandwidth, the greater its capacity for information transfer. The Nyquist relationship between bandwidth and the baud rate on a circuit is

B = 2W, where:
B = baud rate
W = bandwidth in Hertz

5.7 If one pulse represents one bit, then one baud equals one bit/s. If one pulse represents two bits, then one baud represents two bit/s.

5.8 Multilevel coding requires more complex logic for coding and decoding. In addition, it is more susceptible to distortion.

5.9 Nyquist's relationship between bandwidth (W) and baud rate (B) is given by:

B = 2W

Shannon calculated the theoretical maximum capacity of a channel of bandwidth W as:

$$C = W \log_2 \left(1 + \frac{S}{N}\right)$$

where S is the power of the transmitter and N is the power of thermal noise on the circuit. Shannon's formula defines the maximum bit rate (C) which, when divided by the baud rate (B), indicates the number of bits that must be represented by one signal element

$$N = \frac{C}{B}$$

5.10 A modem converts digital pulses into analog tones capable of being transferred on telephone circuits, and reconverts those tones back into digital pulses.

5.11 In asynchronous modems, the timing for synchronization is supplied by the transmitted character, whereas a timing signal is provided by an internal clock for synchronization of synchronous modems.

5.12 The four line-servicing groups and operating speeds of modems are

Subvoice lines	$\leq$	300 bit/s
Voice-grade lines	$\leq$	9,600 bit/s
Wideband lines	$\geq$	19.2 kbit/s
Dedicated lines	$\leq$	1.5 Mbit/s

5.13 Two key causes of signal distortion are signal attenuation (dB) and signal delay (msec or usec).

5.14 Since attenuation is greater at higher frequencies than lower frequencies, a reference frequency permits comparisons of attenuation between circuits.

5.15 Attenuation and delay equalizers and amplifiers can be used to condition leased lines. The attenuation equalizer adds a degree of signal loss to the lower frequencies of a modulated signal so that the loss throughout the transmitted frequency band is almost equal at all transmitted frequencies. To compensate for envelope delay, the delay equalizer introduces an element of delay to some of the transmitted signals so that a uniform delay permits the entire signal to reach the receiver at the same time. Lastly, the amplifier is used to restore the transmitted signal back to its original shape.

5.16 Since leased lines have fixed transmission paths, they can be permanently conditioned. Switched circuits can have transmission routed via an infinite number of paths between the source and transmission receiver, and thus cannot be conditioned to satisfy all possible path characteristics. Modems employ equalizers, usually when designed for data rates of 2,400 bit/s and above. The equalizer is basically an inverse filter used to correct amplitude and delay distortions.

5.17 Through the utilization of equipment conforming to the RS-232-C standard, many types of equipment produced by a variety of equipment vendors can be interfaced to one another with minimal effort.

5.18 Modem handshaking is the exchange of control signals required to establish and maintain a connection between a modem and a business machine, and to disconnect the call at its conclusion.

5.19 Acoustic couplers permit terminal portability, and free a telephone line for other use when not coupled.

5.20 A serial unipolar signal uses a positive voltage to represent a mark and no voltage to represent a space. In bipolar signaling following a return-to-zero pattern, a binary zero is transmitted as zero volts and a binary one as either a positive or negative pulse—opposite in polarity to the previous binary one. Modified, or violated, bipolar signaling is a bipolar signal changed to incorporate network control information.

5.21

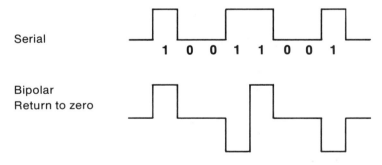

Serial

1   0   0   1   1   0   0   1

Bipolar
Return to zero

5.22 A channel service unit does not contain circuitry necessary to provide timing recovery and detect or generate DDS network control code, but a digital service unit does.

5.23 For an analog extension to AT&T's DDS, a pair of modems, an analog circuit, and a data auxiliary set are required.

ANSWERS TO QUESTIONS AND PROBLEMS IN CHAPTER 6

6.1 A tariff is a schedule of charges, practices, services, and other pertinent data concerning communications services offered to the public. Tariffs are important because they regulate the type and scope of service as well as its cost, permitting the network analyst to plan appropriate action by examining current offerings. Another important tariff feature is that a tariff for interstate service or facility must be approved by the Federal Communications Commission, which normally does not permit subsidized rates on tariffs. This preclusion of subsidized rates prevents large carriers from excluding smaller companies from entering the communications market.

6.2 In the United States, communications common carrier jurisdiction lies with the Federal Communications Commission when communications is interstate, or international with origination in the United States. When communications is intrastate, common carriers may be regulated by state and/or municipal agencies.

6.3 The International Telecommunications Union (ITU) fosters cooperation and compatibility in the areas of radio engineering, data communications, and telephone systems. Several study groups conduct technical and administrative conferences on a periodic basis to develop international operating practices, pricing, policy arrangements, and, most importantly, technical specifications that permit compatibility between telecommunications networks of different nations.

6.4 The Federal Communications Commission's equipment registration program has fostered the proliferation of independent devices that can be connected to the telephone network. By permitting a direct connection via a plug/jack for registered equipment, connection of non-telephone equipment to the telephone network has been simplified.

6.5 Registered equipment can be directly connected to the public switched telephone network via a plug/jack connection, while non-registered equipment must be connected via a data access arrangement.

ANSWERS TO QUESTIONS AND PROBLEMS IN CHAPTER 7

7.1 AT&T has divested itself of its 22 associated telephone companies. In addition, AT&T owns Bell Telephone Laboratories, which is its research arm, as well as Western Electric Co., which is the manufacturing arm. Western Electric, in turn, controls the Teletype Corp., which is one of the largest manufacturers of teleprinters in the United States. AT&T's Long Lines Department provides long distance connections to the 22 formerly associated companies as well as to independent telephone companies. The 2,000 independent telephone companies in the U.S. interconnect with AT&T through one or more of the 22 companies or through the AT&T Long Lines Department.

7.2 Bell Telephone Laboratories is the research and development arm of AT&T. (Included here as part of answer to 7.1.)

7.3 As a result of the 1956 consent decree between the Bell System and the U.S. Department of Justice, the Bell System agreed not to engage in any business activities other than providing communications common carrier offerings. In addition, Western Electric agreed not to manufacture any equipment that was not sold or leased to Bell System operating companies for use in providing common carrier communications services. The establishment of American Bell, and the divestiture by AT&T of operating companies, has largely negated the consent decree.

7.4 Interconnection was the key problem that initially limited the growth of MCI and other specialized carriers. Until a series of legal-ruling-enforced interconnections, telephone companies were reluctant to connect the microwave networks of specialized carriers with their telephone network. This interconnection would cause a loss of revenue for the telephone company and, in effect, would enhance the competition.

7.5 In the context of a value-added carrier, the term value-added means that the carrier uses circuits provided by another carrier and, through special software and hardware devices, improves and adds new capability to the circuit. In most cases, the term value-added carrier is synonymous with packet switching.

7.6 In many foreign countries, telecommunications facilities are provided by a department of the government, whereas in the United States such services are provided by independent companies. Another key difference between foreign countries and the United States concerns the area of communications equipment. In the United States, equipment from many commercial vendors can be considered by a communications subscriber, whereas in many foreign countries only one or at best a few devices manufactured by different vendors are approved for consideration. This situation varies from country to country, and is a result of the few suppliers the national transmission company does business with.

ANSWERS TO QUESTIONS AND PROBLEMS IN CHAPTER 8

8.1

	Switched	FX	WATS
Traffic volume	Low	Medium-heavy	Medium-heavy
Geographical area of terminals	Distributed	Concentrated	Distributed or concentrated

8.2 A. From Table 8.2.1 a station-to-station call with distance between calling and called parties of 575 miles is 62 cents for initial minute and 43 cents for each additional minute. Thus a 20-minute call costs

$$[.62 + (19 \times .43)] = \$8.79$$

For 22 working days/month, total cost is $8.79 × 22, or $193.38.

B. From same table, cost for initial minute is 62 cents, and 43 cents for each additional minute. Thus a 17-minute call costs

$$[.62 + (16 \times .43)] = \$7.50$$

For 20 working days/month, total cost is $7.50 × 20 = $150.00.

C. Here, initial minute costs 62 cents, and each additional minute 43 cents. Thus a 19-minute call costs

$$[.62 + (18 \times .43)] = \$8.36$$

For 21 working days/month total cost is $8.36 × 21 = $175.56.

8.3 A. From Table 8.2.4, Schedule I, the mileage cost for an 851-mile circuit is $252.92 for the first 100 miles plus 94 cents for each additional mile, for a total of $958.86. Two station terminations, each costing $36.05 per month, results in a total monthly cost of $1,030.96.

B. From Table 8.2.4, Schedule II, mileage cost is

[$346.83 + (326 × .94)] = $653.27

Adding two station terminals, each costing $36.05 per month, results in a total monthly expenditure of $725.37.

C. From Table 8.2.5, Schedule III, mileage cost is

[$1,299.38 + (357 × .58)] = $1,506.44

Adding two station terminals, each costing $36.05 per month, results in a total monthly expenditure of $1,578.54.

8.4 A. From Table 8.2.7, the first 15 hours for a New Jersey band 5 WATS costs $20.59 per hour. Thus, an 11-hour call costs $226.49.

B. From Table 8.2.7, the cost of 250 hours for an Oregon band 2 WATS is $3,770.35.

C. From Table 8.2.7, the first 15 hours for a Virginia band 3 WATS costs $286.50 and each additional hour costs $17.45, for a total of $513.35.

8.5 When transmission is via Dataphone digital service, the data travels end to end in its original digital format, and the cost and error problems associated with modulation as required on analog facilities are avoided.

8.6 A. From Table 8.3.1, the monthly cost of the station terminal and DSU is $144.65 for a transmission speed of 2.4 kbit/s. From Table 8.3.2, the channel cost is $252.92 for the first 100 miles plus 94 cents per mile for each mile over 100, for a total channel cost of

[$252.92 + (760 × .94)] = $967.32

Adding the cost of two DSUs and two station terminals, the total monthly cost is

[$967.32 + (144.65 × 2)] = $1,256.62

B. From Table 8.3.1, the monthly cost for each digital station terminal where the DSU is furnished by the customer, is $208.00 when the transmission speed is 4.8 kbit/s. From Table 8.3.2, the circuit cost is $1,098.92 for the first 1,000 miles plus 58 cents for each mile in excess of 1,000, for a total channel cost of

[$1,098.92 + (1,050 × .58)] = $1,707.92

Adding the cost of two digital station terminals, the total monthly cost is

[$1,707.92 + (208 × 2)] = $2,123.92

C. From Table 8.3.1, the monthly cost of each digital station terminal, where the DSU is furnished by the telephone company, is $281.33 for a transmission speed of 9.6 kbit/s. From Table 8.3.2, the cost of a 1,000-mile circuit is $769.20 per month. Adding the cost of two DSUs and two station terminals, the total monthly cost is

$1,098.92 + (428 × 2) = $1,954.92

8.7 **A.** For value-added carrier cost, number of terminals times calls per day per terminal times average call duration times working days per month produces monthly connect time, or

$$2 \times 2 \times 1/2 \times 22 = 44 \text{ hours/month}$$

Since 5,000 characters are transmitted per call and there are two calls per day per terminal and two terminals employed, a total of

$$5,000 \times 2 \times 2 = 20,000 \text{ characters/day}$$

For a 22-day month, this results in 440,000 characters per month.

For the given value-added carrier cost components the monthly cost becomes

Connect time $3.50/hr × 44 hrs/mo =	$154.00
Character transmission ($1.00/10,000) × 440,000	44.00
Central office to customer computer	1,000.00
Total monthly cost:	$1,198.00

For switched telephone network cost, from Table 8.2.1, the cost of an 850-mile call is 62 cents for the first minute and 43 cents for each additional minute. For a 30-minute-call, the cost becomes

$$[.62 + (.43 \times 29)] = \$13.09$$

Since there are two calls per day per terminal, and two terminals operate 22 working days per month, a total of 88 terminal-calls per month are made, each costing $13.09. Thus the total switched telephone cost becomes $13.09 x 88, or $1,151.92 per month.

For leased line cost, consider one connection as an A-A rate center category and the other as a B-B. From Table 8.2.3, the monthly cost of an 850-mile A-A category connection circuit is $252.92 + (.94 × $750), or $957.92. Adding the station termination cost of $36.05 per month per end results in a monthly cost of $1,030.02. For an 850-mile B-B rate category connection, the cost is [$426.38 + (.97 × 750)] or $1,153.88/month. Adding the station terminations results in a cost of $1,225.98 for this circuit, and the cost of the two circuits becomes $2,256.00.

B. For value-added carrier cost:

$$3 \times 3 \times 1/3 \times 21 = 63 \text{ hours per month}$$

$$10,000 \times 3 \times 3 \times 21 = 1,890,000 \text{ characters/month}$$

Total carrier cost becomes

Connect time—$3.50/hr × 63 hrs/mo	$ 220.50
Character cost—(1.00/100,000) × 1,890,000 characters	18.90
Central office to customer computer	1,000.00
Total monthly cost:	$1,239.40

For switched telephone network, from Table 8.2.1, cost for initial minute is 64 cents and each additional minute costs 44 cents. Thus 20 minute call costs .64 + 19 × .44 or $9.00. In a month there are 3 × 3 × 21 or 189 such calls, which result in a total cost of $1,701.00 per month.

For 1,000-mile leased-line costs, from Table 8.2.3

A-A circuit $1,098.92 + $72.10 =	$1,171.02
A-B circuit $1,192.83 + $72.10 =	1,264.93
B-B circuit $1,299.38 + $72.10 =	1,371.48
Total leased-line cost	$3,807.43

C. For value-added carrier cost:

2 × 4 × .41666 × 22 = 73.33 hours per month
20,000 × 2 × 4 × 22 = 3,520,000 characters/month

Total carrier cost becomes

Connect time $3.50/hr. × 73.33 hrs/mo	$ 256.66
Character cost (1.00/100,000) × 3,520,000 characters	35.20
Central office to customer computer	1,000.00
Total monthly cost	$1,291.86

For switched telephone network cost, from Table 8.2.1, cost for initial minute is 74 cents and each additional minute costs 49 cents. Thus a 25-minute call costs [.74 + (24 × .49)], or $12.50. Since there are eight calls per day and 22 working days per month, there are a total of 176 calls per month, each costing $12.50, for a total monthly cost of $2,200.

For leased-line cost, from Table 8.2.3, the cost of a 2,000-mile category A-A circuit is [$1,098.92 + (.58 × 1,000)], or $1,678.92 plus $72.10 per month for station terminations, resulting in a total line cost of $1,751.02. For the A-B rate center circuit, the monthly cost is $1,192.83 + [.58 × 1,000], or $1,772.83 plus $72.10 per month for station terminations, resulting in a total line cost of $1,844.93. Combining the cost of the two circuits results in a total monthly expenditure of $3,595.95.

ANSWERS TO QUESTIONS AND PROBLEMS IN CHAPTER 9

9.1 The four basic groupings of the RS-232-C interface circuits are ground, data, control timing, and secondary operation.

9.2 Protective ground is used to protect the user from being shocked if he touches a device that has a voltage leak. Signal ground is used to establish a common ground reference potential for all interchange circuits except protective ground.

9.3 The request-to-send signal controls the direction of transmission of the local DCE when half-duplex transmission is employed. When the circuit is active, it inhibits receiving of data for half-duplex transmission, whereas it maintains the DCE in the transmit mode for full-duplex transmission.

9.4

Signal	From DCE	To DCE
A. Request to send		X
B. Clear to send	X	
C. Data set ready	X	
D. Received line signal detector	X	
E. Transmit data		X
F. Receive data	X	
G. Data terminal ready		X
H. Ring indicator	X	

9.5 The transmission direction of a reverse channel is opposite that of a primary channel, whereas the transmission direction of a secondary channel is independent of the primary channel.

9.6 Since the bandwidth of a secondary channel is much narrower than that of a primary channel, the transmission speed on the secondary channel is at a much slower rate than that possible on a primary channel.

9.7 The RS-449 standard provides two connectors, a 37-pin one for primary circuits and a 9-pin one exclusively for secondary channels. In comparison, the RS-232-C standard requires a 25-pin connector.

9.8 The mode option permits modems to be employed as either originate- or answer-type modems. Thus a modem connected to a terminal would have an originate mode selection, and a modem connected to a dial-in port at a computer site would be placed in the answer mode of operation.

9.9 If automatic answering—NO option is selected for modems at a computer site, and terminal-to-computer transmission must be conducted manually.

9.10 $\dfrac{200 \times 8}{4,800} = 333$ milliseconds to transmit block

$\left(\dfrac{80}{80 + 333}\right) \times 100 = 19.37\%$ overhead

9.11 $\left(\dfrac{10}{10 + 333}\right) \times 100 = 2.9\%$ overhead

9.12 $\dfrac{300 \times 8}{4,800} = 500$ milliseconds to transmit block

$\left(\dfrac{80}{80 + 500}\right) \times 100 = 13.8\%$ overhead

9.13 $\dfrac{200 \times 8}{9,600} = 167$ milliseconds to transmit block

$\left(\dfrac{80}{80 + 167}\right) \times 100 = 32.4\%$ overhead

ANSWERS TO QUESTIONS AND PROBLEMS IN CHAPTER 10

10.1 A feasibility study is conducted to determine if there is enough justification to proceed with a project and/or select one alternative from many possible solutions based upon performance and economic parameters. A communications plan examines such parameters as the types of transactions to be processed and their urgency, volume, expected growth rates, and other parameters in order to determine a method to implement or revise existing communications. In general, a feasibility study examines data at the macro level in order to obtain a go/no go decision, while a communications plan examines data at a micro level in order to develop a method to implement the feasibility study decision.

10.2 Some of the functions that an intelligent terminal can perform, which normally dumb terminals cannot, include:

A. Formatting input and output—better known as forms mode

B. Data compression/decompression

C. Content-oriented error detection

D. Local editing of data

E. Handling simple computations

10.3 If the intelligent terminal preprocesses data input by checking alphabetic fields for numerics and so on, it can reduce the possibility of incorrectly entered data and thereby not only remove this function from the host computer but also reduce the number and frequency of error messages being transmitted from the host computer to the terminal.

10.4 In general, concentrators combine many low-speed lines into one or more high-speed lines. The functions performed by concentrators range from speed and code conversion to automatic baud recognition, code compression, traffic smoothing, and error control.

10.5 Any of the communications functions listed in the response to 10.4 can be incorporated into front-end processors. In addition, such functions as user password verification can also be incorporated to further reduce the processing burden of the host computer.

10.6 In general, concentrators can physically support more terminal devices than can multiplexers, and are user programmable. Multiplexers are usually programmed by the vendor at the factory.

10.7 Both concentrators and multiplexers combine data from many low- to medium-speed devices into one or more high-speed composite output data channels.

ANSWERS TO QUESTIONS AND PROBLEMS IN CHAPTER 11

11.1 Five data sources that could be candidates for data-stream multiplexing are

1. Data streams from modems connected to leased lines

2. Direct-connect terminals

3. Data from digital service units

4. Data from modems connected to the switched network

5. Data streams from other multiplexers

11.2 The two basic techniques used for multiplexing are frequency division and time division. In frequency-division multiplexing (FDM), the bandwidth is the frame of reference, and it is subdivided into segments with each frequency segment assigned to an output channel. In time-division multiplexing (TDM), time is the frame of reference—input data is positioned into an output channel by time. At any point in time, the output channel holds data for only one input line in TDM, whereas the output channels can hold data for numerous lines when the FDM technique is employed.

11.3 When multiplexers use a bit interleaving technique, minimal buffer storage is required, since each incoming data bit is combined into the high-speed output data stream as the multiplexer receives the bit. In character interleaving, the multiplexer must assemble bits into a character before multiplexing, hence circuitry and buffering is more complex.

11.4 Overhead $= \dfrac{\text{SYNC}}{\text{SYNC} + \text{DATA}} = \dfrac{\text{SYNC}}{\text{TOTAL}}$

A. $\dfrac{2}{2+2} = 50\%$

C. $\dfrac{2}{2+6} = \dfrac{2}{8} = 25\%$

B. $\dfrac{2}{2+4} = \dfrac{2}{6} = 33\%$

D. $\dfrac{2}{2+8} = \dfrac{2}{10} = 20\%$

11.5 When a multiplexer is employed as a front-end substitute, special host software must be developed to make the computer compatible with the multiplexer. Normally, a large quantity of such devices must be used so the software development costs can be spread over many such units.

11.6

4,800
$\underline{\times\ 4}$ reverse compression
19,200 kbit/s

$\dfrac{19{,}200}{1{,}200} = 16$

11.7

	Multiport modem	Multiplexers
Data rates supported	Multiple of 2.4 kbit/s	Unlimited
Transmission mode	Synchronous only	Async/sync
Number of channels	Usually fixed	Not fixed

11.8 Both concentrators and remote network processors perform data concentration; however, only a remote network processor can concurrently perform local batch and remote batch processing.

11.9 A modem-sharing unit permits many terminals to share the common modem in a poll-and-select environment. A multiplexer permits many types of digital data sources, including directly connected terminals and the output data streams of modems, to be combined and to share a common transmission medium.

11.10 A line-sharing unit is normally employed within a computer facility, whereas a modem-sharing unit is normally used at remote locations where terminals are clustered.

ANSWERS TO QUESTIONS AND PROBLEMS IN CHAPTER 12

12.1 As explained in Chapter 12, a good starting point in network design is to construct a table similar to Table 12.3.3, using in our example 22 working days/month. We can refer to Chapter 8 for the relevant cost figures, specifically Tables 8.2.1 and 8.2.4 for switched- and leased-line costs. Completing the table lets us determine on a per-terminal basis the most economic method of connecting each terminal to the computer. For this particular problem, at all four locations, the switched network was determined to be the most economical method to use on an individual basis. The completed table is shown below:

TABLE 12.2

LOCATION	DAILY CONNECT TIME MINUTES	MONTHLY CONNECT TIME NO. OF FIRST MINUTE	NO. OF ADDITIONAL MINUTES	MILEAGE TO COMPUTER CENTER	COST/CALL DAY RATE INITIAL MINUTE	EACH EXTRA MINUTE	MONTHLY SWITCHED NETWORK COST/ TERMINAL	RATE CENTER CATEGORY	MONTHLY LEASED LINE COST	MONTHLY STATION TERMINAL COST	TOTAL MONTHLY LEASED LINE COST	MOST ECONOMICAL TYPE	MONTHLY COST
1	5	22	88	750	.62	.43	51.48	A-A	863.92	72.1	936.02	SWITCHED	51.48
2	20	22	418	400	.59	.42	188.54	B-A	628.83	72.1	700.93	SWITCHED	188.54
3	20	22	418	375	.59	.42	188.54	A-A	511.42	72.1	583.52	SWITCHED	188.54
4	50	22	1078	1,040	.64	.44	488.40	B-A	1,322.58	72.1	1,394.68	SWITCHED	488.40

Next, we can examine the network layout, denote the number of terminals at each location, and try to ascertain if any type of data concentration can be used to reduce costs. The network layout with the number of terminals indicated at each site and the type and cost of the most economical transmission method to the computer center is shown below.

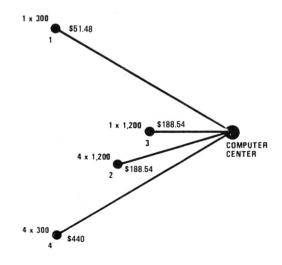

FIGURE I.12.1

Next we can begin to examine the utilization of the data concentration equipment listed as available for consideration in solving this problem— 4- and 8-channel multiplexers. Since there are but single terminals at locations 1 and 3 and the cost of transmission from those locations to the computer is less than the leased-line cost of linking either of those locations to any other location (see the interconnection distances in the problem), we can exclude those two locations not only from being multiplexer locations but also from being connected to multiplexers that may be located at other points in the network.

Based upon the preceding analysis, only locations 2 and 4 can be considered for the installation of multiplexers. Since location 4 is further from the computer site, let us consider that location first as a candidate for multiplexing.

The cost of a 4-channel multiplexer is $100 and a 4,800-bit/s modem rents for $135 per month, resulting in a total cost of $235 per month at location 4 (if we assume that the terminals at the location can be directly cabled to the multiplexer). Since similar equipment is required at the computer site, the modem and multiplexer cost is $470 per month. Adding the cost of a leased line, which from the table was computed as $1,394.68 per month, the total cost of multiplexing data from the four terminals at location 4 becomes $1,864.68, which is less than the switched network cost of 4 × $488.40, or $1,953.60 per month. In addition, the multiplexing cost is fixed, whereas the switched cost is variable and will increase if traffic volume and connection time should rise.

Next, let us similarly examine location 2. Here, the cost of a 4-channel multiplexer and 4,800-bit/s modem would be $235 per month. Again, since similar equipment is required at the computer site, the cost for both sites would be $470 per month. Adding the cost of the leased line from location 2 to the computer site (from the table it was $700.93 per month), the total multiplexing cost becomes $1,170.93 per month. Since the previously computed most-economical cost pointed to the switched network at $188.54 per month per terminal, for the four terminals such service would cost $754.16—which is less than the cost of multiplexing data.

Note that an 8-channel statistical multiplexer was not considered since it rents for $75 per month more than a 4-channel conventional multiplexer and would reduce the modem cost by only $70 per month ($135 for a 4,800-bit/s modem vs. $65 for a 2,400-bit/s modem).

ANSWERS TO QUESTIONS AND PROBLEMS IN CHAPTER 13

13.10 SOLUTION: Using 4-channel TDM
REMOTE SITE

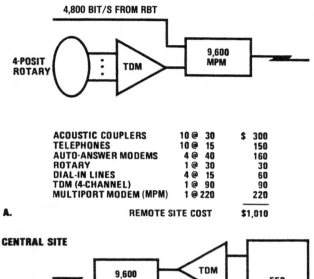

4,800 BIT/S FROM RBT

4-POSIT ROTARY — TDM — 9,600 MPM

ACOUSTIC COUPLERS	10 @ 30	$ 300
TELEPHONES	10 @ 15	150
AUTO-ANSWER MODEMS	4 @ 40	160
ROTARY	1 @ 30	30
DIAL-IN LINES	4 @ 15	60
TDM (4-CHANNEL)	1 @ 90	90
MULTIPORT MODEM (MPM)	1 @ 220	220

A. REMOTE SITE COST **$1,010**

CENTRAL SITE

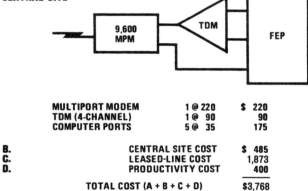

9,600 MPM — TDM — FEP

MULTIPORT MODEM	1 @ 220	$ 220
TDM (4-CHANNEL)	1 @ 90	90
COMPUTER PORTS	5 @ 35	175

B. CENTRAL SITE COST **$ 485**
C. LEASED-LINE COST **1,873**
D. PRODUCTIVITY COST **400**

TOTAL COST (A + B + C + D) **$3,768**

SOLUTION: Using 8-channel TDM

**NO ADDITIONAL INTERACTIVE TERMINALS CAN BE
SERVICED SINCE ANY INCREASE IN TERMINALS WOULD
EXCEED THE CAPACITY OF THE HIGH-SPEED LINE TO
GREENSBORO.**

SOLUTION: Using a statistical multiplexer

REMOTE SITE

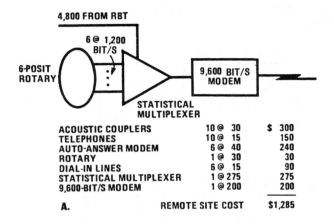

ACOUSTIC COUPLERS	10 @ 30	$ 300
TELEPHONES	10 @ 15	150
AUTO-ANSWER MODEM	6 @ 40	240
ROTARY	1 @ 30	30
DIAL-IN LINES	6 @ 15	90
STATISTICAL MULTIPLEXER	1 @ 275	275
9,600-BIT/S MODEM	1 @ 200	200
A.	REMOTE SITE COST	**$1,285**

CENTRAL SITE

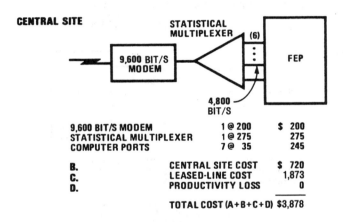

9,600 BIT/S MODEM	1 @ 200	$ 200
STATISTICAL MULTIPLEXER	1 @ 275	275
COMPUTER PORTS	7 @ 35	245
B.	CENTRAL SITE COST	$ 720
C.	LEASED-LINE COST	1,873
D.	PRODUCTIVITY LOSS	0
	TOTAL COST (A+B+C+D)	$3,878

SOLUTION: Using line drivers and a statistical multiplexer

REMOTE SITE

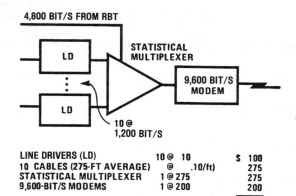

4,800 BIT/S FROM RBT

STATISTICAL
MULTIPLEXER

9,600 BIT/S
MODEM

10 @
1,200 BIT/S

LINE DRIVERS (LD)	10 @ 10	$ 100
10 CABLES (275-FT AVERAGE)	@ .10/ft)	275
STATISTICAL MULTIPLEXER	1 @ 275	275
9,600-BIT/S MODEMS	1 @ 200	200

A. REMOTE SITE COST $ 850

CENTRAL SITE

STATISTICAL
MULTIPLEXER

9,600 BIT/S
MODEM

FEP

(10)
4,800
BIT/S

9,600-BIT/S MODEM	1 @ 200	$ 200
STATISTICAL MULTIPLEXER	1 @ 275	275
COMPUTER PORTS	11 @ 35	385

B.	CENTRAL SITE COST	$ 860
C.	LEASED-LINE COST	1,873
D.	PRODUCTIVITY LOSS	- 100
	TOTAL COST (A + B + C + D)	$3,483

SOLUTION: Summary

COST	4-CHNL TDM SERVING 4 TTY	STAT MUX SERVING 6 TTY	LINE DRIVERS W/STAT MUX SERVING 10 TTY
REMOTE SITE	$1,010	$1,285	$ 850
CENTRAL SITE	485	720	860
LEASED LINE	1,873	1,873	1,873
PRODUCITIVITY	400	0	– 100
TOTAL	3,768	3,878	3,483

13.11 SOLUTION: Multiplexing new traffic with 2nd shift RBT

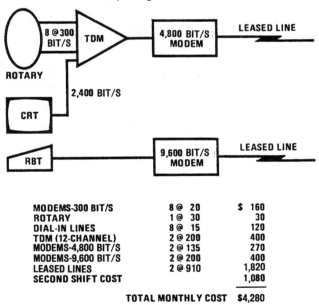

MODEMS-300 BIT/S	8 @ 20	$ 160
ROTARY	1 @ 30	30
DIAL-IN LINES	8 @ 15	120
TDM (12-CHANNEL)	2 @ 200	400
MODEMS-4,800 BIT/S	2 @ 135	270
MODEMS-9,600 BIT/S	2 @ 200	400
LEASED LINES	2 @ 910	1,820
SECOND SHIFT COST		1,080
TOTAL MONTHLY COST		**$4,280**

SOLUTION: Pseudo Wideband utilization

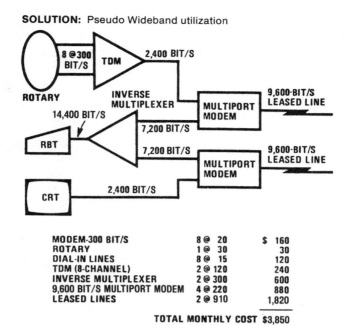

MODEM-300 BIT/S	8 @ 20	$ 160
ROTARY	1 @ 30	30
DIAL-IN LINES	8 @ 15	120
TDM (8-CHANNEL)	2 @ 120	240
INVERSE MULTIPLEXER	2 @ 300	600
9,600 BIT/S MULTIPORT MODEM	4 @ 220	880
LEASED LINES	2 @ 910	1,820
	TOTAL MONTHLY COST	$3,850

13.12 SOLUTION: Using TDMs

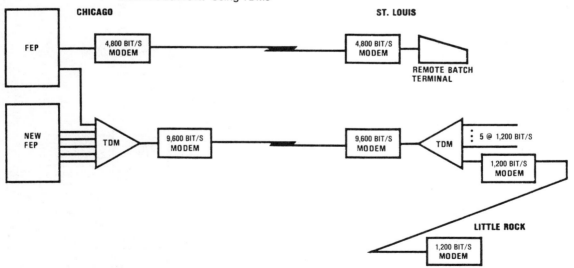

Monthly cost using TDMs

LINE COST

ST LOUIS – CHICAGO	2 @ 404	$808
LITTLE ROCK – ST. LOUIS	1 @ 432	250

MODEM COST

1.200 BIT/S MODEMS	2 @ 40	80
4,800 BIT/S MODEMS	2 @ 120	240
9,600 BIT/S MODEMS	2 @ 200	400

FEP COST

CHANNEL (PORT) COST	7 @ 35	245
ADDITIONAL FEP		1,500

TERMINAL COST

1,200 BIT/S	6 @ 100	600
REMOTE BATCH TERMINAL	1 @ 500	500

MULTIPLEXERS

8-CHANNEL TDM	2 @ 160	320

TOTAL MONTHLY COST $5,125

Clustering the terminals

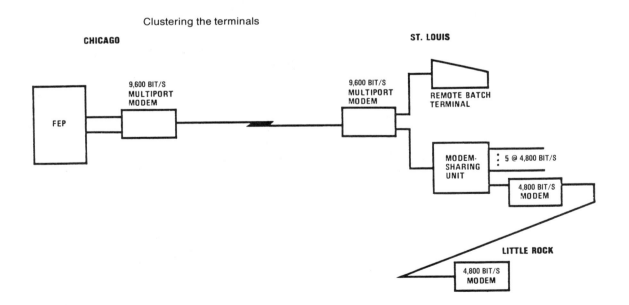

Monthly cost of clustering

LINE COST

ST. LOUIS – CHICAGO	1 @ 404	$404
ST. LOUIS – LITTLE ROCK	1 @ 432	432

MODEM COST

4,800 BIT/S MODEMS	2 @ 120	240
9,600 BIT/S MULTIPORT MODEMS	2 @ 220	440

FEP COST

CHANNEL (PORT) COST	2 @ 35	70

MODEM-SHARING UNIT | 1 @ 35 | 35

TERMINAL COST

4,800 BIT/S	6 @ 125	750
REMOTE BATCH TERMINAL	1 @ 500	500

TOTAL MONTHLY COST $2,871

Cost comparison

	TDM APPROACH	CLUSTER APPROACH
MONTHLY COST	$5,125	$2,871
IF FEP CHANNELS AVAILABLE	–1,500	
	$3,625	$2,871

13.13 SOLUTION: Switching at the remote site

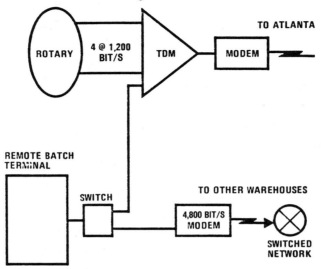

COST

DIAL-UP

5 WAREHOUSES X 12 CALLS X $6.00	$ 360.00
5 MODEMS @ 120	600.00
5 FALLBACK SWITCHES @ $10.00	50.00
MONTHLY COST	**$1,010.00**

SOLUTION: Switching at the central site

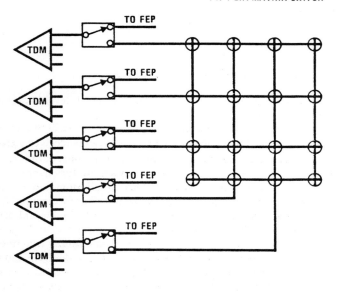

4 X 4 EIA MATRIX SWITCH

COST

DIAL-UP COORDINATION

5 WAREHOUSES X 12 CALLS X 50 CENTS	$ 30
5 FALLBACK SWITCHES @ $10	50
1 MATRIX SWITCH @ $200	200
MONTHLY COST	**$280**

ANSWERS TO QUESTIONS AND PROBLEMS IN CHAPTER 14

14.1 $dB = 10 \log_{10} \dfrac{\text{output power}}{\text{input power}}$

A. $dB = 10 \log_{10} \dfrac{10}{100} = 10 \log_{10} .1 = -10$

B. $dB = 10 \log_{10} \dfrac{100}{1} = 10 \log_{10} 100 = 20$

14.2 Dropouts—sudden, large reductions in signal level that last more than several milliseconds.

Phase hits—sudden, uncontrolled changes in phase of the received signal.

Gain hits—sudden, uncontrolled increases in the received signal level.

Impulse noise—sudden noise "spikes" of very short duration.

14.3 Equalization can be employed to compensate for changes in amplitude and phase response of modulated signals. This equalization can be done by the telephone company when it conditions a circuit, as well as by circuitry in high-speed modems.

14.4 In digital monitoring, one is concerned with the control signals at the RS-232-C interface and the trapping and display of data and control characters between the data circuit-terminating equipment and the data terminal equipment. In analog monitoring, one is concerned with the interface between the DCE and the line, examining the voltage, current, and phase levels of the circuit, as well as other unique line parameters.

14.5 Line monitor/digital test set features one should consider include:

A. Code level—does the device support 5, 6, 7, or 8 bits per character?

B. Stop-length element—can the device support 1, 1.42, 1.5, or 2-bit stop intervals?

C. HDLC/SDLC—can the device support new data link control protocols?

D. Stored-message generator—does the device have a stored-message generator to assist in testing?

E. Character-error counter—does the device have the capability to count errors as they occur, and accumulate totals by time intervals?

14.6 Analog monitoring is specifically concerned with measuring dropouts, phase hits, gain hits, impulse noise, envelope delay, and other communications-line parameters. Since the control of a line normally rests with the communications carrier, most organizations rely on the carrier test center to perform line testing.

14.7 A patchfield provides the means for monitoring lines, injecting signals, and reconfiguring a network, as well as providing access to local equipment interfaces. Usually rack mounted, a patchfield consists of a series of plugs, cords, and jacks that permit the interconnection of components and test set interfaces from one device to another.

ANSWERS TO QUESTIONS AND PROBLEMS IN CHAPTER 15

15.1 Three information collection methods include

A. Personnel interviews—most costly and time consuming, but ferret out most items other methods normally miss.

B. Checklist—usually rigid with little or no room for elaboration of answers.

C. Survey—most flexible method.

15.2 Problems that can occur when a checklist (menu) is employed include no response to a particular question and no means for users to elaborate on answers.

15.3 Advantages of interviews are the personnel contact and ability to ferret out information that can only be gained by face-to-face exposure. Disadvantages include the cost and time required to employ this technique.

15.4 An expansion table may permit one to determine rapidly the capability and cost of upgrading equipment.

15.5 Knowing the protocols supported by a front-end processor will enable the network analyst to consider such line-sharing techniques as multipoint circuits, as well as to plan for the orderly growth of the network to include types of terminals that should be considered based upon protocol support of the front end.

15.6 The assignment of additional software modules to a front-end processor may reduce terminal buffer availability size and thus increase time delays in servicing (responding to) all terminals connected to that device.

15.7 Techniques to alleviate front-end-processor port constraints include the use of line- and modem-sharing units, multipoint circuits, and the operation of a port selector.

15.8 The two primary methods of cutover are parallel and serial. In the parallel cutover method, one has duplicate costs for a period of time. However, one also has a network to fall back to if the new one does not perform as expected and more developmental time becomes necessary.

   In the serial cutover technique, duplicate costs are minimized since, as soon as the new network is ready, the old one is eliminated. Unfortunately, if the new one is not error free or does not work as expected, there is no old one to fall back to.

ANSWERS TO QUESTIONS AND PROBLEMS IN CHAPTER 16

16.1 Sole-source procurements are less time consuming than competitive procurements; however, competitive procurements normally result in lower prices when large quantities of an item are to be obtained.

16.2 A mandatory feature is one essential for the operation of the device. If the device does not have the feature, it is excluded from consideration. A desirable feature is nice to have, but if the device does not have the feature, it is still considered for selection.

16.3 Mandatory features are normally evaluated on a pass-fail basis. For desirable features, a dollar worth is normally assigned to each item, and the price that the vendor bids is adjusted by the value of all the desirable features to obtain the cost-value bid.

16.4

	Vendor A	Vendor B	Vendor C
Bid	$8,750	$8,827	$8,905
Desirable features	$ 350	$ 500	$ 150
Cost-value	$8,400	$8,327	$8,755

Here, Vendor B is selected.

16.5 Assume no effect due to number of terminals.

$$\text{Dept. 1: } \frac{450}{1300} + \frac{750}{1125} = 1.013$$

$$\text{Dept. 2: } \frac{850}{1300} + \frac{375}{1125} = \frac{.987}{2.000}$$

$$\text{Dept. 1: } \frac{1.013}{2} \times \$4,500 = \$2,279.25 \quad \text{pro rata charge}$$

$$\text{Dept. 2: } \frac{.987}{2} \times \$4,500 = \$2,220.75 \quad \text{pro rata charge}$$

INDEX

437

402